SHARP®
CAROUSEL® II

MICROWAVE COOKBOOK

HOW TO USE THIS COOKBOOK

Your Sharp Carousel Convection Microwave Oven can be used as a microwave oven for quick, convenient cooking, as a convection oven for small baked goods and broiling or in combination for roasting and baking.

Your cookbook begins with an introduction to the principles and techniques of microwave cooking, pages 4-24. The next section, pages 1c through 48c, explains convection and combination cooking and includes cooking methods, charts and recipes. The chapters following page 48c focus on microwave-only cooking.

Notice that any recipe listed in the index with a "c" following the page number is a convection or combination recipe. This is a quick way of identifying convection or combination recipes.

For some foods you will find directions for both combination cooking (1c-48c) and microwave cooking. For example, you'll find directions for baking cakes in combination on page 30c, and a recipe for microwaving layer cakes on page 107. Your oven provides you with the option of using either method, depending on the time you have available and your own preferences.

Take a moment to flip through the cookbook to see how it's arranged. As you use the book, be sure to read the captions under the pictures — often that's where you'll find important directions and tips.

PRECAUTIONS TO AVOID POSSIBLE EXPOSURE TO EXCESSIVE MICROWAVE ENERGY

(a) Do not attempt to operate this oven with the door open since open-door operation can result in harmful exposure to microwave energy. It is important not to defeat or tamper with the safety interlocks.

(b) Do not place any object between the oven front face and the door or allow soil or cleaner residue to accumlate on sealing surfaces.

(c) Do not operate the oven if it is damaged. It is particularly important that the oven door close properly and that there is no damage to the: (1) door (bent), (2) hinges and latches (broken or loosened), (3) door seals and sealing surfaces.

(d) The oven should not be adjusted or repaired by anyone except properly qualified service personnel.

Design & Production: Cy DeCosse Incorporated

CONTENTS

How a Microwave Oven Works

Once you've learned how a microwave oven works, you will be better able to make the most of its timesaving versatility. The heart of the microwave oven is a magnetron tube, which converts electricity into high frequency, non-ionizing microwaves. This microwave energy causes food molecules (water, sugar and fat) to vibrate rapidly, creating friction that produces heat to cook the food.

Advantages of the Carousel

Sharp Carousel® II Microwave Ovens are designed with a revolving turntable featuring advanced technology. This remarkable system makes sure food is cooked evenly and thoroughly without hot or cold spots. Since the energy in a microwave oven often is not distributed evenly throughout the cavity, the turntable moves the food through any hot spots. There's no need for you to rotate food to achieve best results.

Once you've become familiar with your microwave oven, you'll soon discover it will make your work in the kitchen easier and more efficient. Included in this book are recipes developed for 600 to 720 watt ovens, plus many tips and techniques. Be sure to read the operation manual that accompanies your oven for specific recommendations.

Microwave Myths

Learning what is fact and what is fiction will help you understand how your microwave oven works and what it can do for you.

Myth 1. Microwaves cook from the inside out.

Actually, it's the reverse. Food prepared in a microwave oven cooks from the outside toward the center. Microwaves penetrate the food from the outside edges to a depth of about ¾ to 1½ inches. Small foods, under 2 inches in diameter, heat more quickly because the microwaves penetrate from all sides. With larger foods, heat moves to the center by conduction.

Myth 2. You can't use metal in a microwave oven.

There are exceptions to the rule of "no metal in a microwave oven." Metal reflects microwave energy, which slows cooking. Small strips of aluminum foil may be used to shield areas of food to keep them from overcooking. (See page 12 for further information.) The use of metal twist ties, pots and pans or metal utensils is not recommended, because they could cause arcing (energy trapped between oven wall and metal, creating blue flashes). Always be sure to check your operation manual for specific recommendations.

Myth 3. Dishes don't get hot in a microwave oven.

Some microwave-safe dishes become hot because they absorb heat from contact with hot food. This is often the case when food is tightly covered during periods of longer cooking.

Myth 4. Microwaved foods don't stay hot.

They cool at the same rate as conventionally heated foods. One advantage of microwaving is that you can cook and serve in the same dish; food stays hot longer because you don't have to transfer it to a cool dish.

Myth 5. Foods don't brown in a microwave oven.

Browning depends on fat content and the amount of cooking time in relation to food volume. Foods such as bacon, turkey or a roast will brown. Many small, moist foods cook so quickly they don't have time to brown.

Do's and Don'ts

Humidity and moisture in food influence the amount of condensation in your oven. This is normal in microwave cooking. Be sure the vent on the back of oven is not blocked. The door seal on your oven is designed to prevent leakage of microwave energy during cooking. Moisture that may occasionally appear around the oven door is normal.

Here are a few do's and don'ts that will start you on your way to learning more about your microwave oven:

Do read the operation manual that accompanies your oven for specific recommendations.

Do follow manufacturer's recommendations for oven cooking bags. Make six ½-inch slits in neck of bag below tie to allow steam to escape during cooking.

Do use small amounts of foil to shield and protect portions of meat and poultry from overcooking; be sure to keep foil at least 2 inches from oven walls and ceiling.

Do pop popcorn only in a microwave popcorn popper or use specially packaged ready-to-pop microwave popcorn. Some ovens include a special feature for popping popcorn. (See owner's manual for further information.) Do not use brown paper bags or glass or plastic bowls for popping popcorn.

Do not dry herbs, wood, gourds or wet papers in the microwave oven.

Do prick foods with skins, such as potatoes or squash, so internal steam that builds up during cooking can escape.

Do hard-poach eggs for salads and casseroles; prick yolk to allow steam to escape. **Do not** cook eggs in the shell or reheat unpeeled hard-cooked eggs in the microwave oven.

Do not use your microwave oven to heat oil or fat for deep-frying. **Do not** can foods in the microwave oven.

Microwave Utensils

The ideal material for a microwave utensil allows energy to pass through the container and heat the food. Many common household items, such as paper plates and glass or plastic bowls, are good choices for warming foods.

When a utensil is used for cooking, it must also be able to withstand contact with hot food or boiling liquid.

Dual-purpose, heat-resistant paper and plastic utensils can be used in microwave and conventional ovens. Look for materials that are marked "safe for microwave or conventional oven up to 400°F." Many traditional cooking containers, such as casseroles and measuring cups, are also suitable for microwaving.

Oven-glass and glass ceramic (Pyroceram®) utensils can be used for microwaving, serving and storing. Oven-glass utensils are inexpensive and widely available. Use them for measuring, mixing and microwaving. Choose clear glass for pies, cakes and breads, so you can easily check for doneness through the bottom of the dish.

Microwave-safe Dish Test. If you are not sure whether your dish is safe to use in the microwave oven, use this test. Place the dish in the oven. Measure ½ to 1 cup water in glass cup. Place on or beside dish. Microwave at HIGH (100%) for 1 to 2 minutes. If dish remains cool, it is suitable for microwaving. Do not use this test for plastic.

Pottery, stoneware and porcelain offer the convenience of cook-and-serve versatility. Serving bowls, platters, casseroles, plates and cups are practical and attractive. Look for dishware that is marked "microwave-safe". If you are not sure if your dish is safe to use, use the dish test above.

Plastic cookware (Thermoset®) marked microwave-safe is designed for microwave oven and conventional oven use and can withstand temperatures up to 400°F. Follow manufacturer's recommendations.

Plastic storage containers and tableware marked "dishwasher-safe" and Styrofoam® may be used for short-term heating to serving temperature. Do not use them for cooking raw foods or for heating foods high in fat or sugar, since they distort at fairly low temperatures. "Original" Tupperware® may melt or distort; Ultra 21® lines from Tupperware are designed for microwave use.

Plastic wrap and oven cooking bags are ideal for microwaving. Plastic food-storage bags should not be used for cooking. Plastic wrap makes a convenient cover for baking dishes; vent so steam escapes. Choose a good-quality plastic wrap or one designed for microwave use; inferior brands may split, become sticky or shrink when used.

Paper plates, hot drink cups, towels and napkins are good choices for short-term cooking and heating. Avoid recycled paper, which may contain metal chips, and wax-coated paper cups or plates. Paper baking cups absorb excess moisture and save clean-ups. Plain white paper towels are excellent for warming breads, cooking bacon or covering to prevent splatters. Wax paper can be used as a light, nonstick cover that holds in steam; it also prevents splattering for dishes such as chili or spaghetti.

Dual-purpose paper products, such as ovenable paperboard containers, are versatile choices. They are freezer-proof and safe for both microwave and conventional ovens up to 400°F.

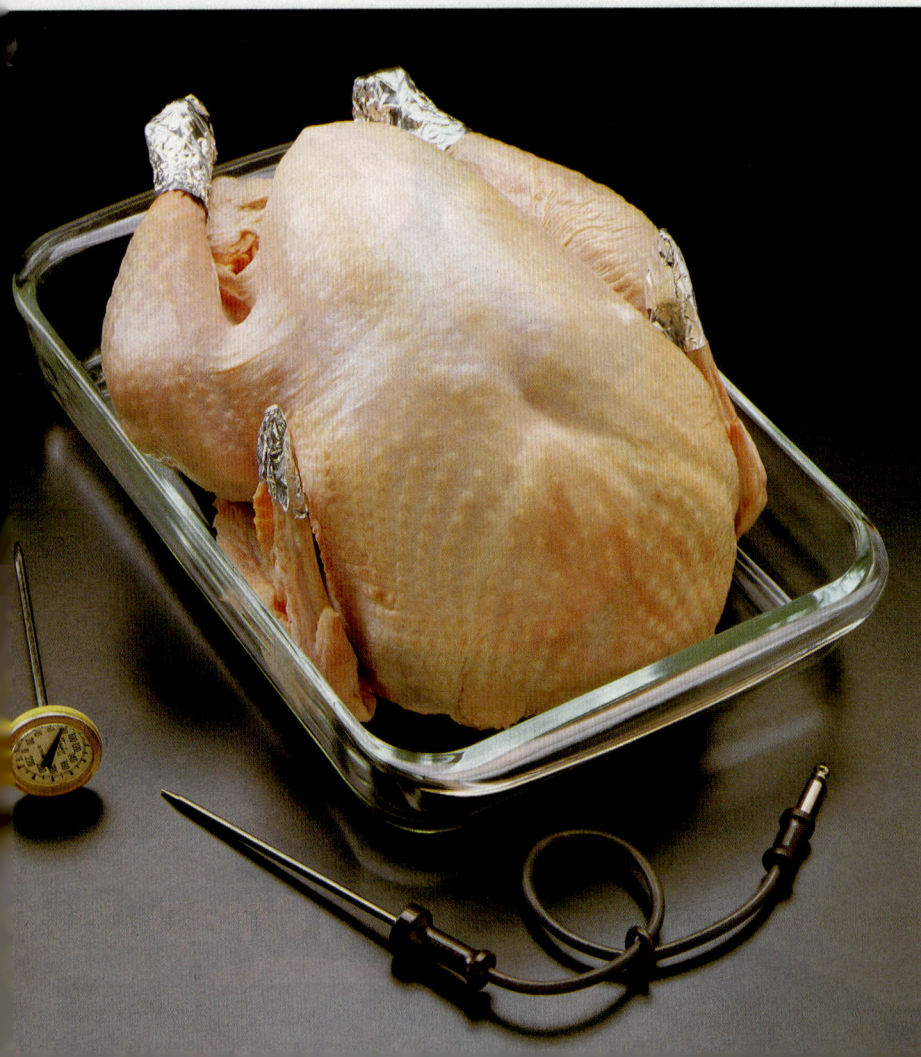

Metal, such as small pieces of aluminum foil, may be used to shield small areas of food (wingtips, leg ends, breast bones) from overcooking and overdefrosting. Metal reflects energy away from food and slows cooking. Special microwave thermometers designed to be left in the oven during cooking and temperature probes are also valuable tools. Shallow (no more than 1¾ inches in depth) foil convenience-food trays may be used. The amount of metal used must be in proportion to the volume of food; foil trays should be two-thirds to three-fourths full. Always keep metal at least 2 inches away from oven walls and ceiling to prevent arcing.

Special Microwave Accessories

Browning dishes and skillets make it easy to sear, brown or crisp foods such as steaks, hamburgers or chops in the microwave oven.

Microwave sandwich grills make it easy to cook and brown a single hamburger or grill a cheese sandwich. Follow manufacturer's instructions for preheating and cooking times.

Microwave popcorn poppers make it fast, easy and safe to pop fresh popcorn. Follow manufacturer's instructions for use.

Microwave coffee makers allow you to prepare two or four cups of freshly brewed coffee in minimum time.

Microwave thermometers and temperature probes are handy for microwave cooking. Instant-read thermometers, microwave meat thermometers and candy thermometers are ideal for testing temperature of meats, poultry, casseroles, soups and candies. Microwave meat and candy thermometers can be left in the microwave oven during cooking. Some instant-read thermometers can only be used outside the microwave oven. Some ovens are equipped with temperature probes. See page 16 or owner's manual for further information.

Roasting racks and bacon racks elevate meats during microwaving so they do not steam in fat and juices.

Not Recommended for Use in the Microwave Oven

Do not use metal pots, pans or bakeware, metal twist ties or dishes with metallic trim. Also avoid utensils with metal screws, bands or handles, metal reinforcement in some baskets or wicker-wrapped handles and conventional meat or candy thermometers. Melamine® or Centura® tableware, plastics that may be sensitive to hot foods, leaded crystal, antique or delicate glassware, fine bone china and ceramic mugs or cups with glued-on handles, brown paper bags and recycled paper products are not recommended for any microwave cooking use.

Microwave Cooking Principles

The key to successful microwave cooking is understanding the basic conditions which may affect cooking results. The speed and evenness of microwave cooking are influenced by characteristics of the food itself and by differences in line voltage. House power varies throughout the country. Voltage fluctuates and is lower during periods of peak consumption.

Microwaves penetrate foods to a depth of about ¾ to 1½ inches on all surfaces: top, bottom and sides. The interior of foods greater than 2 inches in diameter heats by conduction, as it does in conventional cooking. Foods with high water, fat or sugar content respond quickly to microwave energy.

Quantity. Small amounts cook faster than large ones. Microwaving time is always directly related to the amount of food and increases with the quantity. When doubling a recipe, increase time by about one-half and check for doneness.

Size. Small pieces cook faster than large ones. To speed cooking, cut pieces smaller than 2 inches so microwaves can penetrate to the center from all sides. For even cooking, cut vegetables, fruit and meat into pieces of uniform size.

Shape. Foods which are irregular in shape, like fish fillets, chicken breasts or drumsticks, take longer to cook in the thicker parts. To help them cook evenly, place the thickest parts to the outside of the dish, where they will receive more energy.

Starting temperature. Frozen or refrigerated food takes longer to heat than food at room temperature. Cooking times in this book are based on normal storage temperatures. Since rooms, refrigerators and freezers differ in temperature, check for doneness at the minimum time.

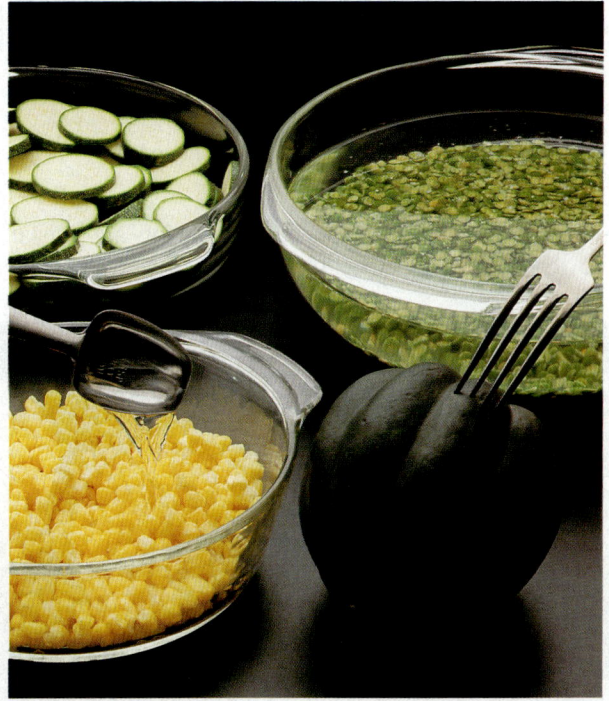

Moisture content. Microwaves are readily attracted to moisture. Naturally moist foods microwave better than dry ones. Add a minimum of liquid to moist foods, as excess water slows cooking.

Fat and bone. Marbling within meat or a thin, even layer of fat on a roast attracts energy and speeds cooking. Drain excess drippings in dish during cooking to speed cooking. Bone conducts heat, so areas next to it may cook faster than other areas.

Density. Porous foods, such as ground beef or mashed potatoes, cook faster than dense foods, such as steak or whole potatoes, since microwaves penetrate them more easily. Turn dense foods over after one-half cooking time to speed and equalize cooking.

11

Microwave Cooking Techniques

Many of the techniques of microwaving are similar to those used in conventional cooking. They help equalize energy in the food so that it cooks evenly and quickly, allowing you the full benefit of microwave speed.

Dish shapes and sizes affect the way foods cook, the amount of attention they require during cooking and the speed at which they cook. The depth of the container is a key to success. Food in a shallow casserole will cook faster than food in a deep dish of the same capacity. Avoid casseroles with sloping sides. A straight-sided casserole keeps the depth of food uniform for even cooking. Whenever possible, choose round dishes. Square or rectangular dishes may lead to overcooking in the corners. Ring shapes are excellent for foods that cannot be stirred during microwaving.

Shielding is a useful technique that protects sensitive areas of food from overcooking. Use small strips of aluminum foil on the wing tips, ends of drumsticks or the breastbone of a turkey, top or edges of a roast, or corners of a square cake or a pan of bar cookies. These small pieces of foil reflect microwave energy away from the food, acting as a protective shield. Heat transfer from other areas of the food cooks shielded areas. Keep foil at least 2 inches from oven walls and ceiling. Covering meats with a sauce also acts as a shield to prevent drying.

Covering

Glass lids will hold in steam to tenderize food, keep moisture in and speed cooking.

Plastic wrap holds in steam to speed cooking and tenderize food. Vent by turning back one edge to form a narrow slot for steam to escape. A tight, unvented plastic cover may split during cooking. Always remove plastic cover away from yourself to prevent steam burns.

Wax paper forms a loose, nonstick cover similar to "partial covering" in conventional cooking. Use it to hold in heat, speed cooking and prevent splatters with foods that do not need to steam.

Paper towels allow steam to escape while they prevent splatters and absorb excess moisture. They are excellent for covering bacon or foods that tend to splatter. Napkins and paper towels are also good for warming bread or rolls. Choose plain white napkins and paper towels. Avoid paper products with heavy dyes and prints.

Microwave Cooking Techniques (continued)

Arrange foods such as individual meat loaves and baking potatoes in a ring around the outside of turntable spacing at least 1 inch apart so energy can penetrate from top and sides.

Turn foods over once during microwaving to speed cooking of medium-size pieces, such as chicken or hamburgers. Large items, such as a turkey, roast or whole cauliflower, should be turned over during cooking time to speed and equalize cooking.

Rearrange closely packed foods, such as meatballs, during cooking, so pieces from the outside are moved to the center. Tuck thin ends of fish fillets under for more even cooking.

Stir foods such as casseroles, vegetables, soups and sauces from the outside to the center of dish once or twice during cooking to equalize heat and speed microwaving. Foods will not scorch or stick, so there's no need to stir constantly as you do in conventional cooking.

Standing time allows food to complete cooking after it is removed from the oven. Since heat is in the food, not the microwave oven, many foods build up enough internal heat so that they continue to cook by themselves. It is important to let roasts, cakes and whole vegetables stand to finish cooking. This will allow the centers to be done without overcooking or drying the outsides.

Standing time can range from 1 to 15 minutes. Recipes direct slight undercooking to compensate for standing times. Tent roasts with foil during standing time. Internal temperature will rise 10 to 20°F. during standing. Cakes will appear moist on top surface, but when they are allowed to stand directly on countertop, heat is trapped and finishes the cooking.

Browning develops on roasts and turkeys or on chops, steaks and hamburgers microwaved in a browning utensil. Many foods cook so quickly in the microwave oven, they do not have time to brown. A browning agent is an easy way to add color and flavor to food. For meats and poultry, use bouquet sauce mixed with water or melted butter; or use soy, Worcestershire,

barbecue or steak sauce. A sprinkling of paprika or dry gravy mix, jelly glaze or a crumb coating also gives a browned appearance. Casseroles can be topped at the end of microwaving with grated cheese or crumbs. Finish cakes and breads with frostings or toppings or grease the cake dish and coat it with graham cracker crumbs.

Microwave Cooking Techniques: Doneness Tests

Many techniques for testing doneness are the same as the ones you use for conventional cooking. One key difference is learning to let standing time finish cooking microwaved foods.

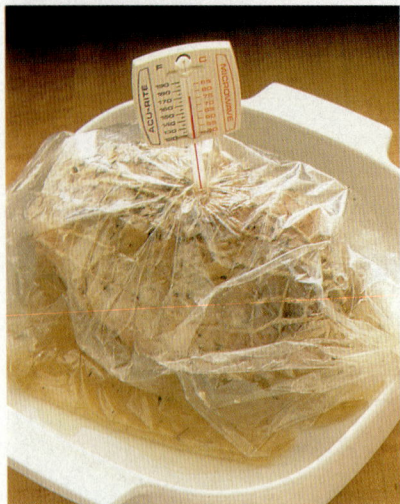

Cook meats to their proper internal temperatures. See chart on pages 36 and 37 for removal and temperatures after standing. Casseroles, soups and stews should be at least 165°F. when removed from the oven.

Fish flakes easily with fork when done. The center is slightly translucent but continues to cook during standing time. Fish toughens and dries if overcooked.

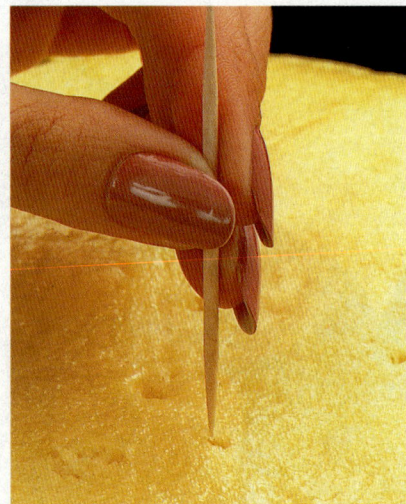

Test cake for doneness by inserting wooden pick in center. If the pick comes out clean and the edges pull away from the dish, cake is done. Let stand directly on countertop to trap heat. Small moist spots on surface will finish cooking during standing time.

Using Temperature Probes

A good way to eliminate guesswork when testing for doneness is to use a temperature probe. If your oven comes with a temperature probe, use it to cook foods such as roasts, casseroles, soups and hot drinks to a given temperature. The probe shuts the oven off automatically when food reaches a preset internal temperature. The tip of the probe should be inserted in the center of the food at least two-thirds of its length. Insert temperature probe in roasts at the center of the meatiest portion, not touching bone or fat. Boneless cuts of pork are advised. For casseroles, soups or beverages, you may want to support the probe by covering casserole with two sheets of plastic wrap, slightly overlapping at center. Insert probe at center where plastic wrap meets.

Recipe Conversion

Many conventional recipes can be converted simply by cutting back on cooking time. The best guide is a microwave recipe similar to the one being converted.

Reduce liquid in conventional recipes which call for raw ingredients, simmering or long baking times. Little evaporation occurs during microwaving, so use two-thirds the liquid and add more, if needed, as you cook.

Omit fat needed to brown foods and prevent sticking in conventional cooking. A small amount of margarine or olive oil may be used for flavor. Since many foods do not brown in the microwave oven, you may want to use a sauce or topping, such as Cheddar cheese, or a browning agent to enhance their appearance or flavor.

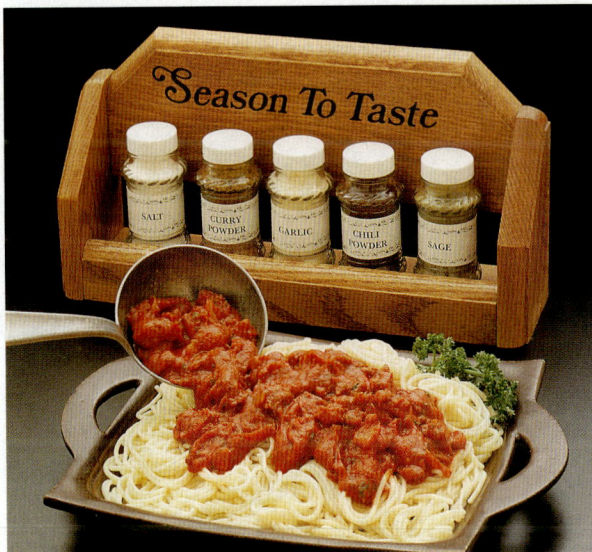

Use less salt, since it attracts microwave energy and draws liquid out of food. To avoid brown specks on vegetables or dry spots on meats, combine salt with a sauce or salt food after cooking. Use less of highly flavored seasonings like garlic, chili, curry powder, sage and pepper. After microwaving, correct seasoning to taste. Small amounts of mild herbs and spices need not be changed.

Reduce power level when microwaving long-cooking dense foods, such as roasts; delicate foods, like egg-based custards, quiches and cream-based sauces or high-protein foods, like cheese-based sauces and fondues. For cakes and quick breads, use lower power level initially for food to rise evenly; finish with higher power level to set structure. At reduced power levels, delicate foods won't overcook, and meats have time to cook evenly without overcooking edges.

17

Reheating

Reheating food is a specialty of the microwave oven. Many Sharp microwave ovens are equipped with special programmed settings or automatic sensors for reheating favorite foods. If your oven has an automatic reheat setting, check your operation manual for specific directions. For freshest-tasting results, use power levels recommended in chart, opposite.

Plates of food. Arrange food with thickest parts of meat and bulky vegetables to outside of plate and quick-to-heat less-dense foods in center. Spread single serving of a main dish in an even layer on plate. Cover with wax paper or plastic wrap. Reheat until bottom of plate feels very warm in the center. Temperature should be at least 165°F.

Pasta, rice and rolls. For leftover rice or pasta, drizzle with 1 tablespoon water per cup and reheat, covered. To reheat bread, rolls or muffins, wrap in paper towel and microwave only until warm to the touch, not piping hot. Breads heat in seconds; overheating can cause breads to become tough, dry and hard.

Meats. Medium (¼-inch) slices reheat best. Cover meat with sauce or gravy to protect from drying out. Meats with sauce should be covered with wax paper to hold in heat. Cover meat slices without gravy with paper towel.

Reheating Chart

Item	Starting Temperature	Microwave Time	Procedure
Plate of Food 1 serving of meat, 2 servings of vegetables	Room temp. Refrigerated	MED.-HIGH (70%) 1½-3 min. 3-4 min.	Meaty portions and bulky vegetables to outside. Cover with wax paper.
Meat (Chicken pieces, chops, hamburgers, meat loaf slices) 1 serving 2 servings	 Refrigerated Refrigerated	MED.-HIGH (70%) 1-2 min. 2½-4½ min.	Cover loosely.
Meat Slices (Beef, ham, pork, turkey) 1 or more servings	 Room temp. Refrigerated	MEDIUM (50%) 45 sec.-1 min. per serving 1-3 min. per serving	Cover with gravy or wax paper. Check after 30 sec. per serving.
Stirrable Casseroles and Main Dishes 1 serving 2 servings 4-6 servings	 Refrigerated Refrigerated Refrigerated	HIGH (100%) 2-4 min. 4-6 min. 6-8 min.	Cover. Stir after half the time.
Nonstirrable Casseroles and Main Dishes 1 serving 2 servings 4-6 servings	 Refrigerated Refrigerated Refrigerated	MEDIUM (50%) 5-8 min. 9-12 min. 13-16 min.	Cover with wax paper.
Soup, Cream 1 cup 1 can (10¾ oz.)	Refrigerated Room temp.	MEDIUM (50%) 3-4½ min. 5-7 min.	Cover. Stir after half the time.
Soup, Clear 1 cup 1 can (10¾ oz.)	Refrigerated Room temp.	HIGH (100%) 2½-3½ min. 4-5½ min.	Cover. Stir after half the time.
Pizza 1 slice 1 slice 2 slices 2 slices	Room temp. Refrigerated Room temp. Refrigerated	HIGH (100%) 15-25 sec. 30-40 sec. 30-40 sec. 45-55 sec.	Place on paper towel on microwave-safe rack.
Vegetables 1 serving 2 servings	Refrigerated Refrigerated	HIGH (100%) ¾-1½ min. 1½-2½ min.	Cover. Stir after half the time.
Baked Potato 1 2	Refrigerated Refrigerated	HIGH (100%) 1-2 min. 2-3 min.	Cut potato lengthwise and then several times crosswise. Cover with wax paper.
Breads (Dinner or breakfast roll) 1 roll 2 rolls 4 rolls	 Room temp. Room temp. Room temp.	HIGH (100%) 8-12 sec. 11-15 sec. 18-22 sec.	Wrap single roll, bagel or muffin in paper towel. To reheat several, line plate with paper towel; cover with another paper towel.
Pie Whole 1 slice	Refrigerated Refrigerated	MED-HIGH (70%) 5-7 min. HIGH (100%) 30 sec.	

Defrosting Frozen Foods

Defrosting food with the microwave oven is not only faster than any other method, it can also give better results. Many microwave ovens are designed with a special automatic defrost setting which makes it safe, quick and easy to defrost meats and poultry. Check your operation manual for specific directions.

Once frozen meat is defrosted, it begins to lose its juices. Microwave ovens give you the advantage of letting you defrost meat just before you cook it for maximum juiciness and quality.

Microwave defrosting is easy, but some attention is needed to make sure that the ice crystals in frozen food melt without the food starting to cook. MEDIUM-LOW (30%) is fast enough to be convenient but gradual enough to give good results. At MEDIUM (50%), meat defrosts in about one-third less time but needs more attention.

Place plastic or paper-wrapped package of frozen food directly in oven. To speed defrosting, remove wrap as soon as possible and cover food with wax paper to hold in heat and prevent moisture loss. Foil wrappings must be removed.

Break up or separate ground beef, cubed meat, chicken pieces or fish fillets after one-third of defrosting time. Remove any defrosted portions and put remainder in baking dish to complete defrosting.

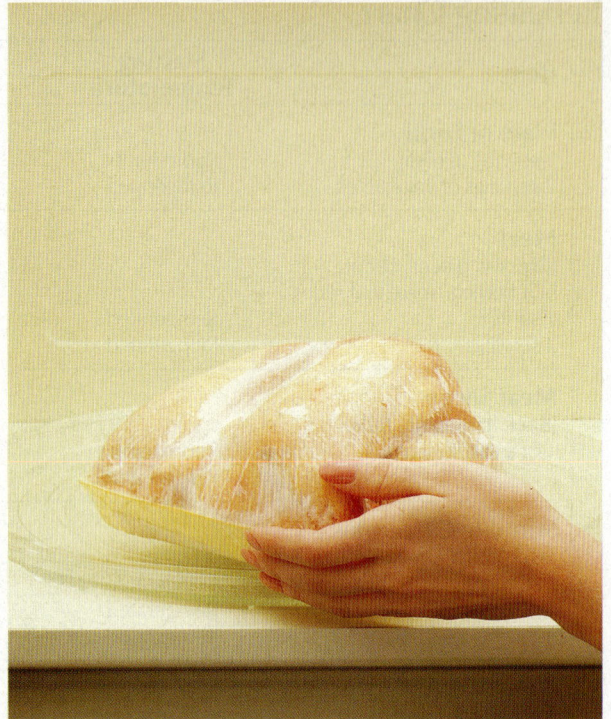

Turn over flat roasts, steaks, chops, whole chickens or Cornish hens after half the defrosting time. If package contains several steaks or chops, separate as soon as possible and place in baking dish.

Remove wrapping from turkey so you can feel warm spots as it defrosts. Metal clamps holding legs should be removed as soon as possible. Start breast side down, shield warm areas with small strips of foil and turn over after each one-fourth of time.

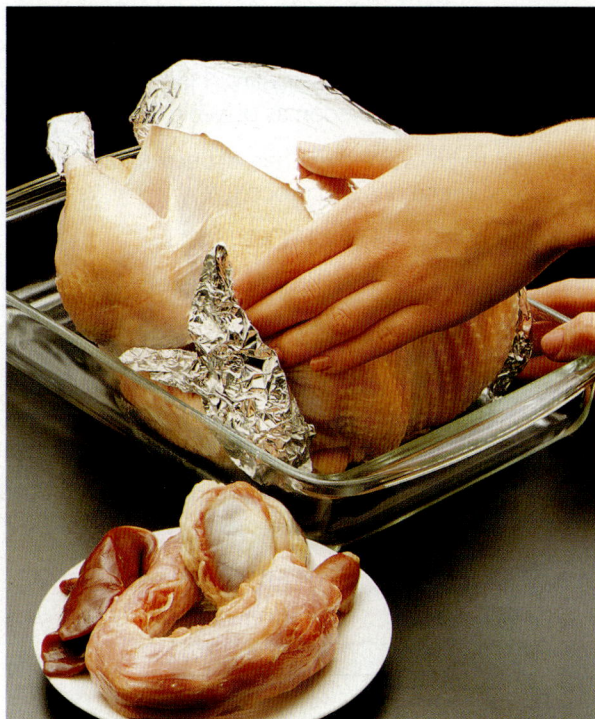

Let turkey stand 20 to 30 minutes submerged in cold water after defrosting, until giblets and neck can be removed and breast meat under wings is completely defrosted. Turkey may be microwaved with clamps if they are difficult to remove.

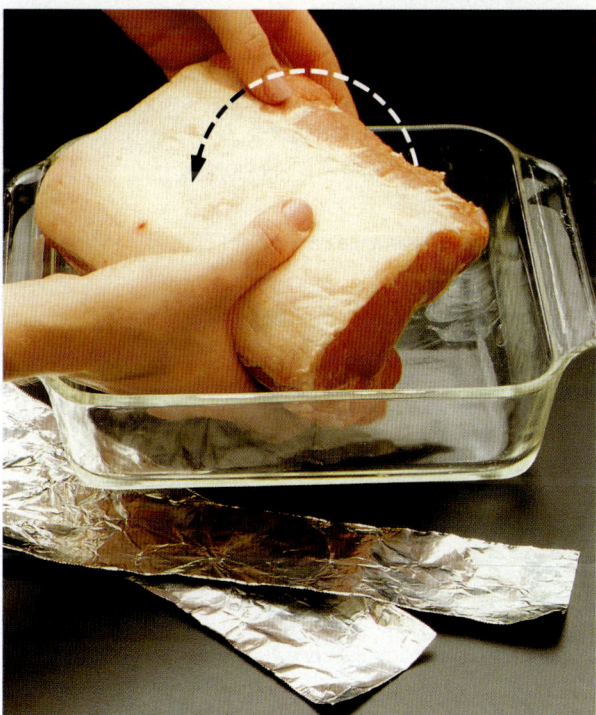

Turn over large roasts after half the defrosting time. As you turn, touch meat for warm areas and shield these with small pieces of foil. Let roasts stand 20 to 30 minutes after second half of defrosting time.

Defrost meats and poultry only until they can be pierced to the center with a skewer or wooden pick. Surface or cavity should feel cool but not icy. Cook immediately after defrosting or refrigerate until cooking time.

Defrosting Frozen Foods Chart

General procedure for defrosting: Place plastic or paper-wrapped packages of frozen food directly in oven. Remove wrappings as soon as possible then place in baking dish. Cover with wax paper. Continue defrosting.

If your microwave oven has a special automatic defrost setting, be sure to read the operation manual for recommendations and procedure.

Power Level: MEDIUM-LOW (30%)

Cut	Microwave Time	Standing Time	Special Instructions
Meats			
Ground Meat	5-10 min. per lb.	5-10 min.	Break apart, remove any defrosted pieces as soon as possible. Place remainder in baking dish.
Chops	5½-8½ min. per lb.	5-10 min.	Separate and turn over once.
Ribs	7-12 min. per lb.	10-15 min.	Separate and rearrange once.
Steaks & Flat Roasts	7-9½ min. per lb.	5-10 min.	Turn over after half the time. Shield as needed.
Thick Roasts	9½-11½ min. per lb.	20-30 min.	Turn over after half the time. Shield as needed.
Cubed Meat	8-12 min. per lb.	5-10 min.	Separate and rearrange once.
Poultry			
Whole Turkey	7½-10 min. per lb.	20-30 min.	Divide total time into 4 parts. Place breast side down in baking dish. Microwave one-fourth of total time. Turn breast side up. Microwave one-fourth of time. Shield warm spots as needed. Let stand 15 minutes. Turn turkey on side. Microwave one-fourth of time. Turn on other side. Microwave remaining time. Remove giblets. Let stand in cool water until cool but not icy, 20 to 30 minutes.
Half Turkey, Turkey Breast	7-10½ min. per lb.	15-20 min.	Breast side down. Turn over after half the time. Shield as needed. Rinse in cool water after defrosting.
Turkey Pieces	7-10½ min. per lb.	5-10 min.	Turn over after half the time. Shield as needed. Rinse in cool water after defrosting.
Whole Chicken	5-9 min. per lb.	10-20 min.	Breast side down. Turn over after half the time. Shield as needed.
Chicken Quarters, Pieces	8-11 min. per lb.	5-15 min.	Separate and rearrange once.
Boneless Breasts	7-11 min. per lb.	15-20 min.	Place on roasting rack. Microwave for half the time. Separate pieces. Microwave remaining time until pliable but cold.
Duck	8-11 min. per lb.	10-20 min.	Breast side down. Turn over after half the time. Shield as needed.
Cornish Hens	9-12 min. per lb.	5-10 min.	Breast side down. Turn over after half the time. Shield as needed.
Fish & Seafood			
Fillets & Steaks	8-10 min. per lb.	5-10 min.	Separate and rearrange once.
Whole Small Fish	7-14 min. per lb.	5-10 min.	Separate and rearrange once.
Scallops & Shrimp	5-9 min. per lb.	5 min.	Separate and rearrange once.

Convenience Foods

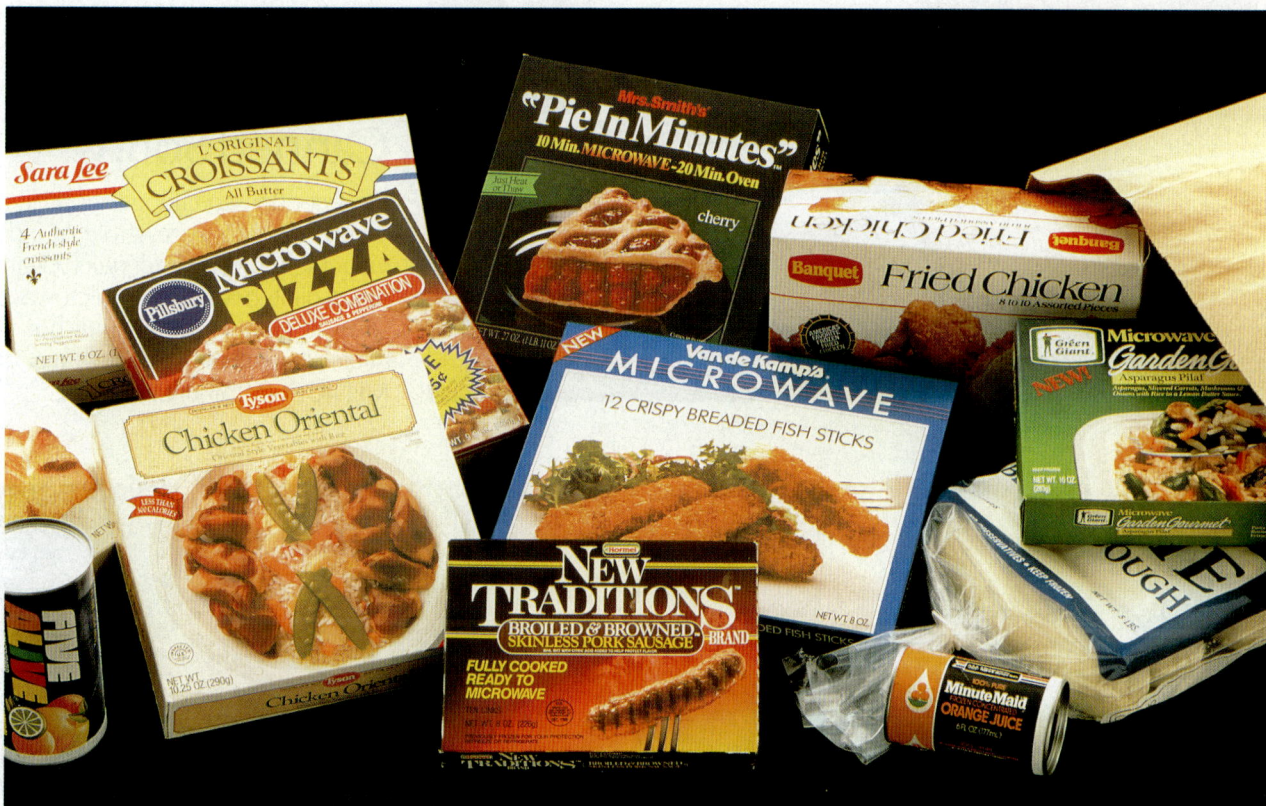

Most convenience foods now include microwave directions, making it easier than ever to enjoy soups, snacks, beverages, entrees and desserts. The package instructions are usually for HIGH (100%) for maximum speed and efficiency.

How to Defrost Bagels and Muffins

Wrap frozen bagel or muffin in a paper towel or napkin. Microwave at HIGH (100%) until just warm to the touch (about 15 to 45 seconds for one, 45 seconds to 1 minute for two). Split bagels or muffins and toast, if desired.

How to Defrost Orange Juice or Lemonade Concentrate

Remove one metal lid from 6-ounce can of frozen juice. Place can upright in oven. Microwave at HIGH (100%) 30 seconds to 1 minute 30 seconds. Concentrate should be softened but not warm. Pour into container and stir in cold water as directed on can.

How to Microwave Canned Soups

Heat condensed canned soups in a 4-cup measure, a casserole or individual serving bowls for quick clean-ups. If diluted with water, microwave soup at HIGH (100%) until hot. If diluted with milk, microwave at MEDIUM (50%) until hot.

How to Pop Popcorn

Now it's faster and easier than ever to pop fresh popcorn in your microwave oven. You can use special microwave popcorn poppers. Be sure to follow the manufacturer's simple instructions. Ready-to-pop packages of microwave popcorn offer maximum convenience. The directions are on the package. "Listen" for the popping to slow. Selected Sharp microwave ovens are equipped with a separate popcorn setting to automatically pop packaged microwave popcorn; corn is done when it stops popping. See owner's manual for exact instructions.

French Fries and Other Favorites

For speedy, crisp French fries and other convenience frozen potato products, first defrost in the microwave and then place under conventional broiler or on a microwave browning tray to crisp.

CONVECTION
MICROWAVE
COOKBOOK

What is Convection Microwave Cooking?

The convection microwave oven is the ultimate cooking team. This state-of-the-art system brings together the best of both worlds. Enjoy the browning and crisping capabilities of convection plus the speed of microwave cooking. Microwaving brings out the natural flavor of foods and keeps them moist and juicy. Convection cooking adds the advantage of browning and crisping food beautifully. Combination settings LOW MIX and HIGH MIX use convection heat to seal and brown the outside while using microwave energy to make sure the interior is cooked.

Breads and cakes are done to perfection; roasts and poultry brown and crisp just right. The results are superior to conventional methods, giving you the widest range of options for creative cooking and timesaving ease. It is not necessary to preheat with combination settings.

When you compare foods cooked in a convection microwave oven with those cooked conventionally, you'll discover the advantages of this advanced system.

Turkey is an excellent example of the superb results you can achieve with this team. The combination oven lets you roast a larger turkey than is possible with microwaving alone. No turning over is needed, and you don't need to baste unless a special seasoning is desired. Turkey roasted conventionally browns well, but white meat often becomes dry in the time needed to cook dark meat completely. Combination settings use hot air roasting for crisp, brown skin plus microwaving speed for moist, juicy meat.

Breads and cakes also turn out beautifully. The convection microwave team bakes bread with a golden brown, crisp crust and fine texture. Cakes are tender, moist and evenly cooked with a nicely browned surface. You can also bake two layers at a time rather than the one-at-a-time method of microwave-only baking.

LOW MIX combines convection heat with microwave power for perfect baking results. Use the Low Mix setting for baked goods that require more than 20 minutes baking time. Angel food and bundt cakes, quick breads and yeast breads and large muffins are examples of foods that bake perfectly at this setting. Check owner's manual for further information.

HIGH MIX combines convection heat with microwave power, providing crisp brown exteriors and superior juiciness for meats. Longer-cooking foods, such as roasts, whole turkey and chicken and poultry pieces, cook in about half of the time with just the right amount of browning. Check owner's manual for further information.

What is Convection Cooking?

With convection cooking, a high-speed fan circulates air past the heat source and around the food. The superheated air browns and crisps the food beautifully.

Convection cooking is ideal for foods requiring 20 minutes or less cooking time. Two sheets of cookies or two pans of muffins bake at the same time, saving you time. Preheating is necessary with convection cooking. Use the convection setting for baked goods such as cookies, biscuits, cupcakes and small muffins or frozen or refrigerated convenience-food items.

What is Convection Broiling?

In convection broiling, food is elevated on the broiling trivet, allowing cooking to occur on all sides simultaneously. It is not necessary to turn foods over during cooking. Fats drip away from the food, providing for great flavor without all the fat.

Convection Broiling is easier than ever with the unique one-step programming broiling feature of Sharp Carousel II Microwave Ovens. Prepare hamburgers, chops, steaks, fish steaks and chicken pieces with ease and minimum attention.

Foods and Best Cooking Methods

There's an easy way to cook each of your favorite foods. Matching the best method and setting to the food is the secret to success time after time. This chart keeps it simple by giving you the everyday guidelines you need. Now you can tell at a glance whether it's best to use the Convection or Microwave only method, the Broil setting or combination cycles of LOW MIX/Bake or HIGH MIX/Roast.

| Convection | ▇ | Low Mix | ▇ | Microwave | ▇ |
| Broil | ▇ | High Mix | ▇ | | |

Food	Convection	Low Mix	High Mix	Broil	Microwave
Breads & Rolls					
Biscuits	▇				
Bread Loaves		▇			
Rolls	▇				
Cakes					
Bundt		▇			
Cupcakes	▇				
Layer Cakes	▇				
Loaf Cakes or Quick Breads		▇			
Muffins (regular size)	▇				
Muffins (bakery-style, large size)		▇			
Tube Cakes		▇			
Cookies					
Bar or Brownies		▇			
All Other Cookies	▇				
Defrosting					▇
Desserts					
Cheesecake		▇			
Cream Puffs or Eclairs	▇				
Crisps or Cobblers		▇			
Frozen Convenience Foods					
Bake under 20 min.	▇				
Bake over 20 min.		▇			

Food	Convection	Low Mix	High Mix	Broil	Microwave
Meat, Fish & Poultry					
Bacon					●
Casseroles			●		
Chicken, Whole Roasting			●		
Chicken Pieces			●	●	
Chops — Lamb, Pork, Veal				●	
Hamburgers				●	
Ham Steak				●	
Hot Dogs					●
Fish & Seafood			●		●
Meat Loaf			●		
Roasts — Beef, Lamb, Pork, Veal			●		
Sausage				●	
Steaks & London Broil				●	
Turkey, Whole & Breast			●	●	
Pies					
Crust	●				
Custard or Pumpkin		●			
Double-Crust			●		
Frozen Prepared Custard		●			
Frozen Prepared Fruit			●		
Variety Pies (pecan, chess, etc.)		●			
Pizza	●				
Potatoes					
Quick					●
Crispy	●				
Reheating Leftovers					●
Vegetables					●

Convection Microwave Utensils

A wide variety of utensils may be used in convection and combination cooking. Many of them are also suitable for microwaving alone. Microwave-only paper and plastic products should not be used for combination cooking or placed in the oven while it is still hot from convection cooking.

Be sure to use hot pads when handling utensils. They become hot from convection and combination cooking.

The Carousel Turntable is a utensil itself: a drip pan under the broiling trivet during roasting and broiling or a baking sheet for breads and cookies.

Baking rack serves as a shelf for two-level cooking, such as layer cakes or cookies. Use it for convection and combination cooking.

Metal and aluminum foil pans are safe for combination as well as convection cooking. During the convection cycle, heat transferred from the pan cooks the bottom and sides of food. During the microwave cycle, energy penetrates from the top.

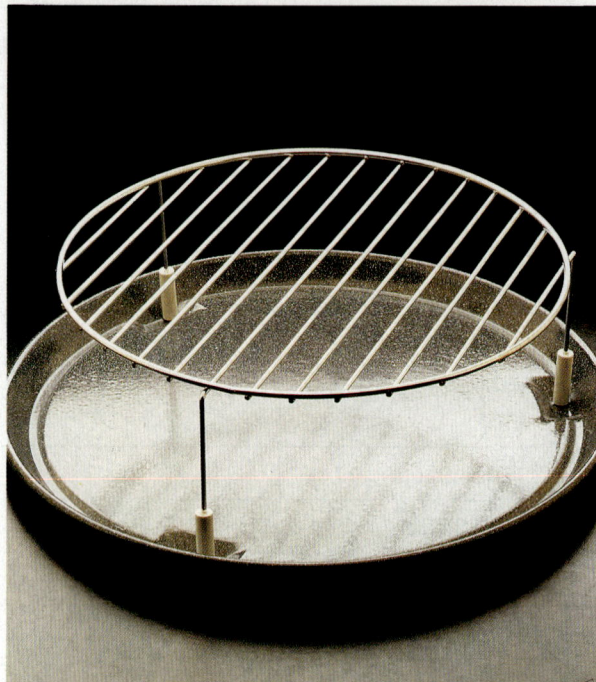

Oven glass is excellent for convection, combination and microwave cooking. Stoneware and pottery utensils may be used if they are also microwave-safe. See the dish test on page 7. Bagged microwave popcorn must be placed on an overturned glass pie plate placed on the turntable.

Glass ceramic (Pyroceram®) casseroles go from oven to table. They are microwave-safe and resist the heat of surface elements as well as ovens.

Ovenable paper is designed for use in both microwave and conventional ovens up to 400°F., so it's suitable for convection or combination cooking, too. Other paper products used for microwaving alone, such as paper napkins and towels, cannot be used with convection heat.

Thermoset® plastics are heat-resistant to temperatures of 425°F. as well as microwave-safe. They are sold as dual-purpose utensils and can be used. Do not use any other plastics for combination and convection cooking.

Dual safe microwave/conventional thermometers may be used in the oven during combination cooking. Other thermometers should only be used outside the oven, since microwave thermometers are not heat-resistant and conventional types are not microwave-safe.

7c

Stuffed Pork Chops, page 19c

Roasting Techniques

Preheating the oven is not necessary for roasted meat and poultry. Place foods on broiling trivet which holds meat out of its juices. You don't even need a pan because the turntable will catch the drippings. For moist, tender, perfectly done meat in a fraction of the conventional time, just season meat and place it in the oven and cook, following the temperature and time in chart on page 11c.

Optional utensils are metal or foil roasting pans, oven-glass baking dishes or Pyroceram® casseroles. Elevate meat on a heat-resistant rack, if desired, and place utensil on turntable.

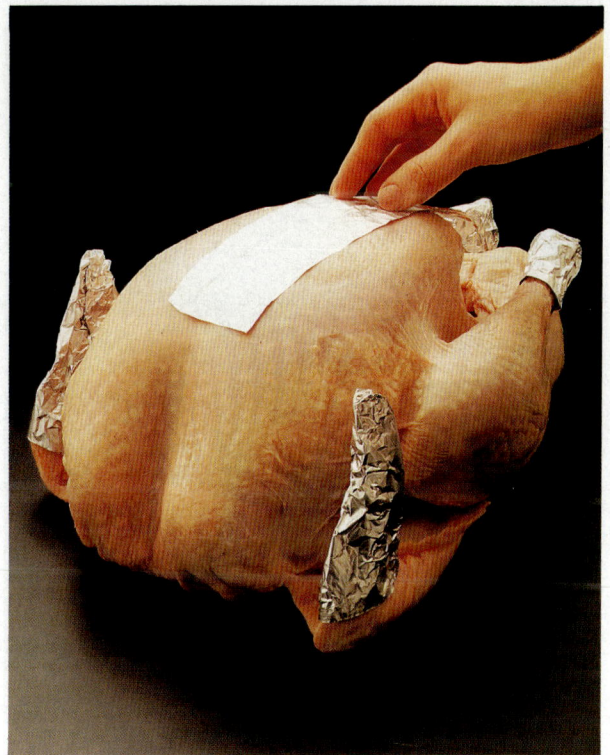

Shield thin or bony areas of roasts or breast, wing tips and legs of birds to prevent overbrowning. Be sure foil does not touch trivet or oven walls.

Roast meat in oven-glass baking dish or shallow Pyroceram® casserole when you wish to make gravy. When meat is done, let it stand on carving board. Microwave gravy in the same dish.

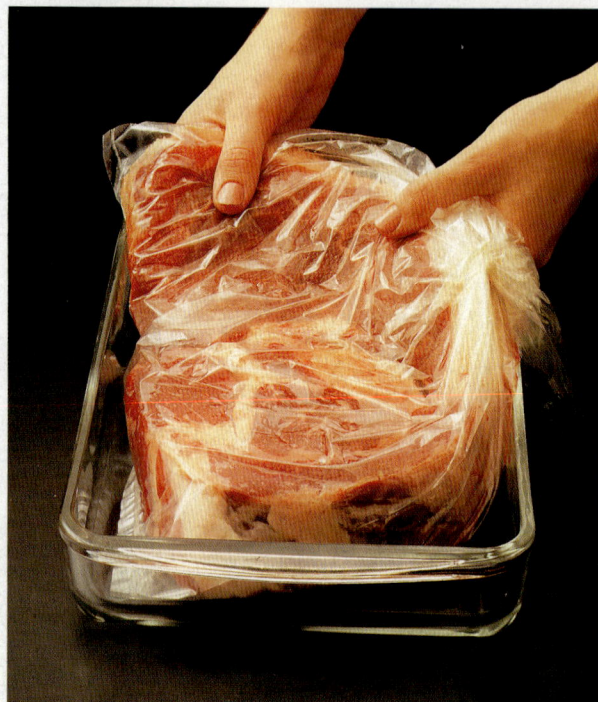

Roast less-tender cuts of beef in heat-resistant and microwave oven-safe covered casserole or in oven cooking bag set in baking dish. Covering helps tenderize meat. You may also use the SLOW COOK setting.

Check doneness after minimum time using a meat thermometer. Removal temperatures are listed on page 11c. If meat is not done, cook 5 minutes longer and check again. Let stand, tented with foil, 5 to 10 minutes before carving.

Dual safe microwave/convection meat thermometer may be inserted in fresh meat before cooking. Other thermometers should only be used outside the oven.

Combination Roasting Chart

Cut		Time	Removal Temperature	Internal Temp. After Standing
Beef				
Roasts (tender cuts)	Rare:	12-14 min. per lb. at HIGH MIX	120°F.	140°F.
	Medium:	13-15 min. per lb. at HIGH MIX	130°F.	150°F.
	Well Done:	14-17 min. per lb. at HIGH MIX	150°F.	160°F.
Roasts (less tender cuts)	Rare:	12-15 min. per lb. at HIGH MIX	120°F.	140°F.
	Medium:	13-17 min. per lb. at HIGH MIX	130°F.	150°F.
	Well Done:	14-18 min. per lb. at HIGH MIX	150°F.	160°F.
Veal				
Roasts (boned, rolled, tied)	Well Done:	14-16 min. per lb. at HIGH MIX	155°F.	165°-170°F.
Breast (stuffed)	Well Done:	11-13 min. per lb. at HIGH MIX	160°F.	170°F.
Pork				
Roasts (boned, rolled, tied or bone-in)	Well Done:	14-16 min. per lb. at HIGH MIX	165°F.	170°F.
Smoked Ham		7-9 min. per lb. at HIGH MIX	130°F.	140°F.
Lamb				
Leg Roasts	Rare:	10-12 min. per lb. at HIGH MIX	120°F.	130°F.
	Medium:	12-14 min. per lb. at HIGH MIX	135°F.	145°F.
	Well Done:	14-16 min. per lb. at HIGH MIX	150°F.	160°F.
Poultry				
Chicken, whole		9-13 min. per lb. at HIGH MIX	175°F.	185°F.
Chicken, pieces		10-12 min. per lb. at *HIGH MIX, 375°F.	175°F.	185°F.
Turkey Breast		13-16 min. per lb. at HIGH MIX	165°F.	170°F.
Turkey (unstuffed)		7-10 min. per lb. at HIGH MIX	175°F.	185°F.

*Necessary to change temperature on HIGH MIX.

Broiling Techniques

Check chart, opposite, for maximum broiling time. Program oven for maximum time, on BROIL or 450°F., following directions in operation manual. Season and slash fat at 1-inch intervals. When audible signal sounds that oven is preheated, quickly put food in oven.

Cook for the minimum time recommended in the chart; then test for doneness. Time varies with the thickness or weight of meat and degree of desired doneness. Turning meat over is not necessary, as moving air cooks it on both sides.

Spray trivet and turntable with nonstick vegetable cooking spray for easy cleanup. Do not cover trivet with aluminum foil, as it blocks the flow of warm air that cooks the food.

Broil food in advance, if desired, then slice. Individual servings may be reheated as needed by microwaving at MEDIUM (50%), following directions on page 19.

Convection Broiling Chart

Cut	Weight/Thickness	Convection Time
Beef		
Rib-eye Steak	¾-1 in. 7-8 oz. each	Rare: 10-13 min. Medium: 14-16 min. Well Done: 17-20 min.
Steaks: Sirloin, Porterhouse, T-bone	1-1½ in.	Rare: 10-13 min. Medium: 14-18 min. Well Done: 19-25 min.
Chuck Steak	1 in.	Rare: 12-14 min. Medium: 15-18 min. Well Done: 19-23 min.
London Broil	1-1¼ in. 2½-3 lbs.	Rare: 23-25 min. Medium: 26-30 min.
Hamburgers	¼ lb. each	Medium: 13-15 min. Well Done: 18-20 min.
Pork		
Chops: loin or center	¾-1 in.	Well Done: 16-20 min.
Bacon	Regular sliced Thick sliced	4-5 min. 7-8 min.
Sausage: Brown 'n Serve	Patties: ½ in., 8 oz. - 1 lb.	8-10 min.
Fresh	Links: 8 oz. - 1 lb.	8-10 min.
Ham slice, fully cooked	¾ in.	10-12 min.
Frankfurters	1 lb.	5-7 min.
Lamb		
Chops: rib, loin or center	¾ in. 3-4 oz. each	Medium: 12-14 min. Well Done 15-17 min.
Chicken		
Broiler-Fryer, halved, quartered or cut up	1-3 lbs.	25-35 min.
Fish		
Fillets	¼-¾ in.	6-7 min.
Steaks	¾ in.	12-14 min.

◄ Pot Roast with Vegetables

4 to 5-pound round or chuck pot roast
½ teaspoon salt
½ teaspoon garlic powder
½ teaspoon dried thyme leaves
⅛ teaspoon pepper
4 potatoes, peeled and quartered
3 onions, quartered
2 carrots, sliced
¾ cup water
2 tablespoons brown bouquet sauce

Makes 8 servings

Place meat in 4-quart casserole. Pat seasonings into meat. Add vegetables. Combine water and browning sauce; pour into casserole dish. Cover.

Roast 20 to 22 minutes per pound on HIGH MIX or until meat is fork-tender. Allow to stand 5 minutes.

Per Serving:			
Calories:	325	Fat:	11 g.
Protein:	36 g.	Cholesterol:	102 mg.
Carbohydrate:	21 g.	Sodium:	227 mg.

Meat Loaf Surprise

1½ pounds ground beef
1 egg
1 small onion, chopped
1 carrot, grated
1 stalk celery, finely chopped
½ cup seasoned bread crumbs
¼ cup catsup
½ teaspoon dried thyme leaves
¼ teaspoon garlic powder
⅛ teaspoon pepper
¼ pound boiled ham, sliced
¼ pound Swiss cheese, sliced

Makes 6 servings

Thoroughly combine all ingredients except ham and cheese. On a sheet of wax paper, press mixture into a 9 × 12-inch rectangle.

Layer sliced ham on meat, then cheese. Roll up, starting at narrow end. Seal ends to form loaf. Place seam side down in loaf pan, 9 × 5 inches. Roast 30 to 35 minutes on HIGH MIX or until internal temperature reaches 155°F. Cover and allow to stand 5 to 10 minutes.

Per Serving:			
Calories:	384	Fat:	23 g.
Protein:	30 g.	Cholesterol:	145 mg.
Carbohydrate:	12 g.	Sodium:	525 mg.

Steak Roulade ▲

¼ cup red wine
¼ cup soy sauce
¼ cup vegetable oil
1½ pounds flank steak
1 medium onion, diced
1 stalk celery, diced
½ green pepper, diced
½ cup sliced mushrooms
2 tablespoons margarine or butter
½ cup seasoned bread crumbs

Makes 4 servings

Combine wine, soy sauce and oil in large dish. Add steak and marinate several hours.

Combine remaining ingredients, except bread crumbs, in small bowl. Microwave at HIGH (100%) until vegetables are tender, 4 to 5 minutes. Stir in crumbs.

Remove meat from marinade. Spread filling evenly over meat. Roll meat up, starting at narrow end. Tie securely with string. Place in glass pie plate and on broiling trivet. Roast 30 minutes on HIGH MIX or until internal temperature reaches 130°F.

Per Serving:			
Calories:	461	Fat:	29 g.
Protein:	35 g.	Cholesterol:	90 mg.
Carbohydrate:	13 g.	Sodium:	536 mg.

Oriental Flank Steak

¼ cup sherry
2 tablespoons packed brown sugar
¾ teaspoon salt
3 tablespoons soy sauce
3 tablespoons Hoisin sauce
3 tablespoons catsup
1 tablespoon minced fresh ginger
2 green onions, thinly sliced
1 to 1½-pound flank steak

Makes 4 servings

Combine all ingredients except flank steak in medium bowl. Pour over steak. Marinate at least 2 hours or overnight. Preheat oven for broiling.

Place flank steak on broiling trivet. Broil in preheated oven 18 to 22 minutes for rare, 22 to 26 minutes for medium, brushing with marinade several times.

Per Serving:			
Calories:	226	Fat:	13 g.
Protein:	22 g.	Cholesterol:	60 mg.
Carbohydrate:	4 g.	Sodium:	421 mg.

◄ Hearty Pizza

1 pound ground beef or
   4 to 6 ounces sliced pepperoni
2 medium onions, chopped
2 cloves garlic, finely chopped
2 tablespoons olive oil
1 can (28 oz.) crushed tomatoes in puree
1 tablespoon dried oregano leaves
1 teaspoon dried basil leaves
½ teaspoon salt
⅛ teaspoon pepper
3 cups all-purpose flour
1 package active dry yeast
½ teaspoon salt
¾ cup milk
¼ cup water
2 tablespoons vegetable oil
2 cups shredded mozzarella cheese (about
   8 ounces)
   Yellow cornmeal

*Makes two 12-inch pizzas,
16 servings*

If using ground beef, place in a medium-sized bowl. Microwave at HIGH (100%) until beef loses pink color, 4 to 6 minutes, stirring to break up beef after half the cooking time. Drain and set aside.

Combine onion, garlic and olive oil in medium bowl. Microwave at HIGH (100%) until vegetables are tender, 4 to 6 minutes. Stir in crushed tomatoes in puree, spices, ½ teaspoon salt and the pepper.

Microwave at HIGH (100%) until bubbly, about 3 minutes. Stir. Reduce power to MEDIUM (50%). Microwave until thickened, 6 to 8 minutes.

Mix flour, yeast and ½ teaspoon salt in large bowl. Stir in milk, water and oil to make a pliable dough. Knead until smooth, about 2 minutes. Place in well-greased large bowl; turn greased side up. Cover with clean, moist towel. Place in oven at 100°F. until double in size, about 40 minutes. (Dough is ready if an indentation remains when touched.)

Remove dough and turntable from oven. Preheat oven to 425°F. Punch down dough. Divide dough in half. With well-greased fingers, pat dough onto 2 greased 12 × ⅝-inch metal pizza pans, which have been sprinkled with cornmeal. Pinch dough to form edge. Prick crust. Bake on turntable and baking rack 12 to 15 minutes or until crusts are golden brown. Top crusts with pizza sauce, ground beef or pepperoni and cheese. Bake at 425°F., 6 to 10 minutes or until cheese is melted and beginning to brown.

Per Serving:			
Calories:	245	Fat:	11 g.
Protein:	12 g.	Cholesterol:	26 mg.
Carbohydrate:	24 g.	Sodium:	333 mg.

Tamale Casserole

1 pound lean ground beef
1 medium onion, chopped
1 small green pepper, chopped
2 cans (8 ounces each) tomato sauce
1 clove garlic, minced
1 teaspoon chili powder
1 teaspoon taco seasoning mix
½ teaspoon sugar
¼ teaspoon salt
¼ teaspoon pepper

Corn Bread:
½ cup yellow cornmeal
½ cup all-purpose flour
2 teaspoons baking powder
1 tablespoon sugar
¼ teaspoon salt
½ cup milk
1 egg
2 tablespoons melted shortening

Topping:
½ cup shredded Cheddar cheese (about
   2 ounces)
¼ cup sliced pitted black olives

Makes 6 servings

Mix ground beef, onion and green pepper in 2-quart casserole. Microwave at HIGH (100%) 5 minutes, stirring to break up beef after half the cooking time. Stir in tomato sauce, garlic, chili powder, taco seasoning mix, sugar, salt and pepper. Microwave at HIGH (100%) 5 minutes. Reduce power to MEDIUM-HIGH (70%). Microwave 5 minutes.

Combine cornmeal, flour, baking powder, sugar and salt in medium bowl. Stir in milk, egg and shortening. Beat mixture until almost smooth.

Pour over beef mixture. Bake 25 minutes on *HIGH MIX, 375°F. or until corn bread is golden. Sprinkle with topping ingredients. Cool 5 minutes before serving.

*Necessary to change temperature on HIGH MIX.

Per Serving:			
Calories:	341	Fat:	16 g.
Protein:	22 g.	Cholesterol:	108 mg.
Carbohydrate:	27 g.	Sodium:	909 mg.

Ginger Pork Kabobs

1 egg, beaten
½ cup crushed chow mein noodles
¼ cup apple juice
2 tablespoons soy sauce
1 tablespoon grated gingerroot
1 pound ground pork
1 can (8 ounces) pineapple chunks (juice pack), drained
1 large red pepper, cut into ¾-inch chunks
½ cup apple juice
2 tablespoons cider vinegar
1 teaspoon cornstarch

Makes 4 servings

Mix egg, crushed noodles, ¼ cup apple juice, soy sauce and gingerroot. Crumble ground pork into mixture; blend thoroughly, shape into 1-inch balls. Set aside.

For glaze, mix ½ cup apple juice, vinegar and cornstarch in small bowl. Microwave at HIGH (100%) until thickened, 1½ to 3 minutes, stirring every 30 seconds.

Preheat oven for broiling. Thread pork balls alternately with pineapple and red pepper chunks on 4 wooden or metal skewers. Place on broiling trivet.

Brush kabobs with glaze. Broil in preheated oven 15 to 20 minutes. Brush with remaining glaze before serving.

Per Serving:			
Calories:	256	Fat:	7 g.
Protein:	29 g.	Cholesterol:	153 mg.
Carbohydrate:	18 g.	Sodium:	652 mg.

Steak Kabobs ▲

¼ cup sugar
¼ cup soy sauce
¼ cup white wine
1 tablespoon vegetable oil
1 teaspoon ground ginger
¼ teaspoon salt
2 pounds lean top beef round steak, cut into 1-inch cubes
2 large green peppers, cut into chunks
2 medium tomatoes, cut into quarters
1 can (8 ounces) pineapple chunks (juice pack), drained

Makes 4 servings

Mix sugar, soy sauce, wine, oil, ginger and salt in medium bowl. Stir in steak cubes; cover. Marinate at room temperature 1 hour or at least 4 hours in refrigerator.

Preheat oven for broiling. Remove steak cubes from marinade; reserve marinade. Thread steak cubes alternately with remaining ingredients on 8 wooden or metal skewers. Place on broiling trivet. Broil 7 to 9 minutes or until desired doneness, brushing with marinade after half the time.

Note: Skewers up to 12 inches can be used.

Per Serving:			
Calories:	432	Fat:	17 g.
Protein:	52 g.	Cholesterol:	153 mg.
Carbohydrate:	15 g.	Sodium:	381 mg.

Stuffed Pork Chops

4 pork chops, 1¼ inches thick
1 cup chopped apple
½ cup soft bread crumbs
½ cup chopped walnuts
¼ cup chopped onion
¼ cup raisins
1 egg
1 teaspoon dried parsley flakes
½ teaspoon dried thyme leaves
¼ teaspoon ground sage
⅛ teaspoon pepper

Makes 4 servings

Make pocket in each chop. Combine remaining ingredients; mix well. Stuff each chop with one-fourth of the mixture. Place chops directly on turntable or round baking pan.

Roast 30 minutes on HIGH MIX or until meat next to bone is no longer pink.

Per Serving:			
Calories:	451	Fat:	26 g.
Protein:	36 g.	Cholesterol:	156 mg.
Carbohydrate:	19 g.	Sodium:	100 mg.

Pineapple Pork Roast

1 cup pineapple preserves
¼ cup prepared mustard
1 tablespoon prepared horseradish
1 tablespoon soy sauce
3 to 5-pound pork roast

Makes 6 servings

Combine all ingredients except pork roast in small bowl. Place roast on broiling trivet.

Roast 14 to 16 minutes per pound on HIGH MIX or until internal temperature reaches 165°F.

Cover roast with sauce during last 20 minutes of cooking. Cover and let stand 10 minutes before serving. Extra sauce may be heated and served with roast.

Per Serving:			
Calories:	394	Fat:	15 g.
Protein:	29 g.	Cholesterol:	93 mg.
Carbohydrate:	36 g.	Sodium:	376 mg.

Convert your own casserole recipes.

Bake 25 to 30 minutes on HIGH MIX or until thoroughly heated.

Glazed Stuffed Cornish Hens ▲

1 cup chopped pecans
¾ cup apricot preserves
¼ cup margarine or butter, melted
3 tablespoons orange juice concentrate
1 tablespoon lemon juice
1 cup seasoned stuffing cubes
½ cup water
2 Cornish hens (1½ pounds each)

Makes 4 servings

Combine pecans, preserves, melted margarine, orange juice concentrate and lemon juice. Combine half the sauce mixture with stuffing cubes and water. Stuff cavity of each bird. Truss birds.

Pour half of the remaining sauce over hens. Brush with remaining sauce halfway through cooking time.

Roast 13 to 15 minutes per pound on HIGH MIX or until meat next to bone is no longer pink. Internal temperature of stuffing should register 165°F.

Per Serving:

Calories:	743	Fat:	36 g.
Protein:	34 g.	Cholesterol:	74 mg.
Carbohydrate:	75 g.	Sodium:	670 mg.

Roast Chicken

1 teaspoon ground ginger
½ teaspoon ground coriander
  Dash of pepper
5 to 6-pound roasting chicken
2 tablespoons margarine or butter
½ cup minced onion
½ cup plain yogurt
½ cup half-and-half
1 teaspoon turmeric
½ teaspoon salt

Makes 6 servings

Combine ginger, coriander and pepper; rub into chicken. Tie legs of chicken; place breast side up on broiling trivet on turntable.

Place margarine in a medium bowl. Microwave at HIGH (100%) until melted, 30 to 45 seconds. Blend in remaining ingredients. Reserve one-fourth cup of the mixture; set aside. Spread remaining mixture over chicken.

Roast 10 to 12 minutes per pound on HIGH MIX or until chicken next to bone is no longer pink. Combine pan drippings and reserved sauce. Microwave at HIGH (100%) until hot, about 1 minute. Serve with chicken.

Per Serving:			
Calories:	284	Fat:	15 g.
Protein:	32 g.	Cholesterol:	100 mg.
Carbohydrate:	4 g.	Sodium:	337 mg.

Mustard and Mayonnaise Chicken

2½ to 3-pound broiler-fryer chicken, cut up
¼ cup spicy prepared mustard
¼ cup mayonnaise

Makes 5 servings

Arrange chicken pieces skin side up on round baking pan or directly on turntable. Combine mustard and mayonnaise; spread on chicken pieces.

Roast 35 minutes on HIGH MIX or until chicken next to bone is no longer pink.

Per Serving:			
Calories:	233	Fat:	15 g.
Protein:	21 g.	Cholesterol:	72 mg.
Carbohydrate:	—	Sodium:	479 mg.

Poultry Pie

Filling:
3 cups diced, cooked boneless chicken or turkey
1 package (10 ounces) frozen peas, defrosted
1 can (10¾ ounces) condensed cream of mushroom soup
½ cup milk
2 tablespoons chopped pimiento
½ teaspoon dried oregano leaves
½ teaspoon dried marjoram leaves
½ teaspoon salt
¼ teaspoon dried thyme leaves
¼ teaspoon garlic powder
⅛ teaspoon pepper

Crust:
1 cup all-purpose flour
1¼ teaspoons baking powder
½ teaspoon salt
¼ cup margarine or butter
3 to 5 tablespoons milk

Makes 8 servings

Combine filling ingredients in a 9-inch deep-dish pie pan; set aside.

Combine flour, baking powder and salt in medium bowl. Cut in margarine until mixture resembles coarse crumbs. Add enough milk to form a soft dough. Roll out on lightly floured surface to fit top of dish. Fit dough onto dish. Trim, seal and flute. Cut small slits in crust.

Place on broiling trivet. Bake 25 to 30 minutes on *LOW MIX, 375°F., or until thoroughly heated and top is browned.

*Necessary to change temperature on LOW MIX.

Per Serving:			
Calories:	284	Fat:	13 g.
Protein:	20 g.	Cholesterol:	49 mg.
Carbohydrate:	21 g.	Sodium:	774 mg.

Broiled Chicken

1 cup dry white wine
1 medium onion, chopped
1 tablespoon dried thyme leaves
½ teaspoon salt
½ teaspoon garlic powder
⅛ teaspoon pepper
2½ to 3-pound broiler-fryer chicken, cut up

Makes 4 servings

Combine all ingredients except chicken. Place chicken skin side down in large dish. Pour marinade over chicken. Marinate 2 hours.

Preheat oven for broiling. Remove chicken from marinade; reserve marinade. Place chicken pieces on broiling trivet. Broil until chicken next to bone is no longer pink, about 30 minutes.

Pour marinade into small bowl. Microwave at HIGH (100%) until onion is soft, about 2 minutes. Pour over chicken pieces.

Per Serving:			
Calories:	235	Fat:	7 g.
Protein:	27 g.	Cholesterol:	81 mg.
Carbohydrate:	5 g.	Sodium:	349 mg.

Herb Roasted Chicken

3 tablespoons margarine or butter, softened
1 clove garlic, minced
3 tablespoons grated Parmesan cheese
½ teaspoon ground sage
¾ teaspoon thyme leaves
¾ teaspoon basil leaves
5 to 6 pound roasting chicken

Makes 6 servings

Cream together margarine, garlic, Parmesan cheese, sage, thyme and basil.

Turn chicken breast side up and work your fingers under the skin at the openings on each side of the breast. Continue into thigh and leg and make the skin as smooth as possible. Using fingers, spread herb mixture evenly under skin.

Place chicken, breast side up on broiling trivet. Bake 9 to 13 minutes per pound on HIGH MIX or until chicken next to bone is no longer pink.

Per Serving:			
Calories:	270	Fat:	15 g.
Protein:	32 g.	Cholesterol:	94 mg.
Carbohydrate:	1 g.	Sodium:	216 mg.

Stuffed Turkey Loaf

1 package (6 ounces) stuffing mix
1½ pounds ground turkey or ground beef
1 egg, slightly beaten
1 small onion, finely chopped
½ cup quick-cooking oats
½ cup applesauce
½ teaspoon salt
⅛ teaspoon white pepper
¼ teaspoon ground thyme
½ teaspoon poultry seasoning
1 teaspoon Worcestershire sauce
  Turkey gravy (1 can, jar or prepared dry mix)

Makes 6 servings

Per Serving:			
Calories:	369	Fat:	17 g.
Protein:	25 g.	Cholesterol:	106 mg.
Carbohydrate:	30 g.	Sodium:	964 mg.

Prepare stuffing according to package directions for microwaving. Set aside 2 cups. Place remaining stuffing in small casserole to be reheated later.

Thoroughly combine remaining ingredients, except for turkey gravy. In a 10-inch glass pie plate, shape ½ of the mixture into an oval. Flatten center being sure to leave one-inch sides.

Place reserved 2 cups of stuffing inside the center. Cover with remaining meat mixture. Press to seal edges and form a loaf shape. Roast 30 to 35 minutes on HIGH MIX or until internal temperature in center of stuffing reaches 170°F. Let stand, covered, 10 minutes before slicing. Slice and serve with heated gravy and reheated leftover stuffing.

Sesame Oven-Fried Chicken ▲

1 egg
½ cup milk
½ cup all-purpose flour
2 tablespoons sesame seed
1 teaspoon baking powder
2 teaspoons paprika
1 teaspoon garlic powder
½ teaspoon salt
2½ to 3½-pound broiler-fryer chicken, cut up
½ cup margarine or butter, melted

Makes 5 servings

Beat egg and milk in medium bowl. Combine flour, sesame seed, baking powder, paprika, garlic powder and salt in plastic or paper bag. Dip chicken pieces in egg mixture, then shake in bag to coat. Arrange chicken pieces skin side up on turntable. Pour margarine evenly over chicken. Bake 35 minutes on *HIGH MIX, 375°F.

*Necessary to change temperature on HIGH MIX.

Per Serving:
Calories:	399	Fat:	27 g.
Protein:	26 g.	Cholesterol:	122 mg.
Carbohydrate:	12 g.	Sodium:	578 mg.

Honey Mustard Chicken

½ cup coarse ground mustard
¼ cup Dijon-style mustard
¼ cup honey
2 to 3 pounds boneless chicken breasts and thighs, skin removed

Makes 4 servings

Combine coarse mustard, Dijon mustard and honey. Set aside.

Preheat oven for broiling. Place chicken in 9-inch oven-safe dish. Put dish on broiling trivet and broil in pre-heated oven 25 to 30 minutes or until chicken is no longer pink. When chicken is about half cooked, pour off any liquid and brush with sauce to cover chicken pieces completely.

Per Serving:
Calories:	368	Fat:	8 g.
Protein:	50 g.	Cholesterol:	133 mg.
Carbohydrate:	19 g.	Sodium:	950 mg.

◀ Broiled Salmon with Basil Sauce

2 tablespoons olive oil
1 clove garlic, minced
¼ cup white wine
2 tablespoons lemon juice
1 cup fresh basil*
¼ cup grated Parmesan cheese
½ teaspoon Dijon-style mustard
4 salmon steaks (1¼ to 1½ pounds) or haddock, halibut, swordfish
  Cayenne pepper

Makes 4 servings

Combine oil, garlic, white wine and lemon juice in blender. Add basil, Parmesan cheese and mustard and blend until smooth. Preheat oven for broiling.

Put one-fourth of basil sauce in bottom of 9-inch oven-safe dish. Arrange steaks on sauce and pour remaining sauce over tops of steaks. Sprinkle with cayenne.

Place dish on broiling trivet and broil in preheated oven 20 to 24 minutes or until fish flakes easily when tested with a fork.

*If not available substitute ½ cup fresh parsley and 2 tablespoons dried basil.

Per Serving:			
Calories:	357	Fat:	21 g.
Protein:	35 g.	Cholesterol:	97 mg.
Carbohydrate:	2 g.	Sodium:	209 mg.

Crunchy Crab Boats

1 can (6 ounces) fancy white crabmeat, drained
1 package (3 ounces) cream cheese, softened
½ cup chopped almonds
2 tablespoons green onions, chopped
1 tablespoon dry white wine
1 teaspoon lemon juice
1 teaspoon prepared horseradish
¼ teaspoon garlic powder
¼ teaspoon salt
  Dash of white pepper
  Dash of cayenne pepper
2 hard rolls, cut in half
¼ cup shredded Swiss cheese

Makes 4 servings

Spicy Shrimp

¼ cup white wine
¼ cup water
3 tablespoons soy sauce
2 tablespoons sugar
1 tablespoon vegetable oil
2 teaspoons dried parsley flakes
⅛ to ¼ teaspoon ground ginger
  Dash of hot pepper sauce
1 pound jumbo raw shrimp, shelled and deveined

Makes 4 servings

Mix all ingredients except shrimp in medium bowl. Stir in shrimp; cover. Marinate at room temperature 45 minutes or 3 hours in refrigerator.

Preheat oven for broiling. Remove shrimp from marinade; reserve marinade. Place shrimp on round baking pan. Broil 6 to 8 minutes, brushing with marinade after half the time.

Microwave remaining marinade at HIGH (100%) 2 minutes. Serve over rice or as a dipping sauce when served as an appetizer, if desired.

Per Serving:			
Calories:	109	Fat:	2 g.
Protein:	18 g.	Cholesterol:	129 mg.
Carbohydrate:	3 g.	Sodium:	319 mg.

Preheat oven for broiling. Remove any bits of shell or cartilage from crab. Combine with next 10 ingredients. Mix well. Set aside.

Spread one-fourth of crab filling on each roll half. Place Swiss cheese on top of each. Place on broiling trivet.

Broil in preheated oven 8 to 10 minutes or until cheese is melted and crab is hot. Sprinkle with paprika and serve.

Per Serving:			
Calories:	292	Fat:	19 g.
Protein:	15 g.	Cholesterol:	57 mg.
Carbohydrate:	15 g.	Sodium:	416 mg.

Cheese Soufflé ▲

¼ cup margarine or butter
¼ cup all-purpose flour
½ teaspoon salt
⅛ teaspoon cayenne pepper
1½ cups milk
2 cups shredded Cheddar cheese (about 8 ounces)
6 eggs, separated

Makes 4 servings

Place margarine in large bowl. Microwave at HIGH (100%) until melted, about 1 minute. Blend in flour, salt and cayenne. Gradually stir in milk. Microwave at MEDIUM-HIGH (70%) until slightly thickened, about 6 minutes, stirring every 2 minutes. Add cheese. Microwave at MEDIUM-HIGH (70%) 2 minutes; stir to blend.

Preheat oven to 325°F. Beat egg yolks. Stir a small amount of hot sauce gradually into egg yolks; return to sauce, blending well. Cool slightly.

Beat egg whites until soft peaks form. With rubber spatula fold egg whites into cheese sauce, half at a time, just until blended. Pour into greased 2-quart soufflé dish. Bake 30 to 35 minutes on *LOW MIX, 325°F. or until top is puffed and golden and center is set. Serve immediately.

*Necessary to change temperature on LOW MIX.

Per Serving:			
Calories:	531	Fat:	41 g.
Protein:	27 g.	Cholesterol:	478 mg.
Carbohydrate:	12 g.	Sodium:	912 mg.

Frittata ▲

¾ cup diced green pepper
¾ cup diced mushrooms
¾ cup diced zucchini
¾ cup diced onion
½ cup diced pimiento
2 tablespoons vegetable oil
6 eggs
2 packages (8 ounces each) cream cheese
¼ cup milk
2 cups cubed bread (3 slices)
1½ cups shredded Cheddar cheese
1 teaspoon salt
½ teaspoon garlic powder
¼ teaspoon pepper

Makes 8 servings

Combine vegetables and oil in medium bowl; cover. Microwave at HIGH (100%) until vegetables are tender, about 5 minutes. Drain liquid.

Beat eggs with cream cheese and milk until smooth. Mix in remaining ingredients. Pour into buttered 9-inch spring form pan.

Bake 30 minutes on LOW MIX or until set in center. Cool 10 to 20 minutes. Cut into wedges.

Per Serving:			
Calories:	426	Fat:	36 g.
Protein:	16 g.	Cholesterol:	292 mg.
Carbohydrate:	12 g.	Sodium:	685 mg.

Strawberry Puff Ring, page 41c

Convection-Only Techniques

Preheating the oven is necessary with convection cooking of smaller, faster-cooking food items that require less than 20 minutes of baking. Foods requiring longer baking time use LOW MIX.

Two-level baking allows baking of two pans of cookies, small muffins or pizzas at the same time. Round baking pans are excellent cooking utensils for many convection-only items.

Convenience foods such as frozen appetizers, pizzas, egg rolls and refrigerated bread products bake and brown quickly with convection-only cooking. Follow package directions for conventional baking times.

Cake Techniques

Layer Cakes. Use a mix or your own conventional recipe. Follow recipe or package directions for preheating and baking instructions. Use baking rack and turntable to bake two layers at once.

Tube or Bundt Cakes. Do not preheat oven. Bake cakes for three-fourths of time on recipe or package directions using LOW MIX. Bake cake on broiling trivet. If arcing occurs with fluted tube pan, place a heat-and-microwave-safe dish or plate between pan and broiling trivet.

Angel Food. Do not preheat oven. Bake your recipe or a mix 25 to 30 minutes on LOW MIX or until crust is golden brown, firm and looks very dry.

Loaf Cakes or Quick Breads. Do not preheat oven. Bake for three-fourths of time on recipe or package directions using LOW MIX. Test for doneness at minimum time. If loaf is not done, let stand in oven a few minutes to complete cooking.

Pie Techniques

Pie Shell. Use mix, frozen pie dough, or your recipe for single crust pie. Prick crust with fork. Preheat oven to 425°F. Place pie shell on broiling trivet; bake with convection heat 8 to 10 minutes or until lightly browned. Cool and fill.

Double Crust or Crumb Top Pies. Prepare pie as you would for conventional baking; make slits in top of two crust pie. Preheat oven to 400°F. Place pie on broiling trivet. Bake double crust or lattice pies 25 to 35 minutes on *HIGH MIX, 400°F.; crumb top pies 20 to 25 minutes on *HIGH MIX, 400°F. (*Necessary to change temperature on HIGH MIX).

Custard Pies. Prebake and cool pie shell as directed above. Fill with uncooked custard. Without preheating, bake pie on round baking pan placed on broiling trivet for 30 to 35 minutes on *LOW MIX, 325°F. If custard is not set, let stand in oven a few minutes to complete cooking. (*Necessary to change temperature on LOW MIX).

Frozen Prepared Custard-Type Pies. Preheat oven to temperature listed on package. Place pie on broiling trivet. Bake three-fourths of package time using LOW MIX set at the package temperature. If filling is not set, let stand in oven to complete cooking. **Frozen Prepared Fruit Pies.** Do not preheat oven. Bake on broiling trivet. Use *HIGH MIX, 375°F. Bake 8-inch, 35 minutes; 9-inch, 40 to 45 minutes. (*Necessary to change temperature on HIGH MIX).

Bread & Baking Techniques

Proofing dough. Use your own recipe or frozen dough. Place in well-greased bowl or loaf pan; cover with damp cloth. Place in oven at *SLOW COOK 100°F. 30 to 45 minutes. Frozen dough will take longer, 2 to 2¾ hours. Dough is doubled when impressions remain after fingers are pressed ½ inch into dough. (*Necessary to change temperature on SLOW COOK.)

Preheating of oven is not necessary. Bake one loaf 25 minutes and two loaves 30 minutes at LOW MIX. After baking, bread should be golden brown and sound hollow when tapped. Do not let bread stand in oven; remove from pans immediately to cool on wire rack.

Braid or other shape. Remove turntable from oven. Shape bread; place directly on turntable. No preheating is needed. Bake for three-fourths of the time in your conventional recipe on LOW MIX.

Combination Baking Chart

Item	Procedure
Cakes: Your recipe or mix	
Tube or Bundt Cakes**	Bake on broiling trivet three-fourths the recommended time on LOW MIX.
Angel Food	Bake 25 to 30 minutes on LOW MIX.
Loaf Cakes or Quick Breads	Bake three-fourths the recommended time on LOW MIX.
Bar Cookies: Your recipe or mix	Bake three-fourths the recommended time or until wooden pick inserted in center comes out clean on LOW MIX.
Pies	
Single Crust: baked before filling, your recipe, mix or frozen prepared	Prick crust with fork. Preheat oven to 425°F. Bake on broiling trivet 8 to 10 minutes or until lightly browned. Let cool before filling.
Double Crust	Preheat oven to 400°F. Bake on broiling trivet 25 to 35 minutes on *HIGH MIX 400°F.
Crumb Top	Preheat oven to 400°F. Bake on broiling trivet 20 to 25 minutes on *HIGH MIX 400°F.
Custard Pie	Prebake, following directions for single crust; cool. Fill with desired uncooked custard. Bake on round baking pan on broiling trivet 35 minutes on *LOW MIX 325°F. If custard is not set, let stand in oven a few minutes.
Pecan Pie	Preheat oven to 350°F. Bake on broiling trivet 25 to 30 minutes on LOW MIX.
Frozen Prepared Fruit Pies	Place on broiling trivet and bake 30 to 40 minutes using *HIGH MIX 375°F.
Frozen Prepared Custard Pies	Preheat oven to package temperature. Place on broiling trivet and bake three-fourths of package time using LOW MIX and package temperature. If not set, let stand in oven a few minutes.
Breads	
Loaf: Your recipe or frozen, defrosted and proofed	Bake 25 to 30 minutes on LOW MIX for 1 to 2 loaves.
Braid or other shape	Remove metal turntable from oven. Place bread directly on metal turntable. Bake on LOW MIX for three-fourths the conventional time.
Muffins	
Large, bakery-style	Bake three-fourths the recommended package or recipe time on LOW MIX.
Desserts	
Cheesecake	Bake three-fourths the recipe time on LOW MIX or until center is nearly set.
Crisps and Cobblers	Bake three-fourths the recipe time on LOW MIX.

**If arcing occurs while using a fluted tube pan, place a heat-resistant dish (Pyrex® pie plate, glass pizza tray or dinner plate) between the pan and the broiling trivet.

*Necessary to change temperature on HIGH MIX and LOW MIX.

Convection Baking Chart

Item (for foods requiring 25 minutes or less)	Baking Time and Temperature
Appetizers: Brown and serve, pastry	Follow package directions.
Biscuits: Your recipe, mix or refrigerator	Follow recipe or package directions.
Cookies: Drop, rolled, refrigerator, spritz, molded	Follow recipe or package directions.
Fish Sticks: Frozen	Follow package directions.
Layer Cakes: Your recipe or mix	Follow recipe or package directions.
Muffins: Your recipe or mix	Follow recipe or package directions.
Pizza: Your recipe or frozen	Follow recipe or package directions.
Puff Pastry: Your recipe or frozen	Follow recipe or package directions.
Rolls: Your recipe, package or refrigerator	Follow recipe or package directions.

◄ Chocolate Chip Bars

2¼ cups all-purpose flour
1 teaspoon baking soda
½ teaspoon salt
¾ cup granulated sugar
¾ cup packed brown sugar
½ cup margarine or butter
½ cup vegetable oil
1 teaspoon vanilla
2 eggs
1 package (12 ounces) chocolate chips
1 cup chopped nuts

Makes 32 bars

Combine flour, soda and salt; set aside. Cream together sugars, margarine, oil and vanilla. Beat until creamy. Beat in eggs. Gradually add flour mixture; mix well. Stir in chocolate chips and nuts.

Spread mixture into 2 ungreased square pans, 8 × 8 inches. Bake 20 to 25 minutes on LOW MIX or until wooden pick inserted in center comes out clean. Let cool in pans. Cut into 32 squares.

Per Serving:			
Calories:	208	Fat:	13 g.
Protein:	2 g.	Cholesterol:	17 mg.
Carbohydrate:	23 g.	Sodium:	108 mg.

◄ Peanut Butter Cookies

½ cup peanut butter
½ cup granulated sugar
½ cup packed brown sugar
¼ cup margarine or butter
¼ cup vegetable shortening
1 egg
1¼ cups all-purpose flour
¾ teaspoon baking soda
½ teaspoon baking powder

Makes 3 dozen

Combine peanut butter, sugars, margarine, shortening and egg; beat until smooth. Blend in flour, baking soda and baking powder. Preheat oven to 375°F.

Shape dough into ¾-inch balls. Place 2 inches apart on lightly greased round baking pans. With fork, flatten in crisscross pattern.

Bake 12 minutes at 375°F. or until set but not hard. Cool on wire racks.

Per Serving:			
Calories:	85	Fat:	5 g.
Protein:	2 g.	Cholesterol:	8 mg.
Carbohydrate:	10 g.	Sodium:	62 mg.

Autumn Treasure Cookies

1 cup all-purpose flour
¼ teaspoon salt
¼ teaspoon baking powder
¼ teaspoon baking soda
½ cup packed brown sugar
½ cup granulated sugar
½ cup butter-flavor shortening
1 egg
1 cup rolled oats
1 teaspoon vanilla
½ cup Reese's Pieces® candy
½ cup M & M® candies (only orange, yellow and browns)

Makes 32 cookies

Preheat oven to 350°F. Grease 2 round baking pans; set aside.

Sift first 4 ingredients. Blend sugars and shortening. Add egg and beat well. Add the sifted mixture and mix well.

Add oats, vanilla and candies. Blend together well.

Drop by rounded tablespoonfuls onto prepared sheets. Bake 12 to 15 minutes at 350°F. or until golden brown. Cool cookies on wire racks.

Per Serving:			
Calories:	112	Fat:	5 g.
Protein:	2 g.	Cholesterol:	9 mg.
Carbohydrate:	15 g.	Sodium:	36 mg.

Orange Oatmeal Chippers

½ cup margarine or butter, softened
⅓ cup oil
¾ cup packed brown sugar
¼ cup granulated sugar
2 eggs
1 teaspoon orange extract
2 cups quick-cooking rolled oats
1 cup all-purpose flour
½ cup whole wheat flour
1 teaspoon baking soda
½ teaspoon salt
1 cup raisins or chocolate chips
1 tablespoon grated orange peel
½ cup coarsely chopped nuts

Makes 4 dozen

Carousel Crackles

1 cup semisweet chocolate chips
1 cup packed brown sugar
⅓ cup vegetable oil
2 eggs
1 teaspoon vanilla
1 cup all-purpose flour
1 teaspoon baking powder
¼ teaspoon salt
½ cup finely chopped walnuts
½ cup powdered sugar

Makes 4 dozen

Place chocolate chips in large mixing bowl. Microwave at HIGH (100%) until melted, about 2 minutes. Blend in brown sugar and oil. Add eggs, 1 at a time, beating well after each. Stir in vanilla. Combine flour, baking powder and salt; stir into chocolate mixture. Mix in nuts. Chill dough at least 1 hour.

Preheat oven to 350°F. Drop dough by rounded teaspoonfuls into powdered sugar; roll to coat. Place 2 inches apart on greased turntable or round baking pans. Bake 10 to 12 minutes at 350°F. Cool on wire racks.

Per Serving:			
Calories:	72	Fat:	4 g.
Protein:	1 g.	Cholesterol:	6 mg.
Carbohydrate:	10 g.	Sodium:	20 mg.

Preheat oven to 350°F. Cream together margarine, oil and sugars. Beat until creamy. Beat in eggs and orange extract; blend well.

Add rolled oats, flours, baking soda and salt; mix well. Stir in raisins or chocolate chips, orange peel and nuts.

Drop dough by teaspoonfuls 2 inches apart on greased round baking pans. Bake 8 to 12 minutes at 350°F. or until light golden brown. Cool on wire racks.

Per Serving:			
Calories:	95	Fat:	5 g.
Protein:	2 g.	Cholesterol:	11 mg.
Carbohydrate:	12 g.	Sodium:	72 mg.

◄ Chocolate Meringue Pie

¾ cup sugar
2 tablespoons cornstarch
2 cups milk
2 squares (1 ounce each) unsweetened chocolate
3 eggs, separated
2 tablespoons margarine or butter
1 teaspoon grated orange peel
1 9-inch baked pie shell
½ teaspoon cream of tartar
6 tablespoons sugar

Makes 8 servings

Mix sugar and cornstarch in medium bowl. Stir in milk. Add chocolate squares. Microwave at HIGH (100%) until smooth and thick, 6 to 8 minutes, stirring after 3 minutes. Stir a small amount of chocolate mixture into egg yolks; return to hot chocolate mixture, blending well. Microwave at MEDIUM-HIGH (70%) 3 minutes, stirring once. Stir in margarine and orange peel until margarine is melted. Pour into pie shell. Set aside.

Preheat oven to 425°F. Beat egg whites and cream of tartar until foamy. Beat in sugar, 1 tablespoon at a time; continue beating until stiff and glossy. Spoon meringue onto chocolate filling; spread over filling, carefully sealing meringue to edge of crust. Bake 8 to 10 minutes at 425°F. or until meringue is brown.

Per Serving:			
Calories:	349	Fat:	17 g.
Protein:	6 g.	Cholesterol:	108 mg.
Carbohydrate:	45 g.	Sodium:	228 mg.

Cheesecake ▲

Crust:
1¼ cups all-purpose flour
¾ cup margarine or butter
¼ cup sugar
1 egg yolk
Grated lemon peel from ½ lemon

Filling:
4 packages (8 ounces each) cream cheese
1¼ cups sugar
2 tablespoons all-purpose flour
4 eggs
1 egg yolk
2 tablespoons heavy cream
Grated lemon peel from ½ lemon

Makes 12 servings

Combine crust ingredients in small bowl; beat until well mixed. Refrigerate, covered, 1 hour.

Preheat oven to 400°F. Press one-third flour mixture into bottom of 9-inch spring form pan. Bake at 400°F. 8 minutes; cool.

In large bowl, beat cream cheese until smooth. Slowly beat in sugar. Add flour and remaining ingredients. Beat 5 minutes. Press remaining dough around side of pan to within 1 inch of top; do not bake. Pour cream cheese mixture into pan.

Bake 35 minutes on LOW MIX or until set. Let cheesecake remain in oven 30 minutes. Remove; cool in pan.

Per Serving:			
Calories:	560	Fat:	42 g.
Protein:	10 g.	Cholesterol:	223 mg.
Carbohydrate:	38 g.	Sodium:	383 mg.

Harvest Fruit Pie ▲

2 cups all-purpose flour
1 teaspoon salt
1 teaspoon ground cinnamon
2/3 cup plus 2 tablespoons vegetable shortening
4 to 5 tablespoons cold water
3/4 cup sugar
1/4 cup all-purpose flour
1/2 teaspoon ground cinnamon
1/2 teaspoon ground nutmeg
6 cups sliced, peeled apples and pears
2 tablespoons margarine or butter
1 tablespoon milk
1 tablespoon sugar

Makes 8 servings

Preheat oven to 400°F. Combine 2 cups flour, the salt and 1 teaspoon cinnamon in medium bowl. Cut in shortening. Sprinkle in water, 1 tablespoon at a time, until flour is moistened. Gather dough into ball; divide in half. Roll each half into 9-inch circle. Ease 1 circle into 9-inch pie pan.

Combine 3/4 cup sugar, 1/4 cup flour, 1/2 teaspoon cinnamon and the nutmeg; mix with apples and pears. Turn into pastry-lined pan; dot with margarine. Cover with top crust. Brush crust with milk; sprinkle with 1 tablespoon sugar. Trim, seal and flute. Cut small slits in top crust.

Place on broiling trivet. Bake 35 minutes on *HIGH MIX, 400°F. or until juices begin to bubble.

*Necessary to change temperature on HIGH MIX.

Per Serving:			
Calories:	469	Fat:	23 g.
Protein:	4 g.	Cholesterol:	—
Carbohydrate:	63 g.	Sodium:	302 mg.

Peach Küchen

1 cup all-purpose flour
1 tablespoon sugar
1/4 teaspoon salt
1/4 teaspoon baking powder
1/4 cup margarine or butter
4 to 5 medium peaches, peeled and sliced or 1 package (20 ounces) frozen peaches, defrosted and drained
1/4 cup sugar
1 teaspoon ground cinnamon
1 cup dairy sour cream
1 egg yolk, slightly beaten
1 teaspoon vanilla

Makes 8 servings

Combine flour, 1 tablespoon sugar, salt and baking powder in medium bowl; mix well. Using a pastry blender, cut in margarine until mixture resembles coarse crumbs. Turn mixture into baking pan, 8 × 8 inches. Pat evenly over bottom and one-fourth way up the sides.

Arrange peaches on top of flour mixture. Combine sugar and cinnamon; sprinkle over peaches. Combine sour cream, egg yolk and vanilla; pour over peach mixture.

Bake 30 minutes on *LOW MIX, 375°F. or until juice begins to bubble. Cool; cut into squares.

*Necessary to change temperature on LOW MIX.

Per Serving:			
Calories:	230	Fat:	13 g.
Protein:	3 g.	Cholesterol:	47 mg.
Carbohydrate:	26 g.	Sodium:	161 mg.

Coconut Oatmeal Pie ▶

3 eggs, well beaten
1 cup packed brown sugar
⅔ cup granulated sugar
⅔ cup quick-cooking oats
⅔ cup shredded coconut
½ cup milk
2 tablespoons margarine or butter, melted
1 teaspoon vanilla
½ cup broken pecans
1 9-inch unbaked pie shell

Makes 8 servings

Preheat oven to 450°F. Combine all ingredients except pecans in large bowl. Add pecans; mix well. Pour into pie shell. Place pie on broiling trivet. Bake at 450°F. 8 minutes, then bake 15 minutes on *LOW MIX, 375°F. or until set.

*Necessary to change temperature on LOW MIX.

Per Serving:			
Calories:	504	Fat:	25 g.
Protein:	7 g.	Cholesterol:	104 mg.
Carbohydrate:	66 g.	Sodium:	215 mg.

Fudge Brownie Pie

¼ cup margarine or butter
¾ cup packed brown sugar
1 tablespoon instant espresso coffee
3 eggs
1 bag (12 ounces) semisweet chocolate chips
¼ cup all-purpose flour
1 cup chopped pecans
1 9-inch unbaked pie shell
1½ teaspoons rum extract
1 cup whipping cream, whipped stiffly
Chocolate sprinkles

Makes 12 servings

Cream margarine and brown sugar until light and fluffy. Stir in espresso. Add eggs, one at a time, beating well after each.

Place chips in 4-cup measure or small bowl. Microwave at MEDIUM (50%) until melted, 1 to 2 minutes, sitrring 2 or 3 times. Stir chocolate, flour and pecans into butter, sugar, egg mixture. Pour into pie shell.

Bake 25 to 30 minutes on broiling trivet on LOW MIX. Cool. Fold rum extract into whipped cream. Spread on top of pie and decorate with sprinkles.

Per Serving:			
Calories:	480	Fat:	35 g.
Protein:	5 g.	Cholesterol:	96 mg.
Carbohydrate:	42 g.	Sodium:	168 mg.

Nut Cake With Mocha Frosting

8 eggs
1½ cups sugar
2 cups hazelnuts or walnuts
¼ cup all-purpose flour
1½ tablespoons baking powder

Frosting:
1 pint heavy cream
½ cup plus 2 tablespoons sugar
¼ cup plus 1 tablespoon
   chocolate-flavor
   drink mix
2½ teaspoons vanilla
1 teaspoon instant coffee

Makes 10 servings

Grease and flour two 9-inch round cake pans; line with wax paper. Combine eggs and sugar in blender; blend until light and fluffy. Add nuts; blend until finely chopped. Add flour and baking powder; blend until just mixed. Pour into prepared pans. Bake 20 to 25 minutes on LOW MIX. If wooden pick inserted in center does not come out clean, let stand in oven a few minutes to complete cooking. Cool.

For frosting, combine remaining ingredients in medium bowl. Beat until stiff. Frost cake and chill. Cake must be refrigerated.

Per Serving:
Calories: 561
Protein: 9 g.
Carbohydrate: 52 g.
Fat: 37 g.
Cholesterol: 285 mg.
Sodium: 216 mg.

Strawberry Puff Ring

½ cup water
2 tablespoons plus 1½ teaspoons margarine or butter
½ cup all-purpose flour
3 eggs
2 cups prepared vanilla pudding or 2 cups sweetened whipped cream
1 pint strawberries, rinsed, hulled and sliced
Powdered sugar

Makes 8 servings

Place water and margarine in medium bowl. Microwave at HIGH (100%) until boiling, about 2 minutes. Blend in flour until smooth. Microwave at HIGH (100%) 1 minute. Add eggs, 1 at a time, beating well after each. Preheat oven to 400°F. Drop dough by tablespoonfuls into 8 equal puffs touching each other in 8-inch circle onto greased round baking pan.

Bake 25 minutes at 400°F. Prick puff with sharp knife in several places to allow steam to escape. Let stand in oven 5 minutes; remove from oven to cool. Cut cooled puff ring in half. Spoon pudding into bottom half of ring; top with strawberries. Replace top half. Sprinkle with powdered sugar.

Per Serving:			
Calories:	186	Fat:	8 g.
Protein:	6 g.	Cholesterol:	111 mg.
Carbohydrate:	25 g.	Sodium:	152 mg.

Preserve Cake ▼

3 cups all-purpose flour
1 teaspoon baking soda
½ teaspoon ground allspice
½ teaspoon ground cinnamon
½ teaspoon ground nutmeg
2 cups sugar
¾ cup margarine or butter, softened
4 eggs
1 cup buttermilk
½ teaspoon vanilla
2 cups preserves (combine 2 or more flavors)
2 cups chopped pecans

Makes 12 servings

Mix flour, baking soda, allspice, cinnamon and nutmeg. Set aside. Beat sugar and margarine until light and fluffy. Add eggs, 1 at a time, beating well after each. Stir in flour mixture alternately with buttermilk, beating well after each addition until smooth. Mix vanilla, preserves and pecans together. Fold mixture into batter until thoroughly blended.

Pour into greased 10-inch tube pan. Bake 50 minutes on LOW MIX. If wooden pick inserted in center does not come out clean, let stand in oven a few minutes to complete cooking. Cool 10 minutes; remove from pan. Cool completely on wire rack.

Per Serving:			
Calories:	647	Fat:	27 g.
Protein:	8 g.	Cholesterol:	92 mg.
Carbohydrate:	97 g.	Sodium:	278 mg.

Sour Cream Pound Cake

4 cups all-purpose flour
2 teaspoons baking powder
1 teaspoon baking soda
½ teaspoon salt
2 cups sugar
1 cup margarine or butter, softened
4 eggs
1 teaspoon vanilla
2 cups dairy sour cream
½ cup sugar
¼ cup finely chopped walnuts
2 tablespoons ground cinnamon

Makes 12 servings

Mix flour, baking powder, baking soda and salt in medium bowl. Set aside. Beat 2 cups sugar and the margarine until light and fluffy. Add eggs, one at a time, beating well after each. Mix in vanilla. Stir in flour mixture alternately with sour cream, beating after each addition until smooth. Set aside.

Combine ½ cup sugar, the nuts and cinnamon. Pour half the batter into well-greased 10-inch tube pan; sprinkle with half of filling. Repeat with remaining batter and filling.

Bake 45 minutes on LOW MIX. If wooden pick inserted in center does not come out clean, let stand in oven a few minutes to complete cooking. Cool 10 minutes; remove from pan. Cool completely on wire rack.

Per Serving:			
Calories:	586	Fat:	28 g.
Protein:	8 g.	Cholesterol:	109 mg.
Carbohydrate:	77 g.	Sodium:	456 mg.

Classic Cranberry Tea Cake

¾ cup margarine or butter, softened
1½ cups sugar
3 eggs
2½ teaspoons almond extract
3 cups all-purpose flour
1½ teaspoons baking powder
1½ teaspoons baking soda
¾ teaspoon salt
1½ cups sour cream
¾ cup canned whole berry cranberry sauce

Makes 16 servings

Thoroughly grease and flour 12-cup fluted bundt cake pan. With an electric mixer, beat margarine. Gradually add sugar and beat until fluffy. Add eggs, one at a time, beating well after each addition. Add extract.

Sift dry ingredients together and add alternately with the sour cream. Fold in cranberries.

Pour into prepared pan and bake on broiling trivet on LOW MIX 35 to 45 minutes or until wooden pick inserted in center comes out clean. Allow to cool on counter 30 minutes. Turn out onto plate and allow to finish cooling before glazing.

Glaze:

¾ cup powdered sugar
½ teaspoon almond extract
2 teaspoons warm water
¼ cup toasted sliced almonds

Combine first 3 ingredients. Drizzle on cake and top with almonds.

Per Serving:			
Calories:	350	Fat:	16 g.
Protein:	5 g.	Cholesterol:	62 mg.
Carbohydrate:	48 g.	Sodium:	360 mg.

Biscuits ▲

5 cups all-purpose flour
3 tablespoons baking powder
3 tablespoons sugar
1 teaspoon salt
1 teaspoon baking soda
1 cup vegetable shortening
2 packages active dry yeast
2 to 4 tablespoons warm water
2 cups buttermilk

Makes 7 dozen biscuits

Combine dry ingredients. Cut in shortening until mixture resembles coarse crumbs. Dissolve yeast in warm water. Add dissolved yeast and buttermilk to dry ingredients; mix well. Roll out desired amount on lightly floured surface to a little over ¼ inch thick. Cut with floured 2-inch biscuit cutter.

Preheat oven to 400°F. Place biscuits on lightly greased baking pans. Let rise 10 minutes. Bake at 400°F. 10 to 12 minutes or until golden brown.

Note: Dough can be refrigerated 1 week in an air-tight plastic bag.

Per Serving:			
Calories:	54	Fat:	3 g.
Protein:	1 g.	Cholesterol:	—
Carbohydrate:	7 g.	Sodium:	78 mg.

Beer Muffins

4 cups buttermilk baking mix
1 can (12 ounces) beer
2 tablespoons sugar

Makes 1 dozen muffins

Preheat oven to 400°F. Combine all ingredients in large bowl. Spoon batter into two 6-cup greased medium muffin pans.

Bake 15 to 20 minutes at *LOW MIX 400°F. or until golden brown.

*Necessary to change temperature on LOW MIX.

Per Serving:			
Calories:	200	Fat:	6 g.
Protein:	3 g.	Cholesterol:	—
Carbohydrate:	30 g.	Sodium:	520 mg.

◀ Caraway Rolls

1 package active dry yeast
¼ cup warm water
1 cup cottage cheese
2 tablespoons sugar
1 tablespoon caraway seed
1 teaspoon salt
¼ teaspoon baking soda
1 egg, slightly beaten
2 cups all-purpose flour

Makes 1 dozen rolls

Dissolve yeast in warm water in large bowl. Microwave cottage cheese at HIGH (100%) until cheese is lukewarm, about 20 seconds; add to yeast mixture. Stir in sugar, caraway seed, salt, soda and egg. Slowly add flour, mixing until dough cleans bowl.

Cover with damp cloth. Place in oven. Let rise at 100°F. until double in bulk, 30 to 45 minutes. Stir down dough. Divide among two 6-cup greased medium muffin pans. Let rise at 100°F. until double in bulk, about 20 minutes.

Bake 15 minutes on LOW MIX or until tops spring back when touched lightly with finger.

Per Serving:			
Calories:	116	Fat:	2 g.
Protein:	5 g.	Cholesterol:	26 mg.
Carbohydrate:	19 g.	Sodium:	287 mg.

Zucchini Muffins

1½ cups all-purpose flour
½ cup sugar
1 teaspoon baking powder
½ teaspoon ground cinnamon
½ teaspoon salt
1 cup grated zucchini
½ cup chopped walnuts
½ cup raisins
1 egg
⅓ cup vegetable oil

Makes 1 dozen muffins

Combine dry ingredients in medium bowl. Mix in remaining ingredients until just moistened. Spoon batter into greased medium muffin pans.

Bake 20 to 24 minutes on *LOW MIX 400°F., or until tops spring back when touched lightly with finger.

*Necessary to change temperature on LOW MIX.

Per Serving:			
Calories:	204	Fat:	10 g.
Protein:	3 g.	Cholesterol:	23 mg.
Carbohydrate:	26 g.	Sodium:	125 mg.

Chocolate Chip Banana Crumb Loaf ▲

1 package (14 ounces) banana bread mix or
   banana muffin mix
¾ cup semisweet chocolate mini morsels
   Ingredients to complete mix

Crumb Topping:

½ cup chopped walnuts
½ cup all-purpose flour
2 tablespoons granulated sugar
2 tablespoons packed brown sugar
¼ cup margarine or butter

Makes 12 servings

Grease and flour 9 × 5-inch loaf pan. For easy removal of finished loaf, place a 2½ × 16-inch strip of wax paper lengthwise in pan with both ends extending above top of pan.

Combine mix and morsels. Prepare bread mix according to package directions or muffin mix according to loaf pan directions. Pour into prepared pan. Combine remaining dry ingredients in small bowl. Cut in margarine until mixture resembles coarse crumbs. Top batter with this mixture.

Bake 35 to 45 minutes on broiling trivet on LOW MIX. If wooden pick inserted in center does not come out clean, let stand in oven a few minutes to complete cooking. Cool 5 minutes; remove from pan by lifting both ends of wax paper. Cool completely on wire rack.

Per Serving:			
Calories:	338	Fat:	19 g.
Protein:	4 g.	Cholesterol:	46 mg.
Carbohydrate:	40 g.	Sodium:	245 mg.

45c

Apricot Pecan Oat Bran Muffins

¾ cup whole wheat flour
1 cup oat bran
¼ cup wheat germ
2 teaspoons baking powder
½ cup orange juice
¼ cup packed brown sugar
1 cup dried apricots, chopped
1 teaspoon grated orange peel
2 tablespoons vegetable oil
½ cup buttermilk
2 eggs
⅓ cup chopped pecans

Makes 1 dozen muffins

Combine whole wheat flour, oat bran, wheat germ and baking powder; set aside.

Place orange juice in small bowl. Microwave at HIGH (100%) 1 minute. Add brown sugar, apricots and orange peel. Cool slightly.

Preheat oven to 400°F. Combine oil, buttermilk and eggs in large bowl. Add apricot, orange and flour mixture. Stir just to combine ingredients.

Spoon batter into two 6-cup greased muffin pans. Sprinkle with pecans.

Bake 15 to 20 minutes at 400°F. or until tops spring back when touched lightly with finger.

Per Serving:			
Calories:	158	Fat:	6 g.
Protein:	5 g.	Cholesterol:	46 mg.
Carbohydrate:	25 g.	Sodium:	76 mg.

No-Knead Cheddar Dill Bread

2½ to 3 cups all-purpose flour
1 tablespoon sugar
2 teaspoons dill weed
1 teaspoon dill seed
1 teaspoon salt
¼ teaspoon baking soda
1 package active dry yeast
1 cup small-curd cottage cheese
¼ cup water
1 tablespoon margarine or butter
1 egg
2 cups shredded sharp Cheddar cheese
1 egg, slightly beaten
Poppy seed

Makes one 8-inch round loaf,
16 servings

Combine 1 cup of flour, sugar, dill weed, dill seed, salt, baking soda and dry yeast in large mixing bowl.

Combine cottage cheese, water and margarine in 2-cup glass measure. Microwave at HIGH (100%) 2 minutes. Add cottage cheese mixture, egg and Cheddar cheese to dry ingredients. Stir well. Add enough flour to make a stiff dough.

Soak a cloth with hot water, wring it out and place it over mixing bowl. Let dough rise in oven at *SLOW COOK 100°F. until double in size, about 1 hour.

Grease well an 8-inch round cake pan. Place in pan bottom a wax paper circle cut to fit. Place a strip of wax paper, 2½ × 25 inches, around pan edge. Grease both wax paper circle and strip. Stir dough down and put in prepared pan, patting the dough to smooth it. Let dough rise in 100°F. oven until double in size, 35 to 45 minutes.

Brush bread lightly with beaten egg and sprinkle top with poppy seed. Bake 25 to 35 minutes on broiling trivet on LOW MIX. Remove from pan. Cool on wire rack.

*Necessary to change temperature on SLOW COOK.

Per Serving:			
Calories:	168	Fat:	7 g.
Protein:	8 g.	Cholesterol:	51 mg.
Carbohydrate:	17 g.	Sodium:	319 mg.

Hearty Cheese Caraway Bread

6¾ cups all-purpose flour
3 tablespoons sugar
2½ teaspoons salt
¼ teaspoon baking soda
1 package rapid rise yeast
2 teaspoons caraway seed
1 cup milk
1 cup water
⅓ cup margarine or butter
1¾ cups grated sharp Cheddar cheese
¼ cup melted margarine or butter (for greasing)

Makes 2 loaves,
24 servings

Set aside 1 cup of flour. In large bowl, mix remaining flour, sugar, salt, baking soda, yeast and caraway seed. Heat milk, water and ⅓ cup of margarine until hot to touch, approximately 2½ to 3 minutes on MEDIUM (50%); stir into dry ingredients. Mix in only enough reserved flour to make soft dough. Turn out onto lightly floured surface; knead until smooth and elastic, about 8 to 10 minutes. Cover; let rise 10 minutes.

Divide dough in half; roll half into a 15 × 9-inch rectangle. Sprinkle ¾ cup of grated cheese evenly over dough. Roll tightly from short end to other. Pinch dough together at ends and along seam. Repeat with second half of dough.

Brush tops of loaves with melted margarine and sprinkle top with 2 tablespoons from the remaining cheese. Press gently on top of loaves. Place each loaf in a buttered 8½ × 4½ × 2-inch loaf pan. Let rise in oven on *SLOW COOK 100°F. 40 minutes.

Bake 25 to 30 minutes on LOW MIX until golden brown. Remove from pans and cool on wire racks.

*Necessary to change temperature on SLOW COOK.

Per Serving:			
Calories:	216	Fat:	8 g.
Protein:	6 g.	Cholesterol:	9 mg.
Carbohydrate:	30 g.	Sodium:	343 mg.

◄ Onion-Cheese Bread

½ cup chopped onion (about 1 medium)

1 tablespoon margarine or butter

1½ cups buttermilk baking mix

½ cup milk

1 egg, well beaten

½ cup shredded sharp Cheddar cheese

2 tablespoons snipped parsley or 1 tablespoon dried parsley flakes

2 tablespoons margarine or butter

½ cup shredded sharp Cheddar cheese

Makes 8 servings

Combine onion and 1 tablespoon margarine in small bowl. Microwave at HIGH (100%) until onion is tender, about 2 minutes. Set onion aside.

Preheat oven to 400°F. Mix baking mix, milk and egg until just moistened in medium bowl. Stir in onion, ½ cup cheese and the parsley. Spread in greased square baking pan, 8 × 8 inches. Dot with 2 tablespoons margarine; sprinkle with ½ cup cheese. Bake at 400°F. until wooden pick inserted in center comes out clean, about 20 minutes.

Per Serving:	
Calories:	210
Protein:	7 g.
Carbohydrate:	15 g.
Fat:	14 g.
Cholesterol:	50 mg.
Sodium:	422 mg.

SNACKS & APPETIZERS

Your microwave oven makes it quick and easy to turn out appetizers that set the mood for the meal ahead. These timesaving recipes adapt well to advance planning and preparing or spur-of-the-moment snacks.

Light and Easy Clam Dip & Liver Pâté, page 26

Light and Easy Clam Dip

4 ounces Neufchâtel cheese
1 can (6½ ounces) minced clams, drained
¼ cup plain lowfat yogurt
¼ cup chopped onion
1 teaspoon prepared horseradish
1 teaspoon Worcestershire sauce

Makes 10 servings

Place cheese in small baking dish. Microwave at MEDIUM (50%) 45 seconds to 1 minute 15 seconds, stirring after half the time. Stir in remaining ingredients. Microwave at MEDIUM (50%) until heated through, 3½ to 5½ minutes, stirring after half the cooking time. Serve hot or cold with assorted fresh vegetables.

Per Serving:			
Calories:	44	Fat:	3 g.
Protein:	3 g.	Cholesterol:	15 mg.
Carbohydrate:	1 g.	Sodium:	67 mg.

Liver Pâté

1 pound chicken livers, rinsed and drained
2 cloves garlic, minced
1 small onion, chopped
2 tablespoons white wine or water
½ teaspoon dried parsley flakes
½ teaspoon salt (optional)
½ teaspoon pepper
1 hard-cooked egg, chopped
1 tablespoon brandy

Makes 16 servings

Combine livers, garlic, onion, wine and seasonings in 2-quart casserole. Cover. Microwave at HIGH (100%) until meat is no longer pink, 5 to 8 minutes, stirring once. Drain well. Place cooked livers, egg and brandy in blender or food processor. Purée until smooth. Turn into serving dish and chill. Pipe or spoon pâté on melba toast, cherry tomatoes or celery sticks.

Per Serving:			
Calories:	46	Fat:	1 g.
Protein:	6 g.	Cholesterol:	142 mg.
Carbohydrate:	1 g.	Sodium:	27 mg.

Tangy Vegetable Dip

¼ cup finely chopped carrot
¼ cup finely chopped green pepper
2 tablespoons finely chopped onion
2 tablespoons water
1 cup low-fat cottage cheese
¼ cup plain low-fat yogurt
2 tablespoons fresh lemon juice
2 teaspoons dried dill weed
¼ teaspoon garlic powder
¼ teaspoon paprika
⅛ teaspoon cayenne pepper
1 large carrot, cut into 4 × ½-inch spears
1 medium cucumber, cut into 4 × ½-inch spears
1 medium jicama, cut into 4 × ½-inch spears or medium green pepper, cut into strips

Makes 12 servings

Combine carrot, green pepper, onion and water in 1-quart casserole. Cover. Microwave at HIGH (100%) until vegetables are tender-crisp, 2 to 3 minutes, stirring once. Drain. Set aside.

Place cottage cheese, yogurt and lemon juice in food processor or blender. Process until smooth. Place in small bowl. Add cooked vegetables and dill weed. Mix well. Cover with plastic wrap and chill.

Combine garlic powder, paprika and cayenne in small bowl. Arrange vegetables on serving platter. Sprinkle with spice mixture. Serve vegetables with dip.

Per Serving:			
Calories:	36	Fat:	1 g.
Protein:	3 g.	Cholesterol:	2 mg.
Carbohydrate:	5 g.	Sodium:	84 mg.

Miniature Pizzas

¼ cup catsup
 1 teaspoon dried oregano leaves
 1 teaspoon wine vinegar
½ teaspoon onion powder
¼ teaspoon sugar
⅛ teaspoon pepper
 2 English muffins, split and crisply toasted
½ cup chopped pepperoni
¼ cup shredded mozzarella cheese (about
    1 ounce)
 4 teaspoons grated Parmesan cheese

Makes 16 servings

Mix catsup, oregano, vinegar, onion powder, sugar and pepper. Spread one-fourth on each muffin half. Top each with one-fourth of the pepperoni. Place 1 table-spoon mozzarella on each muffin half; sprinkle with Parmesan. Place on single layer of paper towels on turntable or on double layer of paper towels on dinner plate.

Microwave at HIGH (100%) until cheese is melted and filling is heated through, 45 seconds to 1 minute 45 seconds. Cut each muffin half into 4 wedges.

Per Serving:			
Calories:	55	Fat:	3 g.
Protein:	3 g.	Cholesterol:	5 mg.
Carbohydrate:	5 g.	Sodium:	159 mg.

◄ Marinated Chicken Wings

12 chicken wings
 1 cup dry sherry
 ½ cup soy sauce
 1 teaspoon ground ginger
 ¼ teaspoon garlic powder
 ¼ teaspoon onion powder

Makes 8 servings

Separate chicken wings at joints into 3 parts each, discarding tip. Mix sherry, soy sauce, ginger, garlic powder and onion powder. Combine chicken and sherry mixture in medium bowl or plastic bag. Cover and refrigerate overnight, stirring once or twice during marinating time.

Drain chicken. Arrange on double layer of paper towels around outer edge of turntable or on roasting rack. Microwave at MEDIUM-HIGH (70%) until juices run clear, 18 to 22 minutes.

Per Serving:			
Calories:	161	Fat:	10 g.
Protein:	14 g.	Cholesterol:	43 mg.
Carbohydrate:	1 g.	Sodium:	299 mg.

Cheese Toasties ▲

 4 slices bacon
 1 cup shredded Cheddar cheese (about
    4 ounces)
 1 tablespoon mayonnaise or salad dressing
 1 tablespoon finely chopped onion
 1 teaspoon milk
 ½ teaspoon Worcestershire sauce
 ¼ teaspoon dry mustard
    Dash of paprika
    Dash of garlic powder
 2 English muffins, split and crisply toasted

Makes 8 servings

Per Serving:			
Calories:	126	Fat:	8 g.
Protein:	6 g.	Cholesterol:	19 mg.
Carbohydrate:	8 g.	Sodium:	152 mg.

Place bacon on triple thickness of paper towels. Cover with paper towel. Microwave at HIGH (100%) until bacon is evenly browned, 3 to 4 minutes; set aside.

Mix cheese, mayonnaise, onion, milk, Worcestershire sauce, mustard, paprika and garlic powder. Spread 2 tablespoons on each muffin half. Crumble 1 piece of bacon on top of each.

Place muffins around outer edge of turntable, leaving center empty or on double thickness of paper towels on dinner plate. Microwave at MEDIUM-HIGH (70%) until cheese melts, 1 to 2 minutes. Cut each muffin half into 4 wedges.

Rumaki ▲

1 cup soy sauce
½ cup packed brown sugar
⅛ teaspoon ground ginger
12 to 13 slices bacon
½ pound chicken livers
1 can (8 ounces) water chestnuts, drained
 and halved

Makes 8 servings

Mix soy sauce, brown sugar and ginger in square baking dish, 8 × 8 inches. Cut bacon slices and chicken livers into halves. Wrap a piece of chicken liver and a water chestnut in each bacon piece. Secure with wooden pick. Place in marinade. Refrigerate, covered, 2 hours; drain.

Place rumaki on double layer of paper towels around outer edge of turntable or on 12-inch round glass plate lined with paper towels. Microwave at HIGH (100%) 5 minutes. Reduce power to MEDIUM-HIGH (70%). Microwave until bacon is evenly browned, 12 to 18 minutes.

Variation: Substitute 1 can (15 ounces) pineapple chunks (juice pack), drained, for chicken livers.

Per Serving:			
Calories:	127	Fat:	6 g.
Protein:	9 g.	Cholesterol:	133 mg.
Carbohydrate:	9 g.	Sodium:	695 mg.

Ham Roll-Ups ▲

1 package (3 ounces) cream cheese
½ cup shredded Cheddar cheese (about
 2 ounces)
1 tablespoon chopped green onion
½ teaspoon prepared mustard
4 slices fully cooked ham

Makes 8 servings

Microwave cream cheese in small bowl at HIGH (100%) until softened, 10 to 15 seconds. Stir in Cheddar cheese, green onion and mustard.

Spread cheese mixture on ham slices. Roll ham from narrow end. Cut each roll into 4 pieces; secure with wooden pick. Place on paper towels on turntable or large dinner plate. Microwave at HIGH (100%) 45 seconds to 1 minute 30 seconds.

Per Serving:			
Calories:	76	Fat:	6 g.
Protein:	4 g.	Cholesterol:	23 mg.
Carbohydrate:	1 g.	Sodium:	166 mg.

Stuffed Mushrooms

12 medium mushrooms
(about 8 ounces)
3 slices bacon, chopped
1/3 cup finely chopped green
onions
1/4 teaspoon salt
1/4 teaspoon pepper
2 to 4 drops red pepper sauce
1 tablespoon all-purpose flour
1/4 cup whipping cream
2 tablespoons shredded
Cheddar cheese

Makes about 12 servings

Wash mushrooms. Remove stems and chop fine. Place mushroom caps on paper towels on turntable or dinner plate. Microwave at MEDIUM-HIGH (70%) 1 minute. Drain and set aside. Place bacon in medium bowl. Microwave at HIGH (100%) until crisp, 2½ to 3 minutes. Drain. Add chopped mushroom stems, onions, salt, pepper and red pepper sauce. Microwave at HIGH (100%) until mushrooms and onions are tender, 2 to 3½ minutes.

Blend in flour; stir in cream until smooth. Reduce power to MEDIUM-HIGH (70%). Microwave until thickened and smooth, 2 to 3 minutes, stirring once or twice during cooking. Stir in cheese.

Fill each mushroom cap with bacon mixture. Place around outer edge of 9-inch pie plate or dinner plate. Microwave at HIGH (100%) until cheese melts, 1 to 1½ minutes.

Per Serving:	
Calories:	39
Protein:	1 g.
Carbohydrate:	2 g.
Fat:	3 g.
Cholesterol:	9 mg.
Sodium:	77 mg.

Chicken Kabobs

1 pound boned chicken breasts, skinned and cut into 1-inch cubes
¼ cup soy sauce
2 teaspoons sugar
¼ teaspoon salt
⅛ teaspoon garlic powder
⅛ teaspoon ground ginger
   Dash of pepper
1 green pepper, cut into ½-inch cubes
15 medium mushrooms (about 4 ounces), halved
2 tablespoons honey

Makes 30 servings

Mix chicken pieces, soy sauce, sugar, salt, garlic powder, ginger and pepper. Let stand 10 to 20 minutes. Drain, reserving soy sauce mixture.

Alternate 1 green pepper cube, 1 chicken cube and 1 mushroom half on round wooden toothpicks. Place kabobs on single layer of paper towels around outer edge of turntable or on roasting rack. Stir honey into reserved soy sauce mixture; brush each kabob generously.

Microwave, uncovered, at HIGH (100%) until chicken is tender and green peppers are tender-crisp, 3½ to 6½ minutes, brushing each kabob with soy sauce mixture after half the cooking time.

Variation: Substitute 1 can (15 ounces) pineapple chunks (juice pack), drained, for mushrooms.

Per Serving:	
Calories:	26
Protein:	4 g.
Carbohydrate:	2 g.
Fat:	—
Cholesterol:	9 mg.
Sodium:	163 mg.

Party Mix ▲

½ cup margarine or butter
2 tablespoons Worcestershire sauce
3 to 5 drops red pepper sauce
2 cups bite-size shredded corn squares
2 cups bite-size shredded wheat squares
2 cups bite-size shredded rice squares
1 cup salted nuts
1 cup thin pretzel sticks

Makes 16 servings

Combine margarine, Worcestershire sauce and red pepper sauce in small bowl. Microwave at HIGH (100%) until margarine melts, 1 to 2 minutes. Stir to blend.

Combine remaining ingredients in 3-quart casserole. Add margarine mixture, tossing to blend. Microwave at HIGH (100%) until cereal is well coated and crisp, 5 to 6 minutes, stirring every minute. Spread evenly onto paper towel-lined tray or cookie sheet. Cool.

Per Serving:					
Calories:	180	Carbohydrate:	20 g.	Cholesterol:	—
Protein:	3 g.	Fat:	10 g.	Sodium:	348 mg.

Spicy Cocktail Meatballs

- 1 pound ground beef
- 1 envelope (1¼ ounces) taco seasoning mix
- 1 egg
- 1 can (4 ounces) whole green chilies, chopped
- ½ cup chopped onion
- 1 tablespoon margarine or butter
- 2 tablespoons all-purpose flour
- ½ cup milk
- 1½ cups shredded Cheddar cheese (about 6 ounces)
- ½ cup shredded Monterey Jack cheese (about 2 ounces)
- 2 tablespoons coarsely chopped tomato

Makes 8 servings

Mix ground beef, taco seasoning mix and egg. Shape into 1-inch balls; place in single layer in 10-inch square casserole. Microwave at HIGH (100%) until meatballs are firm and lose their pink color, 7 to 10 minutes, stirring once or twice during cooking. Drain; cover and set aside.

Combine green chilies, onion and margarine in 2-quart casserole. Microwave at HIGH (100%) until onions are tender, 2 to 3 minutes. Blend in flour; stir in milk until smooth. Microwave at HIGH (100%) until thickened, 3 to 4 minutes, stirring once or twice during cooking.

Stir in Cheddar cheese, Monterey Jack cheese and tomato. Microwave at MEDIUM-HIGH (70%) until cheese is melted and smooth, 1 to 2 minutes, stirring once or twice with a wire whisk. Add meatballs to cheese sauce. Place in chafing dish and serve hot.

Per Serving:	
Calories:	268
Protein:	18 g.
Carbohydrate:	5 g.
Fat:	19 g.
Cholesterol:	100 mg.
Sodium:	447 mg.

Hot Cheese Dip ▲

1 package (8 ounces) process American cheese
   loaf, cubed
¼ cup finely chopped green pepper
¼ cup milk
2 drops red pepper sauce

Makes 12 servings

Mix all ingredients in 1-quart casserole. Microwave at
MEDIUM-HIGH (70%) until cheese melts, 5 to 6 minutes, stirring to blend well once or twice during cooking. Serve with corn chips or snack crackers, if desired.

Variation: Add 2 cans (6½ ounces each) minced clams,
drained, with other ingredients. Microwave as above.

Per Serving:			
Calories:	74	Fat:	6 g.
Protein:	4 g.	Cholesterol:	18 mg.
Carbohydrate:	1 g.	Sodium:	273 mg.

Nachos ▲

16 large tortilla chips
¾ cup shredded Monterey Jack cheese (about
   3 ounces)
¼ cup shredded Cheddar cheese (about 1 ounce)

Makes 16 appetizers

Spread tortilla chips on 10-inch wax paper-lined paper
plate. Sprinkle with cheeses. Microwave at MEDIUM
(50%) until melted, 1½ to 2½ minutes.

Per Serving:			
Calories:	40	Fat:	3 g.
Protein:	2 g.	Cholesterol:	6 mg.
Carbohydrate:	2 g.	Sodium:	62 mg.

Hot Crabmeat Dip

1 package (8 ounces) cream
   cheese
2 cans (6½ ounces each)
   crabmeat, rinsed, drained
   and cartilage removed
¼ cup mayonnaise or salad
   dressing
2 tablespoons lemon juice
1 tablespoon minced green
   onion
1 teaspoon Worcestershire
   sauce
⅛ teaspoon cayenne pepper

Makes 16 servings

Place cream cheese in medium bowl. Microwave at MEDIUM (50%) until
softened, 1 to 2 minutes, stirring once. Shred crabmeat; stir into cream cheese
with remaining ingredients.

Microwave at MEDIUM (50%) until dip is heated through, 4 to 7 minutes,
stirring once. Serve hot with fresh vegetables or wheat crackers, if desired.

Per Serving:					
Calories:	91	Carbohydrate:	1 g.	Cholesterol:	32 mg.
Protein:	4 g.	Fat:	8 g.	Sodium:	117 mg.

33

Lasagna, page 45

MAIN DISHES

The question "what's for dinner?" is easily answered with the help of your Sharp Microwave Oven and these easy-to-prepare recipes. Microwaved meat, poultry and seafood dishes are tender, juicy and perfect for the after-school, after-work rush hour because they're simple and speedy to prepare.

Meat Roasting Chart

Cut	Microwave Time: Start	Microwave Time: Finish	Internal Temp. at Removal	Standing Time	Internal Temp. after Standing
BEEF					
Standing or Rolled Rib (4-6 lbs.)	HIGH (100%) 5 min.	MED. (50%) Rare: 10-14 min. per lb. Med.: 12-15 min. per lb. Well Done: 13-16 min. per lb.	120°F. 135°F. 150°F.	10 min.	140°F. 150°F. 160°F.
Tenderloin (Less than 2 lbs.) (More than 2 lbs.)	HIGH (100%) 3 min. 5 min.	MED.-HIGH (70%) Rare: 6-8½ min. per lb. Med.: 7-10 min. per lb. Well Done: 8-11 min. per lb.	120°F. 135°F. 150°F.	10 min.	140°F. 150°F. 160°F.
Chuck or Pot Roast (cook in ½ cup liquid, covered) (2-3 lbs.)		MED. (50%)			
Without vegetables		22-28 min. per lb.		15 min.	
With 3-4 cups cut-up vegetables		28-32 min. per lb.		15 min.	
Eye of Round (2-3 lbs.)		MED. (50%) Rare: 8 min. per lb. Med.: 9 min. per lb. Well Done: 10 min. per lb.	120°F. 135°F. 150°F.	10 min.	140°F. 150°F. 160°F.
Hamburger (to brown for casserole) (1 lb.)		HIGH (100%) 4-6 min.			
Hamburgers (¼ lb. each) 2 patties 4 patties	1st Side HIGH (100%) 2 min. 3 min.	2nd Side HIGH (100%) 1-3 min. 3-4 min.			

Cut	Microwave Time: Start	Microwave Time: Finish	Internal Temp. at Removal	Standing Time	Internal Temp. after Standing
PORK					
Loin Roast, Boneless	HIGH (100%) 5 min.	MED.-HIGH (70%) 9½-12½ min. per lb.	165°F.	10 min.	170°F.
Tenderloin	HIGH (100%) 3 min.	MED.-HIGH (70%) 9-12½ min. per lb.	165°F.	10 min.	170°F.
Bacon 2 slices 4 slices 6 slices	HIGH (100%) 1½-2½ min. 3-6 min. 3-7 min.				
Ham, Canned		MED. (50%) 6-9 min. per lb.	130°F.	10 min.	135°-140°F.
Boneless Rolled		MED. (50%) 10½-15 min. per lb.	130°F.	10 min.	135°-140°F.

(Meat Roasting Chart continued)

Cut	Microwave Time: Start	Microwave Time: Finish	Internal Temp. at Removal	Standing Time	Internal Temp. after Standing
LAMB					
Rack of Lamb (halved and laced together) (1¼ lbs.)		MED. (50%) Rare: 11-14 min. per lb. Med.: 12-15 min. per lb. Well Done: 16-20 min. per lb.	120°F. 135°F. 150°F.	10 min.	140°F. 150°F. 160°F.
Leg or Sirloin	HIGH (100%) 5 min.	MED. (50%) Rare: 8-11 min. per lb. Med.: 9-12¾ min. per lb. Well Done: 10-14 min. per lb.	120°F. 135°F. 150°F.	10 min.	140°F. 145°F. 160°F.
Chops (1 inch thick)	Preheated browning dish 1st Side	2nd Side			
2 chops	1 min.	½-1½ min.			
4 chops	1 min.	1½-2½ min.			

Poultry Roasting Chart

Cut	Microwave Time: Start	Microwave Time: Finish	Internal Temp. at Removal	Standing Time	Internal Temp. after Standing
CHICKEN					
Whole	HIGH (100%) 5 min.	MED.-HIGH (70%) 7-10 min. per lb.	175°F.	10 min.	185°F.
Pieces		HIGH (100%) 4-8 min. per lb.	175°F.	5 min.	185°F.
TURKEY					
Whole (up to 12 lbs.)	HIGH (100%) 10 min.	MED. (50%) 12-15 min. per lb.	175°F.	15 min.	185°F.
Breast, Bone-in, Boneless	HIGH (100%) 5 min.	MED. (50%) 12½-18 min. per lb.	175°F.	15 min.	185°F.
Legs or Thighs		MED.-HIGH (70%) 13-17 min. per lb.	175°F.	5 min.	185°F.
CORNISH HEN		HIGH (100%) 5½-8 min. per lb.	175°F.	5 min.	185°F.
DUCK	HIGH (100%) 10 min.	MED. (50%) 6½-9½ min. per lb.	175°F.	10 min.	185°F.

Fish and Seafood Cooking Chart

Cut	Microwave Time	Standing Time
FILLETS	HIGH (100%) 3½-6 min. per lb.	3 min.
STEAKS	MED.-HIGH (70%) 7-9 min. per lb.	3 min.
SHRIMP & SCALLOPS	MED.-HIGH (70%) 5-8 min. per lb.	1-2 min.

◄ Peppered Rib Roast

2 teaspoons coarsely ground pepper
¾ teaspoon garlic powder
½ teaspoon salt (optional)
4 to 6-lb. boneless beef rolled rib roast

Makes 12 servings

Combine all ingredients except roast in small bowl. Rub mixture on all sides of roast. Place roast fattiest side down on roasting rack. Estimate total cooking time; divide in half. (See chart page 36).

Microwave at HIGH (100%) 5 minutes. Microwave at MEDIUM (50%) remaining part of first half of total cooking time. Turn roast fattiest side up. Insert microwave meat thermometer.

Microwave at MEDIUM (50%) second half of cooking time or until internal temperature registers desired doneness. Let stand tented with foil 10 minutes before carving. (Internal temperature will rise 10 to 20°F. during standing time.)

Per Serving:			
Calories:	205	Fat:	13 g.
Protein:	21 g.	Cholesterol:	70 mg.
Carbohydrate:	—	Sodium:	60 mg.

Brown Gravy ◄

2 tablespoons fat
1 cup cooking liquid or beef broth
1 tablespoon all-purpose flour
Salt and pepper

Makes 16 servings

After roasting meat, remove from baking dish; cover to keep warm and set aside. Pour cooking liquid from meat into bowl, leaving particles in baking dish. Allow fat to rise to the top. Return 2 tablespoons fat to the baking dish. Skim off any remaining fat and discard. Pour cooking liquid into 1-cup measure. If necessary, add beef broth to measure 1 cup. Set aside.

Blend flour into fat in baking dish. Microwave at HIGH (100%) until lightly browned, 3 to 7 minutes. Gradually stir in reserved cooking liquid. Microwave at HIGH (100%) until slightly thickened and smooth, 3 to 6 minutes, stirring several times during cooking. Sprinkle with salt and pepper to taste. Stir in a few drops brown bouquet sauce, if desired.

Per Serving:			
Calories:	18	Fat:	2 g.
Protein:	—	Cholesterol:	2 mg.
Carbohydrate:	—	Sodium:	49 mg.

Beef Stew

1½ pounds boneless lean beef chuck steak, cut into ½-inch cubes
¼ cup all-purpose flour
½ teaspoon salt
¼ teaspoon pepper
2½ cups hot water
3 medium potatoes, cut into ½-inch cubes
2 medium carrots, thinly sliced
1 stalk celery, cut into ¼-inch slices
¼ cup catsup
1 teaspoon brown bouquet sauce
1 clove garlic, minced
2 tablespoons all-purpose flour
½ cup cold water
1 package (10 ounces) frozen green peas, defrosted and drained

Makes 6 servings

Stir beef, ¼ cup flour, the salt and pepper in 3-quart casserole until beef is coated. Add 2½ cups water, the potatoes, carrots, celery, catsup, bouquet sauce and garlic.

Microwave, covered, at HIGH (100%) 5 minutes. Reduce power to MEDIUM (50%). Microwave until beef is tender, 40 minutes to 1 hour, stirring once or twice during cooking.

Mix 2 tablespoons flour and ½ cup cold water until smooth. Stir flour mixture and peas into stew; cover. Microwave at MEDIUM (50%) until mixture thickens slightly and peas are tender, 10 to 15 minutes. Serve with rice or noodles, if desired.

Per Serving:			
Calories:	322	Fat:	8 g.
Protein:	30 g.	Cholesterol:	76 mg.
Carbohydrate:	31 g.	Sodium:	404 mg.

◄ Swiss Steak

2 pounds boneless beef round steak
¼ cup all-purpose flour
½ teaspoon salt
¼ teaspoon pepper
1 cup thinly sliced celery
1 medium onion, thinly sliced and separated into rings
1 medium green pepper, thinly sliced
1 can (10¾ ounces) condensed tomato soup
⅔ cup water
1 tablespoon Worcestershire sauce

Makes 8 servings

Trim round steak; pound well. Cut into 6 to 8 pieces. Mix flour, salt and pepper. Coat beef with flour mixture. Place meat and any remaining flour mixture in rectangular baking dish, 12 × 8 inches, or 10-inch square casserole.

Combine celery, onion and green pepper in medium bowl. Microwave at HIGH (100%) until vegetables are tender, 3 to 5 minutes. Mix with remaining ingredients. Pour over beef.

Microwave, covered, at HIGH (100%) 5 minutes. Reduce power to MEDIUM (50%). Microwave until beef is tender, 40 to 50 minutes, rearranging pieces after half the cooking time.

Per Serving:			
Calories:	243	Fat:	9 g.
Protein:	28 g.	Cholesterol:	82 mg.
Carbohydrate:	10 g.	Sodium:	476 mg.

Pot Roast

2 to 3-pound beef chuck roast
1 envelope (1.5 ounces) spaghetti sauce mix
¼ cup water

Optional:

3 medium carrots, cut into 1-inch chunks
1 medium onion, cut into eighths
1 large potato, peeled and cut into eighths

Makes 6 servings

Per Serving:			
Calories:	227	Fat:	7 g.
Protein:	24 g.	Cholesterol:	68 mg.
Carbohydrate:	16 g.	Sodium:	660 mg.

Pierce meat deeply and thoroughly on all sides with a fork. Place meat, sauce mix and water in a large oven cooking bag. Place in casserole. Secure bag with nylon tie. Make six ½-inch slits in neck of bag below tie.

Microwave at MEDIUM (50%) 30 minutes. Turn roast over; add vegetables, if desired. Microwave 25 minutes to 1 hour or until meat and vegetables are fork-tender. Let stand, covered, 15 minutes, to tenderize further and develop flavor.

Beef with Peppers and Tomatoes ▲

¼ cup soy sauce
¼ cup water
 2 tablespoons sherry
½ teaspoon garlic powder
 2 pounds beef flank steak, cut across grain into thin strips
 2 medium green peppers, thinly sliced
 2 tablespoons cornstarch
½ cup cold water
 1 tomato, cut into 16 wedges

Makes 8 servings

Mix soy sauce, water, sherry, garlic powder and beef strips in plastic bag or medium bowl; close tightly or cover. Refrigerate 8 hours or overnight.

Combine green peppers, beef and marinade in 2-quart casserole; cover. Microwave at MEDIUM (50%) until beef is tender, 20 to 25 minutes, stirring after half the cooking time. Drain, reserving meat juices. Set beef mixture aside, covered.

Mix cornstarch and cold water in 2-cup measure or small bowl. Stir in reserved meat juices. Microwave at HIGH (100%) until sauce thickens, 2 to 4 minutes, stirring after half the cooking time. Stir sauce and tomatoes into beef and green pepper mixture; cover. Microwave at HIGH (100%) until tomatoes are heated through, 1 to 3 minutes.

Per Serving:			
Calories:	235	Fat:	13 g.
Protein:	23 g.	Cholesterol:	60 mg.
Carbohydrate:	5 g.	Sodium:	591 mg.

Beef Stroganoff

1½ cups fresh sliced mushrooms
 1 medium onion, chopped
 1 clove garlic, minced
 2 tablespoons margarine or butter
 1 pound boneless beef sirloin steak, ½ inch thick, cut across grain into thin strips
 3 tablespoons all-purpose flour
¼ teaspoon salt
¼ teaspoon pepper
 1 cup hot water
 1 tablespoon sherry
 1 tablespoon catsup
 2 teaspoons instant beef bouillon
½ teaspoon Worcestershire sauce
 1 cup dairy sour cream

Makes 6 servings

Combine mushrooms, onion, garlic and margarine in 2-quart casserole; cover. Microwave at HIGH (100%) until mushrooms and onions are tender, 2 to 4 minutes.

Shake beef, flour, salt and pepper in plastic bag until beef is coated. Stir beef and remaining ingredients except sour cream into vegetable mixture.

Microwave, covered, at HIGH (100%) 5 minutes. Reduce power to MEDIUM-HIGH (70%). Microwave until beef is tender, 20 to 30 minutes, stirring after half the cooking time. Let stand 5 to 10 minutes. Stir in sour cream until blended.

Per Serving:			
Calories:	254	Fat:	17 g.
Protein:	17 g.	Cholesterol:	55 mg.
Carbohydrate:	8 g.	Sodium:	332 mg.

Texas Meatballs and Rice

1 pound ground beef
1 egg, slightly beaten
1½ teaspoons chili powder
½ teaspoon salt
¼ teaspoon pepper
1 can (16 ounces) stewed tomatoes
1 large onion, thinly sliced and separated into rings
1 large green pepper, chopped
¾ cup uncooked instant rice

Makes 4 servings

Mix ground beef, egg, chili powder, salt and pepper. Shape into 1½- to 2-inch balls. Place in 2-quart casserole. Microwave at HIGH (100%) until meatballs are set and lose pink color, 4 to 7 minutes, rearranging meatballs after half the cooking time. Drain.

Stir in remaining ingredients; cover. Microwave at HIGH (100%) until mixture is bubbly and onions are tender, 4 to 7 minutes, stirring after half the cooking time. Let stand, covered, until rice is tender, 2 to 3 minutes.

Per Serving:			
Calories:	314	Fat:	17 g.
Protein:	22 g.	Cholesterol:	140 mg.
Carbohydrate:	18 g.	Sodium:	629 mg.

Dressed-Up Meat Loaf ▶

1½ pounds lean ground beef
½ cup soft bread crumbs
½ cup red wine
1 egg, beaten
2 tablespoons chopped onion
2 tablespoons chopped green pepper
1 teaspoon instant beef bouillon
1 teaspoon brown bouquet sauce
½ teaspoon salt
½ teaspoon dry mustard
¼ teaspoon pepper

Makes 8 servings

Thoroughly blend all ingredients. Press into loaf dish, 9 × 5 inches. Microwave at HIGH (100%) until internal temperature reaches 155°F., 11 to 15 minutes. Let stand 3 to 5 minutes covered with aluminum foil. If desired, spread top of meat loaf with ¼ cup catsup during last 2 minutes of cooking time.

Per Serving:			
Calories:	174	Fat:	8 g.
Protein:	19 g.	Cholesterol:	94 mg.
Carbohydrate:	4 g.	Sodium:	245 mg.

Spicy Couscous Pockets

1 can (16 ounces) whole tomatoes, drained
   (reserve juice)
½ cup couscous
1½ tablespoons chili powder
1 teaspoon ground cumin
1 teaspoon dried oregano leaves
1 pound lean ground beef
1 large onion, chopped
¼ cup chopped green pepper
1 clove garlic, minced
1 cup raisins
¾ teaspoon salt
¼ teaspoon pepper
12 mini whole wheat pita pockets
¼ cup snipped fresh parsley
1 pint plain yogurt

Makes 12 servings

Place reserved tomato juice in 4-cup measure. Add enough water to measure ⅔ cup. Microwave on HIGH (100%) until boiling, 1½ to 2 minutes. Add couscous, chili powder, cumin and oregano. Mix well. Cover and set aside.

Combine beef, onion, green pepper and garlic in 3-quart casserole. Microwave on HIGH (100%) until beef is no longer pink, 6 minutes, stirring once. Drain.

Add couscous mixture, tomatoes, raisins, salt and pepper. Mix well. Microwave on HIGH (100%) until hot, 7 to 9 minutes. Let stand 10 minutes.

Spoon beef mixture into warmed pita pockets. Stir parsley into yogurt. Top each pita with yogurt mixture.

Per Serving:			
Calories:	242	Fat:	5 g.
Protein:	14 g.	Cholesterol:	28 mg.
Carbohydrate:	36 g.	Sodium:	254 mg.

43

Swedish Meatballs ▲

1 pound ground beef
½ pound lean ground pork
½ cup dry bread crumbs
1 medium onion, chopped
⅓ cup milk
1 egg, beaten
½ teaspoon salt
¾ teaspoon ground allspice
¼ teaspoon ground nutmeg
¼ teaspoon pepper
2 tablespoons all-purpose flour
½ cup water
1 teaspoon instant beef bouillon
½ teaspoon brown bouquet sauce
1 cup half-and-half

Makes 6 servings

Per Serving:			
Calories:	317	Fat:	18 g.
Protein:	25 g.	Cholesterol:	138 mg.
Carbohydrate:	12 g.	Sodium:	383 mg.

Mix ground beef, ground pork, bread crumbs, onion, milk, egg, salt, allspice, nutmeg and pepper. Shape into 1- to 1½-inch balls. Place in single layer in rectangular baking dish, 12 × 8 inches, or 10-inch square casserole. Microwave at HIGH (100%) until meatballs are set and lose pink color, 9 to 11 minutes, rearranging after half the time.

Remove meatballs, reserving meat juices. Stir flour into meat juices. Stir in water, instant bouillon and bouquet sauce. Microwave at HIGH (100%) until slightly thickened, 3 to 4 minutes, stirring once or twice during cooking. Gradually blend in half-and-half. Reduce power to MEDIUM-HIGH (70%). Microwave until thickened and smooth, 4 to 6 minutes, stirring once or twice during cooking.

Stir meatballs into sauce until coated. Microwave at MEDIUM-HIGH (70%) until heated through, 1½ to 2 minutes.

Lasagna

1 pound ground beef
½ pound bulk hot or regular pork sausage
1 can (16 ounces) whole tomatoes
1 can (6 ounces) tomato paste
½ teaspoon salt
¼ teaspoon pepper
1 clove garlic, minced
1 carton (8 ounces) ricotta or creamed cottage cheese (about 1 cup)
1 egg, beaten
¼ cup grated Parmesan cheese
1 tablespoon dried parsley flakes
½ teaspoon dried oregano leaves
¼ teaspoon dried basil leaves
7 to 9 cooked lasagna noodles
1 cup shredded mozzarella cheese (about 4 ounces)

Makes 6 servings

Mix ground beef and sausage in 2-quart casserole. Microwave at HIGH (100%) until meat loses pink color, 5 to 9 minutes, stirring once to break up meat during cooking. Drain. Stir in tomatoes, tomato paste, salt, pepper and garlic. Microwave at HIGH (100%) until sauce thickens, 7 to 11 minutes, stirring occasionally.

While sauce is cooking, mix ricotta cheese, egg, Parmesan cheese, parsley, oregano and basil.

Layer one-third each of the noodles, meat sauce, ricotta cheese mixture and mozzarella in baking dish, 8 × 8 inches square, or 11 × 7 inches. Repeat twice, ending with mozzarella. Microwave at MEDIUM-HIGH (70%) until sauce bubbles, 12 to 18 minutes.

Per Serving:			
Calories:	478	Fat:	25 g.
Protein:	33 g.	Cholesterol:	133 mg.
Carbohydrate:	30 g.	Sodium:	1022 mg.

Sicilian Supper ▲

1 pound ground beef
½ cup chopped onion
½ cup chopped green pepper
1 package (8 ounces) cream cheese, cubed and softened
1 cup cooked egg noodles
1 can (6 ounces) tomato paste
½ cup water
½ cup milk
¼ teaspoon garlic salt
¼ teaspoon pepper
¼ cup grated Parmesan cheese

Makes 4 servings

Mix ground beef, onion and green pepper in 2-quart casserole. Microwave at HIGH (100%) until beef loses pink color, 5 to 9 minutes, stirring once to break up beef. Drain.

Stir in remaining ingredients except Parmesan. Microwave at HIGH (100%) 2 minutes. Reduce power to MEDIUM-HIGH (70%). Sprinkle with Parmesan. Microwave until heated through, 5 to 7 minutes.

Per Serving:			
Calories:	557	Fat:	39 g.
Protein:	30 g.	Cholesterol:	153 mg.
Carbohydrate:	23 g.	Sodium:	798 mg.

◀ South of the Border Eggplant

1 pound ground beef
4 slices bacon, cut into ½-inch pieces
½ cup chopped onion
½ cup chopped green pepper
1 clove garlic, minced
1 medium eggplant, cut into ½-inch cubes
  (6 to 8 cups)
1 can (16 ounces) tomato sauce
¼ teaspoon pepper
1 cup shredded mozzarella cheese (about
  4 ounces)

Makes 6 servings

Place ground beef in medium bowl. Microwave at HIGH (100%) until beef loses pink color, 4 to 6 minutes, stirring to break up beef after half the cooking time. Drain and set aside.

Mix bacon, onion, green pepper and garlic in rectangular baking dish, 12 × 8 inches, or 10-inch square casserole. Microwave at HIGH (100%) until green pepper is tender and bacon is crisp, 4 to 8 minutes.

Stir in ground beef, eggplant, tomato sauce and pepper. Cover with plastic wrap. Microwave at HIGH (100%) until eggplant is tender, 12 to 16 minutes, stirring once or twice during cooking. Sprinkle with cheese. Microwave at HIGH (100%) until cheese melts, 1 to 2½ minutes.

Per Serving:			
Calories:	269	Fat:	16 g.
Protein:	21 g.	Cholesterol:	61 mg.
Carbohydrate:	12 g.	Sodium:	657 mg.

Stuffed Green Peppers

3 medium green peppers
1 pound lean ground beef
1 can (8 ounces) tomato sauce
½ cup uncooked instant rice
1 egg, slightly beaten
½ teaspoon dried oregano leaves
½ teaspoon salt
¼ teaspoon pepper
⅛ teaspoon garlic powder
¼ cup catsup or tomato sauce

Makes 6 servings

Cut green peppers in half lengthwise. Remove seeds and membranes. Set aside.

Mix ground beef, tomato sauce, rice, egg, oregano, salt, pepper and garlic powder. Spoon into pepper halves. Place on roasting rack. Cover loosely with wax paper.

Microwave at HIGH (100%) until green peppers are tender, 12 to 16 minutes. Rearrange peppers after half the cooking time. Top each green pepper half evenly with catsup during last 2 minutes of cooking.

Per Serving:					
Calories:	178	Carbohydrate:	11 g.	Cholesterol:	96 mg.
Protein:	17 g.	Fat:	7 g.	Sodium:	574 mg.

Fiesta Tamale Pie

- 1 package (8½ ounces) corn muffin mix
- 1 egg
- ⅓ cup milk
- 1 pound ground beef
- ¼ pound bulk pork sausage
- ¼ cup chopped onion
- 1 clove garlic, minced
- 1 can (16 ounces) stewed tomatoes, drained
- 1 can (12 ounces) whole kernel corn, drained
- 1 can (6 ounces) tomato paste
- 1½ teaspoons chili powder
- ½ teaspoon salt
- ¼ cup pitted ripe olives, sliced
- ½ cup shredded Cheddar cheese (about 2 ounces)
  Dash of paprika

Makes 6 servings

Mix corn muffin mix, egg and milk until just moistened. Set aside.

Mix ground beef, sausage, onion and garlic in square baking dish, 8 × 8 inches. Microwave at HIGH (100%) until meat loses pink color, 5 to 9 minutes, stirring once to break up beef. Drain. Stir in tomatoes, corn, tomato paste, chili powder and salt. Microwave at HIGH (100%) until mixture thickens, 4 to 8 minutes. Stir in olives.

Spread corn muffin mixture over beef mixture. Microwave at MEDIUM-HIGH (70%) 5 minutes. Increase power to HIGH (100%). Microwave until center is set, 4 to 8 minutes, sprinkling with cheese and paprika during last 2 minutes of cooking.

Per Serving:			
Calories:	505	Fat:	24 g.
Protein:	24 g.	Cholesterol:	139 mg.
Carbohydrate:	50 g.	Sodium:	1492 mg.

◄ Roast Loin of Pork with Apricot Glaze

1 cup coarsely chopped dried apricots
¾ cup orange juice
½ cup apricot nectar
   Juice and peel of ½ medium lemon, seeds removed
1 tablespoon honey
¼ teaspoon ground cinnamon
3½ pound boneless pork loin roast

Makes 8 to 10 servings

Mix all ingredients except pork roast in medium bowl or 4-cup measure. Microwave at HIGH (100%) until apricots are tender, 8 to 10 minutes, stirring 2 or 3 times during cooking. Remove lemon peel. Set glaze aside.

Place pork roast on roasting rack. Brush with half of the glaze. Place thin strips of aluminum foil over top of each end of roast. Microwave at MEDIUM (50%) until internal temperature reaches 165°F., 60 to 70 minutes, removing foil strips after first 15 minutes and basting 2 or 3 times with glaze during cooking.

Let stand loosely wrapped in aluminum foil until internal temperature reaches 170°F., 10 minutes. Spoon any remaining glaze over roast.

Per Serving:	
Calories:	340
Protein:	35 g.
Carbohydrate:	14 g.
Fat:	16 g.
Cholesterol:	108 mg.
Sodium:	84 mg.

Applesauce-Barbecued Spareribs ▶

- 1 medium onion, thinly sliced and separated into rings
- 1 tablespoon margarine or butter
- 1 cup applesauce
- ½ cup catsup
- 2 tablespoons lemon juice
- 1 tablespoon Worcestershire sauce
- ½ teaspoon salt
- ⅛ teaspoon pepper
- 2½ pounds fresh pork spareribs, cut into 2- or 3-rib pieces

Makes 4 servings

Mix onion and margarine in a medium bowl. Microwave at HIGH (100%) until tender, 3 to 5 minutes. Stir in remaining ingredients except spareribs. Microwave at HIGH (100%) until hot and bubbly, 4 to 6 minutes, stirring 2 or 3 times during cooking. Set barbecue sauce aside.

Arrange spareribs in rectangular baking dish, 12 × 8 inches, or 10-inch square casserole. Spread with ¾ cup of the barbecue sauce. Cover with plastic wrap. Microwave at HIGH (100%) 5 minutes. Reduce power to MEDIUM (50%). Microwave 20 minutes. Rearrange and turn spareribs over. Re-cover.

Microwave at MEDIUM (50%) until fork-tender, 20 to 25 minutes. Drain. Spread remaining barbecue sauce over spareribs. Microwave, uncovered, at MEDIUM (50%) until barbecue sauce is hot and spareribs are glazed, 4 to 6 minutes.

Per Serving:			
Calories:	539	Fat:	37 g.
Protein:	33 g.	Cholesterol:	134 mg.
Carbohydrate:	18 g.	Sodium:	801 mg.

Baked Pork Chops

- 4 pork loin or rib chops, ¾ inch thick
- 2 tablespoons Worcestershire sauce
- ¼ teaspoon dried thyme leaves
  - Dash of pepper

Makes 4 servings

Per Serving:			
Calories:	282	Fat:	16 g.
Protein:	32 g.	Cholesterol:	89 mg.
Carbohydrate:	1 g.	Sodium:	135 mg.

Pork Chops and Sauerkraut

- 1 can (16 ounces) sauerkraut, undrained
- 1 small onion, thinly sliced and separated into rings
- 4 pork chops, about ½ inch thick
- 1 tablespoon water
- ¼ teaspoon brown bouquet sauce
- ½ teaspoon caraway seed
- 1 medium tart apple, cored and cut into thin rings

Makes 4 servings

Layer sauerkraut and onion in square baking dish, 8 × 8 inches. Top with pork chops. Mix water and bouquet sauce; brush over pork chops. Sprinkle with caraway seed. Cover with wax paper.

Microwave at MEDIUM (50%) 10 minutes. Rearrange pork chops; top with apple. Cover. Microwave at MEDIUM (50%) until meat next to bone is no longer pink and apple rings are tender, 5 to 7 minutes.

Per Serving:			
Calories:	255	Fat:	12 g.
Protein:	25 g.	Cholesterol:	67 mg.
Carbohydrate:	11 g.	Sodium:	791 mg.

Arrange pork chops on roasting rack with meatiest portions to outside. Mix Worcestershire sauce, thyme and pepper. Brush half of the mixture over pork chops. Cover with wax paper. Microwave at MEDIUM (50%) 8 minutes. Turn over and rearrange pork chops. Brush with remaining sauce.

Microwave, uncovered, at MEDIUM (50%) until meat next to bone is no longer pink, 4 to 10 minutes.

Peppered Pork and Vegetables with Soft Noodles ▾

8 ounces medium egg noodles, cooked
1 tablespoon vegetable oil
1 cup diagonally sliced celery, ¼-inch slices
½ cup red or green pepper chunks, ¾-inch chunks
⅓ cup coarsely chopped onion
1 jar (7 ounces) sliced shiitake mushrooms, drained
1 jar (7 ounces) whole baby corn, drained
⅛ teaspoon sesame oil
1 pound boneless pork, trimmed and cut into thin strips

Sauce:
½ cup ready-to-serve chicken broth
¼ cup teriyaki sauce
1 tablespoon plus 1½ teaspoons cornstarch
¼ teaspoon pepper
¼ teaspoon sesame oil
⅛ teaspoon instant minced garlic

Makes 6 servings

Toss cooked egg noodles with 1 tablespoon vegetable oil. Cover to keep warm. Set aside. Combine celery, red pepper, onion and 1 tablespoon vegetable oil in 3-quart casserole. Cover. Microwave at HIGH (100%) until vegetables are tender-crisp, 3 to 4 minutes, stirring once.

Stir in mushrooms and corn. Set aside. Combine sesame oil and pork strips in 1-quart casserole. Microwave at HIGH (100%) until meat is no longer pink, about 3 to 5 minutes. Add pork strips to vegetable mixture. Set aside.

Combine all sauce ingredients in 2-cup measure. Mix well. Microwave at HIGH (100%) until sauce is thickened and translucent, 2 to 3½ minutes, stirring twice. Stir sauce into pork and vegetables. Add cooked egg noodles. Toss to combine. Cover. Microwave at HIGH (100%) until hot, 1 to 2 minutes.

Per Serving:			
Calories:	379	Fat:	15 g.
Protein:	23 g.	Cholesterol:	81 mg.
Carbohydrate:	38 g.	Sodium:	559 mg.

Bratwurst in Beer

1 pound fresh bratwurst
1 can (12 ounces) beer
1 can (16 ounces) sauerkraut, drained
4 to 6 hot dog buns

Makes 6 servings

Combine bratwurst and beer in 2-quart casserole; cover. Microwave at HIGH (100%) 5 minutes. Reduce power to MEDIUM-HIGH (70%). Microwave until internal temperature reaches 170°F., 17 to 20 minutes, stirring once during cooking.

Add sauerkraut; cover and let stand 5 minutes. Drain. Serve on buns.

Per Serving:			
Calories:	341	Fat:	21 g.
Protein:	14 g.	Cholesterol:	47 mg.
Carbohydrate:	20 g.	Sodium:	925 mg.

Sweet and Sour Pork

2 tablespoons packed brown sugar
2 tablespoons cornstarch
1 can (8 ounces) pineapple chunks (juice pack), drained (reserve juice)
¼ cup teriyaki sauce
3 tablespoons cider vinegar
1½ teaspoons catsup
1 pound boneless pork shoulder, cut into ¾-inch cubes
2 medium green peppers, cut into ¾-inch chunks

Makes 4 servings

Mix brown sugar and cornstarch in 2-quart casserole. Blend in pineapple juice, teriyaki sauce, vinegar and catsup. Stir in pork and peppers.

Cover. Microwave at HIGH (100%) 5 minutes. Stir in pineapple chunks. Cover. Microwave at MEDIUM (50%) until pork is cooked and sauce is thickened, 12 to 15 minutes, stirring once. Serve over rice, if desired.

Per Serving:			
Calories:	315	Fat:	13 g.
Protein:	23 g.	Cholesterol:	82 mg.
Carbohydrate:	26 g.	Sodium:	781 mg.

Oriental Pork and Tomato Casserole

1 pound boneless pork loin, cut into thin strips
1 cup thinly sliced celery
1 medium onion, thinly sliced and separated into rings
1 clove garlic, minced
1 tablespoon cornstarch
2 tablespoons soy sauce
1 tablespoon water
1 tablespoon packed brown sugar
¼ teaspoon ground ginger
1 medium green pepper, thinly sliced
1 medium tomato, peeled and cut into wedges

Makes 4 servings

Combine pork, celery, onion and garlic in 2-quart casserole. Microwave at HIGH (100%) until pork loses pink color, 5 to 10 minutes, stirring twice during cooking. Drain.

Mix cornstarch, soy sauce and water. Stir soy sauce mixture, brown sugar, ginger and green pepper into pork. Microwave at HIGH (100%) until pepper is tender-crisp and sauce is thickened, 4 to 5 minutes, stirring after half the time.

Stir in tomato wedges. Microwave at HIGH (100%) until tomatoes are hot and green pepper is tender, 1½ to 2 minutes.

Per Serving:			
Calories:	266	Fat:	13 g.
Protein:	26 g.	Cholesterol:	81 mg.
Carbohydrate:	11 g.	Sodium:	607 mg.

◄ Ham-Broccoli Rolls

1 package (10 ounces) frozen broccoli spears
1 tablespoon margarine or butter
2 tablespoons all-purpose flour
2 teaspoons prepared horseradish
2 teaspoons prepared mustard
½ teaspoon Worcestershire sauce
½ teaspoon instant minced onion
1 can (8 ounces) pineapple slices (juice pack),
   drained (reserve juice)
   Pineapple juice
½ cup milk
1 egg, slightly beaten
4 1-ounce slices Swiss cheese (⅛ inch thick)
4 1-ounce slices boiled ham

Makes 4 servings

Place broccoli spears in 1-quart casserole. Microwave at HIGH (100%) until tender, 5 to 7 minutes; drain. Set aside.

Place margarine in a medium bowl. Microwave at HIGH (100%) until melted, 30 to 45 seconds. Stir in flour, horseradish, mustard, Worcestershire sauce and instant onion. Add enough pineapple juice to reserved juice to measure 1 cup. Stir juice and milk into flour mixture. Blend in egg.

Microwave at MEDIUM-HIGH (70%) until thickened, 4 to 5 minutes, stirring twice.

Divide broccoli spears into 4 equal portions. Place a cheese slice on top of each ham slice. Place broccoli spears on top of cheese. Spoon 1 tablespoon sauce over each. Roll ham and cheese around broccoli; place seam side down in loaf dish, 9 × 5 inches.

Pour ¼ cup sauce over ham-broccoli rolls. Top with pineapple slices. Microwave at MEDIUM-HIGH (70%) until cheese is melted and sauce is bubbly, 4 to 6 minutes. Microwave remaining sauce at MEDIUM-HIGH (70%) until hot, 30 seconds to 1 minute. Stir. Serve over ham-broccoli rolls.

Per Serving:			
Calories:	304	Fat:	15 g.
Protein:	19 g.	Cholesterol:	112 mg.
Carbohydrate:	25 g.	Sodium:	537 mg.

Ham Loaf ▲

¾ pound ground ham
½ pound ground veal
¼ pound ground pork
2 eggs, beaten
½ cup dry bread crumbs
½ cup pineapple juice
¼ cup chopped onion
1 teaspoon prepared mustard
⅛ teaspoon pepper
¼ cup packed brown sugar
2 tablespoons pineapple juice
2 teaspoons prepared mustard

Makes 6 servings

Mix ham, veal and pork in medium bowl. Mix eggs, bread crumbs, ½ cup pineapple juice, onion, 1 teaspoon mustard and pepper. Stir into meat mixture. Press into loaf dish, 9 × 5 inches.

Mix brown sugar, 2 tablespoons pineapple juice and 2 teaspoons mustard. Spread over ham loaf. Microwave at MEDIUM-HIGH (70%) until internal temperature reaches 165°F., 15 to 25 minutes. Let stand covered with aluminum foil 5 to 10 minutes.

Per Serving:			
Calories:	285	Fat:	10 g.
Protein:	27 g.	Cholesterol:	163 mg.
Carbohydrate:	21 g.	Sodium:	829 mg.

Leg of Lamb with Sherry-Herb Sauce

◄

    4 to 5-pound leg of lamb
    2 cloves garlic, cut into thin slices
    1 teaspoon dried tarragon leaves
    1 teaspoon dried rosemary leaves
    1 teaspoon margarine or butter
    2 tablespoons margarine or butter
    1 tablespoon all-purpose flour
 1½ cups half-and-half
    1 tablespoon sherry
    ½ teaspoon salt
    ¼ teaspoon dried tarragon leaves
    ¼ teaspoon dried rosemary leaves

Makes 6 servings

Cut small slits in lamb roast. Place garlic slices in slits. Mix 1 teaspoon each tarragon, rosemary and margarine in small bowl. Microwave at HIGH (100%) until margarine is melted, 30 to 45 seconds. Brush over lamb roast. Place roast fat side down on roasting rack. Estimate total cooking time; divide in half. (See chart below.)

Microwave at HIGH (100%) 5 minutes. Reduce power to MEDIUM (50%). Microwave remaining part of first half of cooking time. Turn roast over. Microwave for second half of cooking time or until lamb reaches desired internal temperature. Let stand 10 minutes covered with aluminum foil.

While lamb roast is standing, place 2 tablespoons margarine in 4-cup measure. Microwave at HIGH (100%) until melted, 30 seconds to 1 minute. Blend in flour, half-and-half and sherry. Stir in salt and ¼ teaspoon each tarragon and rosemary. Microwave at MEDIUM-HIGH (70%) until thickened and hot, 3 to 4 minutes, stirring after half the cooking time. Pour over slices of roast.

Doneness	Time/Pound	Internal Temperature
Rare	8-11 min./lb.	120°F.
Medium	9-12¾ min./lb.	135°F.
Well Done	10-14 min./lb.	150°F.

Per Serving:			
Calories:	370	Fat:	18 g.
Protein:	44 g.	Cholesterol:	170 mg.
Carbohydrate:	4 g.	Sodium:	314 mg.

Lamb Chops à l'Orange

    4 lamb rib chops, about 1½ inches thick
    ¼ teaspoon garlic salt
    ½ cup orange marmalade
    4 ¼-inch-thick orange slices

Makes 4 servings

Sprinkle both sides of lamb chops lightly with garlic salt. Place in 10-inch square casserole with meatiest portions toward outside of casserole. Spoon one-fourth of the marmalade on each lamb chop; top each with 1 orange slice. Cover.

Microwave at MEDIUM-HIGH (70%) until lamb chops are desired doneness, 12 to 13 minutes. Rearrange lamb chops once during cooking.

Per Serving:			
Calories:	233	Fat:	5 g.
Protein:	19 g.	Cholesterol:	65 mg.
Carbohydrate:	30 g.	Sodium:	167 mg.

Veal Continental ▲

- 1 cup thinly sliced fresh mushrooms
- ½ cup chopped onion
- 2 tablespoons margarine or butter
- 1½ pounds boneless veal, cut into ¾- to 1-inch cubes
- 1 cup water
- 1 can (8 ounces) tomato sauce
- ¼ cup all-purpose flour
- 2 teaspoons instant beef bouillon
- 1 bay leaf
- ½ teaspoon salt
- ¼ teaspoon pepper
- 1 medium tomato, cut into 8 wedges

Makes 4 servings

Combine mushrooms, onion and margarine in 2-quart casserole. Microwave at HIGH (100%) until onion is tender, 5 to 7 minutes. Stir in remaining ingredients except tomato wedges. Cover. Microwave at HIGH (100%) 5 minutes. Reduce power to MEDIUM-HIGH (70%). Microwave until veal is tender, 20 to 25 minutes, stirring after half the cooking time.

Stir in tomato wedges; cover. Microwave at MEDIUM-HIGH (70%) until tomatoes are tender, 6 to 8 minutes, stirring after half the cooking time. Serve over noodles or rice, if desired.

Per Serving:			
Calories:	375	Fat:	20 g.
Protein:	35 g.	Cholesterol:	122 mg.
Carbohydrate:	14 g.	Sodium:	930 mg.

Veal à la Madelon

- 2 slices bacon, chopped
- ½ cup all-purpose flour
- 1 cup water
- 2 pounds boneless veal, cut into 1-inch cubes
- 1 package (10 ounces) frozen pearl onions
- 8 ounces fresh mushrooms, sliced
- 2 medium carrots, thinly sliced
- 1 clove garlic, minced
- 1 tablespoon dried parsley flakes
- ½ teaspoon salt
- ½ teaspoon grated lemon peel
- ¼ teaspoon pepper
- ½ cup dairy sour cream
- ¼ cup whipping cream

Makes 6 servings

Place bacon in 3-quart casserole; cover. Microwave at HIGH (100%) until bacon is light brown, 3 to 4 minutes. Mix flour and water; stir flour mixture and remaining ingredients except sour cream and whipping cream into casserole; cover.

Microwave at MEDIUM-HIGH (70%) until veal and vegetables are tender and sauce is thickened, 35 to 40 minutes. Blend in sour cream and whipping cream. Serve over rice or noodles, if desired.

Per Serving:			
Calories:	393	Fat:	21 g.
Protein:	33 g.	Cholesterol:	132 mg.
Carbohydrate:	17g.	Sodium:	312 mg.

POULTRY

◄ Roast Turkey

12-pound ready-to-cook turkey,
 giblets removed

Makes 12 to 14 servings

Place turkey breast side down on roasting rack or on saucer in rectangular baking dish, 12 × 8 inches, or 10-inch square casserole. Calculate total cooking time, allowing 12 to 15 minutes per pound. Divide total time in half.

Microwave at HIGH (100%) 10 minutes. Reduce power to MEDIUM (50%). Microwave remainder of first half of the total time. Turn turkey breast side up; baste. Shield turkey with aluminum foil as needed.

Microwave last half of total time or until internal temperature reaches 175° when meat thermometer is inserted in meatiest part of breast and thigh on both sides of turkey. Let stand tented with aluminum foil 15 minutes.

Per Serving:			
Calories:	324	Fat:	9 g.
Protein:	56 g	Cholesterol:	145 mg.
Carbohydrate:	—	Sodium:	134 mg.

Stuffing ◄

8	ounces fresh mushrooms, sliced
½	cup chopped onion
½	cup chopped celery
½	cup margarine or butter
1	egg
1	package (8 ounces) seasoned stuffing mix (about 4 cups)
1	cup hot water
1½	teaspoons instant chicken bouillon
1	teaspoon ground sage

Makes 8 servings

Combine mushrooms, onion, celery and margarine in 2-quart casserole. Microwave at HIGH (100%) until vegetables are tender, 5 to 8 minutes.

Stir in remaining ingredients. Microwave at HIGH (100%) until heated through, 4 to 7 minutes, stirring once during cooking.

Per Serving:			
Calories:	230	Fat:	13 g.
Protein:	5 g.	Cholesterol:	36 mg.
Carbohydrate:	23 g.	Sodium:	598 mg.

Chicken with Rye Stuffing

1	tablespoon margarine or butter
1	tablespoon brown bouquet sauce
3	tablespoons margarine or butter
½	cup chopped onion
½	cup chopped celery
3	cups cubed rye or pumpernickel bread
2	tablespoons water
1	teaspoon instant chicken bouillon
¼	teaspoon pepper
¼	teaspoon caraway seed
2½	to 3-pound broiler-fryer chicken

Makes 4 servings

Combine 1 tablespoon margarine and the bouquet sauce in custard cup. Microwave at HIGH (100%) until margarine is melted, 30 seconds to 1 minute. Set aside. Combine 3 tablespoons margarine, the onion and celery in medium bowl. Microwave at HIGH (100%) until celery is tender, 3 to 6 minutes. Stir after half the time. Stir in bread cubes, water, bouillon, pepper and caraway.

Fill chicken cavity loosely with stuffing. Close body cavity with wooden skewers. Coat chicken with bouquet sauce mixture. Place breast side up on roasting rack in rectangular baking dish, 12 × 8 inches, or 10-inch square casserole.

Microwave at HIGH (100%) 5 minutes. Reduce power to MEDIUM-HIGH (70%). Microwave until internal temperature reaches 175° and chicken next to bone is not pink, 20 to 30 minutes. Rye stuffing should register 165°F. Let stand loosely covered with aluminum foil 5 to 10 minutes.

Per Serving:			
Calories:	365	Fat:	19 g.
Protein:	30 g.	Cholesterol:	82 mg.
Carbohydrate:	20 g.	Sodium:	492 mg.

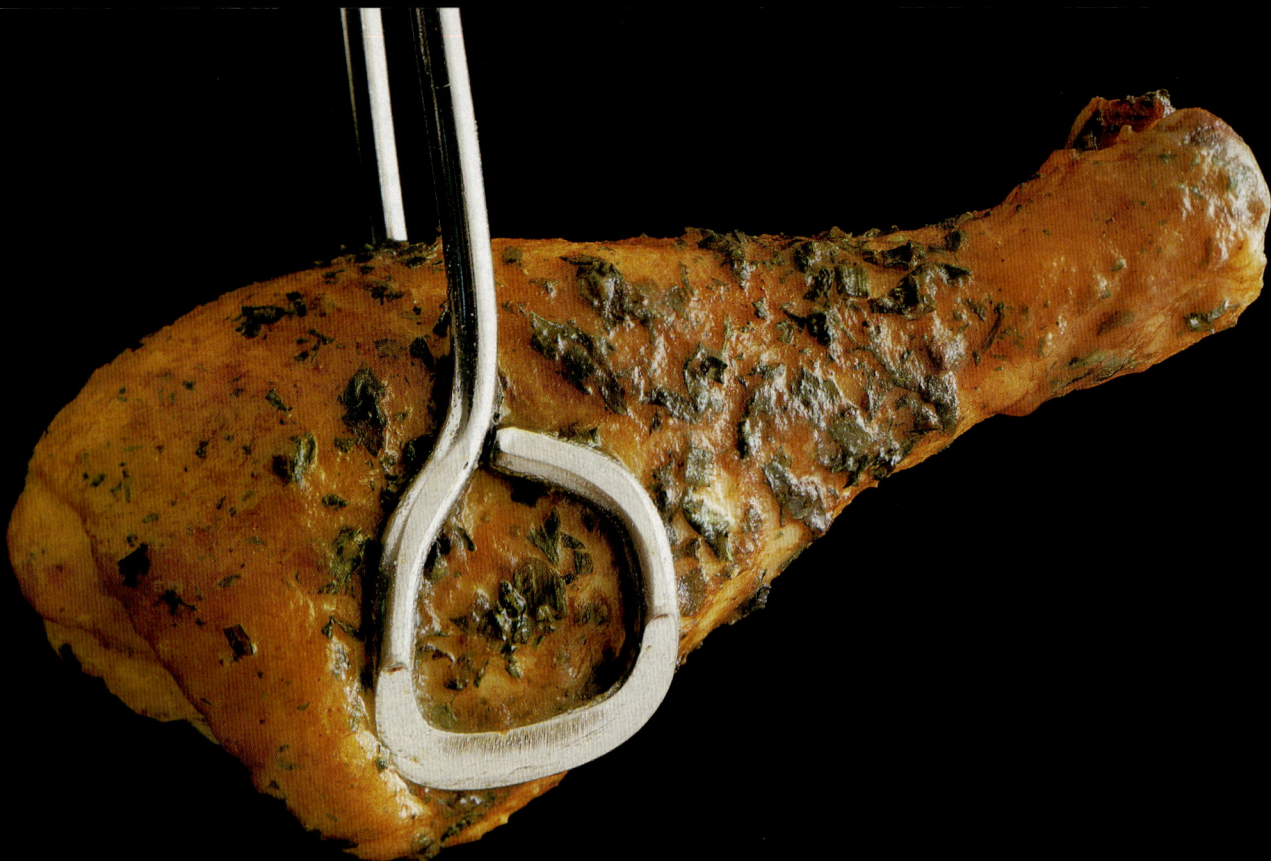

Herbed Drumsticks ▲

¼ cup margarine or butter
1 tablespoon dried parsley flakes
2 teaspoons chopped chives
1 teaspoon dried tarragon leaves
¼ teaspoon salt
¼ teaspoon pepper
¼ teaspoon brown bouquet sauce
8 chicken drumsticks

Makes 4 servings

Place margarine in small bowl. Microwave at HIGH (100%) until melted, 45 seconds to 1 minute 30 seconds. Stir in remaining ingredients except chicken. Set aside.

Place chicken drumsticks in rectangular baking dish, 12 × 8 inches, or 10-inch square casserole with meatiest portions to outside of dish. Brush with half of the margarine mixture. Microwave at MEDIUM-HIGH (70%) until chicken next to bone is not pink, 15 to 20 minutes, turning over, rearranging and brushing with remaining margarine mixture after half the cooking time.

Per Serving:			
Calories:	257	Fat:	16 g.
Protein:	25 g.	Cholesterol:	82 mg.
Carbohydrate:	1 g.	Sodium:	347 mg.

Teriyaki Chicken

½ cup packed brown sugar
½ cup soy sauce
½ cup sherry
1 teaspoon ground ginger
1 teaspoon garlic powder
2½ to 3-pound broiler-fryer chicken, cut up

Makes 4 servings

Mix all ingredients except chicken in medium bowl. Microwave at HIGH (100%) until sugar dissolves, 1 to 1½ minutes. Place chicken in large plastic bag. Pour marinade over chicken. Tightly close bag. Refrigerate 8 hours or overnight, turning chicken over occasionally.

Drain chicken; place in 10-inch square casserole. Cover with wax paper. Microwave at MEDIUM-HIGH (70%) until chicken next to bone is not pink, 21 to 24 minutes, rearranging pieces after half the cooking time.

Per Serving:			
Calories:	216	Fat:	7 g.
Protein:	27 g.	Cholesterol:	81 mg.
Carbohydrate:	8 g.	Sodium:	596 mg.

Chicken Breasts Parmesan

1 can (8 ounces) tomato sauce
1 teaspoon Italian seasoning
¼ teaspoon garlic salt
⅓ cup cornflake crumbs
¼ cup grated Parmesan cheese
1 teaspoon dried parsley flakes
2 large boneless chicken breasts (1½ to 2 pounds),
   split and skin removed
1 egg, beaten
½ cup shredded mozzarella cheese (about
   2 ounces)
   Grated Parmesan cheese

Makes 6 servings

Mix tomato sauce, Italian seasoning and garlic salt in
2-cup measure. Cover with wax paper. Microwave
at HIGH (100%) 2 minutes. Stir. Reduce power to
MEDIUM (50%). Microwave 5 minutes; stirring once.
Set sauce aside.

Mix cornflake crumbs, ¼ cup Parmesan cheese and
the parsley flakes. Dip chicken breasts in beaten egg,
then in crumb mixture. Place in rectangular baking
dish, 12 × 8 inches, or 10-inch square casserole. Cover
with wax paper. Microwave at MEDIUM-HIGH (70%)
until chicken is tender, 9 to 14 minutes, rearranging after
half the cooking time. (Do not turn over.)

Pour sauce over chicken. Sprinkle mozzarella over
chicken breasts. Sprinkle with Parmesan cheese. Microwave at MEDIUM-HIGH (70%) until mozzarella melts
and sauce is hot, 2 to 5½ minutes.

Per Serving:			
Calories:	217	Fat:	7 g.
Protein:	30 g.	Cholesterol:	119 mg.
Carbohydrate:	8 g.	Sodium:	572 mg.

Brunswick Stew ▲

    1 package (10 ounces) frozen whole kernel corn
    1 package (10 ounces) frozen lima beans
    1 package (10 ounces) frozen okra
2½ to 3-pound broiler-fryer chicken, cut up
    2 cups hot water
    1 medium onion, thinly sliced and separated into
      rings
    ½ teaspoon salt
    ¼ teaspoon pepper
    ⅛ teaspoon garlic powder
    1 bay leaf
    2 medium tomatoes, each cut into 8 wedges
    ¼ cup all-purpose flour

Makes 6 servings

Place corn, lima beans and okra in 2-quart casserole in oven. Microwave at HIGH (100%) until defrosted, 6 to 8 minutes. Drain. Cut okra into ½-inch pieces. Set aside.

Combine chicken, water, onion, salt, pepper, garlic powder and bay leaf in 3- to 5-quart casserole; cover. Microwave at HIGH (100%) until chicken next to bone is not pink, 18 to 25 minutes. Remove bay leaf. Remove bones and skin from chicken; cut meat into 1-inch pieces. Add chicken, tomatoes, flour, corn, lima beans and okra to chicken broth mixture.

Microwave, uncovered, at HIGH (100%) until stew is slightly thickened, 18 to 24 minutes, stirring after half the cooking time.

Per Serving:			
Calories:	261	Fat:	5 g.
Protein:	24 g.	Cholesterol:	54 mg.
Carbohydrate:	31 g.	Sodium:	261 mg.

Chicken Curry

    1 medium green pepper, chopped
    1 medium onion, thinly sliced and separated into
      rings
    1 clove garlic, minced
    1 tablespoon margarine or butter
    2 medium tomatoes, peeled and thinly sliced
    1 medium apple, chopped
    ¼ cup all-purpose flour
    1 tablespoon curry powder
    1 tablespoon ground allspice
    1 teaspoon ground ginger
    ½ teaspoon salt
    ¼ teaspoon pepper
2½ to 3-pound broiler-fryer chicken, cut up
1½ cups hot water
    2 teaspoons instant chicken bouillon

Makes 6 servings

Place green pepper, onion, garlic and margarine in deep 3- to 5-quart casserole. Microwave at HIGH (100%) until onion and green pepper are tender, 3 to 5 minutes, stirring once during cooking. Stir in tomatoes and apple.

Mix flour, curry powder, allspice, ginger, salt and pepper. Add flour mixture to vegetables; toss to coat. Add remaining ingredients; cover. Microwave at MEDIUM-HIGH (70%) until chicken next to bone is not pink and sauce is thickened, 24 to 29 minutes, stirring twice during cooking.

Per Serving:			
Calories:	201	Fat:	7 g.
Protein:	19 g.	Cholesterol:	54 mg.
Carbohydrate:	16 g.	Sodium:	381 mg.

Chicken and Shrimp in Red Wine Sauce ▶

¼ cup margarine or butter
1 medium onion, chopped
2 cloves garlic, minced
2½ to 3-pound broiler-fryer
   chicken, cut up
1 can (8 ounces) tomato sauce
¾ cup rosé wine
¼ cup all-purpose flour
2 tablespoons snipped parsley
½ teaspoon salt
1 teaspoon dried basil leaves
½ teaspoon Italian seasoning
¼ teaspoon pepper
1 pound raw shrimp, shelled
   and deveined, fresh or
   frozen, defrosted

Makes 6 servings

Combine margarine, onion and garlic in 3- to 5-quart casserole. Microwave at HIGH (100%) until onion is tender-crisp, 3 to 5 minutes. Stir in remaining ingredients except shrimp.

Microwave at MEDIUM-HIGH (70%) until chicken next to bone is not pink, 24 to 29 minutes, turning and rearranging chicken pieces after half the cooking time. Remove chicken pieces and place in serving dish. Cover; set aside.

Add shrimp to wine sauce. Microwave at HIGH (100%) until shrimp turns pink (do not overcook or shrimp will become tough), 3 to 4 minutes, stirring after half the cooking time. Skim any fat from surface of sauce. Pour shrimp sauce over chicken pieces.

Per Serving:	
Calories:	327
Protein:	34 g.
Carbohydrate:	10 g.
Fat:	14 g.
Cholesterol:	169 mg.
Sodium:	663 mg.

Chicken Cacciatore

2 cups thinly sliced fresh
   mushrooms
½ cup chopped onion
1 clove garlic, minced
1 can (15 ounces) tomato sauce
1 can (6 ounces) tomato paste
½ cup water
½ cup red wine
1½ teaspoons dried oregano
   leaves

1½ teaspoons dried parsley flakes
1 teaspoon sugar
½ teaspoon salt
¼ teaspoon pepper
¼ teaspoon dried thyme leaves
2½ to 3-pound broiler-fryer
   chicken, cut up

Makes 4 servings

Combine mushrooms, onion and garlic in 3- to 5-quart casserole. Microwave at HIGH (100%) until tender, 4 to 6 minutes. Stir in remaining ingredients except chicken. Add chicken pieces, stirring to coat.

Microwave at MEDIUM-HIGH (70%) until chicken next to bone is not pink, 24 to 29 minutes, rearranging after half the cooking time.

Per Serving:					
Calories:	289	Carbohydrate:	22 g.	Cholesterol:	81 mg.
Protein:	31 g.	Fat:	8 g.	Sodium:	1328 mg.

Chicken à la King ▼

- 3 tablespoons margarine or butter
- 3 tablespoons all-purpose flour
- ¾ teaspoon salt
- ⅛ teaspoon pepper
- ¾ cup half-and-half
- ½ cup hot water
- 1 teaspoon instant chicken bouillon
- 2 cups cut-up cooked chicken
- 1 can (4 ounces) mushroom stems and pieces, drained
- 2 tablespoons finely chopped pimiento
- 4 baked puff pastry shells

Makes 4 servings

Place margarine in medium bowl. Microwave at HIGH (100%) until melted, 30 seconds to 1 minute. Blend in flour, salt and pepper. Gradually stir in half-and-half, water and bouillon. Microwave at MEDIUM-HIGH (70%) until thickened, 4 to 6½ minutes, stirring twice.

Stir in chicken, mushrooms and pimiento. Microwave at MEDIUM-HIGH (70%) until chicken is heated through, 5 to 8 minutes, stirring once during cooking. Serve over pastry shells.

Per Serving:			
Calories:	596	Fat:	39 g.
Protein:	27 g.	Cholesterol:	79 mg.
Carbohydrate:	34 g.	Sodium:	1114 mg.

Chicken Livers and Mushrooms

- 3 slices bacon, chopped
- ½ medium onion, chopped
- 1 pound chicken livers
- 1 can (10¾ ounces) condensed cream of chicken soup
- 1 can (4 ounces) sliced mushrooms, drained
- ½ cup water
- 2 tablespoons snipped parsley
- ⅛ teaspoon pepper

Makes 4 servings

Place bacon and onion in 2-quart casserole. Cover. Microwave at HIGH (100%) until bacon is crisp and onion is tender, 3 to 6 minutes. Stir in remaining ingredients.

Microwave at MEDIUM-HIGH (70%) until chicken livers are firm and tender and sauce is thickened, 17 to 22 minutes, stirring once or twice. Serve over rice or noodles, if desired.

Per Serving:			
Calories:	253	Fat:	11 g.
Protein:	25 g.	Cholesterol:	508 mg.
Carbohydrate:	12 g.	Sodium:	873 mg.

Chicken and Dumplings ▲

2½ to 3-pound broiler-fryer chicken, cut up
3 medium carrots, thinly sliced
2 cups hot water
6 peppercorns
2 bay leaves
½ teaspoon salt
¾ cup water
6 tablespoons all-purpose flour
½ teaspoon dried sage leaves
1 cup frozen peas, defrosted
1 can (4 ounces) sliced mushrooms, drained
1 cup buttermilk baking mix
1 tablespoon dried parsley flakes
⅓ cup milk

Makes 6 servings

Per Serving:			
Calories:	269	Fat:	8 g.
Protein:	22 g.	Cholesterol:	55 mg.
Carbohydrate:	27 g.	Sodium:	581 mg.

Place chicken, carrots, 2 cups water, the peppercorns, bay leaves and salt in 3- to 5-quart casserole; cover. Microwave at HIGH (100%) until chicken next to bone is not pink, 18 to 25 minutes, stirring after half the cooking time. Remove bones and skin from chicken; cut into small pieces. Return chicken meat to casserole. Remove bay leaves and peppercorns. Skim excess fat from chicken broth.

Blend ¾ cup water, the flour and sage until smooth. Stir into chicken mixture. Cover. Microwave at HIGH (100%) until slightly thickened, 15 to 18 minutes. Stir 2 or 3 times during cooking. Stir in peas and mushrooms.

Stir baking mix, parsley flakes and milk with fork just until moistened. Drop dough in 6 spoonfuls onto hot chicken mixture. Cover. Microwave at MEDIUM-HIGH (70%) until dumplings are set, 4 to 6 minutes.

◂ Turkey Divan

2 tablespoons margarine or butter
2 tablespoons all-purpose flour
⅓ cup hot water
1 to 2 teaspoons instant chicken bouillon
¼ cup whipping cream
2 tablespoons sherry
⅛ teaspoon nutmeg
¼ cup grated Parmesan cheese
1 pound sliced cooked turkey or chicken
1 package (10 ounces) frozen broccoli spears,
  defrosted
2 tablespoons grated Parmesan cheese
  Dash of paprika

Makes 4 servings

Place margarine in medium bowl. Microwave at HIGH (100%) until melted, 30 seconds to 1 minute. Blend in flour. Stir in water, bouillon, cream, sherry and nutmeg. Microwave at MEDIUM-HIGH (70%) until thickened, 4 to 7 minutes, stirring 2 or 3 times. Stir in ¼ cup Parmesan. Set aside.

Place turkey slices in square baking dish, 8 × 8 inches. Arrange broccoli spears over top. Pour cream sauce over broccoli. Sprinkle with 2 tablespoons Parmesan cheese and the paprika. Microwave at MEDIUM-HIGH (70%) until heated through, 6 to 8 minutes.

Per Serving:			
Calories:	381	Fat:	20 g.
Protein:	40 g.	Cholesterol:	114 mg.
Carbohydrate:	8 g.	Sodium:	434 mg.

Turkey Tetrazzini ◂

¼ cup margarine or butter
¼ cup all-purpose flour
1 teaspoon instant chicken bouillon
¼ teaspoon salt
¼ teaspoon pepper
½ cup hot water
1½ cups milk
3 cups spaghetti, cooked and drained
2 cups cut-up cooked turkey or chicken
1 can (4 ounces) sliced mushrooms, drained
1 tablespoon dried parsley flakes
2 tablespoons sherry
2 tablespoons grated Parmesan cheese
2 tablespoons shredded Cheddar cheese

Makes 4 servings

Place margarine in 2-quart casserole. Microwave at HIGH (100%) until melted, 30 seconds to 1 minute. Blend in flour, instant bouillon, salt and pepper. Gradually stir in water and cream. Microwave at MEDIUM-HIGH (70%) until thickened, 6 to 9 minutes, stirring once or twice during cooking.

Stir in spaghetti, turkey, mushrooms, parsley and sherry. Sprinkle with Parmesan and Cheddar. Microwave at MEDIUM-HIGH (70%) until heated, 8 to 10 minutes.

Per Serving:			
Calories:	538	Fat:	20 g.
Protein:	34 g.	Cholesterol:	66 mg.
Carbohydrate:	53 g.	Sodium:	636 mg.

FISH & SEAFOOD

◄ Shrimp Scampi

¼ cup margarine or butter
2 tablespoons dried parsley flakes
2 tablespoons lemon juice
1 large clove garlic, minced
¼ teaspoon salt
1 pound jumbo raw shrimp, shelled and deveined
Paprika (optional)

Makes 4 servings

Place margarine in 2-quart casserole. Microwave at HIGH (100%) until melted, 45 seconds to 1 minute 30 seconds. Stir in parsley, lemon juice, garlic and salt. Add shrimp; toss to coat. Cover.

Microwave at MEDIUM-HIGH (70%) until shrimp are pink, opaque and tender (do not overcook or shrimp will become tough), 5 to 8 minutes, stirring twice. Sprinkle with paprika.

Per Serving:			
Calories:	197	Fat:	13 g.
Protein:	18 g.	Cholesterol:	129 mg.
Carbohydrate:	2 g.	Sodium:	397 mg.

Teriyaki Fish

½ cup water
¼ cup soy sauce
¼ cup dry sherry
2 tablespoons packed brown sugar
½ teaspoon ground ginger
⅛ teaspoon garlic powder
12 ounces fish fillets, fresh or frozen, defrosted

Makes 4 servings

Combine all ingredients except fish in square baking dish, 8 × 8 inches. Stir until blended. Add fish, coating both sides. Cover; refrigerate 1 hour.

Place fish fillets on roasting rack. Microwave at HIGH (100%) until fish flakes easily in center with fork, 5 to 7 minutes.

Per Serving:			
Calories:	128	Fat:	1 g.
Protein:	17 g.	Cholesterol:	37 mg.
Carbohydrate:	9 g.	Sodium:	1085 mg.

Fillet of Flounder with Broccoli

1 package (10 ounces) frozen chopped broccoli
¼ cup margarine or butter
¼ cup all-purpose flour
1 teaspoon dried tarragon leaves
½ teaspoon salt
⅛ teaspoon pepper
¼ teaspoon paprika
1 cup milk
¼ cup dry white wine
1 tablespoon lemon juice
12 ounces flounder fillets, fresh or frozen, defrosted

Makes 4 servings

Place frozen broccoli in 1-quart casserole; cover. Microwave at HIGH (100%) until broccoli is tender, 5 to 7 minutes. Drain. Set aside. Place margarine in medium bowl. Microwave at HIGH (100%) until melted, 45 seconds to 1 minute 30 seconds. Blend in flour, tarragon, salt, pepper and paprika. Gradually stir in milk, wine and lemon juice. Microwave at MEDIUM-HIGH (70%) until thickened, 5 to 7 minutes, stirring once or twice. Set sauce aside.

Place fish in rectangular baking dish, 12 × 8 inches, or 10-inch square casserole. Cover with wax paper. Microwave at HIGH (100%) until fish flakes easily in center with fork, 5 to 7 minutes. Drain and remove fish fillets.

Spread reserved broccoli in baking dish. Arrange fish fillets over top. Pour reserved sauce over fish and broccoli. Microwave at MEDIUM-HIGH (70%) until heated through, 2 to 4 minutes.

Per Serving:			
Calories:	271	Fat:	14 g.
Protein:	21 g.	Cholesterol:	45 mg.
Carbohydrate:	14 g.	Sodium:	516 mg.

Salmon-Stuffed Sole ▲

¼ cup chopped onion
¼ cup chopped celery
2 tablespoons margarine or butter
1 can (7¾ ounces) salmon, drained and bones removed
3 tablespoons dry bread crumbs
1 teaspoon grated lemon peel
⅛ teaspoon pepper
2 fresh sole fillets (8 ounces each)
⅛ teaspoon paprika
2 tablespoons margarine or butter
1½ tablespoons all-purpose flour
¼ teaspoon salt
⅛ teaspoon pepper
⅛ teaspoon paprika
¾ cup half-and-half
¼ cup white wine

Makes 4 servings

Place onion, celery and 2 tablespoons margarine in medium bowl. Microwave at HIGH (100%) until tender, 2 to 4 minutes. Stir in salmon, crumbs, lemon peel and pepper.

Place 1 fillet on roasting rack. Top with stuffing and remaining fillet. Sprinkle with ⅛ teaspoon paprika. Cover with wax paper. Microwave at HIGH (100%) until fish flakes easily, 5½ to 7½ minutes. Let stand, covered.

Place 2 tablespoons margarine in medium bowl. Microwave at HIGH (100%) until melted, 30 seconds to 1 minute. Stir in flour, salt, ⅛ teaspoon pepper and paprika. Blend in half-and-half and wine. Microwave at HIGH (100%) until thickened, 2½ to 5 minutes, stirring once.

Per Serving:			
Calories:	380	Fat:	22 g.
Protein:	33 g.	Cholesterol:	91 mg.
Carbohydrate:	10 g.	Sodium:	652 mg.

Trout Almondine

¼ cup margarine or butter
½ cup slivered almonds
2 teaspoons almond liqueur
2 packages (10 ounces each) frozen whole pan-dressed trout, defrosted or 4 fresh pan-dressed trout (5 ounces each)

Makes 4 servings

Per Serving:			
Calories:	404	Fat:	28 g.
Protein:	32 g.	Cholesterol:	82 mg.
Carbohydrate:	5 g.	Sodium:	209 mg.

Place margarine in 1-quart casserole or small bowl. Microwave at HIGH (100%) until melted, 45 seconds to 1 minute 30 seconds. Stir in almonds and liqueur. Microwave at HIGH (100%) until almonds are light brown, 3 to 3½ minutes, stirring after every minute. Remove almonds with a slotted spoon. Set almonds and margarine aside.

Arrange trout in rectangular baking dish, 12 × 8 inches, or 10-inch square casserole. Pour reserved margarine over trout. Cover with wax paper. Microwave at HIGH (100%) until fish flakes easily in center with a fork, 5 to 9 minutes, turning over and rearranging after half the time. Sprinkle with almonds.

Fillet of Sole in Lemon Parsley Butter

½ cup margarine or butter
2 tablespoons all-purpose flour
2 tablespoons fresh lemon juice
1 tablespoon snipped parsley
¼ teaspoon salt
⅛ teaspoon pepper
⅛ teaspoon celery seed
1 pound sole or flounder fillets, fresh or frozen, defrosted

Makes 4 servings

Place margarine in rectangular baking dish, 12 × 8 inches, or 10-inch square casserole. Microwave at HIGH (100%) until melted, 45 seconds to 1 minute 30 seconds. Blend in remaining ingredients except fish fillets.

Coat both sides of fish fillets with butter sauce. Arrange in the baking dish. Cover with wax paper. Microwave at HIGH (100%) until fish flakes easily in center with fork, 5 to 6 minutes.

Per Serving:			
Calories:	324	Fat:	24 g.
Protein:	22 g.	Cholesterol:	54 mg.
Carbohydrate:	4 g.	Sodium:	494 mg.

◄ Crab Newburg

2 tablespoons margarine or butter
2 tablespoons all-purpose flour
¼ teaspoon salt
¼ teaspoon paprika
    Dash of cayenne pepper
1 cup half-and-half
½ cup milk
¼ cup sherry
2 egg yolks, beaten
2 cans (7½ ounces each) crabmeat, drained and cartilage removed

Makes 4 servings

Place margarine in 1½-quart casserole. Microwave at HIGH (100%) until melted, 30 seconds to 1 minute. Stir in flour, salt, paprika and cayenne pepper. Blend in half-and-half, milk and sherry. Microwave at MEDIUM-HIGH (70%) until thickened, 4 to 7 minutes, stirring with the wire whisk 2 or 3 times during cooking.

Stir small amount of hot mixture into egg yolks; return to mixture. Microwave at MEDIUM-HIGH (70%) until thickened, 1 to 3 minutes, stirring once or twice. Stir in crabmeat. Serve over toast points or puff pastry shells, if desired.

Per Serving:			
Calories:	300	Fat:	17 g.
Protein:	23 g.	Cholesterol:	241 mg.
Carbohydrate:	8 g.	Sodium:	537 mg.

Poached Fish

12 ounces fish fillets, fresh or frozen, defrosted
½ cup dry white wine
¼ teaspoon salt
⅛ teaspoon pepper

Makes 4 servings

Place fish fillets in square baking dish, 8 × 8 inches. Pour wine over fish fillets. Sprinkle with salt and pepper.

Cover with plastic wrap. Microwave at MEDIUM (50%) until fish flakes easily in center with fork, 10 to 15 minutes.

Per Serving:			
Calories:	95	Fat:	1 g.
Protein:	15 g.	Cholesterol:	37 mg.
Carbohydrate:	1 g.	Sodium:	181 mg.

Shrimp de Jonghe ▲

½ cup margarine or butter, cut into 4 pieces
4 cloves garlic, sliced
½ cup sherry
1 tablespoon snipped parsley
½ teaspoon salt
1 teaspoon chopped chives
¼ teaspoon dried tarragon leaves
¼ teaspoon instant minced onion
    Dash of ground nutmeg
    Dash of dried thyme leaves
¾ cup dry bread crumbs
2 pounds raw shrimp, shelled and deveined

Makes 6 servings

Combine margarine and garlic in 1½-quart casserole. Microwave at HIGH (100%) until garlic is browned, 4 to 5 minutes. Remove and discard garlic. Stir in sherry, parsley, salt, chives, tarragon, instant onion, nutmeg and thyme. Remove ¼ cup of seasoned margarine; stir into bread crumbs.

Mix shrimp into remaining margarine in casserole until coated. Microwave at MEDIUM-HIGH (70%) 5 minutes. Stir. Sprinkle with bread crumbs. Microwave at MEDIUM-HIGH (70%) until shrimp is pink and opaque, 1 to 4 minutes. Let stand 2 minutes.

Per Serving:			
Calories:	335	Fat:	18 g.
Protein:	25 g.	Cholesterol:	173 mg.
Carbohydrate:	13 g.	Sodium:	617 mg.

Shrimp Creole ▲

1 medium onion, chopped
¾ cup chopped green pepper
¼ cup chopped celery
3 tablespoons margarine or butter
1 can (16 ounces) whole tomatoes
1 can (6 ounces) tomato paste
1 cup water
2 tablespoons all-purpose flour
2 tablespoons dried parsley flakes
1½ teaspoons sugar
½ teaspoon salt
½ teaspoon chili powder
⅛ teaspoon pepper
⅛ teaspoon dried thyme leaves
⅛ teaspoon red pepper sauce
12 ounces raw shrimp, shelled and deveined

Makes 4 servings

Combine onion, green pepper, celery and margarine in 3-quart casserole. Microwave at HIGH (100%) until vegetables are tender, 3 to 6 minutes. Add tomatoes, tomato paste, water and flour, stirring to break up tomatoes. Mix in remaining ingredients except shrimp. Cover.

Microwave at HIGH (100%) until mixture is bubbly, 8 to 10 minutes, stirring twice during cooking. Stir in shrimp; cover. Microwave at HIGH (100%) until shrimp is opaque and tender (do not overcook or shrimp will become tough), 4 to 6 minutes, stirring once or twice during cooking. Let stand 2 minutes. Serve with rice, if desired.

Per Serving:			
Calories:	241	Fat:	11 g.
Protein:	17 g.	Cholesterol:	97 mg.
Carbohydrate:	22 g.	Sodium:	997 mg.

Coquilles St. Jacques

1 tablespoon margarine or butter
1 tablespoon chopped onion
1 pound scallops
1 cup sliced fresh mushrooms
⅓ cup white wine
1½ teaspoons lemon juice
¼ teaspoon salt
Dash of dried marjoram leaves
Dash of paprika
3 tablespoons margarine or butter
2 tablespoons all-purpose flour
½ cup whipping cream
1 tablespoon snipped parsley

Makes 4 servings

Combine 1 tablespoon margarine and onion in 1½-quart casserole. Microwave at HIGH (100%) 1 minute. Stir in scallops, mushrooms, wine, lemon juice, salt, marjoram and paprika. Microwave, covered, at HIGH (100%) 3 minutes. Drain and reserve liquid.

Place 3 tablespoons margarine in small bowl. Microwave at HIGH (100%) until melted, 30 seconds to 1 minute. Blend in flour. Stir in ½ cup reserved scallop liquid, cream and parsley. Microwave at MEDIUM-HIGH (70%) until thickened, 3 to 5 minutes, stirring once. Stir sauce into scallops.

Spoon scallop mixture into 4 ramekins or small bowls. Microwave at MEDIUM-HIGH (70%) until heated through, 2 to 3½ minutes. (Do not overcook.)

Per Serving:			
Calories:	342	Fat:	23 g.
Protein:	21 g.	Cholesterol:	78 mg.
Carbohydrate:	9 g.	Sodium:	464 mg.

Scalloped Oysters

2 tablespoons margarine or butter
½ cup dry bread crumbs
¼ teaspoon paprika
¼ cup chopped celery
1 tablespoon margarine or butter
1 pint shucked oysters, drained
1 can (10½ ounces) condensed cream of chicken
   soup
¼ cup dry bread crumbs
2 tablespoons half-and-half or milk
1 tablespoon dried parsley flakes
¼ teaspoon salt
⅛ teaspoon pepper

Makes 4 servings

Place 2 tablespoons margarine in small bowl. Microwave at HIGH (100%) until melted, 30 seconds to 1 minute. Stir in ½ cup bread crumbs and the paprika. Set aside.

Place celery and 1 tablespoon margarine in 1-quart casserole. Microwave at HIGH (100%) until celery is tender, 2 to 4 minutes. Add oysters; cover. Microwave at HIGH (100%) until edges of oysters are curled, 3 to 4 minutes. Stir in soup, ¼ cup bread crumbs, the half-and-half, parsley, salt and pepper.

Microwave at HIGH (100%) until hot and bubbly, 5 to 7 minutes, stirring after half the cooking time. Sprinkle with buttered bread crumbs during last 2 minutes of cooking time.

Per Serving:			
Calories:	307	Fat:	17 g.
Protein:	13 g.	Cholesterol:	70 mg.
Carbohydrate:	25 g.	Sodium:	1084 mg.

Steamed Clams ▼

2 pounds shell clams (cherrystone or littleneck)
½ cup water

Makes 6 servings

Per Serving:			
Calories:	63	Fat:	1 g.
Protein:	11 g.	Cholesterol:	29 mg.
Carbohydrate:	2 g.	Sodium:	48 mg.

Wash shells of clams thoroughly, discarding any broken or open clams. Set aside.

Pour water into 2-quart casserole; cover. Microwave at HIGH (100%) until water boils, 3 to 4 minutes. Add clams; cover. Microwave at HIGH (100%) until clams open, 4 to 6 minutes, stirring after half the cooking time.

73

EGGS, CHEESE & SAUCES

This section includes favorite egg and cheese dishes that are as great for a late-day supper as they are for breakfast. You'll learn how easy it is to turn out smooth, memorable sauces without worrying about scorching, sticking or overcooking.

Scrambled Eggs

Eggs	Butter	Milk	Time
1	1 tbsp.	1 tbsp.	1/2-3/4 min.
2	1 tbsp.	2 tbsp.	1 1/4-1 3/4 min.
4	1 tbsp.	2 tbsp.	2-3 min.
6	2 tbsp.	1/4 cup	3 1/4-4 1/4 min.

Place butter in casserole or serving dish. Microwave at HIGH (100%) until butter melts, about 30 seconds. Add eggs and milk and scramble with a fork. Following the chart, microwave at HIGH (100%) half the time.

Eggs will start to set around edge of dish. Break up cooked portions with fork; stir them to center of dish. Microwave remaining time, stirring once or twice more from outside to center.

Stop cooking while eggs still look moist, soft and slightly underdone. If cooked until they are as firm as you like, they will be overcooked and tough when served. Let stand 1 to 4 minutes; stir again. If not firm enough, microwave a few seconds more.

Per Serving:			
Calories:	189	Fat:	17 g.
Protein:	7 g.	Cholesterol:	276 mg.
Carbohydrate:	1 g.	Sodium:	211 mg.

Poached Eggs

1/2 cup hot tap water
1 teaspoon white vinegar
4 eggs

Makes 4 servings

Place 2 tablespoons water and 1/4 teaspoon vinegar in each of four 6-ounce custard cups. Arrange in oven in a circle. Microwave at HIGH (100%) until water boils, 1 to 1 1/2 minutes.

Break 1 egg into each custard cup. Prick yolk. Cover each loosely with plastic wrap. Reduce power to MEDIUM-HIGH (70%). Microwave until egg whites are opaque and egg yolks are soft-set, 1 1/2 to 2 1/2 minutes.

Per Serving:			
Calories:	79	Fat:	6 g.
Protein:	6 g.	Cholesterol:	275 mg.
Carbohydrate:	1 g.	Sodium:	69 mg.

Puffy Omelet ▲

1 tablespoon margarine or butter
4 eggs
1/4 cup milk or half-and-half
1/4 teaspoon baking powder
1/4 teaspoon salt
  Dash of pepper

Makes 4 servings

Place margarine in 9-inch pie plate. Microwave at HIGH (100%) until melted, 30 to 45 seconds. Separate eggs, placing egg whites in large mixing bowl and egg yolks in medium bowl. Blend remaining ingredients into egg yolks. Beat whites with electric mixer until stiff but not dry.

Fold egg yolk mixture into beaten egg whites with rubber spatula. Pour into pie plate. Microwave at MEDIUM (50%) until center is set, 4 to 6 minutes.

Cheese Omelet Variation: Sprinkle 1/2 cup shredded cheese over cooked omelet. Microwave at MEDIUM-HIGH (70%) until cheese melts, 30 seconds to 1 minute.

Western Omelet Variation: Combine 1/2 cup chopped onion, 1/2 cup chopped green pepper and 1 tablespoon olive oil in medium bowl or 4-cup measure. Microwave at HIGH (100%) until vegetables are tender, 2 1/2 to 3 minutes. Stir in 1 cup diced fully cooked ham. Sprinkle over omelet during last minute of cooking time. If necessary, microwave an additional 30 seconds to 1 minute.

Per Serving:			
Calories:	113	Fat:	9 g.
Protein:	7 g.	Cholesterol:	276 mg.
Carbohydrate:	1 g.	Sodium:	276 mg.

Cheese Fondue ▲

   1 clove garlic, cut in half
   4 cups shredded Swiss cheese (about 16 ounces)
  ¼ cup all-purpose flour
  ¼ teaspoon salt
  ¼ teaspoon ground nutmeg
  ⅛ teaspoon pepper
1½ cups white wine
     French bread, cut into 1-inch cubes

Makes 6 servings

Rub inside of 2-quart casserole with garlic. Discard garlic. Combine cheese, flour, salt, nutmeg and pepper in plastic bag. Shake to coat cheese. Set aside.

Pour wine into 2-quart casserole. Microwave at MEDIUM-HIGH (70%) until wine is very hot but not boiling, 2 to 4 minutes. Add all ingredients from plastic bag. Blend with wire whisk.

Microwave at MEDIUM-HIGH (70%) until bubbly, 4 to 9 minutes. Stir with wire whisk until smooth. Serve with bread cubes.

Per Serving:			
Calories:	354	Fat:	21 g.
Protein:	22 g.	Cholesterol:	70 mg.
Carbohydrate:	9 g.	Sodium:	288 mg.

Macaroni and Cheese

   3 tablespoons margarine or butter
   2 tablespoons all-purpose flour
  ¼ teaspoon salt
  ½ teaspoon dry mustard
  ¼ teaspoon pepper
   4 drops red pepper sauce
1½ cups milk
   2 cups shredded Cheddar cheese or 1 cup each shredded Cheddar and Swiss cheese (about 8 ounces)
   7 ounces elbow macaroni, cooked and drained
   3 tablespoons margarine or butter
  ½ cup seasoned dry bread crumbs

Makes 6 servings

Place 3 tablespoons margarine in 2-quart casserole. Microwave at HIGH (100%) until melted, 30 seconds to 1 minute. Blend in flour, salt, mustard, pepper and red pepper sauce. Stir in milk.

Microwave at HIGH (100%) until thickened, 4 to 6 minutes, blending with wire whisk once or twice during cooking. Stir in cheese. Microwave at HIGH (100%) to soften cheese, 30 seconds to 1 minute 30 seconds. Stir in macaroni.

Place 3 tablespoons margarine in small bowl. Microwave at HIGH (100%) until melted, 30 seconds to 1 minute. Stir in bread crumbs; sprinkle over casserole. Microwave at MEDIUM-HIGH (70%) until heated through, 5 to 7 minutes.

Per Serving:			
Calories:	450	Fat:	26 g.
Protein:	17 g.	Cholesterol:	45 mg.
Carbohydrate:	37 g.	Sodium:	551 mg.

Sauces

Medium White Sauce ▶

2 tablespoons margarine or butter
2 tablespoons all-purpose flour
¼ teaspoon salt
1 cup milk

Makes 6 servings

Place margarine in 1-quart casserole. Microwave at HIGH (100%) until melted, 30 seconds to 1 minute. Stir in flour and salt. Blend in milk.

Microwave at HIGH (100%) until thickened, 3 to 6 minutes, stirring once or twice during cooking.

Cheese Sauce Variation: Stir ¾ cup shredded Cheddar cheese and a dash of cayenne pepper into cooked white sauce. Microwave at HIGH (100%) to melt cheese, 30 seconds to 1 minute.

Per Serving:			
Calories:	64	Fat:	5 g.
Protein:	2 g.	Cholesterol:	3 mg.
Carbohydrate:	4 g.	Sodium:	154 mg.

Hollandaise Sauce

3 egg yolks
1 tablespoon lemon juice
¼ teaspoon salt
    Dash of cayenne pepper (optional)
½ cup margarine or butter

Makes 4 servings

Blend egg yolks, lemon juice, salt and cayenne pepper in small bowl. Set aside. Place margarine in another small bowl. Microwave at HIGH (100%) just until melted, 15 seconds to 1 minute, stirring once or twice.

Blend egg yolk mixture into margarine with wire whisk. Microwave at MEDIUM-LOW (30%) until thickened, 45 seconds to 2 minutes 15 seconds, blending with wire whisk every 15 seconds. Check sauce often when it begins to thicken. Blend with wire whisk before serving.

Per Serving:			
Calories:	252	Fat:	27 g.
Protein:	2 g.	Cholesterol:	204 mg.
Carbohydrate:	1 g.	Sodium:	408 mg.

Mornay Sauce ▲

2 tablespoons margarine or butter
2 tablespoons all-purpose flour
1 cup chicken stock or broth
¼ cup half-and-half
¼ cup grated Romano cheese
¼ cup shredded Swiss cheese (about 1 ounce)
1 tablespoon dried parsley flakes

Makes 8 servings

Place margarine in 2-cup measure. Microwave at HIGH (100%) until melted, 30 seconds to 1 minute. Stir in flour. Blend in chicken stock or broth and half-and-half.

Microwave at MEDIUM-HIGH (70%) until thickened and smooth, 4 to 7 minutes, stirring 2 or 3 times. Stir in Romano and Swiss cheese and parsley. Microwave at MEDIUM-HIGH (70%) 1 minute. Stir until cheese melts.

Per Serving:			
Calories:	73	Fat:	6 g.
Protein:	3 g.	Cholesterol:	9 mg.
Carbohydrate:	2 g.	Sodium:	181 mg.

SOUPS &
BEVERAGES

Quickly cook satisfying soups in your Sharp Microwave Oven that taste like they've simmered all day. Try Irish coffee, hot buttered rum or cocoa for a late-night warm-up.

◄ Confetti Soup

3 tablespoons butter or margarine
1 cup cubed carrots, ¼-inch cubes
1 cup cubed rutabaga, ¼-inch cubes
½ cup chopped onion
½ cup chopped celery
1 cup fresh broccoli flowerets or cauliflowerets
¼ cup all-purpose flour
½ teaspoon salt
½ teaspoon pepper
¼ teaspoon sugar
4 cups milk
1 cup shredded pasteurized process American cheese
1 cup frozen corn
½ cup cubed fully cooked ham, ¼-inch cubes
½ cup frozen peas

Makes 6 servings

Combine butter, carrots, rutabaga, onion, celery and broccoli in 3-quart casserole. Cover. Microwave at HIGH (100%) until vegetables are tender, 9 to 14 minutes, stirring 3 times. Stir in flour, salt, pepper and sugar. Blend in milk. Reduce power to MEDIUM-HIGH (70%). Microwave, uncovered, until mixture is slightly thickened, 15 to 18 minutes, stirring after every 4 minutes. Stir in cheese, corn, ham and peas. Microwave at MEDIUM-HIGH (70%) until heated through and cheese melts, 3 to 5 minutes, stirring once.

Per Serving:			
Calories:	302	Fat:	16 g.
Protein:	15 g.	Cholesterol:	36 mg.
Carbohydrate:	27 g.	Sodium:	786 mg.

Split Pea Soup

6 cups water
1 pound dried green split peas (about 2½ cups)
3 medium carrots, coarsely grated
1 medium onion, thinly sliced
½ teaspoon salt
¼ teaspoon pepper

Makes 8 servings

Combine all ingredients in 3-quart casserole; cover. Microwave at HIGH (100%) 10 minutes.

Reduce power to MEDIUM (50%). Microwave until vegetables are tender and soup is thickened, 1 hour to 1 hour 10 minutes, stirring 2 or 3 times during cooking.

Per Serving:			
Calories:	156	Fat:	—
Protein:	10 g.	Cholesterol:	—
Carbohydrate:	29 g.	Sodium:	159 mg.

New England Clam Chowder

3 slices bacon, chopped
2 cans (6½ ounces each) minced clams, drained (reserve ⅓ cup liquid)
1½ cups cubed potatoes, ½-inch cubes
½ cup chopped onion
3 tablespoons all-purpose flour
1½ cups milk
⅛ teaspoon pepper
1 cup half-and-half

Makes 4 servings

Place bacon in 2-quart casserole. Microwave at HIGH (100%) until bacon is crisp, 3 to 4 minutes. Add reserved clam juice, potatoes and onion. Cover. Micro-wave at HIGH (100%) until potatoes are tender, 8 to 10 minutes, stirring after half the cooking time.

Blend in flour. Stir in milk and pepper. Microwave at HIGH (100%) until thickened, 5 to 7 minutes, stirring twice during cooking time.

Blend in half-and-half; stir in clams. Microwave at MEDIUM-HIGH (70%) until thickened and heated through, 4 to 5 minutes.

Per Serving:			
Calories:	297	Fat:	12 g.
Protein:	21 g.	Cholesterol:	66 mg.
Carbohydrate:	26 g.	Sodium:	282 mg.

Vegetable Soup

3 slices bacon, chopped
1 cup chopped celery
¼ cup chopped onion
2 cups cubed potatoes, ½-inch cubes
1 cup thinly sliced carrots
¼ cup water
3 tablespoons all-purpose flour
3 cups vegetable juice cocktail
2 cups water
1 package (10 ounces) frozen green peas
1 teaspoon salt
¼ teaspoon pepper

Makes 8 servings

Combine bacon, celery and onion in 5-quart casserole. Microwave at HIGH (100%) until bacon is crisp and vegetables are tender, 4 to 6 minutes.

Add potatoes, carrots and ¼ cup water; cover. Microwave at HIGH (100%) until potatoes are tender, 12 to 15 minutes, stirring after half the cooking time.

Blend in flour. Stir in vegetable juice, 2 cups water, the green peas, salt and pepper. Cover. Microwave at HIGH (100%) until soup is slightly thickened and peas are heated through, 8 to 10 minutes, stirring after half the cooking time.

Per Serving:

Calories:	107	Fat:	1 g.
Protein:	4 g.	Cholesterol:	2 mg.
Carbohydrate:	20 g.	Sodium:	418 mg.

Autumn Soup ▲

1 pound lean ground beef
1 cup chopped onion
1 cup chopped celery
4 cups hot water
2 cups cubed potatoes, ½-inch cubes
1 cup thinly sliced carrots
½ teaspoon salt
½ teaspoon dried basil leaves
¼ teaspoon pepper
1 bay leaf
3 tomatoes, cut into eighths and sliced in half

Makes 8 servings

Mix ground beef, onion and celery in 5-quart casserole. Microwave at HIGH (100%) until ground beef loses its pink color, 5 to 7 minutes, stirring after half the cooking time.

Add hot water, potatoes, carrots, salt, basil, pepper and bay leaf; cover. Microwave at HIGH (100%) until potatoes are tender, 18 to 20 minutes.

Add tomatoes. Microwave at HIGH (100%) until tomatoes are tender, 8 to 10 minutes. Remove and discard bay leaf.

Per Serving:			
Calories:	141	Fat:	5 g.
Protein:	13 g.	Cholesterol:	38 mg.
Carbohydrate:	12 g.	Sodium:	184 mg.

Onion Soup

¼ cup margarine or butter
2 medium onions, thinly sliced
4 cups hot water
1 package (1⅜ ounces) onion soup mix
1½ teaspoons instant beef bouillon
1 teaspoon Worcestershire sauce
4 ½-inch slices toasted French bread
¼ cup grated fresh Parmesan cheese

Makes 4 servings

Combine margarine and onion in 2-quart casserole. Microwave at HIGH (100%) until onions are tender-crisp, 4 to 6 minutes.

Add water, onion soup mix, instant bouillon and Worcestershire sauce; cover. Microwave at HIGH (100%) 5 minutes. Reduce power to MEDIUM (50%). Microwave until onions are tender and flavors are blended, 15 to 20 minutes.

Ladle soup into 4 individual serving bowls. Place toast on top. Sprinkle each with 1 tablespoon Parmesan cheese. Microwave at HIGH (100%) until cheese softens, 5 to 7 minutes.

Per Serving:			
Calories:	227	Fat:	15 g.
Protein:	6 g.	Cholesterol:	6 mg.
Carbohydrate:	19 g.	Sodium:	1367 mg.

81

Canadian Cheese Soup ▲

  1 cup water
  1 large potato, shredded
  1 medium onion, chopped
  1 medium carrot, grated
  1 stalk celery, finely chopped
  1 cup chicken consommé or broth*
  ½ cup half-and-half
1½ cups shredded sharp Cheddar cheese (about 6
    ounces)

Makes 4 servings

Combine water, potato, onion, carrot and celery in 2-quart casserole; cover. Microwave at HIGH (100%) until potatoes are tender, 12 to 17 minutes, stirring after half the cooking time.

Stir in consommé and half-and-half; cover. Microwave at MEDIUM-HIGH (70%) until heated through, 6 to 8 minutes. Mix in cheese, stirring until melted.

*Or use 2 teaspoons instant chicken bouillon dissolved in 1 cup hot water.

Per Serving:			
Calories:	281	Fat:	18 g.
Protein:	14 g.	Cholesterol:	56 mg.
Carbohydrate:	16 g.	Sodium:	490 mg.

Quick Corn Chowder

  3 slices bacon, chopped
  ¼ cup finely chopped onion
  2 tablespoons all-purpose flour
  1 package (10 ounces) frozen whole kernel corn
1½ cups milk
1½ teaspoons snipped parsley
  ½ teaspoon salt
  ¼ teaspoon pepper

Makes 4 servings

Combine bacon and onion in 2-quart casserole. Microwave at HIGH (100%) until bacon is crisp and onion is tender, 4 to 6 minutes, stirring after half the cooking time.

Blend in flour. Stir in corn, milk, parsley, salt and pepper. Microwave at HIGH (100%) until slightly thickened and corn is tender, 7 to 12 minutes, stirring twice during cooking time.

Per Serving:			
Calories:	147	Fat:	4 g.
Protein:	7 g.	Cholesterol:	11 mg.
Carbohydrate:	22 g.	Sodium:	259 mg.

Coffee

Spoon instant coffee into 1 to 4 cups or mugs. Add hot tap water. Place in oven. When heating more than 2 cups, space them around the edge of the turntable, leaving the center empty. Microwave at HIGH (100%) until very hot but not boiling. (See chart below.)

1 cup	½-1¼ min.
2 cups	1-1¾ min.
3 cups	1¼-2¼ min.
4 cups	1¾-2½ min.

Per Serving:			
Calories:	2	Fat:	—
Protein:	—	Cholesterol:	—
Carbohydrate:	—	Sodium:	2 mg.

Hot Cocoa for One

2 tablespoons sugar
2 teaspoons cocoa
2 tablespoons cold water
¾ cup milk

Makes 1 serving

Mix sugar, cocoa and cold water in large mug or cup. Microwave at HIGH (100%) until thickened, 30 seconds to 1 minute.

Blend in milk. Microwave at HIGH (100%) until hot, 2 to 3 minutes, stirring once or twice.

Per Serving:			
Calories:	196	Fat:	4 g.
Protein:	7 g.	Cholesterol:	14 mg.
Carbohydrate:	35 g.	Sodium:	117 mg.

Hot Buttered Rum

⅔ cup apple cider
1 tablespoon packed brown sugar
1 1-inch stick cinnamon
1½ ounces rum
1 teaspoon butter
  Dash of ground nutmeg

Makes 1 serving

Stir cider and brown sugar in large mug or cup. Add cinnamon stick.

Microwave at HIGH (100%) until cider boils, 2 to 2½ minutes. Stir in rum. Top with butter and ground nutmeg.

Per Serving:			
Calories:	267	Fat:	4 g.
Protein:	—	Cholesterol:	10 mg.
Carbohydrate:	33 g.	Sodium:	49 mg.

Irish Coffee ▲

¾ to 1 cup strong black coffee
1½ ounces Irish whiskey
1 teaspoon sugar
1 tablespoon whipped cream

Makes 1 serving

Mix coffee, whiskey and sugar in large mug or cup.

Microwave at HIGH (100%) until hot, 1½ to 2 minutes. Top with whipped cream.

Per Serving:			
Calories:	147	Fat:	3 g.
Protein:	—	Cholesterol:	10 mg.
Carbohydrate:	4 g.	Sodium:	5 mg.

VEGETABLES

Fresh in color, texture and flavor, vegetables are naturals for microwave cooking. Vegetables cook quickly in a minimum of liquid, so they retain more vitamins and minerals.

Vegetable Chart

Vegetable	Amount	Cooking Procedure	Microwave Time at HIGH (100%)	Standing Time, Covered
Artichokes				
Fresh	2 medium	Trim and rinse. Wrap in plastic wrap. Arrange in oven with space between.	5½-8½ min.	3 min.
Asparagus				
Fresh Spears	1 lb.	12 × 8-in. dish, ¼ cup water. Cover. Rearrange after 4 min.	7-10 min.	3 min.
Frozen Spears	10-oz. pkg.	1-qt. casserole. 2 tbsp. water. Cover. Separate after 3 min.	7-9 min.	3 min.
Beans				
Fresh, Green and Wax	1 lb.	1½-in. pieces. 2-qt. casserole. ¼ cup water. Cover. Stir after 4 min.	12½-17½ min.	5 min.
Frozen, Green	9-oz. pkg.	1-qt. casserole. 2 tbsp. water. Cover. Stir after 3 min.	4-7 min.	3 min.
Frozen, Lima	10-oz. pkg.	1-qt. casserole. 2 tbsp. water. Cover. Stir after 2 min.	5-8 min.	3 min.
Beets				
Fresh, Whole	5 medium	Wash; cut off tops. 2-qt. casserole. ½ cup water. ½ tsp. salt. Cover. Rearrange every 7 min.	15-20 min.	3-5 min.
Broccoli				
Fresh, Spears	1½ lbs.	12 × 8-in. dish. 2 tbsp. water. Cover. Rearrange after 5 min.	6-8 min.	2-3 min.
Fresh, Pieces	1 lb.	1-in. pieces. 2-qt. casserole. 2 tbsp. water. Cover. Stir after 4 min.	6-8 min.	3-5 min.
Frozen, Spears, Cuts, Chopped	10-oz. pkg.	1-qt. casserole. 2 tbsp. water. Cover. Stir after 2 min.	5-7 min.	3 min.
Brussels Sprouts				
Fresh	4 cups	2-qt. casserole. ¼ cup water. Cover. Stir after 3 min.	4-8 min.	3 min.
Frozen	10-oz. pkg.	1-qt. casserole. 2 tbsp. water. Stir after 3 min.	6-8 min.	3 min.
Cabbage				
Shredded	1 lb.	2-qt. casserole. 2 tbsp. water. Cover. Stir after 5 min.	7½-13½ min.	3 min.
Wedges	1 lb.	12 × 8-in. dish. ¼ cup water. Cover. Rearrange after 6 min.	12½-15½ min.	2-3 min.
Carrots				
Fresh, Slices	2 cups	1-qt. casserole. 2 tbsp. water. Cover. Stir after 3 min.	4-8 min.	3 min.
Frozen, Slices	2 cups	1-qt. casserole. 2 tbsp. water. Stir after 3 min.	6-8 min.	3 min.
Cauliflower				
Fresh, Flowerets	2 cups	1-qt. casserole. 2 tbsp. water. Cover. Stir after 3 min.	5-7 min.	3 min.
Fresh, Whole	1 lb.	Wrap in plastic wrap. Turn over after 3 min.	5½-7½ min.	3 min.
Frozen, Flowerets	10-oz. pkg.	1-qt. casserole. 2 tbsp. water. Cover. Stir after 3 min.	5-8 min.	3 min.

Vegetable Chart

Vegetable	Amount	Cooking Procedure	Microwave Time at HIGH (100%)	Standing Time, Covered
Corn				
Fresh, on Cob	2 ears	12 × 8-in. dish. ¼ cup water.	7-10 min.	5 min.
	4 ears	Cover. Turn over, rearrange after 3 and 6 min.	12-16 min.	5 min.
Frozen, on Cob	2 ears	12 × 8-in. dish. 2 tbsp. water.	5½-7½ min.	3 min.
	4 ears	Cover. Turn over, rearrange after 3 and 6 min.	10½-12½ min.	3 min.
Frozen, Whole Kernel	10-oz. pkg.	1-qt. casserole. 2 tbsp. water. Cover. Stir after 2 min.	4-6 min.	3 min.
Okra				
Fresh, Whole	¾ lb.	1-qt. casserole. ¼ cup water. ¼ tsp. salt. Cover. Stir after 3 min.	6½-10 min.	3-5 min.
Frozen, Whole or Slices	10-oz. pkg.	1-qt. casserole. 2 tbsp. water. Cover. Stir after 2 and 4 min.	5-7 min.	3 min.
Peas, Black-eyed				
Frozen	10-oz. pkg.	1-qt. casserole. ¼ cup water. Cover. Stir at 2 min. intervals.	8-9 min.	2 min.
Peas, Green				
Fresh	2 cups	1-qt. casserole. ¼ cup water. Cover. Stir after 3 min.	4-6 min.	3 min.
Frozen	10-oz. pkg.	1-qt. casserole. 2 tbsp. water. Cover. Stir after 2 min.	6-8 min.	3 min.
Potatoes				
Baked	2 medium	Prick; place on paper towels. Turn	6½-8 min.	5-10 min.
	4 medium	over, rearrange after 4 or 5 min. Let stand, wrapped in foil.	10-14 min.	5-10 min.
Boiled	4 medium	Peel and quarter potatoes. 2-qt. casserole. ¼ cup water. ½ tsp. salt. Cover. Rearrange after 5 min.	9-12 min.	3 min.
Spinach				
Fresh	1 lb.	3-qt. casserole. 2 tbsp. water. Cover. Stir after 3 min.	6-9 min.	3 min.
Frozen, Leaf or Chopped	10-oz. pkg.	1-qt. casserole. 2 tbsp. water. Cover. Stir after 4 min.	7-9 min.	2-5 min.
Squash				
Fresh, Acorn	1 whole	Halve; remove seeds. Wrap each	8½-11 min.	5-10 min.
	2 whole	half with plastic wrap. Rotate, rearrange after 5 or 6 min.	13-16 min.	5-10 min.
Fresh, Zucchini, Slices	2 cups	2-qt. casserole. 2 tbsp. margarine. Cover. Stir after 2 min.	3½-5½ min.	3 min.
Frozen, Mashed	10-oz. pkg.	1-qt. casserole. Cover. Break apart after 2 min., then stir at 2 min. intervals.	6-8 min.	2 min.
Sweet Potatoes				
Baked	2 small	Prick; place on paper towels. Turn	5-9 min.	5-10 min.
	4 small	over, rearrange after 4 min.	8-13 min.	5-10 min.
Tomatoes				
Fresh	2 medium	Halve tomatoes. Round dish.	3-5 min.	2 min.
	4 medium	Cover. Rearrange once.	5-10 min.	2 min.
Canned Vegetables	15 to 16 oz.	1-qt. casserole. Drain all but 2 tbsp. liquid. Stir once.	2-4 min.	2 min.

Zesty Squash ▲

¼ cup margarine or butter
1 clove garlic, minced
1 teaspoon dried oregano leaves
½ teaspoon dried basil leaves
¼ teaspoon salt
⅛ teaspoon pepper
2 medium zucchini, thinly sliced
1 medium yellow summer squash, thinly sliced
1 large tomato, cut into 8 wedges

Makes 4 servings

Place margarine and garlic in 2-quart casserole. Microwave at HIGH (100%) until margarine is melted, 1 to 1½ minutes. Mix in oregano, basil, salt and pepper. Add remaining ingredients except tomato. Toss to coat. Cover.

Microwave at HIGH (100%) until squash is tender, 5 to 10 minutes, stirring after half the cooking time. Stir in tomato. Cover; let stand 2 minutes.

Per Serving:			
Calories:	126	Fat:	12 g.
Protein:	2 g.	Cholesterol:	—
Carbohydrate:	5 g.	Sodium:	273 mg.

Wilted Spinach Salad

1 pound fresh spinach
6 slices bacon, chopped
3 tablespoons chopped onion
⅓ cup vinegar
⅓ cup water
2 tablespoons sugar
¼ teaspoon pepper

Makes 4 servings

Wash spinach. Remove thick stems and bruised leaves. Drain well and set aside in salad bowl.

Place bacon pieces in 1-quart casserole. Microwave at HIGH (100%) until bacon is crisp, 6 to 8 minutes, stirring after half the cooking time. Remove bacon and set aside on paper toweling.

Add onion to bacon fat. Microwave at HIGH (100%) until tender, 1½ to 2½ minutes. Add vinegar, water, sugar and pepper. Microwave on HIGH (100%) until boiling, 3 to 6 minutes. Immediately pour over spinach. Add bacon and toss well. Serve immediately.

Per Serving:			
Calories:	109	Fat:	5 g.
Protein:	6 g.	Cholesterol:	8 mg.
Carbohydrate:	12 g.	Sodium:	241 mg.

Italian Zucchini ▶

4 medium zucchini (about 1½ pounds), thinly
  sliced
1 tablespoon margarine or butter
1 tablespoon olive oil
2 teaspoons snipped parsley
½ teaspoon dried basil leaves
½ teaspoon dried oregano leaves
¼ teaspoon salt

Makes 6 servings

Place zucchini in 1½-quart casserole; cover. Microwave at HIGH (100%) until tender-crisp, 4 to 6 minutes. Drain.

Stir in remaining ingredients. Microwave at HIGH
(100%) until vegetables are tender, 2 to 4 minutes, stirring after half the cooking time.

Per Serving:			
Calories:	50	Fat:	4 g.
Protein:	1 g.	Cholesterol:	—
Carbohydrate:	3 g.	Sodium:	109 mg.

Ratatouille

1 medium eggplant (1 to 1½ pounds), peeled and
  cut into 1-inch cubes
1 medium onion, thinly sliced and separated into
  rings
1 green pepper, thinly sliced
1 large clove garlic, minced
¼ cup olive oil
1 medium zucchini (½ to ¾ pound), thinly sliced
1½ teaspoons dried basil leaves
1½ teaspoons dried marjoram leaves
½ teaspoon salt
¼ teaspoon pepper
1 large tomato, chopped

Makes 8 servings

Mix eggplant, onion, green pepper, garlic and olive oil
in 3-quart casserole. Microwave, covered, at HIGH
(100%) until onion and green pepper are tender, 8 to
10 minutes, stirring once or twice during cooking time.

Add zucchini, basil, marjoram, salt and pepper. Microwave, covered, at HIGH (100%) until eggplant and zucchini are tender, 5 to 7 minutes. Gently stir in tomato.
Let stand 5 minutes.

Per Serving:			
Calories:	86	Fat:	7 g.
Protein:	1 g.	Cholesterol:	—
Carbohydrate:	6 g.	Sodium:	138 mg.

Creamed Spinach ▲

2 packages (10 ounces each) frozen chopped
  spinach
½ cup chopped onion
2 tablespoons margarine or butter
6 ounces cream cheese
¼ teaspoon salt
¼ teaspoon pepper
¼ teaspoon ground nutmeg
⅓ cup milk

Makes 6 servings

Place spinach on plate in oven. Microwave at HIGH
(100%) until completely defrosted, 6 to 9 minutes. Drain
thoroughly and set aside.

Place onion and margarine in 1-quart casserole. Microwave at HIGH (100%) until onion is tender, 3 to 4 minutes. Add cream cheese. Microwave at MEDIUM (50%)
until softened, 1 to 1½ minutes. Stir in salt, pepper and
nutmeg until smooth. Blend in milk. Mix in spinach.

Microwave at MEDIUM-HIGH (70%) until heated
through, 4 to 6 minutes, stirring once. Stir before serving.

Per Serving:			
Calories:	162	Fat:	14 g.
Protein:	5 g.	Cholesterol:	32 mg.
Carbohydrate:	5 g.	Sodium:	276 mg.

Cauliflower Scramble

2 packages (10 ounces each) cauliflower in cheese sauce
1 medium zucchini, thinly sliced
¼ cup chopped onion
2 tablespoons margarine or butter
2 medium tomatoes, each cut into 8 wedges
¼ teaspoon dried thyme leaves

Makes 6 servings

Remove cauliflower pouches from boxes. Place both pouches in oven. Microwave at HIGH (100%) until defrosted but not hot, 4 to 6 minutes, rearranging pouches once. Set aside.

Combine zucchini, onion and margarine in 2-quart casserole. Microwave at HIGH (100%) until vegetables are tender-crisp, 2½ to 4 minutes. Stir in cauliflower, tomatoes and thyme. Microwave, covered, at HIGH (100%) until heated through, 4½ to 6½ minutes. Stir before serving.

Per Serving:			
Calories:	98	Fat:	5 g.
Protein:	2 g.	Cholesterol:	—
Carbohydrate:	11 g.	Sodium:	425 mg.

Glazed Carrots ▶

4 large carrots (1 pound)
3 tablespoons packed brown sugar
2 tablespoons margarine or butter
1 tablespoon water
¼ teaspoon salt
⅛ teaspoon ground cinnamon

Makes 6 servings

Cut carrots into long thin strips. Set aside. Combine brown sugar, margarine, water, salt and cinnamon in 2-quart casserole.

Microwave at HIGH (100%) until margarine is melted, 45 seconds to 1 minute 30 seconds. Stir to blend. Stir in carrots until coated. Cover. Microwave at HIGH (100%) until carrots are tender, 5 to 8 minutes, stirring once.

Per Serving:			
Calories:	92	Fat:	4 g.
Protein:	1 g.	Cholesterol:	—
Carbohydrate:	14 g.	Sodium:	162 mg.

Fresh Cauliflower au Gratin

1 medium head cauliflower (about 1 pound),
    separated into flowerets
2 tablespoons water
1 tablespoon margarine or butter
1 tablespoon all-purpose flour
½ cup milk
1 teaspoon prepared mustard (optional)
¼ teaspoon salt
½ cup shredded Cheddar cheese (about
    2 ounces)
⅛ teaspoon paprika

Makes 4 servings

Place cauliflowerets and water in 1-quart casserole; cover. Microwave at HIGH (100%) until tender, 5 to 7 minutes, stirring after half the cooking time. Drain and set aside.

Place margarine in 2-cup measure. Microwave at HIGH (100%) until melted, 30 seconds to 1 minute. Stir in flour. Blend in milk, mustard and salt. Reduce power to MEDIUM-HIGH (70%). Microwave until thickened, 2 to 5 minutes, stirring every minute. Stir in cheese until melted. Pour over cauliflowerets; sprinkle with paprika.

Per Serving:			
Calories:	125	Fat:	8 g.
Protein:	6 g.	Cholesterol:	17 mg.
Carbohydrate:	7 g.	Sodium:	283 mg.

Orange Carrots

4 large carrots (1 pound), cut in thin slices
¼ cup margarine or butter
1 tablespoon grated orange rind
1 teaspoon sugar

Makes 6 servings

Combine all ingredients in 1-quart casserole.

Cover. Microwave at HIGH (100%) until carrots are tender, 4 to 8 minutes, stirring after half the cooking time.

Per Serving:			
Calories:	103	Fat:	8 g.
Protein:	1 g.	Cholesterol:	—
Carbohydrate:	9 g.	Sodium:	116 mg.

◄ Artichokes with Mustard Sauce

 4 medium artichokes
¼ cup water
½ cup prepared brown mustard
¼ cup mayonnaise or salad dressing
 1 tablespoon horseradish sauce (optional)

Makes 4 servings

Slice 1 inch from top of artichokes; trim stem even with base. Cut off sharp tips of outer leaves. Rinse artichokes under cold water. Arrange in upright position in square baking dish, 8 × 8 inches. Pour ¼ cup water into baking dish. Cover with plastic wrap.

Microwave at HIGH (100%) until lower leaves can be pulled off with a slight tug and base is fork-tender, 10 to 16½ minutes, rearranging artichokes once during cooking. Mix remaining ingredients. Serve with artichokes.

Per Serving:			
Calories:	260	Fat:	14 g.
Protein:	9 g.	Cholesterol:	8 mg.
Carbohydrate:	33 g.	Sodium:	670 mg.

Broccoli in Lemon Sauce

 2 packages (10 ounces each) frozen broccoli
    spears
 2 tablespoons water
 2 tablespoons margarine or butter
 1 tablespoon all-purpose flour
½ cup milk
 2 teaspoons grated lemon rind
⅛ teaspoon salt

Makes 6 servings

Place broccoli and water in 2-quart casserole; cover. Microwave at HIGH (100%) until heated through, 8 to 12 minutes, stirring to break apart after half the time. Drain and set aside.

Place margarine in small bowl or 2-cup measure. Microwave at HIGH (100%) until melted, 30 seconds to 1 minute. Stir in flour. Blend in remaining ingredients. Reduce power to MEDIUM-HIGH (70%). Microwave until thickened, 2½ to 3 minutes, stirring every 30 seconds to 1 minute. Pour over broccoli. Microwave at MEDIUM-HIGH (70%) until heated through, 2 to 3 minutes.

Per Serving:			
Calories:	72	Fat:	4 g.
Protein:	3 g.	Cholesterol:	2 mg.
Carbohydrate:	7 g.	Sodium:	119 mg.

Sunshine Brussels Sprouts ▶

2 packages (10 ounces each) frozen Brussels
  sprouts
2 tablespoons water
¼ cup chopped onion
1 tablespoon margarine or butter
¼ cup half-and-half
2 egg yolks, slightly beaten
1 tablespoon fresh lemon juice
⅛ teaspoon salt
  Dash of pepper

Makes 6 servings

Place Brussels sprouts and water in 2-quart casserole;
cover. Microwave at HIGH (100%) until tender, 8 to 10
minutes, stirring after half the cooking time. Drain and
set aside.

Place onion and margarine in 2-cup measure. Microwave at HIGH (100%) until onion is tender, 1 to 2 minutes. Blend in remaining ingredients. Reduce power to
MEDIUM-HIGH (70%). Microwave until thickened,
30 seconds to 2 minutes, stirring every 30 seconds. Pour
over Brussels sprouts. Microwave at HIGH (100%) until
heated through, 1 minute.

Per Serving:			
Calories:	93	Fat:	5 g.
Protein:	5 g.	Cholesterol:	95 mg.
Carbohydrate:	9 g.	Sodium:	83 mg.

Scalloped Asparagus

2 packages (10 ounces each) frozen cut asparagus
2 tablespoons water
2 tablespoons margarine or butter
¼ cup slivered almonds
1 tablespoon margarine or butter
1 tablespoon all-purpose flour
¼ teaspoon salt
½ cup milk
½ cup shredded sharp Cheddar cheese (about
  2 ounces)

Makes 6 servings

Per Serving:			
Calories:	155	Fat:	12 g.
Protein:	7 g.	Cholesterol:	11 mg.
Carbohydrate:	7 g.	Sodium:	233 mg.

Place asparagus and water in 2-quart casserole; cover.
Microwave at HIGH (100%) until heated through, 8 to
10 minutes, stirring to break apart after half the time.
Drain and set aside.

Place 2 tablespoons margarine in small bowl. Microwave
at HIGH (100%) until melted, 30 seconds to 1 minute.
Mix in almonds until coated. Microwave at HIGH
(100%) until light brown, 2 to 3 minutes. Set aside.

Place 1 tablespoon margarine in small bowl or 2-cup
measure. Microwave at HIGH (100%) until melted,
30 seconds to 1 minute. Stir in flour and salt. Blend in
milk. Reduce power to MEDIUM-HIGH (70%). Microwave until thickened, 2 to 3½ minutes, stirring every
30 seconds to 1 minute. Stir in cheese until melted.
Pour over asparagus. Sprinkle with almonds. Microwave at MEDIUM-HIGH (70%) until heated through,
2 to 3 minutes.

Parsley Potatoes

6 medium red potatoes (about 2½ pounds),
  peeled and quartered
¼ cup water
¼ cup margarine or butter
1 tablespoon dried parsley flakes
¼ teaspoon salt
⅛ teaspoon pepper

Makes 6 servings

Place potatoes and water in 2-quart casserole; cover. Microwave at HIGH (100%) until fork-tender, 12 to 15 minutes, stirring after half the time. Let stand 5 minutes. Drain and set aside.

Place margarine in 2-cup measure. Microwave at HIGH (100%) 1 to 1½ minutes. Stir in remaining ingredients. Pour over potatoes. Toss to coat.

Per Serving:			
Calories:	187	Fat:	8 g.
Protein:	3 g.	Cholesterol:	—
Carbohydrate:	27 g.	Sodium:	188 mg.

Stuffed Baked Potatoes

4 baking potatoes (about 6 to 8 ounces each)
½ cup half-and-half
¼ cup shredded Cheddar cheese (about 1 ounce)
2 tablespoons margarine or butter
2 teaspoons dried parsley flakes
½ teaspoon salt
¼ teaspoon pepper
¼ teaspoon dry mustard
¼ cup shredded Cheddar cheese (about 1 ounce)
⅛ teaspoon paprika

Makes 4 servings

Bake potatoes as directed in chart on page 87. Cut thin slice from the top of each potato. Scoop out inside with a spoon, leaving a thin shell. Add remaining ingredients except ¼ cup cheese and paprika to potatoes. Mash until no lumps remain.

Spoon one-fourth of the potato mixture into each shell. Place stuffed potatoes in square baking dish, 8 × 8 inches. Sprinkle with remaining ¼ cup cheese and the paprika. Microwave at MEDIUM-HIGH (70%) until cheese is melted and potatoes are heated through, 3 to 4 minutes.

Per Serving:			
Calories:	267	Fat:	14 g.
Protein:	8 g.	Cholesterol:	26 mg.
Carbohydrate:	29 g.	Sodium:	443 mg.

German Potato Salad ▲

6 slices bacon, chopped
½ cup chopped green onions
¼ cup white vinegar
2 tablespoons sugar
¼ teaspoon salt
6 medium potatoes (about 2½ pounds), peeled and cut into ¼-inch slices
¼ cup water

Makes 6 servings

Place bacon and green onions in small bowl or 1-quart casserole; cover. Microwave at HIGH (100%) until bacon is light brown, 5 to 7 minutes. Stir in vinegar, sugar and salt. Set aside.

Place potato slices and water in 2-quart casserole; cover. Microwave at HIGH (100%) until potatoes are fork-tender, 10 to 15 minutes, stirring after half the cooking time. Drain. Pour bacon and vinegar mixture over potato slices. Toss to coat.

Per Serving:			
Calories:	174	Fat:	3 g.
Protein:	5 g.	Cholesterol:	5 mg.
Carbohydrate:	32 g.	Sodium:	199 mg.

Green Beans Almondine ▲

1½ pounds fresh green beans
½ cup hot water
¼ teaspoon salt
⅓ cup slivered almonds
3 tablespoons margarine or butter
¼ teaspoon ground nutmeg (optional)
¼ teaspoon pepper

Makes 6 servings

Wash beans and break off ends. Break beans into 1-
to 1½-inch pieces. Place in 2-quart casserole. Stir water
and salt until salt is dissolved. Stir into beans. Cover.

Microwave at HIGH (100%) until beans are tender-
crisp, 13 to 16 minutes, stirring once. Let stand 2 to 3
minutes. Drain.

Mix in almonds, margarine, nutmeg and pepper until
margarine is melted. Microwave at HIGH (100%) until
heated through, 1 minute.

Per Serving:			
Calories:	124	Fat:	9 g.
Protein:	3 g.	Cholesterol:	—
Carbohydrate:	10 g.	Sodium:	164 mg.

Sautéed Green Beans

1½ pounds fresh green beans
¼ cup margarine or butter
¼ teaspoon salt
¼ teaspoon dried savory leaves
⅛ teaspoon dried oregano leaves
⅛ teaspoon pepper

Makes 6 servings

Wash beans and break off ends. Break beans into 1-
to 1½-inch pieces. Place in 2-quart casserole. Place
margarine in small bowl or 2-cup measure. Microwave
at HIGH (100%) until melted, 1 to 1½ minutes. Blend
in remaining ingredients.

Pour seasoned margarine mixture over beans. Toss to
coat. Cover. Microwave at HIGH (100%) until beans
are tender-crisp, 13 to 16 minutes, stirring once. Cover;
let stand 2 to 3 minutes.

Per Serving:			
Calories:	104	Fat:	8 g.
Protein:	2 g.	Cholesterol:	—
Carbohydrate:	8 g.	Sodium:	185 mg.

Sweet Potato Casserole ▲

4 medium sweet potatoes or yams (about 2 pounds)
¼ cup packed brown sugar
¼ cup margarine or butter
½ teaspoon salt
1 can (8 ounces) crushed pineapple
1 tablespoon packed brown sugar
1 tablespoon margarine or butter
1 teaspoon water
½ teaspoon ground cinnamon
¼ teaspoon ground nutmeg
1½ cups miniature marshmallows
¼ cup chopped pecans

Makes 6 servings

Wash sweet potatoes. Prick each 2 or 3 times with fork to allow steam to escape. Arrange in oven at least 1 inch apart. Microwave at HIGH (100%) until fork-tender, 8 to 13 minutes. Cover and let stand 5 minutes.

Peel and slice potatoes. Place in 2-quart casserole. Add ¼ cup brown sugar, ¼ cup margarine and the salt. Mash until no lumps remain. Mix in pineapple. Microwave at HIGH (100%) 2 minutes. Stir and set aside.

Place 1 tablespoon brown sugar, 1 tablespoon margarine, the water, cinnamon and nutmeg in medium bowl. Microwave at HIGH (100%) until margarine is melted, 1 to 1½ minutes, stirring after half the time. Add marshmallows; toss to coat. Top sweet potato mixture with marshmallows. Microwave at HIGH (100%) until marshmallows are melted and potatoes are heated through, 2 to 4 minutes. Sprinkle with pecans.

Per Serving:			
Calories:	301	Fat:	13 g.
Protein:	2 g.	Cholesterol:	—
Carbohydrate:	46 g.	Sodium:	309 mg.

Acorn Squash with Cranberry Filling ▶

2 large acorn squash (about 2 pounds each)
1 can (16 ounces) whole cranberry sauce
1 tablespoon honey
¼ teaspoon ground allspice

Makes 4 servings

Prick squash several times with fork to allow steam to escape. Place in oven. Microwave at HIGH (100%) until soft when pricked with fork, 11 to 13 minutes, turning squash over and rotating after half the cooking time. Let stand 5 minutes. Cut in half and remove seeds. Place cut side up in 10-inch square casserole. Set aside.

Combine cranberry sauce, honey and allspice in small bowl. Microwave at HIGH (100%) until hot and bubbly, 3 to 4 minutes, stirring after half the cooking time. Spoon into squash halves. Microwave at HIGH (100%) until heated through, 2 to 3 minutes.

Per Serving:			
Calories:	274	Fat:	—
Protein:	2 g.	Cholesterol:	—
Carbohydrate:	71 g.	Sodium:	40 mg.

Squash Parmesan

3 small yellow summer squash (about 1 pound), thinly sliced
¼ cup chopped onion
2 tablespoons water
2 tablespoons grated fresh Parmesan cheese

Makes 4 servings

Place squash, onion and water in 1-quart casserole; cover. Microwave at HIGH (100%) until vegetables are tender, 3 to 6 minutes.

Sprinkle with Parmesan cheese. Microwave at HIGH (100%) until cheese melts, 1 to 2 minutes.

Per Serving:			
Calories:	32	Fat:	1 g.
Protein:	2 g.	Cholesterol:	2 mg.
Carbohydrate:	4 g.	Sodium:	60 mg.

PASTA, GRAINS & CEREALS

Help your family eat right by preparing delicious pasta and rice dishes and steaming hot cereals in your Sharp microwave oven. Cleanups for hot cereals, rice and pasta dishes are easy . . . no scrubbing!

**Hot Pasta Salad,
page 103**

Oatmeal with Prunes & Raisins

2½ cups hot water
1⅓ cups old-fashioned rolled oats
¼ cup instant nonfat dry milk powder
¼ cup chopped pitted prunes
2 tablespoons raisins
2 teaspoons margarine or butter
¼ teaspoon salt
¼ teaspoon ground cinnamon

Makes 4 servings

In 2-quart casserole, combine all ingredients. Mix well. Microwave at HIGH (100%) for 8 to 10 minutes or until desired consistency, stirring after half the time.

Per Serving:			
Calories:	183	Fat:	4 g.
Protein:	7 g.	Cholesterol:	1 mg.
Carbohydrate:	32 g.	Sodium:	194 mg.

Cereal Cooking Chart

Power Level: HIGH (100%)

Select a large bowl or casserole when microwaving cereals which boil over easily. Stir cereal once during cooking and again before serving.

	Amount	Salt (tsp.)	Water (cups)	Time (min.)
Quick Oatmeal				
1 serving	⅓ cup	¼	¾	2-2½
4 servings	1⅓ cups	¾	3	6-7
Old-Fashioned Oatmeal				
1 serving	⅓ cup	¼	¾	4-6
4 servings	1⅓ cups	1	2½	8-9
Regular Cream of Wheat				
1 serving	2½ tbsp.	⅛	1	4-6
4 servings	⅔ cup	½	3½	9-12
Oat Bran				
1 serving	⅓ cup	⅛	1	2-2½
4 servings	1⅓ cups	½	3-4	8-10

Spiced Creamy Cereal

2 cups skim milk
⅓ cup regular cream of wheat cereal
2 tablespoons chopped dried apricots
⅛ teaspoon salt
Dash ground nutmeg
Dash ground allspice

Makes 2 servings

In 2-quart casserole, combine all ingredients. Microwave at HIGH (100%) for 6 to 8 minutes or until cereal thickens, stirring after every 2 minutes.

Per Serving:			
Calories:	141	Fat:	1 g.
Protein:	10 g.	Cholesterol:	4 mg.
Carbohydrate:	24 g.	Sodium:	261 mg.

Sunny Couscous Cereal

¾ cup water
¼ cup fresh orange juice
½ cup uncooked couscous
1 teaspoon grated orange peel
2 tablespoons finely chopped blanched almonds
1 tablespoon honey
1 tablespoon frozen apple juice concentrate
Dash of ground cinnamon

Makes 4 servings

Combine all ingredients in 1-quart casserole. Cover. Microwave at HIGH (100%) until liquid is absorbed and couscous is tender, 5 to 6 minutes. Let stand, covered, 1 minute.

Per Serving:			
Calories:	122	Fat:	2 g.
Protein:	3 g.	Cholesterol:	—
Carbohydrate:	23 g.	Sodium:	1 mg.

Spanish Rice with Shrimp ▶

1 can (16 ounces) stewed tomatoes
1½ cups water
⅔ cup uncooked long grain rice
⅓ cup finely chopped onion
¼ cup chopped celery
3 tablespoons tomato paste
¼ teaspoon salt
1 teaspoon sugar
1 teaspoon instant chicken bouillon
½ teaspoon dried oregano leaves
¼ to ½ teaspoon garlic powder
1 can (4½ ounces) small shrimp, rinsed and
 drained

Makes 8 servings

Combine all ingredients except shrimp in 2-quart casserole. Mix well. Cover. Microwave at HIGH (100%) 10 minutes. Reduce power to MEDIUM (50%). Microwave until liquid is absorbed and rice is tender, 28 to 35 minutes. Stir in shrimp. Let stand, covered, 5 minutes. Fluff with fork before serving.

Per Serving:			
Calories:	101	Fat:	1 g.
Protein:	6 g.	Cholesterol:	28 mg.
Carbohydrate:	19 g.	Sodium:	337 mg.

Instant Rice

1¼ cups uncooked instant rice
1¼ cups hot water
1 teaspoon salt
1 teaspoon margarine or butter (optional)

Makes 4 servings

Combine all ingredients in 2-quart casserole. Cover. Microwave at HIGH (100%) until water boils, 4 to 8 minutes. Let stand, covered, 5 minutes. Fluff with fork before serving.

Per Serving:			
Calories:	111	Fat:	—
Protein:	2 g.	Cholesterol:	—
Carbohydrate:	25 g.	Sodium:	533 mg.

Brown Rice

1 cup parboiled long grain brown rice
2¾ cups hot water
1 tablespoon margarine or butter (optional)
½ teaspoon salt

Makes 4 servings

Combine all ingredients in 3-quart casserole. Cover. Microwave at HIGH (100%) 5 minutes. Reduce power to MEDIUM (50%). Microwave until liquid is absorbed and rice is tender, 25 to 35 minutes. Fluff with fork before serving.

Per Serving:			
Calories:	167	Fat:	1 g.
Protein:	3 g.	Cholesterol:	—
Carbohydrate:	36 g.	Sodium:	271 mg.

Long Grain Rice

1 cup uncooked long grain rice
2 cups hot water
1 tablespoon margarine or butter (optional)
1 teaspoon salt

Makes 4 servings

Combine all ingredients in 2-quart casserole. Cover. Microwave at HIGH (100%) 5 minutes. Reduce power to MEDIUM (50%). Microwave until liquid is absorbed and rice is tender, 10 to 13 minutes. Fluff with fork before serving.

Per Serving:			
Calories:	168	Fat:	—
Protein:	3 g.	Cholesterol:	—
Carbohydrate:	37 g.	Sodium:	535 mg.

Rice Oregano ▲

2 cups hot water
1 cup uncooked long grain rice
¼ cup finely chopped onion
2 tablespoons butter or margarine
4 teaspoons instant chicken bouillon
½ teaspoon dried oregano leaves
⅛ teaspoon pepper

Makes 6 servings

Combine all ingredients in 2-quart casserole. Mix well. Cover. Microwave at HIGH (100%) 5 minutes. Reduce power to MEDIUM (50%). Microwave until liquid is absorbed and rice is tender, 13 to 19 minutes. Let stand, covered, 5 minutes. Fluff with fork before serving.

Per Serving:			
Calories:	152	Fat:	4 g.
Protein:	2 g.	Cholesterol:	—
Carbohydrate:	26 g.	Sodium:	294 mg.

Rice Pilaf ▲

¼ cup chopped onion
¼ cup chopped celery
¼ cup chopped green pepper
2 tablespoons margarine or butter
1 cup hot water
1 can (4 ounces) sliced mushrooms, drained
⅓ cup uncooked long grain rice
1 tablespoon instant chicken bouillon

Makes 3 servings

Combine onion, celery, green pepper and margarine in 1-quart casserole. Microwave at HIGH (100%) until vegetables are tender-crisp, 3 to 5 minutes. Stir in remaining ingredients; cover.

Microwave at HIGH (100%) 5 minutes. Reduce power to MEDIUM (50%). Microwave until liquid is absorbed, 10 to 12 minutes. Let stand, covered, 5 minutes. Fluff with fork before serving.

Per Serving:			
Calories:	166	Fat:	8 g.
Protein:	3 g.	Cholesterol:	—
Carbohydrate:	21 g.	Sodium:	613 mg.

Fried Rice

2 tablespoons chopped onion
1 tablespoon margarine or butter
2 teaspoons instant chicken bouillon
1⅔ cups hot water
2 cups uncooked instant rice
2 tablespoons finely chopped green onion
2 eggs, beaten
1 tablespoon plus 2 teaspoons soy sauce

Makes 6 servings

Combine onion and margarine in 2-quart casserole. Microwave at HIGH (100%) until onion is tender, 1 to 3 minutes. Set aside.

Stir bouillon into hot water until dissolved. Add bouillon mixture, rice and green onion to casserole; cover. Microwave at HIGH (100%) until mixture boils, 4 to 8 minutes. Let stand, covered, until liquid is absorbed, 5 to 6 minutes.

Stir in eggs and soy sauce. Microwave, uncovered, at HIGH (100%) until eggs are set, 2 to 4½ minutes, stirring several times during cooking. Fluff with fork before serving.

Per Serving:			
Calories:	85	Fat:	4 g.
Protein:	3 g.	Cholesterol:	92 mg.
Carbohydrate:	9 g.	Sodium:	455 mg.

Mushroom Tetrazzini ▶

    1 package (7 ounces) spaghetti
    ¼ cup margarine or butter
    1 cup sliced fresh mushrooms
    ½ cup chopped onion
    ¼ cup all-purpose flour
    2 tablespoons sherry
    ½ teaspoon salt
    ⅛ teaspoon pepper
    1½ cups milk
    4 ounces Provolone cheese, cut into ¼-inch
        cubes
    4 ounces mozzarella cheese, cut into ¼-inch
        cubes
    2 tablespoons snipped parsley

Makes 6 servings

Prepare spaghetti as directed on package. Rinse and drain. Cover. Set aside. Combine margarine, mushrooms and onion in 2-quart casserole. Microwave at HIGH (100%) until mushrooms are tender, 4 to 6 minutes, stirring once. Stir in flour, sherry, salt and pepper. Blend in milk. Microwave at HIGH (100%) until mixture thickens and bubbles, 4 to 6 minutes, stirring every 2 minutes. Stir in Provolone and mozzarella cheeses. Microwave at HIGH (100%) until mixture can be stirred smooth, 1½ to 2 minutes, stirring after every minute. Pour cheese mixture over spaghetti. Toss to coat. Microwave at HIGH (100%) until heated through, 1 to 2 minutes. Sprinkle with parsley.

Per Serving:			
Calories:	374	Fat:	18 g.
Protein:	17 g.	Cholesterol:	28 mg.
Carbohydrate:	35 g.	Sodium:	565 mg.

Hot Pasta Salad

    1 medium green pepper, cut into ¼-inch strips
    ½ medium red onion, cut in half lengthwise and
        thinly sliced
    2 tablespoons margarine or butter
    2 teaspoons poppy seed
    ⅛ teaspoon salt
    ¾ cup cooked spaghetti
    1 medium tomato, cut into thin wedges

Makes 4 servings

Combine all ingredients except spaghetti and tomato in 1-quart casserole. Cover. Microwave at HIGH (100%) until pepper and onion are tender, 3 to 5 minutes, stirring once. Add remaining ingredients. Toss lightly. Re-cover. Microwave at HIGH (100%) until hot, 2 to 3 minutes. Let stand, covered, 1 minute.

Per Serving:			
Calories:	110	Fat:	7 g.
Protein:	2 g.	Cholesterol:	—
Carbohydrate:	11 g.	Sodium:	137 mg.

Light Cheese-Stuffed Manicotti ▲

8 uncooked manicotti shells

Sauce:
1 can (16 ounces) whole tomatoes, undrained and cut up
1 can (8 ounces) tomato sauce
1 tablespoon Burgundy wine
2 teaspoons olive oil
½ teaspoon dried basil leaves

Filling:
1 carton (15 ounces) lite ricotta cheese (1 gram fat per ounce)

½ cup low-fat cottage cheese, drained
2 egg whites (¼ cup)
2 tablespoons snipped parsley
1 tablespoon grated Parmesan cheese
⅛ teaspoon garlic powder
½ cup shredded hard farmer cheese (2 ounces)

Makes 4 servings

Prepare manicotti shells as directed on package. Rinse. Let stand in warm water while preparing sauce and filling.

Combine sauce ingredients in 2-quart casserole. Microwave at HIGH (100%), uncovered, until flavors are blended and sauce is slightly thickened, 6 to 8 minutes, stirring twice. Set aside.

Combine filling ingredients in small mixing bowl. Stuff each cooked manicotti shell with scant ⅓ cup cheese filling.

Reserve ⅓ cup tomato sauce. Set aside. Pour remaining sauce into 10-inch square casserole. Arrange stuffed shells in sauce. Spoon reserved sauce over manicotti. Cover. Microwave at MEDIUM-HIGH (70%) until hot, 12 to 14 minutes, rotating dish twice. Sprinkle with farmer cheese. Let stand, covered, until cheese melts, 5 minutes.

Per Serving:					
Calories:	367	Carbohydrate:	39 g.	Cholesterol:	32 mg.
Protein:	27 g.	Fat:	12 g.	Sodium:	836 mg.

Fresh Vegetable Alfredo

½ pound fresh asparagus, cut into ¾-inch lengths
¼ cup margarine or butter
1 can (16 ounces) pitted black olives, drained
½ cup whipping cream
2 eggs, beaten
½ cup grated Parmesan cheese
⅛ teaspoon garlic powder
⅛ teaspoon pepper
8 ounces uncooked fettucini
1 cup quartered cherry tomatoes

Makes 4 servings

Place asparagus and margarine in 2-quart casserole. Cover. Microwave at HIGH (100%) until margarine is melted and asparagus is tender-crisp, 3 to 4 minutes, stirring once. Add olives. Set aside. Blend whipping cream, eggs, Parmesan cheese, garlic powder and pepper in small mixing bowl. Add to asparagus mixture. Mix well. Set aside.

Prepare fettucini as directed on package. Rinse and drain. Add to asparagus mixture. Toss to coat. Microwave at MEDIUM (50%) until hot, 4 to 6 minutes, stirring every 2 minutes. Add cherry tomatoes. Toss to combine. Before serving, sprinkle with additional grated Parmesan cheese, if desired.

Per Serving:	
Calories:	583
Protein:	19 g.
Carbohydrate:	49 g.
Fat:	36 g.
Cholesterol:	188 mg.
Sodium:	749 mg.

Lasagna Primavera ▲

Nonstick vegetable cooking spray
9 uncooked lasagna noodles
2 cups fresh broccoli flowerets
2 cups sliced fresh mushrooms
1 yellow summer squash (about 4 ounces), sliced (1 cup)
1 zucchini (about 4 ounces), sliced (1 cup)
¼ cup shredded carrot
¼ cup water
1 large clove garlic, minced
¼ teaspoon salt
¼ teaspoon pepper
½ cup nonfat dry milk powder
1 tablespoon plus 1 teaspoon all-purpose flour
½ teaspoon dried basil leaves
½ teaspoon fennel seed, crushed
½ teaspoon dried oregano leaves
1 cup water
1 cup lite ricotta cheese (1 gram fat per ounce)
2 tablespoons snipped parsley
1 cup shredded mozzarella cheese (4 ounces)

Makes 6 servings

Spray 11 × 7-inch baking dish with nonstick vegetable cooking spray. Set aside. Prepare lasagna noodles as directed on package. Rinse. Let stand in warm water.

Combine broccoli, mushrooms, squash, zucchini, carrot, ¼ cup water, the garlic, salt and pepper in 3-quart casserole. Cover. Microwave at HIGH (100%) until vegetables are tender, 8 to 10 minutes, stirring once. Set aside.

Place dry milk, flour, basil, fennel and oregano in 4-cup measure. Blend in 1 cup water. Microwave at HIGH (100%) until mixture thickens and bubbles, 3 to 5 minutes, stirring with whisk every minute. Set aside.

Combine ricotta cheese and parsley in small mixing bowl. Mix well. Set aside. Place lasagna noodles on paper towels to drain.

Layer 3 noodles, half of vegetable mixture, half of ricotta mixture, ½ cup mozzarella cheese and half of sauce in prepared dish. Top with 3 noodles, remaining vegetable and ricotta mixtures. Top with remaining noodles, sauce and mozzarella cheese.

Cover with plastic wrap. Microwave at MEDIUM-HIGH (70%) until lasagna is hot, 10 to 12 minutes. Let stand, covered, 10 minutes.

Per Serving:			
Calories:	273	Fat:	6 g.
Protein:	19 g.	Cholesterol:	18 mg.
Carbohydrate:	37 g.	Sodium:	280 mg.

BAKING & DESSERTS

There's a happy ending to a perfect meal when you use your microwave oven to prepare homemade favorites, such as puddings, cheesecakes and cobblers that bring back memories of your grandmother's kitchen. Use the microwave oven for melting chocolate or butter or toasting nuts or coconut.

Two-Layer Pineapple Upside-Down Cake

1 can (15½ ounces) crushed pineapple (juice pack), drained (reserve juice)
1 tablespoon cornstarch
2 tablespoons packed brown sugar
1 tablespoon honey
½ teaspoon lemon juice
2 tablespoons margarine or butter
¼ cup packed brown sugar
1 can (8 ounces) pineapple slices (juice pack), drained (reserve juice)
7 maraschino cherries, drained
1 package (18½ ounces) yellow cake mix

Makes 12 servings

Blend juice from crushed pineapple and cornstarch in small bowl. Stir in crushed pineapple, 2 tablespoons brown sugar, the honey and lemon juice. Microwave at HIGH (100%) until thickened, 4 to 5 minutes, stirring after half the time. Set aside. Place margarine in round baking dish, 9 × 1½ inches. Microwave at HIGH (100%) until melted, 30 to 45 seconds. Stir in ¼ cup brown sugar; spread evenly in dish. Arrange pineapple slices and cherries over brown sugar. Set aside.

Line round baking dish, 9 × 1½ inches, with wax paper. Add enough additional water to juice reserved from pineapple slices to equal amount of water needed for preparing cake mix. Prepare cake mix according to package directions using pineapple juice-water mixture. Pour half of the batter into wax paper-lined baking dish and half over pineapple slices.

Microwave first layer (wax paper-lined baking dish) at MEDIUM-HIGH (70%) 5 minutes. Increase power to HIGH (100%). Microwave until wooden pick inserted in center comes out clean, 1 to 4 minutes. Invert onto serving plate; spread with crushed pineapple mixture. Microwave pineapple layer at MEDIUM-HIGH (70%) 4 minutes. Increase power to HIGH (100%). Microwave until wooden pick inserted in center comes out clean, 5 to 8 minutes. Cool 2 minutes. Invert second layer on top of first.

Per Serving:			
Calories:	381	Fat:	18 g.
Protein:	4 g.	Cholesterol:	69 mg.
Carbohydrate:	53 g.	Sodium:	220 mg.

Carrot Bread

½ cup whole wheat flour
½ cup all-purpose flour
½ cup granulated sugar
¼ cup packed brown sugar
1 teaspoon baking soda
1 teaspoon baking powder
1 teaspoon ground cinnamon
½ teaspoon salt
½ cup vegetable oil
2 eggs
1 teaspoon vanilla
2 cups grated carrots
⅓ cup raisins (optional)

Makes 12 servings

Lightly grease bottom of loaf dish, 9 × 5 inches. Combine flours, sugars, baking soda, baking powder, cinnamon and salt in medium mixing bowl. Add remaining ingredients except carrots and raisins. Beat at low speed until just blended. Stir in carrots and raisins. Pour into loaf dish.

Place loaf dish on saucer or roasting rack in oven. Microwave at MEDIUM-HIGH (70%) 6 minutes. Cover ends of loaf dish with 2-inch strips of aluminum foil and mold to fit around handles. Microwave at MEDIUM-HIGH (70%) until no uncooked batter can be seen through bottom of dish and wooden pick inserted in center comes out clean, 3 to 8 minutes. Cool on countertop 5 minutes. Remove from dish. Store in refrigerator.

Per Serving:			
Calories:	187	Fat:	10 g.
Protein:	2 g.	Cholesterol:	46 mg.
Carbohydrate:	22 g.	Sodium:	227 mg.

Chocolate Chip Zucchini Cake ▶

¼ cup margarine or butter
1 cup sugar
¼ cup vegetable oil
1 cup all-purpose flour
2 tablespoons cocoa
½ teaspoon baking soda
¼ teaspoon baking powder
¼ teaspoon ground cinnamon
1 cup shredded zucchini
¼ cup buttermilk
1 egg
½ teaspoon vanilla
6 tablespoons semisweet chocolate chips

Frosting:

2 tablespoons all-purpose flour
½ cup milk
2 tablespoons margarine or butter
½ cup sugar
  Dash of salt
¼ cup vegetable shortening
½ teaspoon vanilla

Makes 12 servings

Place margarine in medium mixing bowl. Microwave at MEDIUM-LOW (30%) until softened, 15 to 45 seconds, checking after every 15 seconds. Add sugar and oil. Beat at medium speed of electric mixer until light and fluffy. Add remaining cake ingredients except chocolate chips. Beat at low speed until moistened. Beat at medium speed 1 minute, scraping bowl occasionally. Stir in choco-

late chips. Spread batter into square baking dish, 8 × 8 inches. Shield corners of dish with triangles of foil.

Place dish on saucer in microwave oven. Microwave at MEDIUM (50%) 6 minutes. Remove foil. Increase power to HIGH (100%). Microwave until top appears dry and center springs back when touched lightly, 5 to 10 minutes. Let stand on counter. Cool completely.

Place flour in medium mixing bowl. Blend in milk. Microwave at HIGH (100%) until mixture becomes very thick and pastelike, 2 to 2½ minutes, stirring with whisk after every minute. Chill 45 minutes. Place margarine in small bowl. Microwave at MEDIUM-LOW (30%) until softened, 15 to 30 seconds. Add margarine and remaining frosting ingredients to flour mixture. Beat at high speed until light and fluffy, 3 minutes. Spread frosting over top of cooled cake.

Per Serving:			
Calories:	293	Fat:	15 g.
Protein:	3 g.	Cholesterol:	24 mg.
Carbohydrate:	38 g.	Sodium:	154 mg.

Bran Muffins

2¼ cups whole bran cereal
¼ cup packed dark brown sugar
1 cup buttermilk
⅓ cup dark molasses
1¼ cups all-purpose flour
1 teaspoon baking powder
1 teaspoon baking soda
½ teaspoon salt
½ cup dark raisins
½ cup vegetable oil
1 egg, slightly beaten

Makes 2 dozen muffins

Mix bran cereal, brown sugar, buttermilk and molasses in medium bowl. Let stand until all liquid is absorbed. Combine flour, baking powder, baking soda and salt. Stir raisins, oil and egg into bran mixture. Stir in flour until evenly moist.

Spoon batter into 24 paper-lined muffin cups, 2½ × 1¼ inches, filling each half full. Microwave 6 muffins at HIGH (100%) until wooden pick inserted in center comes out clean, 2 to 3 minutes. Repeat with remaining muffins.

Per Serving:			
Calories:	113	Fat:	5 g.
Protein:	2 g.	Cholesterol:	12 mg.
Carbohydrate:	17 g.	Sodium:	179 mg.

Pudding from a Mix ▲

1 package (3 to 3⅝ ounces)
   pudding mix

Makes 4 servings

Prepare mix according to package directions in 4-cup measure or 2-quart casserole. Microwave at HIGH (100%) 3 minutes. Stir. Microwave until mixture boils, 1 to 4 minutes, stirring every minute. Pour into serving dishes. Chill. Mixture will thicken while standing.

Nutritional information varies with flavor of mix. See package for specific nutritional information.

Applesauce

 4 cups sliced peeled tart apples
½ cup water
¼ to ½ cup sugar
¼ teaspoon ground cinnamon

Makes 6 servings

Place all ingredients in 1-quart casserole; cover.

Microwave at HIGH (100%) until apples are tender, 7 to 10 minutes. Mash apples to desired consistency. Serve warm or chilled.

Variation: Add 3 tablespoons red cinnamon candies to applesauce. Microwave at HIGH (100%) 30 seconds to 1 minute 30 seconds. Stir until candies are dissolved.

Per Serving:			
Calories:	74	Fat:	—
Protein:	—	Cholesterol:	—
Carbohydrate:	19 g.	Sodium:	—

Apple Crisp ▶

 4 cups sliced peeled apples
 2 tablespoons lemon juice
½ cup packed brown sugar
½ cup uncooked quick-cooking or old-fashioned
   oats
¼ cup all-purpose flour
¼ cup margarine or butter
 1 teaspoon ground cinnamon
½ teaspoon salt
⅛ teaspoon ground nutmeg

Makes 6 servings

Place apples in 1-quart casserole. Sprinkle with lemon juice. Microwave at HIGH (100%) until apples are tender-crisp, 2½ to 4 minutes. Set apples aside.

Combine remaining ingredients in small bowl. Microwave at HIGH (100%) until hot and bubbly, 1½ to 3½ minutes, stirring after half the cooking time. Spread over apples. Microwave at HIGH (100%) until apples are tender and topping is bubbly, 4 to 6 minutes.

Per Serving:			
Calories:	227	Fat:	8 g.
Protein:	1 g.	Cholesterol:	—
Carbohydrate:	39 g.	Sodium:	273 mg.

Cherry Cobbler

 6 tablespoons margarine or butter
 1 cup all-purpose flour
⅔ cup coarsely chopped nuts
⅓ cup packed dark brown sugar
¾ teaspoon ground cinnamon
¼ teaspoon ground allspice
 1 can (21 ounces) cherry pie filling
 2 teaspoons cornstarch
½ teaspoon lemon juice

Makes 6 servings

Place margarine in small bowl. Microwave at HIGH (100%) until melted, 45 seconds to 1 minute 15 seconds. Stir in flour, nuts, brown sugar, cinnamon and allspice. Set topping aside.

Mix cherry pie filling, cornstarch and lemon juice until smooth in 1-quart casserole. Microwave at HIGH (100%) 1 minute. Sprinkle with topping. Reduce power to MEDIUM-HIGH (70%). Microwave until filling is translucent and bubbly, 6 to 8 minutes. Serve warm or cold with ice cream or whipped topping, if desired.

Per Serving:			
Calories:	608	Fat:	20 g.
Protein:	4 g.	Cholesterol:	—
Carbohydrate:	105 g.	Sodium:	165 mg.

Cinnamon Baked Apples

4 large baking apples (2½- to 3-inch diameter)
4 tablespoons red cinnamon candies

Makes 4 servings

Core apples without cutting through bottom skin and peel about 1-inch strip of skin from stem end of each apple. If necessary, cut thin slice from bottom of each apple so it will stand upright.

Arrange apples in shallow baking dish. Place 1 tablespoon of the cinnamon candies in center of each apple. Microwave at HIGH (100%) until apples are tender, 4 to 6 minutes.

Per Serving:	
Calories:	150
Protein:	—
Carbohydrate:	38 g.
Fat:	1 g.
Cholesterol:	—
Sodium:	30 mg.

Deep Dish Apple Pie ▲

1 tablespoon sugar
½ teaspoon ground cinnamon
5 cups sliced peeled apples
½ cup sugar
2 tablespoons all-purpose flour
½ teaspoon ground cinnamon or cloves
¾ cup buttermilk biscuit baking mix
⅓ cup milk
2 tablespoons sugar

Makes 6 servings

Mix 1 tablespoon sugar and ½ teaspoon cinnamon; set aside. Combine apples, ½ cup sugar, the flour and ½ teaspoon cinnamon or cloves in 1-quart casserole. Cover. Microwave at HIGH (100%) until apples are tender and sauce is bubbly, 3 to 4 minutes.

Mix buttermilk biscuit baking mix, milk and 2 tablespoons sugar just until moistened. Drop by spoonfuls onto hot apple mixture. Sprinkle with cinnamon-sugar mixture. Microwave at HIGH (100%) until topping is set, 4 to 6 minutes. Serve with whipped cream, if desired.

Per Serving:				
Calories:	217	Fat:	3 g.
Protein:	2 g.	Cholesterol:	1 mg.
Carbohydrate:	48 g.	Sodium:	182 mg.

Graham Cracker Crust ▲

3 tablespoons margarine or butter
1 cup fine graham cracker crumbs
¼ cup granulated or packed brown sugar

Makes 9-inch pie crust,
6 servings

Place margarine in 9-inch pie plate. Microwave at HIGH (100%) until melted, 30 seconds to 1 minute. Add graham cracker crumbs and sugar; mix thoroughly. Press mixture firmly against bottom and side of pie plate.

Microwave at MEDIUM-HIGH (70%) until hot, 2 to 4 minutes. Cool completely before filling.

Chocolate Cookie Crust Variation: Follow recipe for Graham Cracker Crust, except increase margarine to ¼ cup and substitute 1¼ cups fine chocolate wafer cookie crumbs for graham cracker curmbs and brown sugar.

Per Serving:			
Calories:	140	Fat:	7 g.
Protein:	1 g.	Cholesterol:	—
Carbohydrate:	19 g.	Sodium:	165 mg.

Baked Pie Shell ▲

⅓ cup shortening
2 tablespoons margarine or butter, softened
1 cup all-purpose flour
½ teaspoon salt
3 tablespoons cold water
3 or 4 drops yellow food coloring (optional)

Makes 9-inch pie shell,
6 servings

Cut shortening and margarine into flour and salt until particles are size of small peas. Combine water and food coloring; sprinkle over flour mixture; toss with fork until particles are just moist enough to cling together. (It may not be necessary to use all the water.) Shape pastry into ball. Flatten to ½ inch. Roll out on floured pastry cloth to scant ⅛-inch-thick circle, 2 inches larger than inverted pie plate, with stocking-covered rolling pin.

Fold pastry into quarters. Lift carefully into pie plate. Unfold and fit loosely into plate; press firmly against bottom and side. Do not stretch pastry or it will shrink while microwaving. Let pastry relax about 10 minutes to reduce shrinkage.

Trim overhanging edge of pastry to generous ½ inch. Fold under, even with plate, to form standing rim. Flute, keeping rim high to contain bubbling. Prick crust with fork on bottom and side ½ inch apart. Microwave at HIGH (100%) until crust appears dry and opaque through bottom of plate, 5 to 7 minutes.

Per Serving:			
Calories:	208	Fat:	15 g.
Protein:	2 g.	Cholesterol:	—
Carbohydrate:	16 g.	Sodium:	223 mg.

Cheesecake ▾

Graham Cracker Crust (page 113)
2 packages (8 ounces each) cream cheese, softened
½ cup sugar
2 eggs, separated
1 tablespoon lemon juice
1 teaspoon grated lemon peel
½ cup dairy sour cream
1 tablespoon sugar
½ teaspoon vanilla

Makes 8 servings

Prepare crust. Set aside. Beat cream cheese and ½ cup sugar in large mixing bowl until light and fluffy. Beat in egg yolks, lemon juice and peel until smooth.

Beat egg whites in small mixing bowl until stiff peaks form. Fold beaten egg whites into cream cheese mixture. Spread evenly in prepared crust.

Microwave at MEDIUM (50%) until center is set, 10 to 15 minutes. Refrigerate several hours before serving. Mix sour cream, 1 tablespoon sugar and the vanilla. Carefully spread over cheesecake before serving.

Per Serving:			
Calories:	408	Fat:	30 g.
Protein:	7 g.	Cholesterol:	138 mg.
Carbohydrate:	31 g.	Sodium:	315 mg.

Crème de Menthe Pie ▴

3 cups miniature marshmallows
⅓ cup half-and-half
¼ cup green crème de menthe
3 tablespoons white crème de cacao
Chocolate Cookie Crust (page 113)
1 cup chilled whipping cream

Makes 8 servings

Combine marshmallows and half-and-half in medium bowl. Microwave at MEDIUM-HIGH (70%) until marshmallows are melted, 2 to 4 minutes, stirring once or twice during cooking. Blend in crème de menthe and crème de cacao. Refrigerate until cool and thickened but not set. Prepare crust while filling cools.

When marshmallow mixture is thickened but not set, beat whipping cream in chilled bowl until stiff. Fold marshmallow mixture into whipped cream. Pour into crust. Refrigerate until set, 2 to 4 hours. Garnish with chocolate curls, if desired.

Per Serving:			
Calories:	274	Fat:	14 g.
Protein:	2 g.	Cholesterol:	29 mg.
Carbohydrate:	35 g.	Sodium:	102 mg.

Quick Cherry Pie ▲

Baked Pie Shell (page 113)
1 cup sugar
¼ cup cornstarch
⅛ teaspoon salt
2 cans (16 ounces each) pitted tart red cherries (water pack), drained
½ teaspoon almond extract
⅓ cup sliced almonds

Makes 6 servings

Bake pie shell. Set aside. Blend sugar, cornstarch and salt in medium bowl. Stir in cherries.

Microwave at HIGH (100%) until mixture is translucent, 8 to 11 minutes, stirring once or twice during cooking. Stir in almond extract. Pour into pie shell. Sprinkle with almonds. Chill.

Per Serving:			
Calories:	448	Fat:	19 g.
Protein:	5 g.	Cholesterol:	—
Carbohydrate:	69 g.	Sodium:	279 mg.

Pumpkin Cheese Pie ▲

Graham Cracker Crust (page 113)
1 package (8 ounces) cream cheese
1 cup canned pumpkin
¾ cup packed brown sugar
3 eggs
1½ tablespoons all-purpose flour
1 teaspoon ground cinnamon
½ teaspoon ground nutmeg
½ teaspoon vanilla

Makes 6 servings

Prepare crust. Set aside. Place cream cheese in medium bowl. Microwave at MEDIUM (50%) until softened, 1 to 2 minutes. Add remaining ingredients. Beat at medium speed of electric mixer until smooth and well blended.

Microwave at MEDIUM-HIGH (70%) until hot and thickened, 6 to 8 minutes, stirring every 2 minutes. Pour into crust. Reduce power to MEDIUM (50%). Microwave until filling is firm to the touch, 10 to 15 minutes. Center may appear soft-set. Garnish with pecan halves, if desired. Refrigerate until set.

Per Serving:			
Calories:	435	Fat:	23 g.
Protein:	8 g.	Cholesterol:	179 mg.
Carbohydrate:	52 g.	Sodium:	319 mg.

Peaches
with Raspberry Sauce ▲

1 package (10 ounces) frozen sweetened
    raspberries
4 peaches, peeled and cut into halves
2 teaspoons cornstarch
½ teaspoon grated lemon peel

Makes 4 servings

Remove raspberries from package and place in 1-quart container. Microwave at MEDIUM (50%) until raspberries are defrosted, 2 to 4 minutes, turning over every minute and gently breaking apart as soon as possible. Let stand 5 minutes.

Place peach halves in rectangular baking dish, 12 × 8 inches, or 10-inch square casserole. Cover with plastic wrap. Microwave at HIGH (100%) until peaches are heated through, 2 to 6 minutes. Set aside.

Drain raspberry juice in small bowl. Blend in cornstarch and lemon peel. Microwave at MEDIUM-HIGH (70%) until thick and bubbly, 2 to 4 minutes, stirring once or twice during cooking. Place 2 peach halves in each of 4 small bowls. Stir raspberries gently into sauce. Top each bowl of peaches with one-fourth of raspberry mixture. Top with whipped cream, if desired.

Variation: Substitute 8 canned peach halves and omit cooking peaches.

Per Serving:			
Calories:	97	Fat:	—
Protein:	1 g.	Cholesterol:	—
Carbohydrate:	25 g.	Sodium:	1 mg.

Blueberries
and Vanilla Cream

½ cup water
1 envelope (0.25 ounces) unflavored gelatin
¾ cup sugar
1 cup half-and-half
½ teaspoon vanilla
¼ teaspoon salt
¾ cup dairy sour cream
2 cups frozen blueberries
¾ teaspoon lemon juice
⅓ cup sugar
2 teaspoons cornstarch

Makes 4 servings

Microwave water at HIGH (100%) until boiling, 45 seconds to 1 minute 15 seconds. Stir in gelatin until dissolved. Combine gelatin mixture and ¾ cup sugar in medium bowl; stir to dissolve sugar. Stir in half-and-half, vanilla and salt. Chill until mixture begins to set. Beat with electric mixer until smooth. Beat in sour cream. Spoon into 4 lightly oiled individual dishes. Chill at least 4 hours.

Microwave blueberries at MEDIUM-HIGH (70%) until completely defrosted, 4 to 5½ minutes. Let stand 5 minutes. Drain well, reserving juice. Mash ⅓ cup of the blueberries in small bowl. Add reserved juice and lemon juice. Blend in ⅓ cup sugar and the cornstarch. Microwave at HIGH (100%) until thick and bubbly, 45 seconds to 1 minute 30 seconds. Let stand until cool. Stir in remaining blueberries. Unmold vanilla cream onto dessert plates. Top each with one-fourth of the blueberry mixture.

Per Serving			
Calories:	432	Fat:	17 g.
Protein:	5 g.	Cholesterol:	42 mg.
Carbohydrate:	68 g.	Sodium:	185 mg.

Chocolate Almond Fondue ▸

1 package (12 ounces) milk chocolate chips
2 tablespoons half-and-half
¼ cup almond liqueur
    Pound cake squares
    Ladyfingers, split
    Banana chunks, sprinkled with lemon juice
    Mandarin orange sections, drained
    Pineapple slices, drained and quartered

Makes 8 servings

Combine chocolate chips and half-and-half in small bowl or 1-quart casserole.

Microwave at MEDIUM-HIGH (70%) until chocolate is melted, 2 to 4 minutes, blending with wire whisk once or twice during cooking. Stir in liqueur. Serve from bowl, reheating as needed, or in fondue pot over low heat. Dip pound cake squares, ladyfingers, banana chunks, mandarin orange sections and pineapple slices into fondue with fondue forks or skewers.

Variation: Omit liqueur. Increase half-and-half to ⅓ cup. Add ½ teaspoon almond extract.

Per Serving:			
Calories:	244	Fat:	14 g.
Protein:	3 g.	Cholesterol:	10 mg.
Carbohydrate:	30 g.	Sodium:	40 mg.

Butterscotch Fondue

1 package (12 ounces) butterscotch chips
⅓ cup half-and-half
    Ladyfingers, split
    Banana chunks, sprinkled with lemon juice
    Marshmallows

Makes 8 servings

Combine butterscotch chips and half-and-half in small bowl or 1-quart casserole.

Microwave at MEDIUM-HIGH (70%) until butterscotch chips are melted, 2 to 6 minutes, stirring once or twice. Serve from bowl, reheating as needed, or in fondue pot over low heat. Dip ladyfingers, banana chunks and marshmallows into fondue with fondue forks or skewers.

Per Serving:			
Calories:	238	Fat:	14 g.
Protein:	—	Cholesterol:	4 mg.
Carbohydrate:	26 g.	Sodium:	4 mg.

◄ Chocolate Sauce

2 ounces unsweetened chocolate
¼ cup milk
½ cup sugar
Dash of salt
¼ teaspoon vanilla

Makes 6 servings

Combine chocolate and milk in 2-cup measure or small bowl. Microwave at MEDIUM (50%) until melted, 1 to 2 minutes, stirring 2 or 3 times.

Blend in sugar and salt. Microwave at MEDIUM-HIGH (70%) until sugar is dissolved, 45 seconds to 1 minute 30 seconds. Stir in vanilla. Serve over cake or ice cream, if desired.

Per Serving:			
Calories:	117	Fat:	5 g.
Protein:	1 g.	Cholesterol:	1 mg.
Carbohydrate:	20 g.	Sodium:	28 mg.

Hot Vanilla Sauce

½ cup packed brown sugar
1 tablespoon plus 1½ teaspoons all-purpose flour
Dash of ground nutmeg
½ cup milk
¾ cup half-and-half
1½ teaspoons vanilla or rum extract

Makes 8 servings

Combine sugar, flour and nutmeg in medium bowl. Stir in ¼ cup of the milk until smooth. Stir in remaining milk and half-and-half.

Microwave at HIGH (100%) until thickened, 5 to 7 minutes, stirring 2 or 3 times. Stir in vanilla. Serve over cake or fruit, if desired.

Per Serving:			
Calories:	94	Fat:	3 g.
Protein:	1 g.	Cholesterol:	10 mg.
Carbohydrate:	16 g.	Sodium:	21 mg.

Lemon Sauce ▶

½ cup sugar
1 tablespoon cornstarch
  Dash of salt
½ teaspoon grated lemon peel
1 cup water
1 tablespoon lemon juice
2 tablespoons margarine or butter
1 egg yolk, slightly beaten

Makes 8 servings

Combine sugar, cornstarch, salt and lemon peel in deep 1-quart bowl. Blend in water and lemon juice.

Microwave at HIGH (100%) until sauce is thickened and clear, 2½ to 4½ minutes, stirring after half the cooking time. Stir in margarine and egg yolk. Microwave at HIGH (100%) until bubbly, 30 seconds to 1 minute.

Per Serving:			
Calories:	86	Fat:	4 g.
Protein:	—	Cholesterol:	34 mg.
Carbohydrate:	14 g.	Sodium:	51 mg.

Cherry Sauce

1 can (17 ounces) pitted dark sweet cherries
1 tablespoon cornstarch
1½ teaspoons lemon juice
1 teaspoon grated lemon peel

Makes 8 servings

Drain cherry juice into 1-quart bowl; blend in cornstarch until smooth. Microwave at HIGH (100%) until clear and thickened, 2½ to 4 minutes, stirring once during cooking.

Stir in cherries, lemon juice and peel. Microwave at HIGH (100%) until sauce bubbles and cherries are hot, 1 to 2 minutes. (For thicker sauce add 1 teaspoon additional cornstarch.)

Per Serving:			
Calories:	36	Fat:	—
Protein:	1 g.	Cholesterol:	—
Carbohydrate:	9 g.	Sodium:	2 mg.

Rocky Road Candy

1 package (6 ounces) semisweet or milk
  chocolate chips
2 tablespoons half-and-half
1 teaspoon vanilla
2 cups miniature marshmallows
1½ cups chopped nuts
1 cup shredded coconut

Makes 2 dozen pieces

Combine chocolate chips and half-and-half in medium bowl. Microwave at MEDIUM-HIGH (70%) until chocolate chips are melted, 1 to 3 minutes, stirring once during cooking.

Stir in vanilla and remaining ingredients until coated. Press into greased square baking dish, 8 × 8 inches. Chill. Cut into squares.

Per Serving:			
Calories:	113	Fat:	8 g.
Protein:	2 g.	Cholesterol:	1 mg.
Carbohydrate:	10 g.	Sodium:	4 mg.

Chocolate Bourbon Balls

½ cup margarine or butter
4 cups powdered sugar
1 cup finely chopped nuts
¼ cup bourbon
1 package (6 ounces) milk chocolate chips
3 tablespoons half-and-half

Makes 3 dozen candies

Place margarine in medium bowl. Microwave at HIGH (100%) until melted, 1 to 2 minutes. Mix in sugar, nuts and bourbon. Refrigerate until firm.

Shape into 1-inch balls. Refrigerate until firm. Combine chocolate chips and half-and-half in small bowl. Microwave at MEDIUM-HIGH (70%) until chocolate chips are melted, 1 to 2½ minutes, stirring once or twice. Stir until smooth. Drizzle chocolate over candies. (Reheat chocolate as needed.) Chill.

Per Serving:			
Calories:	117	Fat:	6 g.
Protein:	1 g.	Cholesterol:	1 mg.
Carbohydrate:	14 g.	Sodium:	35 mg.

Fudge

3 cups semisweet or milk chocolate chips
1 can (14 ounces) sweetened condensed milk
¼ cup margarine or butter
1 cup chopped walnuts

Makes 2 dozen pieces

Place all ingredients except nuts in large bowl. Microwave at MEDIUM (50%) until chocolate chips are melted, 3 to 5 minutes, stirring once or twice during cooking. Stir in nuts. Pour into well-greased square baking dish, 8 × 8 inches. Refrigerate until set.

Variation: Substitute 1 cup peanut butter chips for 1 cup of the chocolate chips.

Per Serving:			
Calories:	219	Fat:	14 g.
Protein:	3 g.	Cholesterol:	7 mg.
Carbohydrate:	24 g.	Sodium:	49 mg.

Peanut Brittle

1 cup sugar
½ cup light corn syrup
    Dash of salt
1 to 1½ cups shelled raw peanuts
1 tablespoon margarine or butter
1½ teaspoons baking soda
1 teaspoon vanilla

Makes 1 pound,
16 servings

Grease baking sheet heavily. Combine sugar, corn syrup and salt in 3-quart casserole. Stir in peanuts. Microwave at HIGH (100%) until light brown, 8 to 10 minutes, stirring once or twice.

Stir in remaining ingredients until light and foamy. Quickly spread on greased baking sheet. Spread as thin as possible for brittle candy. Cool; break into pieces.

Per Serving:			
Calories:	135	Fat:	5 g.
Protein:	2 g.	Cholesterol:	—
Carbohydrate:	22 g.	Sodium:	130 mg.

Microwave Tips:
Combine Microwave with Conventional Cooking

Microwave fillings and sauces for crepes you prepare with a crepe maker or skillet.

Soften brown sugar. Place apple slice in bag. Close tightly with string or plastic strip. Microwave at HIGH (100%) until lumps soften, 15 seconds.

Many foods are prepared most efficiently when you do part of the cooking by microwave and part conventionally. Use microwaving for its speed, easy cleanup and for unique jobs that cannot be done conventionally.

Prepare and fill crepes in advance. Refrigerate until serving time, then microwave until hot.

Toast coconut. Spread coconut evenly in 9-inch pie plate. Microwave at HIGH (100%) until golden brown, 3 to 5 minutes, tossing with fork after every minute.

Toast bread conventionally. Prepare sandwiches and microwave to heat fillings and melt cheese.

Warm syrup for pancakes in serving pitcher or uncapped bottle. Reheat leftover pancakes, too.

Plump raisins. Sprinkle 1 or 2 teaspoons of water over fruit. Cover tightly. Microwave at HIGH (100%) 30 seconds to 1 minute.

Brown meats in a Pyroceram® casserole on the conventional range. Microwave to complete cooking, but reduce time by one-fourth to one-third.

Blanch almonds. Microwave 1 cup water until boiling. Add nuts. Microwave at HIGH (100%) 30 seconds. Drain and skin.

Make instant mashed potatoes right in the measuring cup. Place water, butter and salt in 4-cup measure. Microwave until boiling. Add milk to correct measure. Stir in flakes.

Peel tomatoes or peaches easily. Put enough water to cover food in casserole or measuring cup. Microwave until boiling. Drop in food for a few seconds. Peel strips off quickly.

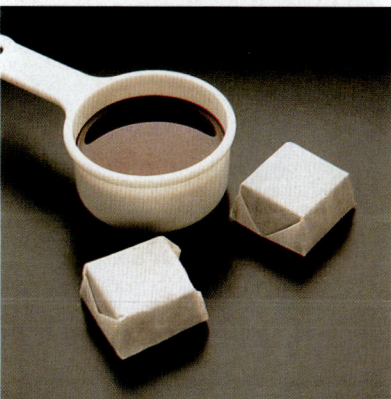

Melt 2 ounces baking chocolate in a plastic cup used to measure shortening. It won't scorch, and you'll save dishwashing. Microwave at MEDIUM (50%) until melted, 2½ to 3½ minutes.

Melt butter for blender hollandaise, basting sauces and frostings for conventional cakes.

Microwave sauces while you cook pasta conventionally. Reheat pasta without flavor loss.

Dissolve gelatin. Sprinkle unflavored gelatin over ¼ cup cold water in 1-cup measure. Let stand 5 minutes. Microwave at HIGH (100%) 30 seconds to 1 minute 15 seconds.

Microwave chicken or ribs until almost done. Finish on the barbecue grill for charcoal flavor. The interior will be fully cooked without overbrowning.

Grill extra hamburgers while the coals are hot. Undercook meat slightly and freeze. Defrost and finish by microwaving.

Soften cream cheese directly from the refrigerator. Microwave 3 ounces at HIGH (100%) 10 to 15 seconds; microwave 8 ounces at MEDIUM (50%) 1 to 2 minutes.

Get more juice from lemons. Microwave at HIGH (100%) 30 to 45 seconds before cutting and squeezing.

INDEX

"c" following the page number indicates convection/combination recipe.

"c" following the page number indicates convection/combination recipe.

"c" following the page number indicates convection/combination recipe.

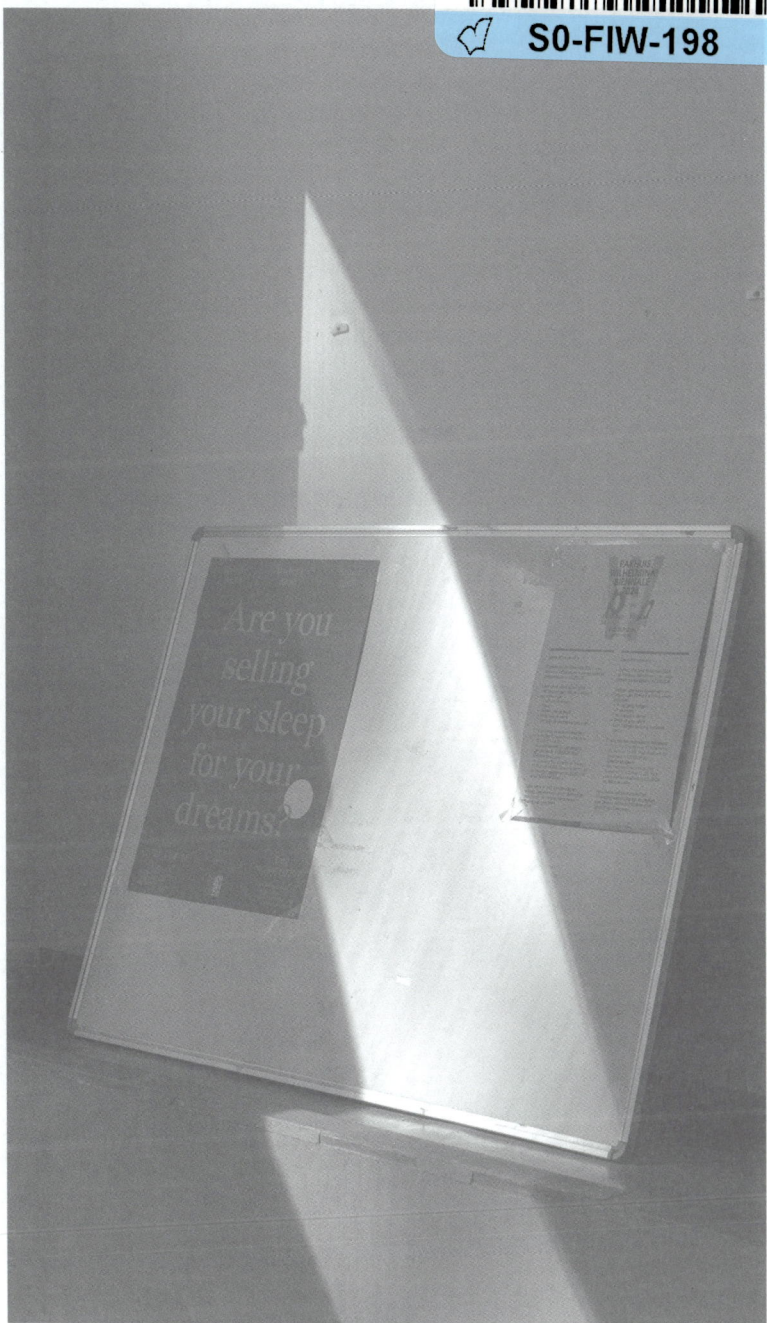

Sunrise
08:20

Edited by
ANDREA KNEZOVIĆ & AGATA BAR

Sunset
18:28

Nocturnalities
Bargaining Beyond Rest

Nocturnalities
Bargaining Beyond Rest

Nocturnalities
Bargaining Beyond Rest

Lat
52° 21' 41.4" N

20:02

Long
4° 53' 26.8" E

TABLE OF CONTENT

Introduction. Nocturnalities: Bargaining Beyond Rest, Bargaining Beyond Self?

Lat
52° 22' 44.4" N

17:26

Long
4° 54' 1.02" E

What is the value of rest in the age of late capitalism? And who claims ownership over certainty in a reality that seems so precarious? In a world that rarely pauses, where the relentless pace of life often demands more than the traditional hours of daylight can offer, the concept of bargaining extends far beyond mere economic transactions. While bargaining prospects entered biopolitical spheres, our privacy became transactional scores co-opted by the shifting mechanism of today's expanding late capitalism. The currency of rest in today's lifestyle is framed as a meritocratic luxury for the labouring crowds. At the same time, it is portrayed as an exoticized act of the outdated bourgeoisie prone to *unproductive* leisure time. Rest and its embodiment became extensively polarized, and its geographical, socio-economy, and cultural assets became more perplexing within techno-globalizing frameworks.

As someone who has worked as an artist, researcher, and advisor in Amsterdam and the European cultural sector in the past decade, the reality of such a predicament is far from just nonchalant, detached discursive gesturing. The frameworks of care, leisure, and free resting time have become commodified for a range of market transactions. Since there has already been a variety of discursive elaborations relating to the critique of financial capital, labour, or its contemporary mechanisms – from Marx to Bifo and Marazzi to Terranova, Melamed, and others – I would like to move away from yet another self-indulgent discursive dictum and give space for imagining intellectual attitudes that are perhaps a bit different.[1]

In 2019, I embarked on an explorative journey of the politics of rest through academic research and artistic practice. Initially, in 2022, I created an exhibition and nocturnal event under the title *Nocturnalities: Bargaining Beyond Rest* that was facilitated by ŠKUC Gallery in Ljubljana. Scholars and thinkers such as Jonathan Crary and Katija Praznik, as well as various artists and the general public, were invited to activate the gallery from dusk until dawn and reflect on the topic of labour and rest. This was a symbolic departure point of what would become a larger umbrella platform; a book, an online REST Archive, and several exhibition programmes and public events dedicated to rest and care.

....

[1] Here I am referring to the extensive political and economic legacy of German philosopher Karl Marx and his discursive critique of capitalism; Franco ´Bifo´ Berardi, an Italian Marxist philosopher who focused on media and information technology; Christian Marazzi, a Swiss economist and political scientist who explored the effects and violence of financial capital; Tiziana Terranova, an Italian theorist and activist who examined information technology and digital labour; and scholar and author Jodi Melamed who focused on decolonial frameworks and investigating the effects of racial capitalism.

Working in the arts and being involved in institutional policy-making, I have often witnessed and experienced the harsh effects of the work-life imbalance within the cultural sector. Those conditions are familiar to any cultural worker, educator, freelancer, or any other individual dipped into the greasy reality of neoliberal toxicity. Side effects of ambitious, fast-paced lifestyles – such as overworked mentality and burnout, already embedded in our late-capitalist condition – are often systemically and infrastructurally anticipated and pre-assumed as part of the labouring norm, or as accompanying the reality of pursuing a professional career. In some countries, such as the Netherlands and Belgium, insurance companies already offer 'burnout packages' that provide pre-emptive healthcare for young and mid-career professionals who are deemed high-risk for a burnout.[2]

The ever-growing impact of burnout has become more normalized and embraced within the colloquialism of the professional strata – especially in cultures driven by productivity and meritocratic attitudes. Scholar Byung-Chul Han refers to such phenomenon as 'the burnout society'; a society that thrives on competitiveness and service-oriented mentalities while neglecting healthy boundaries due to the precarious condition of the late-capitalist framework, consequently producing varieties of mental health deficiencies and disorders for late-capitalist individuals.[3]

----

[2] On some level, institutional and corporate social responsibility is continuously rising, and companies are being more and more pushed to address questions regarding mental health care and work-life balance within their labour policies. An example is the Belgian consultant agency Simplex that specializes in employee benefits and actuarial advice that amongst other things advises on insurances and non-statutory benefits. See: "Am I insured against burnout?," Simplex, www.simplexeb.be/en/nieuwsbrief/am-i-insured-against-burnout.

[3] Byung-Chul Han, *The Burnout Society* (Stanford, CA: Stanford University Press, 2020).

I also suffered a severe burnout just as the coronavirus pandemic started to unfold. As I watched myself dissolve into the abyss of late capitalism, and consequently tried to repair and heal from the unbalanced behaviour and lifestyle, I found myself in a peculiar situation. My ambitious go-getting alter-ego was faced with some fundamental changes. In this process, I couldn't help but notice the constant need – inside of me as well as around me – to determine or speculate certainty. What I mean here by the notion of certainty is the strong epistemic belief and determination that a particular outcome or reality will come into being. This outcome and belief not only secure and provide reassurance and a controlled setting to our restless minds, but rather sets illusionary parameters of future expectations beyond our grasp.

The notion of certainty and its mythologization somehow became the prime asset of any relational dynamic and urgency that has to be consistently determined. This became especially accentuated during the coronavirus pandemic, where the uncertainty of our livelihood and the conditions of our global prospects became a speculative currency for yet another late-capitalist acquisition. Reflecting on those moments in time, it became evident that I shared the same urge for needing to know how things would be, end, stay, become, and transform. However, it wasn't just me trying to negotiate certainty. It seemed the whole world around me was extensively busy with its ontological framework and monetary prospects. As the pandemic crisis raged across the globe and its restricting social conditions penetrated our intimate realms, our lives shifted from often mundane corporal encounters into techno-social and digital intimacies. Suddenly, certainty became a battlefield of hopes, dreams, and petty expectations – a precarious currency in the ever-expanding 24/7 digital reality and the world that never sleeps.

Perhaps the reason why the politics of rest has been a keen interest of mine is because it showcases something much more than just the intimate relationship between boundaries and labour. Contrary to care-oriented practices, it discloses a whole new set of individual (epigenetic) and institutional (hereditary infrastructural, systemic, and educational) intergenerational traumas and misconducts. Situated in behavioural tropes and lack of infrastructural care, the notion of restlessness or *unrest* is perpetually recurring throughout our systemic, legislative, and psycho-cultural environments, often manifesting most evidently in/on the most vulnerable parts of our society.

We can witness these effects on an individual level, as generational struggles are presented through health issues, memory interruptions (both on a biological level and in the preservation of intellectual legacy), socio-economic precarity, or the way one assumes personal responsibility for their well-being. This is visible in the broader socio-cultural anxiety caused by constant geopolitical destabilization. We also encounter such tropes in infrastructural and educational conditioning that often present themselves through economic articulations, class and labour strategies, and organizational routines of a particular culture (especially pronounced in the way values and ethics are expressed through the social dialectic).[4]

....

[4] The Netherlands, for example, is a Western, predominantly Calvinist culture that has a strong work ethic and places productivity at the centre of social values and ambitions. A good illustration of this mentality is the Dutch adjective *druk*, meaning *busy* or *having a lot of work*, which is continuously expressed in contemporary colloquial settings, and provides people with a sense of pride and duty. On the other hand, a culturally diametrically opposite is Croatia and their term *fjaka* meaning a relaxed state of body, mind, spirit, and heart. Unlike the Dutch term *druk*, *fjaka* maintains a perspective where there is no rush or busyness. This term is expressed in contemporary Croatian society with equal pride and diligence as the Dutch relate to and emphasize the notion of busyness.

As we unfold these conditions, we can notice that the current late-capitalist politics of 'rest' is not exclusively the recent side-effect of our restless society but rather a historical, intergenerational build-up, embedded in the way we have organized, economized, and negotiated our societal structures and consequently taxonomized emotions. With today's lifestyle, we are reaching even further. We are not just oriented toward the hyper-production of material value but are faced with the utter co-option and monetarization of what we find dearest: our individuality. As modes of production shifted from industrial capitalism to cognitive capitalism, capitalist production infiltrated the domestic sphere like never before, by blurring the boundaries between working hours and leisure, and commodifying personal routines.

Cognitive capitalism, a term popularized by scholar Yann Moulier Boutang, is a form of capitalism that focuses on the extraction of information, knowledge, and intellectual capacities as the primary sources of value and economic expansion.[5] Unlike industrial capitalism, which relies heavily on physical labour and the production of material goods, cognitive capitalism focuses on the manipulation and production of knowledge. The exploits of mental labour, creativity, and intellectual property have transformed how we conceptualize and generate value and consequently embody labour. The radical expansion of globalization extensively shifted the metric of power. Characterized by the shrinking of distances, lowered costs, and increased information exchange and market interconnectivity, it has created the illusion of spatial multimodality and transnationalism, including impacting our relationship towards the intimate capacities of labour. Suddenly, with more access and information, we felt the need to equilibrate the expansion of our internal clock as well. Otherwise, how would we keep up?

---

[5] Yann Moulier Boutang, *Cognitive Capitalism* (Cambridge: Polity Press, 2011).

Moulier Boutang argued that globalization "'de-territorialises' and 'ire-territorialises' spaces, and disarticulates homogeneities and cohesions instantaneously, both at the centre and at the periphery."[6]

As technological development progressed, our relationship to the natural or biological order shifted as well. We became trapped in the rhythm of translating parameters of techno-economic growth onto our own mortal bodies. In less than half a century, we have gone from goods and services-oriented production to a data-driven economy. This did not just affect the way we structure labour and the supply chain, but the way we organize our mentality, culture, and society at large. As Moulier Boutang articulated, cognitive capitalism leveraged technological advancements to perpetuate a system where human cognitive functions are continuously extracted and monetized, leading to an economy that thrives on the constant engagement of cognitive resources.[7]

These frameworks inevitably unfolded various other challenges, such as an uprising of a new form of necropolitical economy (ecocides and climate crisis) endorsed by late techno-scotosis.[8] By 'scotosis,' I do not just insinuate a denial of the drastic impact technology has on contemporary labour conditions, mental health, and well-being of societies at large, but it increasingly also implies a blindness towards human ethos and our primordial need for perseverance and safety, justifying our fixation and mythologization of certainty.

....

[6] Ibid., 49.

[7] Ibid.

[8] Scotosis, coming from Ancient Greek σκότος (skótos, "darkness"), is commonly understood as intellectual blindness, denial or oblivious attitude toward particular truths. It can be also interpreted as a hardening of the mind against unwanted wisdom. In this instance, I'm referring to the work of Babette Babich, *On Necropolitics and Techno-Scotosis*, and the term techno-scotosis which relates to a particular type of technopolitical blindness — or blindness towards technological advances fuelled by the malicious mechanisms of late capitalism. Babette Babich, "On Necropolitics and Techno-Scotosis," *Philosophy Today* 65, no. 2 (Spring 2021): 305-24.

The protection of selfhood is perhaps the most primordial and instinctual need every living creature has. In recent years, it has become evident that the non-stop, never-asleep tentacles of late capitalism are overtaking our intimacy and autonomous critical reasoning. In his work, *24/7: Late Capitalism and the Ends of Sleep*, Jonathan Crary comments on the psycho-cultural implication of late capitalism and its 24/7 modes of production. Crary suggests that the dehumanizing aspect of non-interpreted market conditions is reshaping the very essence of human nature, and insists on its automated, almost mechanical qualities – including the rejection of the body's need for rest and sleep.[9]

As we slowly drift toward the realm of technological trans-temporality or post-temporality – going beyond the regular notion of time or erasing the sense of relatability between time and space – we must stop for a moment and look at the softer sides of individuality, away from the material/corporal conquests, to the prospect of intimate care. Let's be honest here; we are all suffering from the agonizing grip of late capitalism. So how can we avoid such an anxious predicament? Are we coming toward the end of the autonomous Self and barging into the frontiers of the age of awake?

This whole circumstance, regardless of how potentially grim it sounds, offers another tipping point to consider; by reimagining the frameworks of the economy of care, can we reinvent the way we relate to value production? In his continuous elaboration and critique of post-capitalist society, Slavoj Žižek notes that the financial collapse is not the end of reality but rather the end of the reality of capital. Perhaps Žižek is right, perhaps we are unable to imagine any kind of existing framework that goes beyond bargaining prospects, and in particular capital exchange. It might also be that we are so deep in, that the intimate Self, and consequently, rest, have become an ultimate prize in the battle for power. Or, are we so anxious to secure a sense of certainty that we willingly bargained away our birthright for rest, only to reach yet another dopamine hit for control?

....

[9] Jonathan Crary, *24/7 Late Capitalism and the Ends of Sleep* (London: Verso, 2013), in particular chapters 1 and 2.

It seems that operating under a constant rush of adrenaline and anxiety can only lead toward one road: burnout. The psychopathologies of our daily life are exponentially multiplying and becoming a primary asset in economic transactions, due to the divergence of occurring mental health urgencies (surges of depression, anxiety, burnouts, and personality disorders amongst the younger generation).[10] And the global corporate industries seem to keep up with the occurring trends. Our contemporaneity has become characterized by the increasing tensions between the social hallmark of production and the intimate dispositions for continuous accumulation. Tiziana Terranova identifies this through the negotiation of socio-economic binaries: "Cognitive capitalism is crossed by a constituent tension between the tendency to exploitation, subsumption and proletarianization on one side, and autonomy, self-reference, and self-creation on the other."[11]

....

[10] Panagiota Koutsimani, Anthony Montgomery, Katerina Georganta, "The Relationship Between Burnout, Depression, and Anxiety: A Systematic Review and Meta-Analysis," *Frontiers in Psychology* 10 (13 March 2019), doi.org/10.3389/fpsyg.2019.00284; "Mental health has worsened among young people," Statistics Netherlands, 1 June 2022, cbs.nl/en-gb/news/2022/22/mental-health-has-worsened-among-young-people.

[11] Tiziana Terranova, "Ordinary Psychopathologies of Cognitive Capitalism," in *The Psychopathologies of Cognitive Capitalism Part 1*, eds. Arne de Boever, Warren Neidich (Berlin: Archive Books, 2013), 50.

Decolonial thinking is certainly concerned with the way in which we deal with current systemic and intimate negotiations of rest and certainty; especially seen in the way we articulate ambition through gender performativity, the notion of ownership, and territorial demarcations.[12] Decades have passed and several technological and social revolutions have occurred and yet we are still thinking within the binary framework of the Darwinist dictum of evolutionary competition. We are pushing hard to prevent the collapse of financial capital by prolonging the extractivism of *form* and *content* and using social energy as a collateral asset in the process. Cultivated social energy and intellect are the last untouched frontiers in this extractivist mission.

As the 'pathologies of attention' become more and more recurring contemporary issues, one must wonder, what did opaque sides of the democratization of capital and technology do to our social well-being?[13] I ask such questions not to subvert the democratic ideals of modern society, but rather to question the malignancy of late-capitalist mechanisms and their employment of exploitative strategies in the legislative and socio-economic prospect of modern democracy.

----

[12] For further research see: Jodi Melamed, *Represent and Destroy: Rationalizing Violence in the New Racial Capitalism*; Sabelo J. Ndlovu-Gatsheni's article *The cognitive empire, politics of knowledge and African intellectual productions: reflections on struggles for epistemic freedom and resurgence of decolonisation in the twenty-first century*; Warren Neidich's book *The Glossary of Cognitive Activism*; Danilo Correale's book *No More Sleep No More*; and the work of writer and poet Tricia Hersey, *Rest Is Resistance*.

[13] Here I refer to the information overload and side effects of regularly occurring cognitive deficiencies instigated by the contemporary attention economy. In his book *The Ecology of Attention*, Yves Citton explains these parameters through a depiction of cognitive labour and invested attention. He elaborates further how the attention economy is closely elevated by its vocabulary and its specificity, drawing connections between commodification of language and digital performativity. See: Yves Citton, *The Ecology of Attention* (Cambridge: Polity, 2021).

As we move away from a disciplinary society into a society of control, which Maurizio Lazzarato notes as 'noo-politics,' we constantly encounter capitalist transgressions on our attention and psychic life.[14] Assuming that we cannot interpret our reality anymore according to the classic labour theory of value production and its demarcations of time – working with the frameworks of employed productivity – we are now immersed in what I would call an excessive 24/7 *cognitive liminal labour* and its ever-expanding immeasurable potentialities. By this I mean intellectual and psychic labour that is in a continuous liminal state of performance. Where ritualization of classical material labour is absent, another type of labour is in place; one that does not have an initial start, middle, and end, but is rather a form of non-resolutionary labour, a state betwixt and between future speculations and cognitive value production.

We are increasingly pushed into collective insomnia by the grips of the global economy, technological expansion, and information extractivism. Under the premise of tailored living and comfort-economy we are eliminating clear frameworks of work performance and hybridizing our notions of workspace, while at the same time, our internal clocks are blurring the boundaries between automation and life, autonomy and control, rest and productivity. Gilles Deleuze and Félix Guattari once said that capitalism is something like a special form of pathological delirium.[15] It seems that the delirium of capitalist imagination and its anxiety is reaching its crescendo, and we are observing its final acts. Perhaps it is exactly the imagination of such a predicament that has been lacking. Are we ready to start slowly grieving late capitalism and its invasive yet ephemeral form of imagination, almost as a post-relationship grief that is required before entering the healing stage of one's life?

....

[14] Here I refer to the intersection of technology and power through a network-based geopolitics of knowledge. Noo-politics is a form of power, tapping into the assets of information strategies and attention economy.

[15] Gilles Deleuze, "Capitalism: A Very Special Delirium," in Felix Guattari, *Chaosophy: Texts and Interviews 1972-1977*, ed. Sylvère Lotringer (Los Angeles: Semiotext(e), 2009), 35-36.

In the end, it could be that the notion of grief is the remedy to our exhausted minds. It is not just that we have to grieve our private losses and the exhaustion that is carved into our bodies and minds; there is a need to mourn temporality at large. To say goodbye to the old ways of reading and relating to time, memory, and landscapes, and the badges of value and ownership we once carried with pride. Re-examining our identity protocols, behavioural patterns, and systems of worth articulation will ease the grief and mourning of the Self we are so intensely experiencing. In the end, bargaining beyond rest is not just bargaining against Self, but rather gambling the future potentialities and heritage that we just do not yet possess.

Heritage is what we make of our present, and the present is the only truth we can be certain of.

Bedtime Stories for Restless Souls

We are two cultural workers in the Netherlands, living together and sharing our freelance lives. Often, we take our work to bed, and many nights, the stress keeps us awake. To pass the time, we tell each other stories about rest. We find that it helps to dream of rest together.

We know that we are not the only ones experiencing sleeplessness. Actually, you are one of us, aren't you? Would you like a hit of our copium? It's your pick! Do you want to hear the story of Aeio in Busytown? Or the one about the artist who preferred not to work? Or, maybe, you're interested in our story about the Xanax residency?

IN SEARCH OF RADICAL REST

So, you want to know how I started my quest for radical rest? I will tell you. The year was 2023. A prestigious art academy hosted a lecture by the Nap Bishop inside a giant bathtub.[1] The Bishop took the stage and addressed her audience with fervour: "Down with grind culture! Rest is radical! Rest is care! We need to create space in our institutions for rest, sleep, naps, daydreaming, and slowing down!" Like myself, everyone in the audience was either burnt out or nearly burnt out. We ate up the Bishop's every word. For years, the call to naps continued to bounce through the echo chambers of social media.[2]

Soon after the lecture, I ordered a copy of the Nap Bishop's book and started reading:

> The more we think of rest as a luxury,
> the more we buy into the systemic lies of grind
> culture. Our bodies and Spirits do not belong
> to capitalism, no matter how it is theorized
> and presented. Our divinity secures this,
> and it is our right to claim this boldly.
> I'm not grinding ever. I trust the Creator and
> my Ancestors to always make space for my
> gifts and talents without needing to work
> myself into exhaustion. [3]

....

[1] The Nap Bishop is Tricia Hersey, the bestselling author of *Rest Is Resistance* and the founder of The Nap Ministry. Hersey was one of the speakers during the 2023 Gerrit Rietveld Academy Studium Generale, which took place at the Stedelijk Museum Amsterdam.

[2] The strategy of subversive sleep has had some niche popularity within Dutch art academies for some time. See for instance, the 2017-2018 COOP study group "Sleeping with a Vengeance, Dreaming of a Life" at DAI, initiated by Ruth Noack, dutchartinstitute.eu/page/10208/2017-2018-coop-study-group-sleeping-witha-vengeance-dreaming-of-a.

[3] Tricia Hersey, *Rest Is Resistance: A Manifesto* (New York: Little Brown Spark, 2022), 28-29.

I was surprised. Despite her clerical title, I hadn't realized that the Nap Bishop really was an evangelist. Then I remembered the words of a philosopher: "Contrary to protestant work ethics, postmodern work ethics are basically some kind of tolerated guided laziness. The enigmatic and tragic character of Bartleby has changed into a farce, into the absurdity of contemporary corporate life."[4]

....

[4] Aaron Schuster, "Zelo težko je početi nič," quoted in Bojana Kunst, *Artist at Work: Proximity of Art and Capitalism* (Winchester: Zero Books, 2015), 188.

I started to wonder: How am I being guided to rest? Why do I need a US preacher to cope with my grind culture anxieties? Why is my messiah a nap entrepreneur?[5] Is solitary rest really resistance, or is it just self-help? Can rest be a collective practice – not just by resting together, but as a form of organization?[6] Can I turn my nap into a strike? These questions never left me. And so, my quest for radical rest started. It's a journey along the borderline of productive refusal and corporate neutralization.[7] I try to take slow and careful steps. Time will tell whether I am dismantling capitalism, or only helping to rejuvenate it.

....

[5] The Nap Ministry offers a range of services including installations, workshops, lectures, and coaching. It has also established the Resurrect Rest School. On her blog, Hersey writes: "In 2023 I had 30 bookings, flew close to 100,000 airline miles, boarded 26 round trip flights. I lectured in Amsterdam and participated in a theater festival in Melbourne, Australia, was in residency as a scholar-artist at NYU for the Fall 2023 semester."

[6] I have later found that it can! I recommend reading Jenny Odell, *How to Do Nothing: Resisting the Attention Economy* (Hoboken, NJ: Melville House, 2019).

[7] In 2021, A Walk Space created a series of 'Guides to Rest.' They asked five 'tired Nigerian artists' to come up with guidelines for rest based on their personal experiences. In the resulting publications, very different approaches are presented as part of a unified discursive programme. In Volume 1, Ayodele Olofintuade recommends: sex, sleep, travel, to define boundaries, but also "shop as therapy." In Volume 4, Olatunde Alara suggests: read more feminist theory, avoid art exhibitions, be critical when engaging with non-black people, avoid cis-heterosexual male tropes, make art that de-centers the privileged gaze, have a strong sense of class consciousness, avoid the well travelled person stereotype, create for yourself, say 'no' more often, and think about art from the human perspective. The bundling of these politically disparate arguments is just one small example to illustrate a general lack of shared understanding of the political dimensions of rest. It goes to show that the discourse of rest as resistance is both fascinating and tricky. Rahima Gambo and Innocent Ekejiuba, eds., *A Guide for Rest*, vol. 1-5, A Walk Space Studio in collaboration with IDFA DocLab and MIT Open Documentary Lab, November 2021. Also available online: www.arestguide.com.

A REAL ARTIST
(PART I)

A long time ago, in a country that no longer exists, there was an artist who tried to reach a state of perfect laziness, which is to say, to not produce anything, which is to say, to really be an artist.[8] One day, on a strangely productive whim, the artist photographed his attempts at laziness while sleeping in his bed. He later exhibited these pictures as an artwork called *Artist at Work*.[9]

....

[8] The artist Mladen Stilinović defined laziness as "the absence of movement and thought, just dumb time – total amnesia, indifference, staring at nothing, non-activity, impotence, sheer stupidity, a time of pain, futile concentration." In his quest for laziness, he was inspired by Marcel Duchamp and Kazimir Malevich, but mostly by Paul Lafargue, author of the 1883 pamphlet *The Right to Be Lazy*. In this pamphlet, Lafargue tried to formulate a Marxist-humanist theory against the social-democratic demands for full employment, arguing for an appreciation of different types of productivity. Until the rise of postworkerist theory after WWII, Lafargue was mostly considered to be a funny anomaly in Marxism with a cult following among artists and bohemians. See: Mladen Stilinović, "In Praise of Laziness," *Mladen Stilinović*, mladenstilinovic.com/works/10-2; Kazimir Malevich, "Laziness as the Truth of Mankind," 1921, www.workaffair. greteaagaard.net/satelite_files/malevich_laziness.pdf; Paul Lafargue, "The Right to Be Lazy," translated by Charles Kerr, marxist.org, 2000, www.marxists.org/archive/lafargue/1883/lazy.

[9] We can easily see analogies between Stilinović's *Artist at Work* from 1978, and Yoko Ono and John Lennon's 'bed-ins for peace' from 1969, as well as more recent art practices. In 2016, for example, Carolyn Lazard created *Support System (for Tina, Park, and Bob)*, during which they rested in a bed in a Brooklyn apartment. Every half an hour, a group of visitors was led in and invited to share 'crip time' with the artist. Lazard's work has been associated with 'third wave' institutional critique. In each of these cases, the bed becomes a performative site of production. See: Karen Archey, *After Institutions* (Berlin: Floating Opera Press, 2022), 88.

They were admired, discussed, critiqued, exhibited, and traded around the world, even until long after the artist had passed away. To his satisfaction, the artist had achieved total contradiction. As the boundaries between productivity and non-productivity faded, his work and non-work became inseparable. The artist had reached a state of perfect laziness and perfect artistic productivity at one and the same time.[10]

....

[10] Bojana Kunst takes Stilinović as a case study in *Artist at Work: Proximity of Art and Capitalism*. She acknowledges "the martyr-like total appropriation of art by capitalism" but arrives at a more positive assessment. To Kunst, Stilinović is a representative of the former East before the totalization of capitalism, and argues that his laziness should serve as an example and reminder for artists today: "The lazy artist of socialism was still able to hold up a mirror of irony to the ideological hypocrisy of the celebration of work; with the absence of the institutions that could provide work, the artist actually needed to remain without work if he or she wanted to remain an artist. Today, the artist cannot remain without work if he or she wants to remain an artist. [...] In this constant striving to expel any trace of laziness from his or her useless work, the artist overlooks the fact that this is how he or she loses any critical power to hold up a mirror to the true layabouts at the core of the capitalist system." Kunst, *Artist at Work*, 187.

A REAL ARTIST
(PART II)

Not so long ago, in a country that still exists, there was an artist who accepted a commission to create a public artwork, which is to say, to be a public servant, which is to say, to really be an artist.[11] But a few months later, a neo-fascist party won the elections in the artist's country. In loyalty and solidarity with those repressed by the new overlords, the artist resigned from the commission.[12]

....

[11] The artist, Matthijs de Bruijne, has a long track-record of creating artworks in the service of exploited social groups and communities (for instance, designing campaign materials for the union of Dutch domestic workers), and planned to create a 'Parade of Diversity.' In the Dutch context, a small group of art workers is consequently, and vocally advocating for the understanding of artists as public servants. See, for instance, Alina Lupu, "Subtle Schemes to Derail Funds But by No Means Structural Solutions," *The Office of Alina Lupu*, 2022, theofficeofalinalupu.com/download/HFFM-FINAL-WEB-SINGLE.pdf.

[12] De Bruijne announced his resignation with a public statement in which he expressed his frustration with the new, openly racist chairman of the Dutch parliament. He concludes: "Dan maar iets minder, minder, minder werk voor mij," reappropriating the racist slur used by the neofascist leader Geert Wilders, who infamously called for "minder, minder, minder Marokkanen" (less, less, less Moroccans) in 2014. Matthijs de Bruijne, "Aan wie blijf ik trouw?" *Metropolis M*, 26 January 2024, metropolism.com/nl/opinie/aan-wie-blijf-ik-trouw.

To his satisfaction, the artist immediately attained the simple clarity of total politicization. The planned artwork was never created, nor was the artist's withdrawal celebrated as a radical artistic gesture. There was no interest from art critics, institutions, or the market.[13] By performing a rejection of work that not even the art world could absorb and neutralize, the artist had successfully tested the limits of capital growth.

....

[13] In *The ABC of the Projectariat*, Kuba Szreder also discusses Stilinović's Artist at Work under the entry "A is for Art Strikes (Lessons to Be Taken)." Szreder points out that Stilinović is one of many artists who made withdrawal from the art world a central theme in their art practice (along with figures like Lee Lozano and Maurizio Cattelan) and argues, in line with Boltanski and Chiapello's *The New Spirit of Capitalism*, that these individual withdrawals are in fact mere affirmations of artistic genius that allow the art world to expand and rejuvenate. Whereas Kunst emphasized the role of art as a mirror held up to reality, Szreder insists that art is a hammer with which to shape reality. To really engage in 'productive withdrawal,' Szreder suggests that artistic withdrawal must be both collectivized and politicized, turning them into social strikes. The examples he gives include the practices of Occupy Museums, Chto Delat?, G.U.L.F, Decolonize This Place, and the Polish Days Without Art.
    Kuba Szreder, *The ABC of the Projectariat: Living and Working in a Precarious Art World* (Manchester: Manchester University Press, 2021), 25–29 and 187–191.

LIFE ISN'T ALWAYS
A BED OF ROSES

As you read this, there are millions of beds trapped in optimization. Optimization that creates efficient resting pods, ergonomically adequate working stations, chill-out zones for online meet-ups, and a horizontal backbone for a vertical window into the world. The vertical window opens every time a person connects to social media over their phone while in bed. The whole universe has become concentrated onto the smallest screen, with the bed floating in an endless sea of information. The demands of biological reproductive labour have, if not been replaced, at least been multiplied by Silicon Valley's demands for digital reproductive labour. To lay down is not to rest but to move, to produce, to datafy.[14] We have reached the end of sleep.[15]

---

[14] In "The 24/7 Bed," architectural historian Beatriz Colomina convincingly made the point that beds have turned into quintessential workstations. She traced the evolution of the bed from its basic functional purpose of providing rest to its symbolic and ideological significance throughout history as an intermediary between technology, media, and the human body. Beatriz Colomina, "The 24/7 Bed," *Urbane Künste Rurh*, no date, www.urbanekuensteruhr.de/en/magazine/das-24-7-bett.

[15] The 'end of sleep,' as declared by Jonathan Crary in *24/7*, is most obvious in high-discipline contexts, such as the military, where sleep deprivation is promoted as a sign of strength and loyalty. For instance, an officer in the Indian Naval Marine reported on his recent experience as a cadet: "Us mortals? We perfected the art of sleeping upright, even with eyes open. Woe betides the unfortunate soul caught napping." Sailor Signh, "Life at Indian Naval Academy: From Cadets to Captains, A Sailor's Odyssey," *Sailor Speaks*, 3 January 2024, sailorspeaks.com/2024/01/03/life-at-indian-naval-academy-from-cadets-to-captains-a-sailors-odyssey; Jonathan Crary, *24/7: Late Capitalism and the Ends of Sleep* (London: Verso, 2013).

With the rise of mass media and hyper-connectivity, the lines between private and public space have blurred. The bed is no exception to this rule. As the stage for bed-ins, online shopping sprees, and zoom-calls, the bed has become the epicentre of productivity and consumption. We are subjected to advice on how to improve rest for more productive work, where to spend our time, and what to impulsively purchase next, all while in bed. The bed has, in fact, transformed into the quintessential working station of modern times.

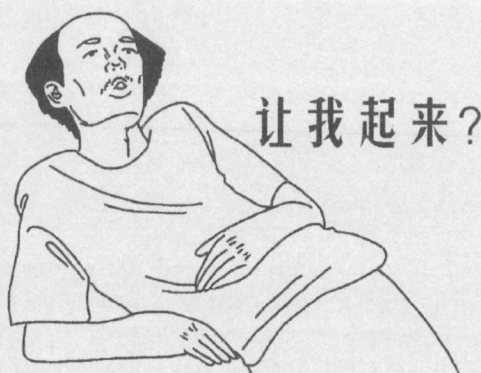

让 我 起 来？

这 辈 子 没 可 能 了

The 'lying flat' meme is part of the online anti-work movement.
Source: 163.com/dy/article/G9ADFRI90545KZQY.html.
See also: knowyourmeme.com/memes/cultures/antiwork.

The 'lying flat' meme went viral on Baidu in May 2022.
The text reads: "You want me to get up? That's not possible
in this lifetime."[16]

....

[16] The tangpingist or 'lying flat' movement was jumpstarted in April
2021 when a post by Mr. Luo on Baidu titled "Lying Flat Is Justice"
went viral. As a manifesto of renunciation, the post shared the author's
lessons from two years of joblessness. The extraordinary stresses
of contemporary life, the author concluded, were unnecessary, the
product of the old-fashioned mindset of the previous generation. It was
possible, even desirable, he argued, to find independence in resignation:
"I can be like Diogenes, who sleeps in his own barrel taking in the sun."
Discussions about 'lying flat' picked up pace in May 2021, as young,
over-worked Chinese people weighed the merits of relinquishing
ambition, spurning effort, and refusing to bear hardship. For the
English translation of the manifesto, see: Anonymous Tangpingist,
"Tangpingist Manifesto: Tangpingists of the world, unite!"
The Anarchist Library, 2022, theanarchistlibrary.org/library/
anonymous-tangpingist-manifesto.

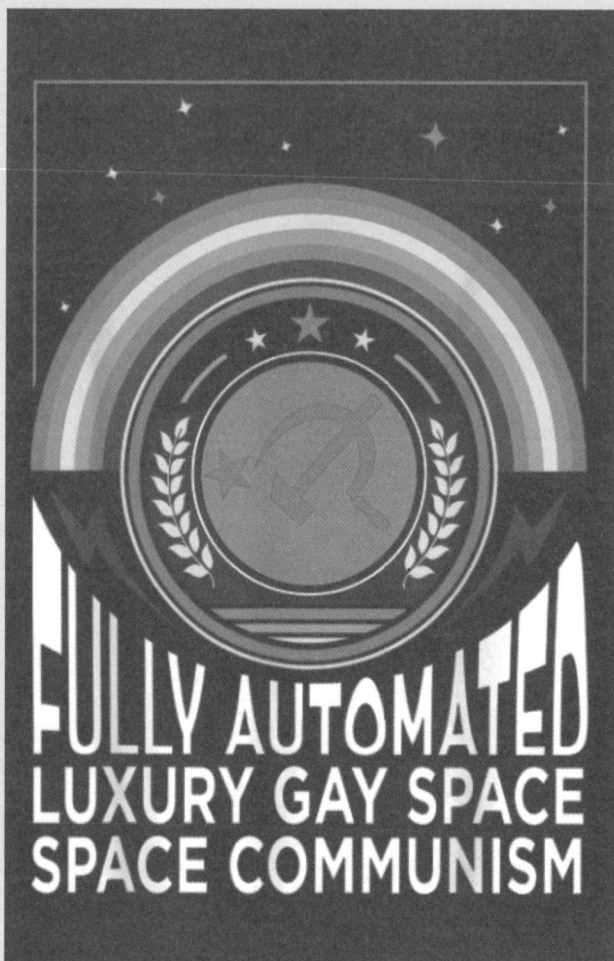

The 'fully automated luxury gay space communism' meme is a queer utopian take on Aaron Bastani's book *Fully Automated Luxury Communism: A Manifesto* (London: Verso, 2019). This version is the cover of a notebook offered by Mike Heaverlo on Amazon: amazon.nl/en/Mike-Heaverlo/dp/B0B5KK3Y7l. Find other versions of the meme and background information on Know Your Meme: knowyourmeme.com/memes/cultures/fully-automated-luxury-gay-space-communism.

THREE
DREAMS

Some people dream of fully automated luxury gay space communism. They write cybernetic post-work theories and seek to emancipate homo ludens.[17] They own the future and the power of imagination. We call these people: the accelerationists.

....

[17] To get an idea of accelerationist theory, you could read Srnicek and Williams', *Inventing the Future*. In Europe, the stronghold of post-workerism is Italy, best known for scholars like Franco 'Bifo' Berardi. Homo ludens ('man the player') is a concept invented by the cultural historian Johan Huizinga in 1938. It has since inspired generations of artists and activists. In the 1960s and 1970s, it was used by the Situationist International and the Provo movement. In the digital age, cultural play theory has merged with social and economic game theory and gamification studies into the field of 'ludology'. Nick Srnicek and Alex Williams, *Inventing the Future: Postcapitalism and a World Without Work* (New York: Verso, 2015).

Illustration from the eight-hour day movement in the UK, ca. 1880.
At the time, child labour was common and the working day
could range from 10 to 16 hours.

Other people dream of an eight-hour working day, regular
breaks, and a pension plan. They have an unwavering belief
in traditional Marxist theory and seek to liberate homo faber.
They own the heroic legacy of the workers' movements and
the power of the trade unions. We call these people:
organized workers.

Alina Lupu, *Work, Rest, What We Will* at Eight Cubic Meters,
Amsterdam, 2022. Courtesy of Alina Lupu.

A growing group of workers, belonging to the flex work vanguard of mobility, food delivery, distribution, and the arts, can no longer afford to accept the choice between accelerationism and labour organizing. They cunningly resort to a tactic of promiscuity, challenging history using imagination and challenging the future using historic achievement. They ask: "Where are we now, juggling as we seem to be in between the real and the virtually embedded, at times money-rich, time-poor, other times experiencing poverty all over? When does an artist's workday start, and when does it end? And can an artist strike to regulate their hours? What sort of division of hours would they choose? Would they ever choose to stop working?"[18]

....

[18] A lightly edited citation from Alina Lupu's exhibition text for *Work, Rest, What We Will* at Eight Cubic Meters, theofficeofalinalupu.com/projects/work-play-what-we-will-eight-cubic-meters

THE XANAX
RESIDENCY

A pretty, young woman lives by herself in an apartment on the Upper East Side of Manhattan. She's a recent art history graduate, and deeply dissatisfied with her life. She decides to spend a year under the influence of self-medicated prescription drugs. She calls it: my year of rest and relaxation.[19]

Our protagonist feels that opting out is the only way to resist. But who is funding the rent? Who is paying for the medication? Where does she get the money for a year's worth of groceries? Is it a sponsor deal? A Xanax residency?[20]

Maybe the company could fund your year of rest and relaxation as well. Would you accept the grant?[21]

....

[19] This is the plot of the best-selling novel *My Year of Rest and Relaxation* by Ottessa Moshfegh. Ottessa Moshfegh, *My Year of Rest and Relaxation* (London: Penguin, 2018).

[20] The protagonist of *My Year of Rest and Relaxation* is a recent orphan, living off a sizeable inheritance. It brings home the point that radical retreat is a copium for the privileged (for instance, I'm thinking of small groups of white rich kids going to the mountains for a 'digital detox'). But it is not unthinkable that the aggressive pharmaceutical industry would find it opportune to fund the medication retreats of micro-influencers.

[21] We could consider the Xanax residency as the ultimate consequence of accepting individual resistant rest as a valid form of copium. According to Jia Tolentino's review of *My Year of Rest and Relaxation*, Moshfegh "builds a façade of beauty and privilege around her characters, forcing the reader to locate repulsion somewhere deeper: in effort, in daily living, in a world that swings between tragic and banal." Jia Tolentino, "Ottessa Moshfegh's Painful, Funny Novel of a Young Woman's Chemical Hibernation," *The New Yorker*, 11 July 2018, www.newyorker.com/ books/page-turner/ottessa-moshfeghs-painful-funny-novel-of-a-young-womans-chemical-hibernation.

A
IS FOR ATTENTION

Aeio Ttntn walked down the street in Busytown. She had lived in this place all her life, but never felt so distant from it. She remembered how colourful the trees were before they were covered in smog. She remembered the smell of the wet pavement before all sidewalks were covered by arcades. She remembered the gentle sound of silence before it was replaced with the impatient, never-ending sound of rushing footsteps.

As she travels through what it was, Aeio is stopped by what it is. She halts. Her eyes wide open, she suddenly sees how everyone around her moves. Why is she the only one standing still? Hordes of people, all of them tired, stuck in busywork.[22] She sees them, but they don't see her. They're too busy to notice.

Now that Aeio pays attention, she can clearly see how the bodies moving around her are shaped by a restricted experience of time and space. Vulnerability and precarity have eroded their sense of agency. When standing still, it's so easy to see things for what they are, and how they can be different.

....

[22] 'Busywork,' coined by Byung-Chul Han, is activity that creates the appearance of productivity without actually adding value or contributing meaningful outcomes. Busywork is a symptom of 'achievement societies' that equate activity and performance to moral value. Han's critique of grind culture and his call for a more reflexive use of time are aligned with David Graeber's economic critique of 'bullshit jobs.' Byung-Chul Han, *The Burnout Society* (Standford, CA: Stanford UP, 2015).

Aeio tilts her head, her perspective changes, and, right there, time changes. It becomes vertical. And she can move around freely. Because movement in vertical time – unproductive, attentive movement – is invisible to the machine of grind culture.[23] In the newfound freedom of vertical time, Aeio can imagine a place where no one wastes their time on time not to be wasted. A time that is present.

Aeio wishes that people would not be so busy. She craves that they would stop, just for a second, and see her.[24] Will you look out for Aeio Ttntn?

....

[23] The distinction between horizontal and vertical time was made by Jenny Odell in *Saving Time*. Horizontal time refers to the linear, productive, and goal-oriented perception of time. It's the time spent working, achieving tasks, and moving forward on a predetermined path. Vertical time, on the other hand, is a deeper, more contemplative understanding of time. It involves slowing down, being present, and connecting with the world around us on a more profound level – in other words, meaningful experiences that aren't necessarily tied to productivity or progress. Odell argues that in our fast-paced, hyper-connected world, horizontal time often overshadows vertical time, which results in the specific form of alienation (between human and environment) that we call 'burnout.' She suggests that by embracing moments of vertical time – whether it's through spending time in nature, engaging in creative pursuits, or simply being present – we can reclaim a more balanced and fulfilling relationship with time. Jenny Odell, *Saving Time: Discovering a Life Beyond the Clock* (London: The   Bodley Head, 2023).

[24] "Everyone knows what attention is. It is the taking possession by the mind, in clear and vivid form, of one out of what seems several simultaneously possible objects or trains of thought. Focalization, concentration, and consciousness are of its essence. It implies withdrawal from some things in order to deal effectively with others." William James, *The Principles of Psychology*, Vol. 1, (New York: Henry Holt, 1890), 403-404.

23/7

Initiated in 2015, *23/7* is a series of artistic interventions that challenge the concept of continuous, homogeneous time that flows uninterruptedly, 24 hours a day, 7 days a week. These actions question the notion of total and constant availability, offering an approach that introduces disruptions and irregularities in our perception of time. A prime example is the artist's website, mariosantamaria.net, which is programmed to be accessible only 23 hours a day, blocking any connections outside that window. Intriguingly, it is never disclosed how these 23 hours are allocated within the daily cycle, leaving visitors in a state of uncertainty. Similarly, the artist's contact email has been set to a perpetual 'out of office' mode since 2016. Every incoming message receives an automatic reply stating: "Thanks for your email. I'm sleeping," regardless of the sender's identity or the email's content. These interventions provoke reflection on the overwhelming saturation of time in the digital age, and the potential to reclaim control over our temporal experience by embracing irregularities and disconnections.

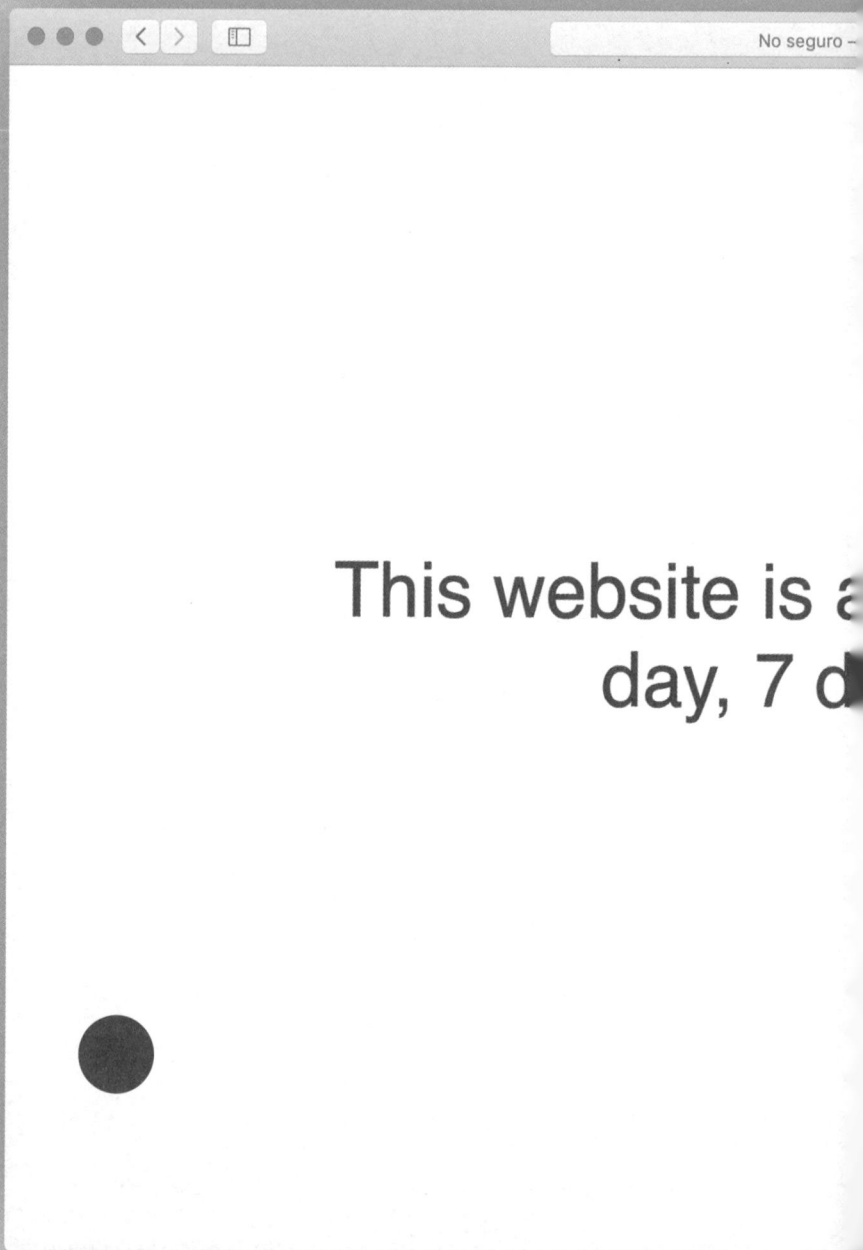

This website is a
day, 7 d

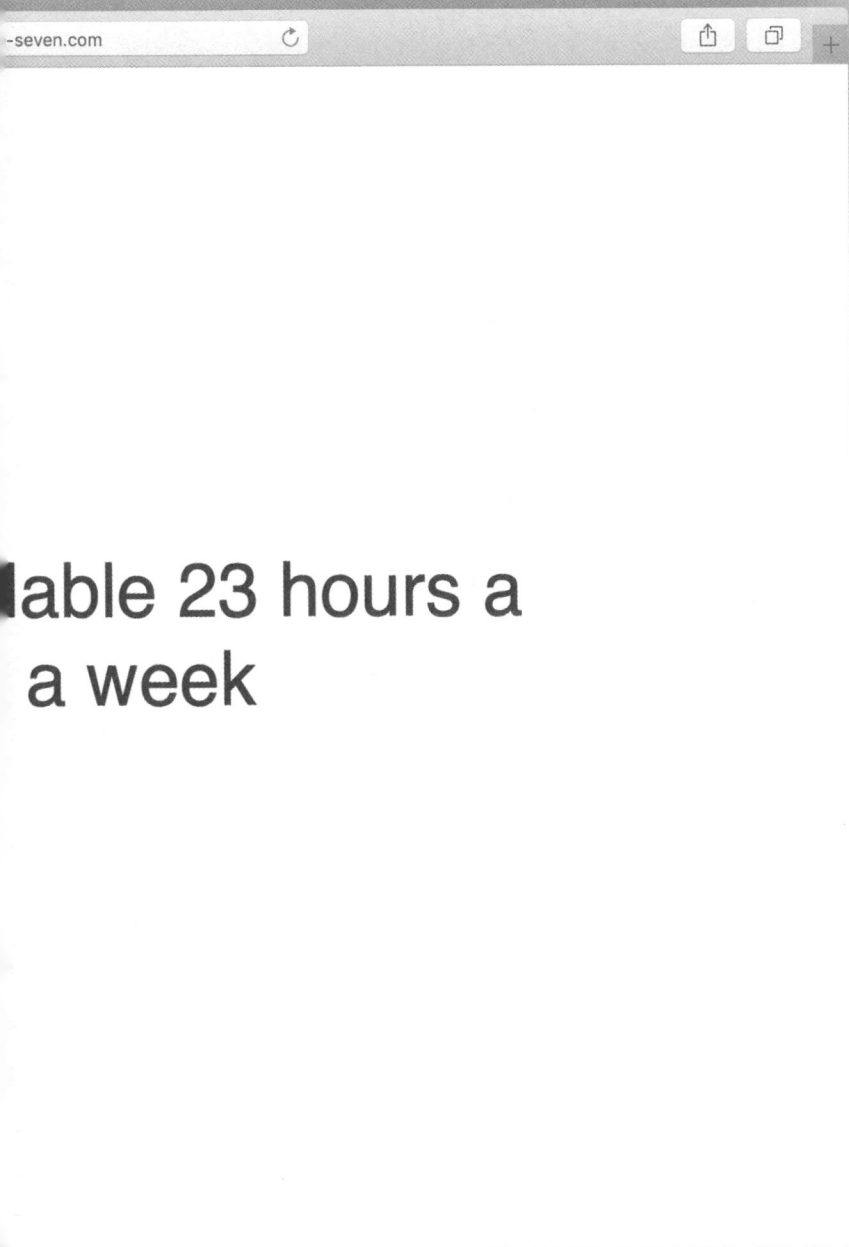

-seven.com

lable 23 hours a
a week

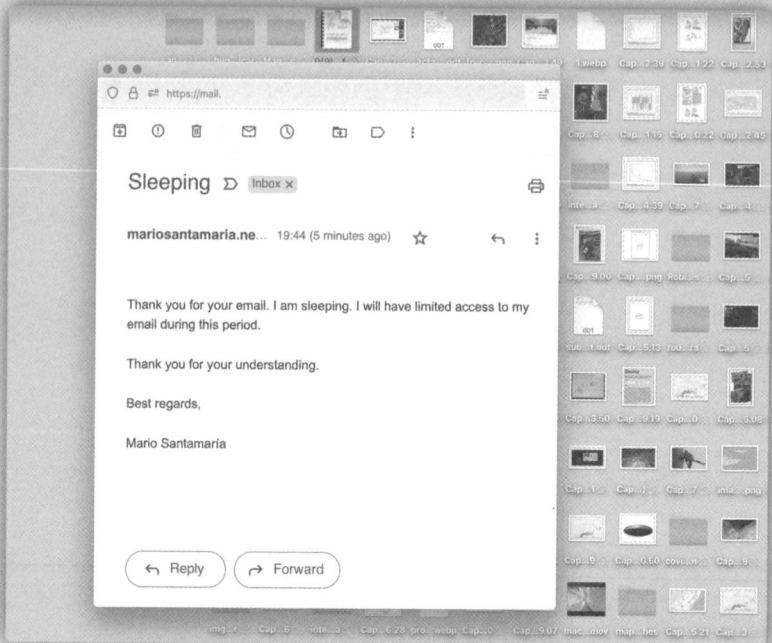

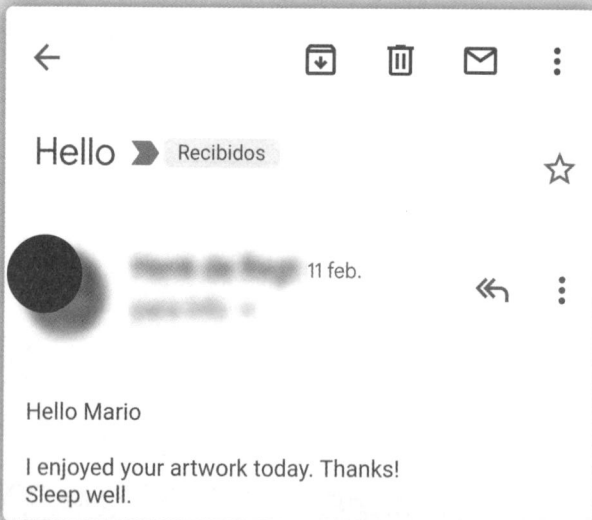

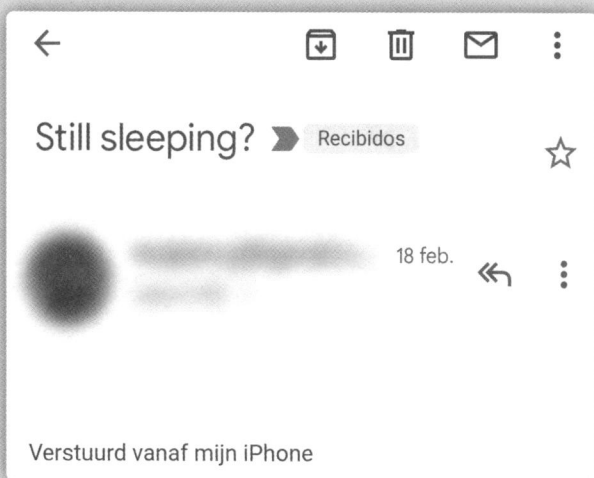

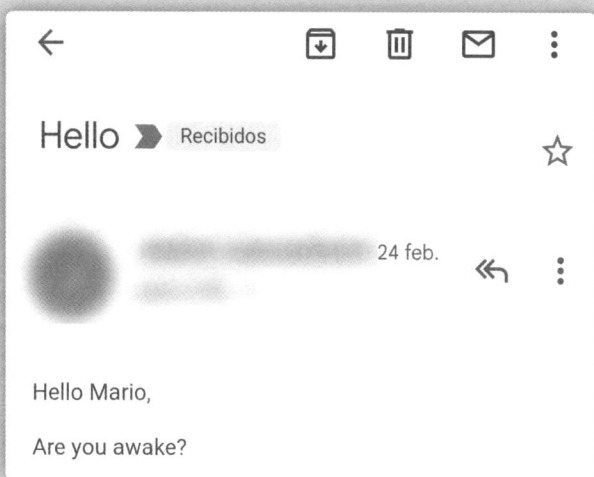

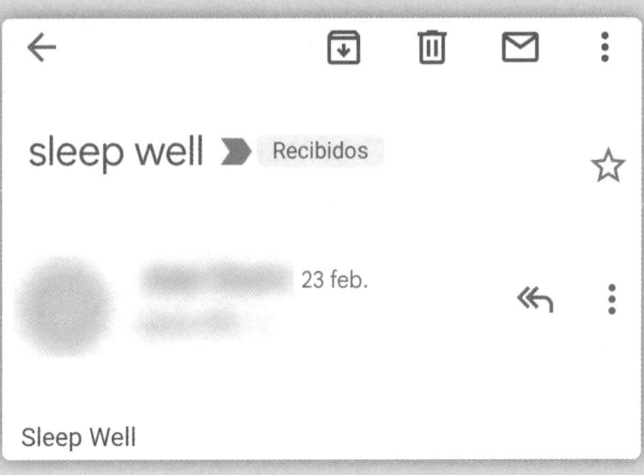

sleep well ➤ Recibidos ☆

23 feb.

Sleep Well

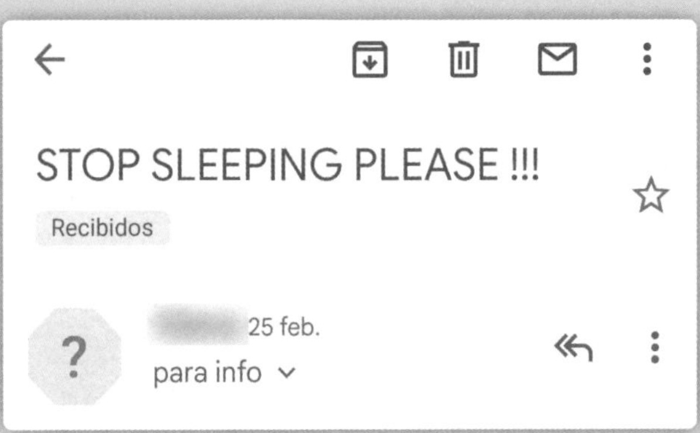

STOP SLEEPING PLEASE !!!

Recibidos ☆

? 25 feb.
para info ⌄

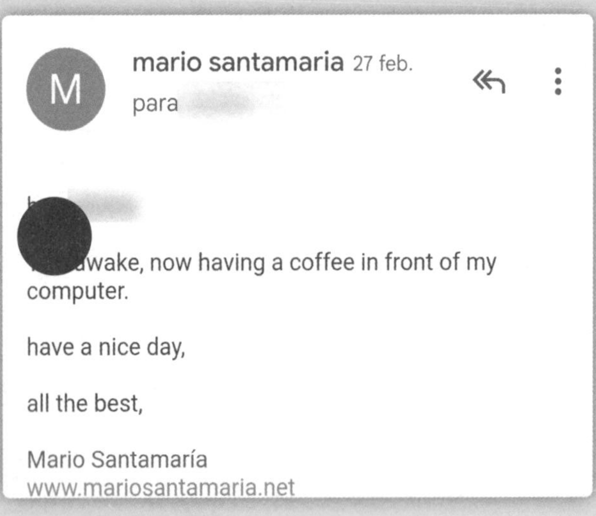

---

mario santamaria 27 feb.

para

awake, now having a coffee in front of my computer.

have a nice day,

all the best,

Mario Santamaría
www.mariosantamaria.net

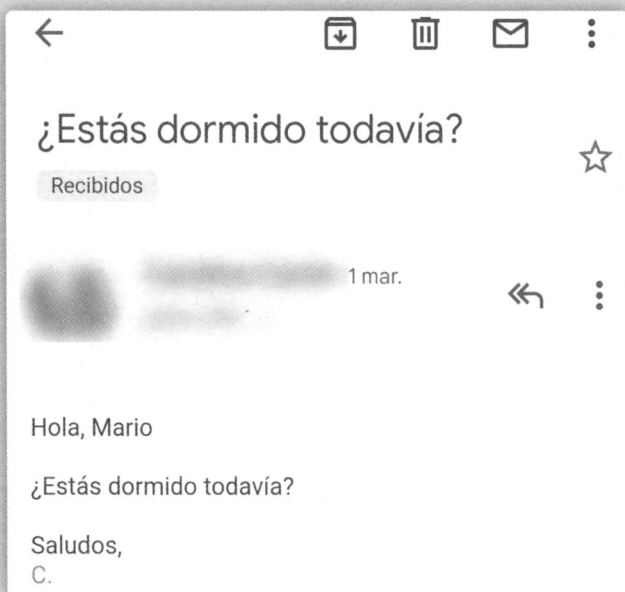

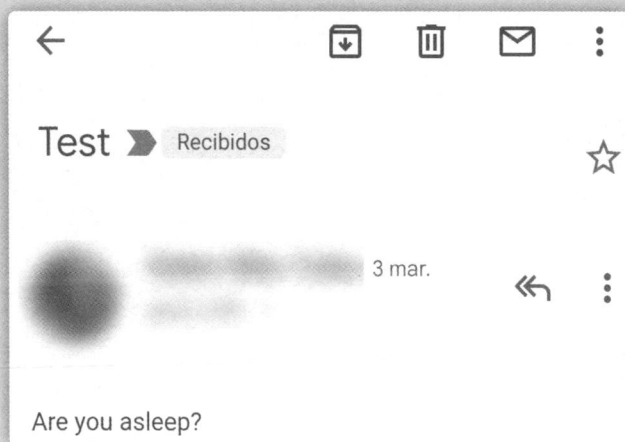

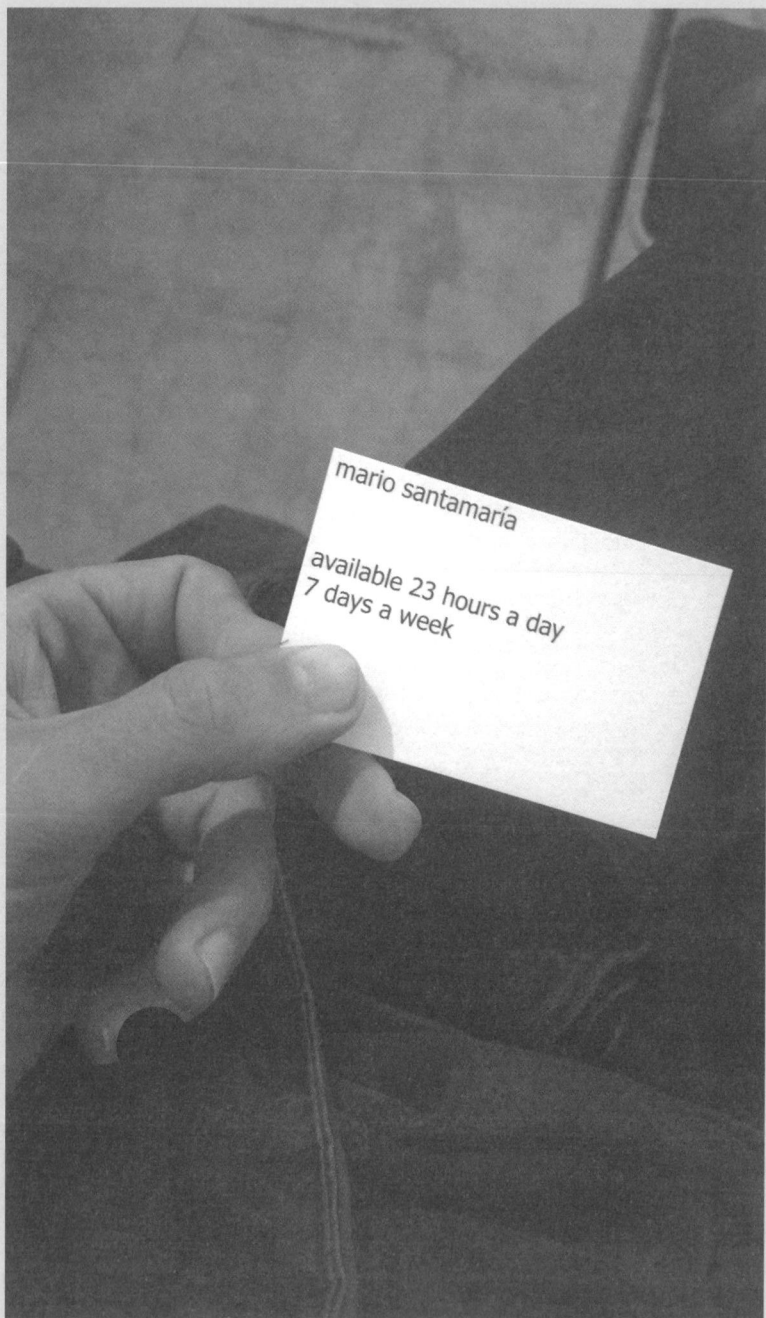

mario santamaría

available 23 hours a day
7 days a week

Extracted, Extracted

Dream of 23 January, Venice

In the middle of the night, it's dark but some orange light filters through the window. I open my eyes. There is a presence in my room, between my bed and the window. I feel I belong to someone else. My eyes are wide open, this phantom has an arm lifted, menacing, showing me fear in a handful of dust. I can't move, I try again and again, but my body is blocked.

I dreamt this during an overworked period of research in Venice, while we were in residence at the Hellenic Institute of Byzantine and Post-Byzantine Studies. It is one of the most fearful nightmares I have ever experienced. Still, now, I cannot fully grasp what happened. My conscious self would say that there was something unresolved in my psyche, that I was overworked and exhausted, and that feeling emerged through sleep paralysis. However, my unconscious self would say I saw a phantom that kept me immobilized with terrifying power.

I was experiencing an intensely stressful moment, which mirrored the conversations I had with my colleague, particularly around frameworks of human resource extraction and their direct connection to economic and environmental instability. While I was getting exhausted by relentless cognitive work and stimulations, Venice was visibly sinking around us.

The shockwave arrived at night. My sleep being under attack seemed an improbable idea. Minute after minute, the phantom grew bigger. Pulling, forcing, pressing, breaking. Perhaps I gave in, for that long instant. What if I stopped to breathe before fully grasping the core of capital legacy? Extraction, depletion, time-devouring, planet-killing, toxic, and annihilative energies pushing all around me. But this I know; Death/Thanatos has a close grip on my body. It came to stop me, it knocked me down, and it obliged me to stop working. Perhaps the ghost has been a resolution of some kind.

1) EXTRACTED, EXTRACTED,
original drawing,
pen on paper,
30 × 41 cm, 2024

The drawing references the nightmare
experienced in Venice.
A three-headed monster pulls and
misforms our collective body while
Hypnos caresses our hair.

2) HYPNOS/THANATOS,
original drawing,
pen on paper,
30 × 41 cm, 2021

Brothers Hypnos/Thanatos (Sleep/Death)
play a circular form of eternal struggle.

3) UNTITLED,
16 mm film still,
2022
Two eyes are wide open through a VR headset.

4) DETAIL OF A FRENCH MINIATURE,
author unknown,
ca. 1300
A demon possesses a sleeping person.
An early depiction of sleep paralysis.

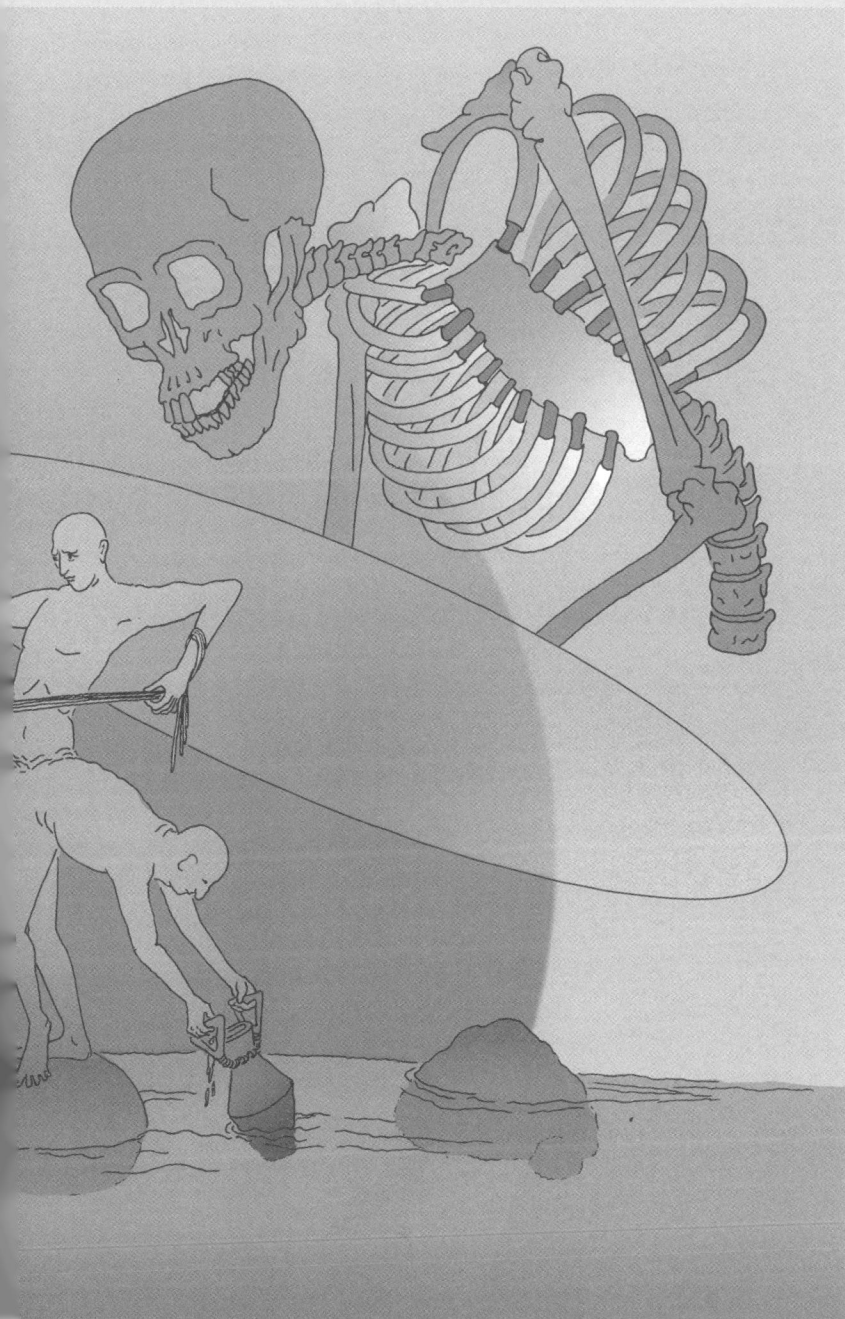

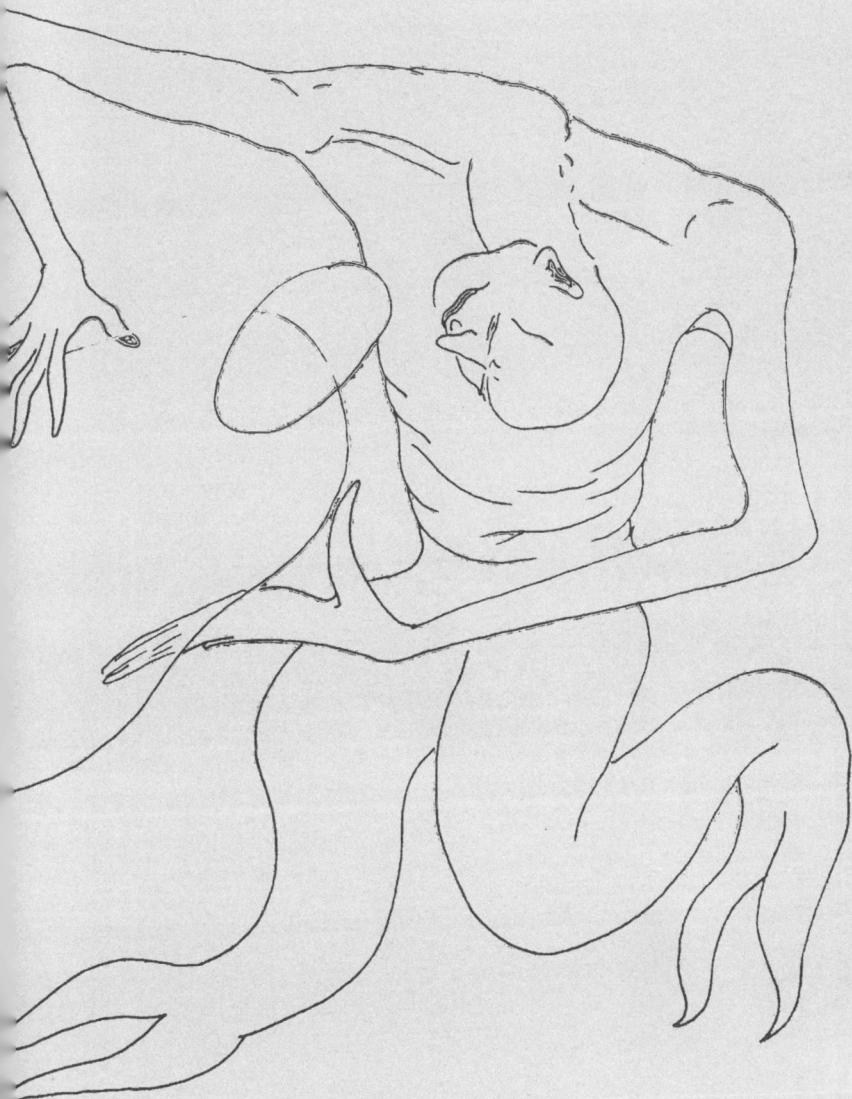

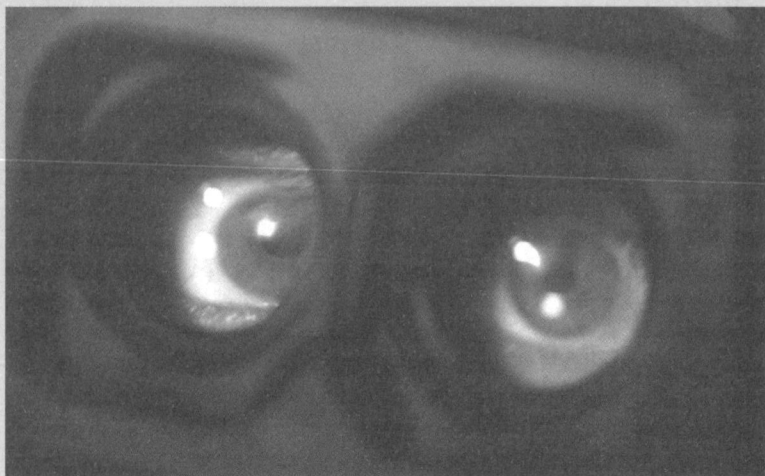

Dark Mode: Living with Eye Floaters

I don't like the colour white for two reasons: first, I get dirty when I eat, like a child; second, I have floaters in my eyes. When I look at a white wall, I feel a bit sad as I become aware of these elusive particles that traverse the aqueous humour of my eyes, casting their ominous silhouette on the canvas of the retina. Generally referred to as eye floaters or *muscae volitantes* (Latin for 'flying flies'), these diaphanous shadows become particularly visible against the backdrop of a blue sky, or an empty Word document. Perverse irony, since they are partly caused – it seems – by the extended exposure to screens. The symbiotic relationship between screens and vision is, in fact, what I want to explore in this short essay. I want to look at the eye itself as a screen, and consider the behaviours and feelings provoked by a mild yet permanent alteration of one's vision.

"Floaters may seem to be alive, since they move and change shape, but they are not alive."[1] This is how an educational YouTube video explains the flies in my eyes. Mine mostly look like semi-transparent squiggly lines, but they can have different shapes such as spots, rings, or even cobwebs, like those of a cheap, black and white horror movie. Floaters are small concretions of collagen stuck in the vitreous body of the eye, moving gently like snow in a snow globe. They are not to be confused with moving dots of light followed by a black tail, an anomaly known as blue field entoptic phenomenon, which is in fact the opposite of floaters, since the latter are shadows and the former is light. Myodesopsia, the perception of floaters, is not uncommon: a 2002 UK survey indicated that, on average, fourteen patients every month reported floaters symptoms to their optometrist.[2]

....

[1] Michael Mauser, "What are those floaty things in your eye?" *TED-Ed*, 1 December 2014, youtu.be/Y6e_m9iq-4Q.

[2] Amaral Alwitry, H. Chen, and S. Wigfall, "Optometrists' Examination and Referral Practices for Patients Presenting with Flashes and Floaters," *Ophthalmic and Physiological Optics 22*, no. 3 (April 2002): 183–188, doi.org/10.1046/j.1475-1313.2002.00027.x.

There is no known unintrusive remedy for eye floaters, and so they are almost never treated. Generally, a doctor would tell you that the brain will eventually 'tune them out,' but it is hardly able to, since floaters don't have a fixed position within the eye. So, tuned out or not, you have to learn to live with them. Some companies have promoted laser vitreolysis as a solution, but, despite the aggressive marketing, there's currently insufficient evidence supporting the use of such a technique for treating floaters. While searching for therapies, I stumbled on 'the floater doctor' who uses laser and promises to take the issue seriously – unlike the American Academy of Ophthalmology.[3] Another oculist from Hawaii offers a review of a Taiwanese study suggesting that a pineapple-based diet might alleviate the condition.[4] I like pineapple, so I might give it a try. Better than laser anyway.

In one of his novels, Emmanuel Carrère tells the story of Erica, a middle-aged woman affected by a stroke. Frequently, all of a sudden and out of nothing, she turns her head to the left because she *feels* there is a shadowy presence there, at the edge of her field of vision, "something like a bear, a black bag, thick smoke, a cloud of wasps, something indistinct, menacing and vaguely unclean, that swarms and crawls and swells and scares her."[5] However, as soon as she tries to catch it, the shadow recedes. I started noticing something similar, but clearly not as dramatic. In full daylight, I perceived something that I couldn't focus on, and it made me scared. I thought it was neurological, and I was afraid of it getting worse. I remember crying on a Skype call with my girlfriend from Italy, desperate about going either blind or mad.

....

[3] James H. Johnson, "American Academy of Ophthalmology says Eye Floaters are not a problem. We disagree," *The Floater Doctor*, 29 March 2023, youtu.be/-HH9lLyj7x4.

[4] Rupa Wong, "Natural Cure For Eye Floaters? Eye Doctor Explains," *Dr. Rupa Wong*, 16 December 2022, youtu.be/u2l7kN5_HD4.

[5] Emmanuel Carrère, *Yoga* (London: Vintage, 2023).

Hence, I retreated to what was already my comfort zone: night-time, when I couldn't see the shadows and still work on my laptop. It was only much later that I discovered the term 'eye floater' and its medical explanation, thus realizing that it likely wouldn't get worse and that I might even get used to this condition. Being able to give a somewhat reassuring name to these shadows, a permanent souvenir of countless hours of cognitive (and primarily visual) work, was already something: my brain didn't zone them out. I never got fully used to them, but the fear was gone. Many people had eye floaters and could live a normal life nonetheless: eye floaters were *benign*.

But how come myodesopsia is so common and yet not at all present in popular culture? After all, it's something that a lot of people perceive at all times. To make a comparison, there are many popular references to misophonia, a condition characterized by negative emotional reactions to specific sounds, like chewing.[6] For example, the protagonist of *Tár*, a despotic conductor interpreted by Cate Blanchett, has it.[7] While there is no Simpsons episode featuring floaters, a few obscure references to them exist. Net artist Anthony Antonellis dedicated an online artwork to the condition, which happens to be the best eye floater simulator out there, as it is realistic and dynamic.[8] The website replicates the perception of floaters against the backdrop of the iconic Microsoft Windows XP Bliss wallpaper. The title of the piece is also a dark pun that combines the cutting-edge tech of the time (2012, I believe) with some serious plagues which can be related to myodesopsia: *Floaters: Detached Retina Display*. I find the artwork brilliant because it conjures the default experience of looking at a computer screen, while reflecting (literally) on the very act of seeing, obstructed by the floaters that nonchalantly follow the mouse cursor.

[6] Silvio Lorusso, "The Other as Noise," Real Life, 6 February 2020, reallifemag.com/the-other-as-noise.

[7] Tár, directed by Todd Field (Universal Pictures, 2022).

[8] Anthony Antonellis, Floaters: Detached Retina Display, 2012, www.anthonyantonellis.com/floaters.

Antonellis links perception to technology, but there are people who go further. Swiss author Floco Tausin, for instance, considers floaters as a door to an elevated state of consciousness. In the book *Mouches Volantes: Eye Floaters as Shining Structure of Consciousness*, they write:

> I tried to figure out whether there is more to the phenomenon of *mouches volantes* than just 'particles in the eye' [...] that the *eye floaters* are the initial parts of a shining basic structure formed by our consciousness which organizes our everyday perception of objects in our field of vision, making them appear sensible; and that the mystical entering into one sphere of this structure will enable us human beings to maintain our consciousness beyond the point of physical death.[9]

I know what you're thinking, Tausin is going wild here, but let's cautiously give their argument a chance. After all, they are right to emphasize awareness, in that floaters are a constant reminder – a curse for some people – of the act of seeing, of perception itself. A reminder that the eye is a screen. A meme comes to mind that depicts the monitor-based lives of the cognitive-visual worker. For half of the day, they're glued to a 'bad screen,' namely, that of the computer used for office work, the other half to a 'good screen' devoted to videogames, Netflix or porn. But there is another screen, one that goes beyond good and evil: the absolute retina screen of our eye, which is physical and subject to damage and fatigue.

---

[9] Floco Tausin, *Mouches Volantes: Eye Floaters as Shining Structure of Consciousness* (Bern: Leuchtstruktur-Verlag, 2009).

A feedback loop exists between the eye and the computer screen: the monitor radiates light that gleams on our eyes, making them tired and more sensitive, so we lower the brightness of the screen. From this perspective, the screen is not just an extension of the gaze, but something that shapes it. It doesn't let us just see more, but in a different way, with a specific rhythm, and while doing so, it makes us aware of this very act. Computer vision, understood here not as the vision *of* a computer but the vision directed *at* a computer screen, is also characterized by novel forms of coordination. I notice for instance that my eyes move automatically in sync with my scrolling thumb, provoking a feeling of physical discomfort when, for some reason, the digital page remains still.

Not to be constantly reminded of my floaters, I still seek dimly lit environments: murky cafes, obscure dens, and gloomy settings. I act as the protagonist of a gothic novel. And so my work acquires a crepuscular quality. Luckily, devices followed suit. Nowadays, almost every software and operating system includes a 'dark mode' option, an almost paradoxical attempt to emanate darkness instead of light. Users can now recreate their own digital Castle of Otranto. My photophobia drives me to work in an ambience of rest, blending labour with leisure. But unlike ten years ago, when I first got eye floaters, I'm unable to work at night. Not only have my eyes changed, my whole body has: I'm not a night owl anymore. What is this darkness without night in which I operate? What is this leisure without rest? Eye floaters are a haunting presence that lurks in the recesses of ⬤ vision, but the actual ghost behind all of this is labour, that spirit that forces you to trade day for night, sunlight for screen light. It's time to defeat the ghost, at least for today. It's time to close this ivory Word window and shut down my laptop like you would turn off an *abat-jour*, literally 'the day destroyer.'

Sleep Streams: Seismographs of Digital States of *Veille*

The way in which the flows of our clicks, likes, and scrolls are counted and interpreted is no longer a secret of our online digital condition. In between exhaustiveness and exhaustion, the visual and sound accumulation interweaves several cadences, confronting us with the arrhythmia of our technological prostheses. According to Louise Merzeau, "we devote more and more energy to negotiating changes of cadence, rhythmic variations and irregularities, in order to make machine time habitable." These technologies take the pulse of our actions, as well as our absences and hesitations. Even non-choice has become a form of data. As evidenced by our browser tabs that are never closed, our online experiences are punctuated by moments of waiting and procrastination.[1]

---

[1] Louise Merzeau, "Le Flâneur impatient," *Médium*, Rythmes, no. 41, (April 2014): 22, English translation by the author.

The vulnerability of our digital condition is highlighted in sleep streams, a practice consisting of filming and streaming oneself sleeping via platforms such as Twitch, TikTok, or YouTube. It is difficult to identify and locate the origins of the phenomenon. While vlogs, the online streaming of our daily activities, are becoming more and more common, sleep streams may have started accidentally. During one of his streams on Twitch, Jesse Daugherty, known as @JesseDStreams, became famous for falling asleep while playing Hearthstone – an online trading card game. For several hours, his subscribers watched his sleeping face, noting and commenting on this unexpected situation. When he woke up, Jesse had over 2,400 new followers and 50 new subscribers (who pay a monthly subscription fee of $5 via the platform). This may seem a pittance when you consider the number of followers/subscribers of successful streamers; but for Jesse, who was only followed by a handful of people, the difference counted even more because he had simply fallen asleep. In the midst of a massive flow of content, videos of people sleeping stand out in the mediascape, generating a popular success tinged with a certain strangeness. Pushing the concept of the attention economy to its limits, where even our sleep is suddenly monetized and rewarded with thousands of views, subscriptions, and donations, sleep streams nevertheless need to be studied beyond their weird aura.

ELOÏSE VO

THE MACHINERY
OF SLEEP STREAMS

Twitch is a video streaming platform created in 2007. Although it was originally designed to broadcast video game content, it is now possible to watch lifestyle blogs, concerts, and political programmes. Unlike previous platforms such as YouTube, Twitch allows content producers, known as 'streamers,' to simultaneously stream two videos in fluxs: the screencast of their computer and the video feedback of their webcam. The platform also stands out by offering an architecture of interaction, allowing the viewers to react, discuss, and exchange in real-time with the streamers by using the chat; an instant messaging system located in the column next to the video window. This interaction space enables the experience shared between streamers and viewers to be re-synchronized in time, if not in space.[2] The arrival of streaming platforms such as Twitch has also helped to reshape the business model of content production platforms. It is no longer just a matter of monetizing the streamer's channel based on the number of subscribers through partnerships and advertising collaborations, it is now possible to pay streamers directly by subscribing to their favourite channel for a few dollars a month, or to make one-off payments in the form of donations. Platforms such as Twitch have thus contributed to the development of immaterial work, through so-called communicational forms, where the value-producing gesture consists of offering comments or making donations in exchange for certain rewards such as unlocking a customised GIF or emoji, or giving more visibility to someone's comment.[3]

....

[2] Bruno Bachimont, "Separating Bodies, Synchronising Minds: The Role of Digital Technology in Mediating Distance," *IMG Journal*, no. 3 (2020): 54–69, img-journal.unibo.it/article/view/12247.

[3] Streamers often produce personalized GIFs or emojis in reference to their videos and their community. For a few dollars or euros, viewers or followers can buy them and then use them in a chat.

Given the profitability unlocked by the online popularity of sleep streams, some streamers have expanded their production to an industrial scale. Every night from 11 p.m. to 6 a.m., Jakey Boehms streams his sleep on TikTok. He was one of the first to apply the concept of interactive streaming to sleep videos, offering the possibility of directly interacting with his bedroom. In return for donations ranging from $0.60 to $600, viewers can turn on LED lights, raise the electric blinds, trigger a bubble machine, or play music at different volumes. The platform's interface acts like a dashboard for a remote control of the streamer's room. With a community of around one million subscribers, Jakey Boehms' sleep is disturbed every ten to twenty seconds. And for $600, the most expensive option, you can trigger all the actions at the same time for a duration of five minutes. By extending these interactive principles to his entire channel, whether for lifestyle videos or video games, Jakey Boehms claims to earn up to AU$50,000 per month, of which TikTok takes a 50 per cent commission.

Because of the publicity generated by these excessive remunerations, the sleep streams are attracting both fascination and scepticism. They highlight how one of the most intimate activities is being turned into a productive one in alignment with the liberal logic of the digital platform economy. It's hard not to see the failure of sleep in these practices to be one of what Marx, quoted by Jonathan Crary, called "the last 'natural barriers' to the full realisation of 24/7" capitalization of our rhythms, emotions and attention.[4] These videos are becoming the visible manifestation of the radical reorientation and weaponization of our time off. In order to generate a new source of income, streamers are prepared to stream their sleep online, even if it means sacrificing the quality of their physical and mental recovery. On the other side of the screen, viewers are ready to buy the right to disturb someone else's sleep, a questioning attitude in between trolling practises and the satisfaction of a scopic vision.

....

[4] Jonathan Crary, 24/7: *Late Capitalism and the Ends of Sleep* (London: Verso Books, 2013); Eva Illouz, *Cold Intimacies: The Making of Emotional Capitalism* (Cambridge: Polity Press, 2007); Yves Citton, ed., *L'économie de l'attention. Nouvel horizon du capitalisme?* (Paris: La Découverte, 2014). Alice Leney,

FLUXES OF EXHAUSTION
AND EXHAUSTIVENESS

Behind this dramatization of the exploitation of sleep, most of the videos are rather banal and ordinary. They are just very long videos of people sleeping. Nothing more is visible than fragmented bodies seen from a distance: a dark mass of hair, an arm or a foot escaping from the blanket. Whereas videos on Twitch tend to offer a 'face-cam' view, accentuating the effects of proximity by tightening the angle on the streamer's face and expression, the distanced bodies of the sleep streams resist the inquisitive gaze of the camera and the viewer. By maintaining a certain distance, the sleeping body remains a black box. The dispositif is only revealed by a peripheral vision and attention to the slight movements of a duvet, lifted at regular intervals by the movements of a breath. Of course, this sleeping body, whose image is streamed online, is never entirely unproductive or passive. The set-up, the frame, and the lighting have to be staged. The camera turned on. While the quality and length of videos are no longer technically limited, streamers are under considerable pressure to produce ever more content. These videos reveal their own exhaustion in the attention economy, where the important thing is to animate the networks by generating as much flux as possible, whatever it may be. If no one can presume that the streamer is really asleep, or what their motivations are, the streamer as content producer disappears. Defying the platform's economy, they are no longer there to entertain and chat with their audience. Their presence remains only in the background, allowing the viewers to inhabit this uncanny space.

While sleep streams show the inactivity of the sleeping body of the streamer, the presence of the viewers reflects their own state of insomnia and the difficulty that some people have in resting and sleeping. A ton of literature warns about the consequences of blue light from screens, which disturb the production of melatonin, known as the sleeping hormone. While five lumens are enough to disturb our sleep, the light emitted by a phone is between twelve and twenty lumens. In contrast to these assumptions, TikToker Elisa Diaz claims her sleep streams offer a safe place to accompany her followers during their insomnia, loneliness, or anxiety.

Followed by 467,400 subscribers, Elisa Diaz is a 'sleepfluencer,' sharing her advice to help her community. This cathartic effect of the sleep stream, expressed on numerous occasions in the comments, is also evident in the choice of the tag 'visual ASMR' used to label her videos. This acronym, which stands for autonomous sensory meridian response, usually defines a sensation of tingling and pleasure experienced in response to certain sound stimuli, such as pen noises, zips, or whispers. Here, they are displaced into the visual field, where the benefits of sound stimuli are replaced by the sedative effect of long and slow videos. In a context of repeated eruptions of new content, these videos seem to produce a hypnotic effect through their fixed and immobile frame and the long hours of streaming, which can last all night, but also all day. According to artist and researcher Alice Leney, the main therapeutic aspect of these videos comes from this companionship through images: "companion videos" that open up "an intimate space, within the slow rhythm of the infra-ordinary," by offering "'an on-demand *presence* service".[5] If sleep streams fail to make sleep more accessible to the viewer, they seem to allow the experience of a certain absence. Sleep streams highlight the way in which attention is channelled within platforms. Chatboxes in particular can be used to map the shared presence of viewers, and thus become a sensor for digital wakefulness: GIFs, messages, and emojis reveal the co-presence of other viewers. The mechanisms of 'playbour,' a contraction between *play* and *labour*, produce a frenetic digital environment that constantly demands a reaction or interaction. Conversely, sleep streams seem to be a refuge for staying connected without having to actively participate. They allow a temporary withdrawal from the exchange of information and communication, without requiring a total disconnection, which is simply impossible.

---

[5] "Le public des vidéos 'ASMR': Des sentinelles sensibles?" *Multitudes 2*, no. 79 (2020): 99, doi.org/10.3917/mult.079.0093.

Twitch and TikTok thus operate on the principle of interpassivity, whereby viewers get pleasure from watching someone else play a video game, for example. These transfer effects have been described by philosophers Slavoj Žižek and Robert Pfeller.[6] Rather than letting others do it for them, they let them enjoy it for themselves. In other words, they delegate passivity rather than the activity itself. Sleep and its benefits can't be transferred from one body to another. The viewers delegate passivity and the possibility of rest to the sleeping body on screen because they themselves are unable to escape their wake state and the trap of relentless exhaustion. When sleep has never seemed so difficult to conquer, despite the many injunctions and attempts to quantify, control, and optimise it, sleep streams channel the experience of passivity by externalizing the need for sleep and regeneration to a proxy body. The sleep streams open up a space that is always, at the same time, already there; making possible a certain form of inanimity, a fusion of the terms inanimate and intimacy. Facing the impossibility of disconnection, and by acknowledging our interconnected conditions, the experience of the inanimity provided by sleep streams enables a temporary withdrawal from these injunctions to participate.

....

[6] Robert Pfaller, *Interpassivity: The Aesthetics of Delegated Enjoyment* (Edinburgh: Edinburgh University Press, 2018).

COLLECTIVE DIMINISHMENT:
THE DIGITAL STATE OF *VEILLE*

The experience of this inanimity is akin to the 'digital lethargy' defined by philosopher and poet Tung-Hui Hu. Lethargy describes these experiences of waiting and time-out, resulting from a form of endurance and perseverance.[7] If Anson Rabinbach demonstrated how the concept of fatigue has mainly been described in terms of body management and economy, Jonathan Sterne reminds us that for the "chronically fatigued subject, fatigue is not an absence of energy: it is a presence."[8] The fatigue that is expressed in sleep streams is far from being simply a state of inaction in which you are too tired to do anything. While waiting to be recharged and re-energized, sleep streams alleviate the pressure to rush towards solutions and force us to listen to the unresolved present.

....

[7] Tung-Hui Hu. *Digital Lethargy. Dispatches from an Age of Disconnection* (Massachusetts: MIT Press, 2022).

[8] Anson Rabinbach, *The Human Motor. Energy, Fatigue, and the Origins of Modernity* (Berkeley: University of California Press, 1992); Jonathan Stern, *Diminished Faculties. A Political Phenomenology of Impairment* (Durham: Duke University Press, 2021).

In French, this is embedded in the ambivalence of the oddly enchanting term *veiller*, which designates a transient, fleeting state that is neither sleep nor wakefulness. The etymology of the word *veiller* comes from the Latin vigilare, meaning to watch, to be awake, on guard, attentive. Sharing the same root as *vigil*, or 'night watchman,' it implies the presence of an outside eye. Describing both a state of inaction, withdrawal, or rest, as well as a state of active attention, the action of *veiller* (to watch) is located in between 'sur-*veillance*' and 'sous-*veillance*' (under-veillance). At this threshold, *nous veillions* (we watch over) can relate to a growing seed, an injured animal, a dead person, an inactive volcano or a sleeping child. Online states of *veille* nestle in the margins of ASMR videos and sleep streams. Sleep streams thus become the meeting point for distributed and atomized viewers. While being unable to rest or sleep by themselves, they are nourishing a 'soft attention,' by inventing new ways of being anonymously-alone-together. These multiple states of digital *veille* shape an affective infrastructure, which may remain diffuse, ambient, or unrealized, but which nevertheless allows us to recharge a certain potential for collective action.*Veiller* invites a speculative exploration of the importance of care while living in more-than-human technical arrangements.

CONCLUSION

Sleep streams are no different from other forms of data extraction that are taking place on social platforms.
They are symptomatic of the extraction processes of cognitive and emotional capitalism, where every moment of inaction is rendered valuable by attention detection algorithms. The value of the supposedly unproductive body of the sleeper is rendered by the interactions of the viewers, who are themselves kept in a state of insomnia by the platform. Like the ASMR videos analysed by Alice Leney, the consumption of sleep streams can be understood as an "adaptation mechanism within our digital condition of late capitalism."[9]

....

[9] Tasha Bjelić, "Digital Care," *Women & Performance: a journal of feminist theory*, no. 26 (2016), p. 101-104, available at www. womenandperformance.org/ampersand/tash a-bjelic, cited in Leney, "Le public."

The sleeping bodies who haunt our platforms thus operate at the threshold of this unconscious exhaustion; and my own attraction to sleep streams lies precisely in this possibility to collectively inhabit these bubbles of absence and disengagement.

At the intersection of the media, somatic and socio-political spheres, sleep streams act as sensitive seismographs. These videos allow us to monitor the states of fatigue and wakefulness, activity and idleness that punctuates our online experiences. These fluxes of presence and absence allow certain intimacies to circulate through and beyond the filters and barriers of the Internet. The sleep streams trace the contours of a certain techno-sensitivity, connected, atomized, and distributed, which operates through more-than-human cognitive arrangements. While we are not able to stay fully awake, digital states of *veille* multiply possibilities of dismediations.[10] By preventing us from stabilizing defined states, *veiller* allows us to experience incomplete and discontinuous modes of communication, and to rethink rhythms and continuums with dissonances. Wherever we are, no matter the time of day in our longitudes, we can rest reassured and comforted; because in the shadow of these digital communities, there is always someone sleeping, and therefore, someone watching.

....

[10] Mara Mills and Jonathan Sterne, "Dismediation. Three Proposals, Six Tactics," in *Disability Media Studies*, eds. Elizabeth Ellcessor, Bill Kirkpatrick (New York: New York University Press, 2017).

Hypersomnia

Aurélien Lepetit's body of work aims to transcribe his sleep cycles, which he records and compiles methodically into textiles. Data collected through a tracking device – an automated surveillance system – structures his plastic work, where the weave recalls the graphic nature of his digital diagrams. Analysed and translated into fabric through weaving, the resulting patterns resemble a form of language developed by the artist. His work reveals this second life that escapes us, where the loss of control over our bodies and thoughts leads to a state of wakefulness. This installation evokes sleep, often associated with rest and reverie, as a space of vulnerability that also includes anxiety and waiting when experiencing insomnia. This autobiographical series addresses issues related to rest and the right to withdraw from a reality driven by productivity pressure.

Extract from the exhibition text written by Camille Velluet for the group exhibition *The Sound of Fabrics* at Punt WG, Amsterdam, that took place between 29 June-22 July 2024.

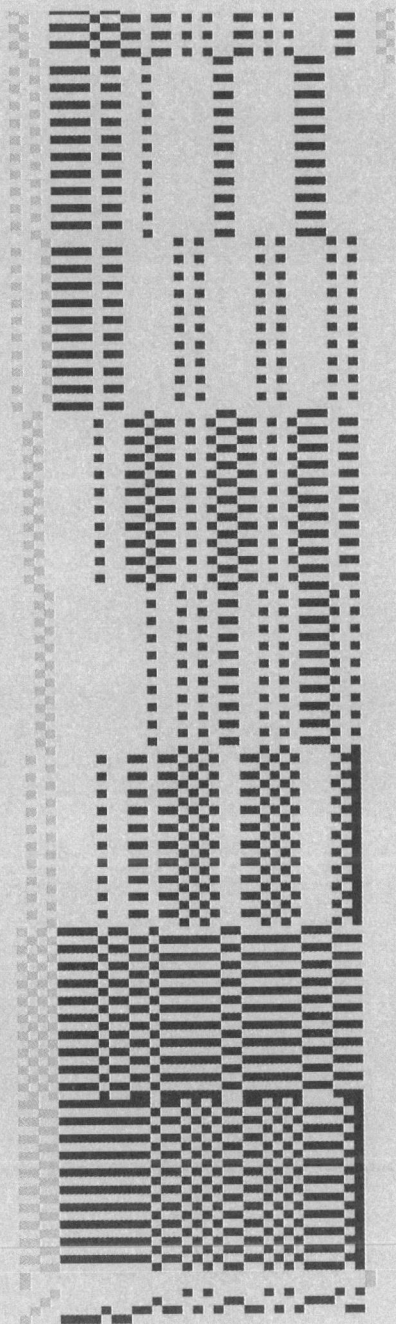

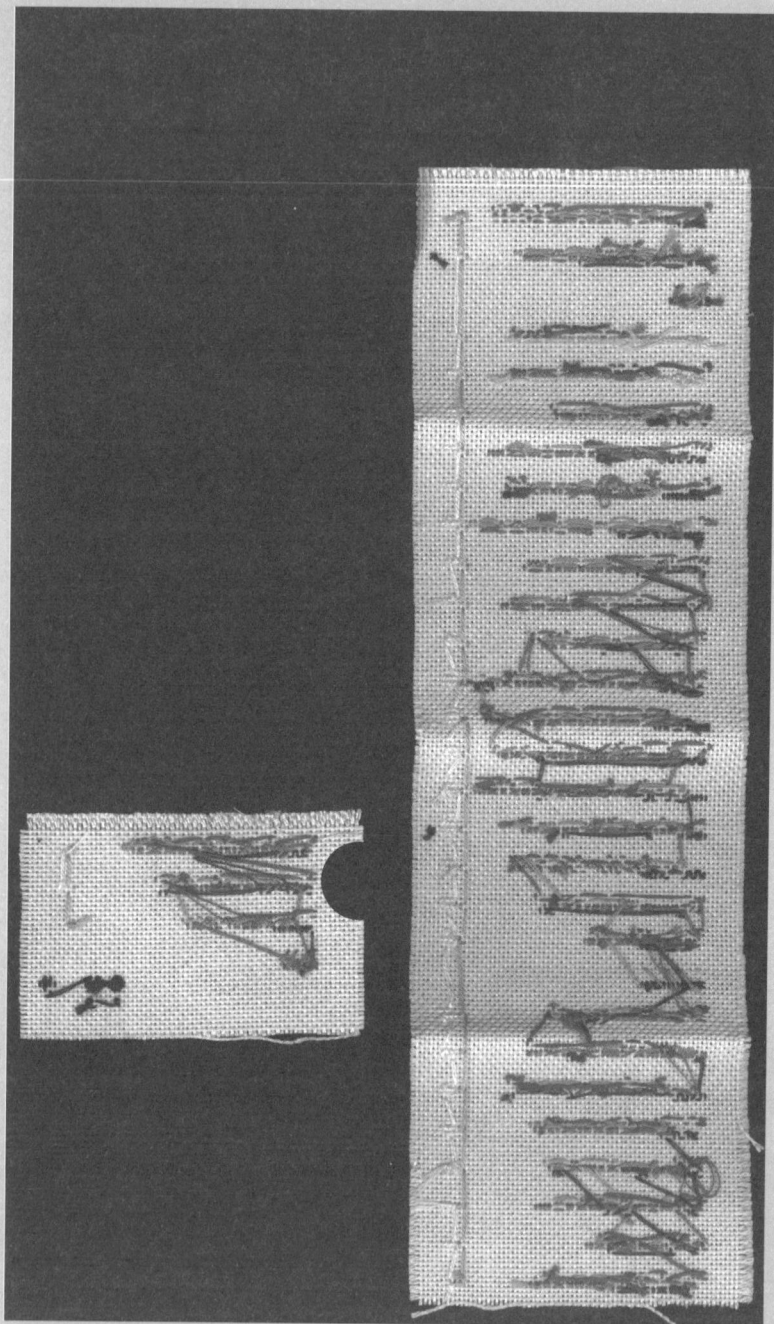

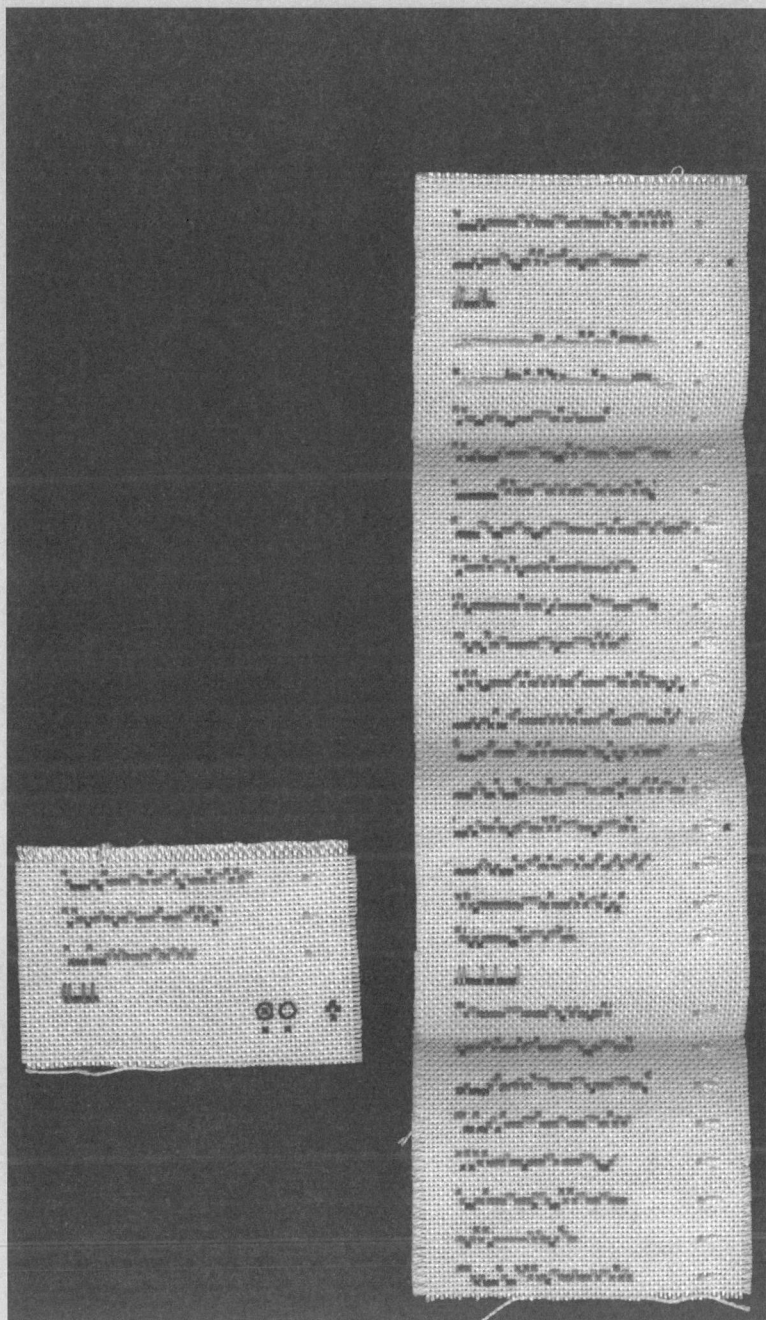

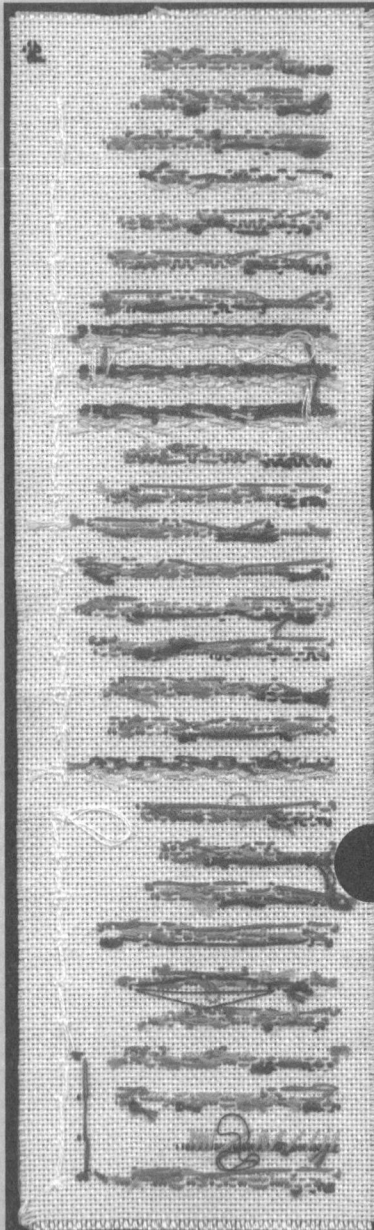

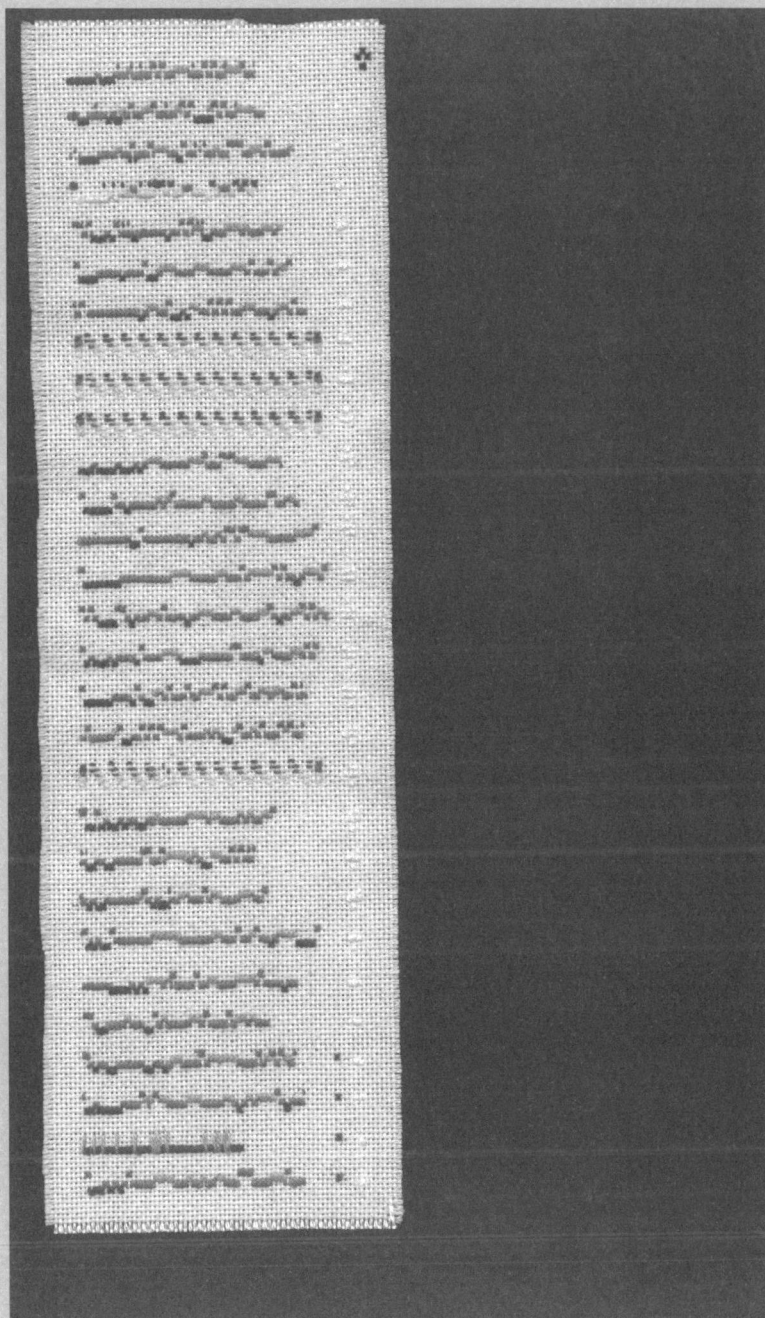

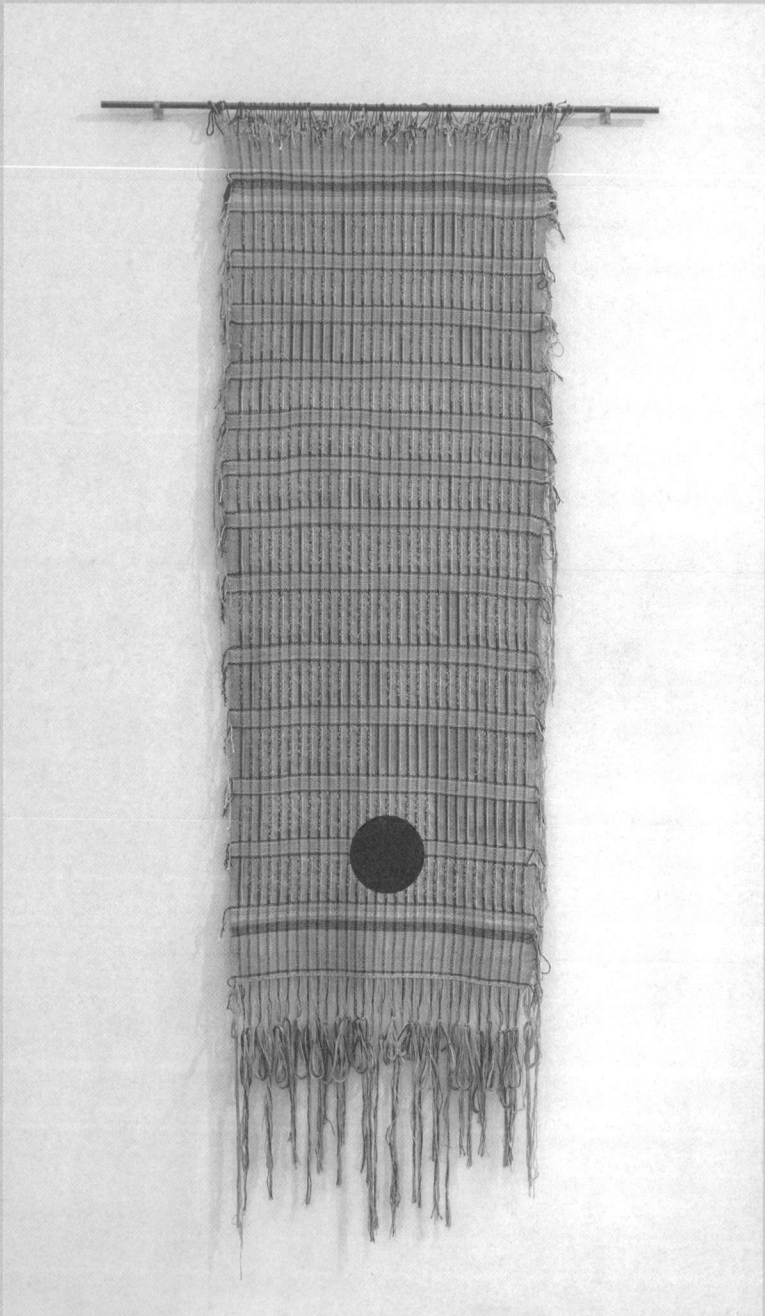

Amator Archives: Work, Rest, Sleep

Archiving and counter-archiving are central to WERKER's practice. Their work revolves around an ever-expanding collection of books, photographs, magazines, and other printed matter on subjects such as labour, solidarity, and the body. Comprising several thousand documents, the archive is continuously activated by people working in different constellations; to collectively explore marginalized histories and to generate new political imaginaries. These explorations take the form of workshops and publications, performances, and installations. The archive is physically located in the Nieuwmarkt neighbourhood of Amsterdam and is open by appointment: info@werkercollective.net.

Der Bauarbeiter
(zweiter von lin
seinen Kollegen

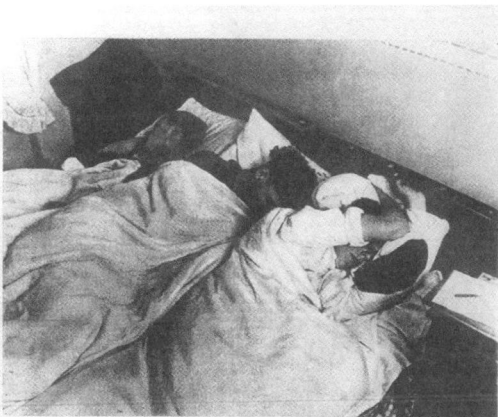

den, wobei man praktischer auch die größtmögliche Blende nehmen müßte, um die Sache nicht zu sehr in die Länge zu ziehen. Selbstverständlich würden nun bei gewöhnlicher Entwicklung die Lichter zu kräftig gedeckt, so daß

...durch Ausstellung eines Reflektors, in Form eines Bettlakens usw., erreicht worden. Diese weiße Fläche müßte ihren Platz ungefähr an der linken Bildkante erhalten, natürlich so, daß sie nicht mit auf das

Übermüdel
April, 20 Uhr, 100 Watt Osram, 20 Sekunden, Obj. 4,5. Blende, 12,5

H. E. Bireman

MARSEILLE LE 12.10.1983.-ATTENTAT-Un attentat à l'explosif qui n'a pas fait de victime,a été commis dans la cité "La Bricarde" oh habitent de nombreuses famil-les magrébines.L'explosion s'est produite jeudi vers 3H du matin.Notre photo: Les enfants de l'immeuble montrant les débris de l'explosion. P.CIOT A.F.P.
A.F.P. téléphoto P.CIOT A.F.P.

NAT F.

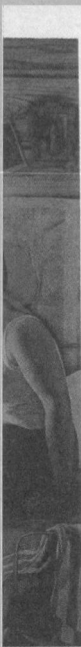

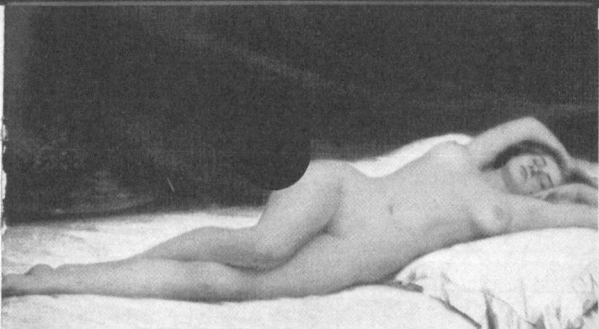

us, der seine Hoffnung auf
s aus dem Westen", das
Makel", setzt, das durch
s Amida-Buddhas erlangt
Zen (Meditation)-Buddhis-
reitet.

ebieten, die der Buddhis-
erobert hatte, wurde er
rahmanismus und den *Is*-
verdrängt.   Andererseits
nfluß bis nach Europa. Da
örigkeit zu anderen Reli-
ausschließt, ist die Zahl
ger kaum zu bestimmen;
gen liegen zwischen 120
nen.

ten Prinzip nach ist er sin-
Eine Erlösung von allen
irde vor allem eine Abto-
alität bedeuten. Wenn das
eltflucht liegt, ist nicht ein-
lerung der Gesellschaft in
nden mehr wichtig. Aber
us kennt keine Dogmen,
einzelne seinen Weg zur
für sich selbst gehen kann,
keinen Druck durch Ge-
eine „Kirche". Die Tole-
ddhismus brachte keine
rpflichtenden Sexualein-
hervor, wie sie im christ-
aum entstanden.

Anfang an traten in der
n Kunst erotische Frauen-
die von den alten Mutter-
rkeitskulten übernommen
. In der Form des Maha-
nus wurden sie später als
heiten in den tantrischen
erinnen der Buddhas,
und Schutzgottheiten.

nung für den femininen
herab, etwa wie „warm
Erst später sprach man
den — geliebten Frau
Goethes „König in Th
bei Hans Sachs ind
„Buhllied". Noch heu
manchmal als Gleich
nerisches Werben gel
ein Rivale „Neben-buh
Aber im allgemeinen s
„Buhle" zu abschätzi
worden. „Buhle" oder
das moderne Verstä
sane, Mätresse oder *Di*
Dieser Bedeutungswa

The boy . . . remained asleep. He lay
unashamed, embraced and penetrated by
the sun. The lips were parted, the down
on the upper was touched with gold, the
hair broken into countless glories, the
body was a delicate amber. To anyone he
would have seemed beautiful . . .

'Don't forget
to take your
pills, darling'

DRUGS
AND
DRIVING

ol.3 no.9 DECEMBER 1971
T CLEANERS

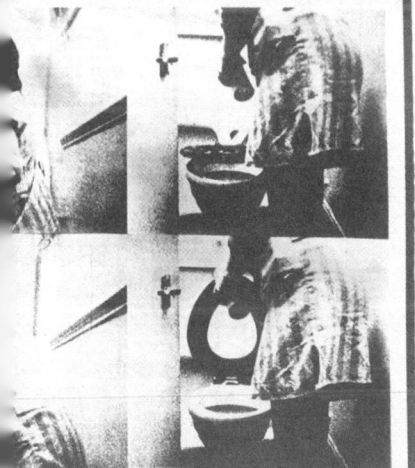

Podlednou, kjer so obešale Mežnarjeve perice.

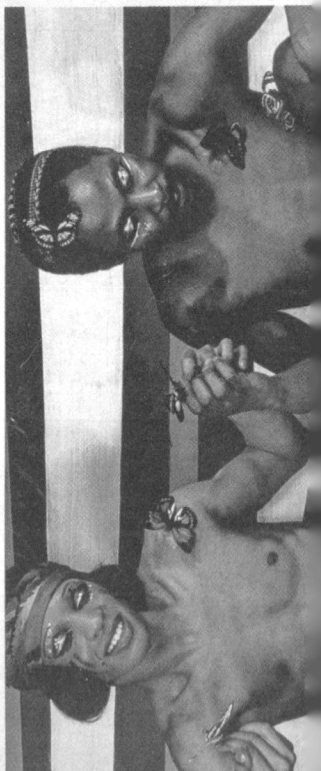

fiction

NIGHTS

North London 1975

I save my sleeps for when Bill comes. The rest of the time I get along by way of small strategies not very different from those used by other women I know who spend nights alone. I read a lot, new and old books written by women, novels and autobiographies mainly. Not much theory — I read more theory when I always slept with Bill. Male novelists don't do either, they're too grand, too self-destructive, and I don't like the way they're always talking about being alone, that complacency, there's something deceitful about it.

Those nights when I know I have to be up early the next day to take the three children to their two schools, like tonight, or when I have to catch the bus to work — those are the worst. I rarely get to sleep before three. So the exhaustion builds throughout the week, and I let it all out on the nights Bill stays.

a strange house — I'd spend long minutes working out how to use a facecloth or a toothbrush so that it looked as if they hadn't been wetted and as if I'd brought my own as I imagined proper guests did; and Jean's mother was a nervous, fussy woman.

So we lay there in the glare of the bedside lamp, staring at this and that, at the brown shutters, the anaglypta wallpaper, the black night, the pear tree branch at the window.

"I can't sleep with the light on." Bill's voice was flat, hating.

"I can't sleep with the light off."

"I can't bear this."

"Christ."

"You know I can't sleep with the light on."

I could sense Bill's disbelief and hysteria mounting. I am very afraid of his rages, but I would not give in.

"Why not?"

I started being afraid of men's rage years ago when I slipped my husband, half-joking, and he floored

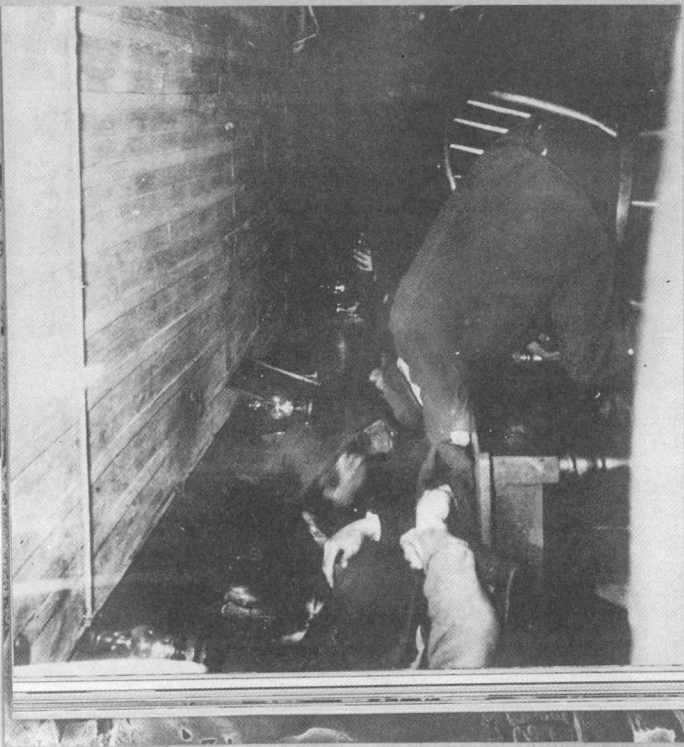

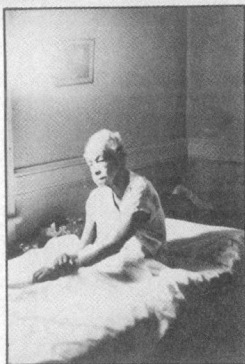

Melinda Hoder

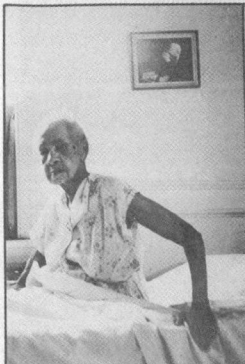

Melinda Hoder

The woman in these photographs is Espy Williams. When she was younger, she worked hard as a domestic and cook for a wealthy family, making her own living. In her life she has seen everything from horse-and-buggy to space travel. Until two years ago, she lived with her older sister. When Espy's sister died she had a mild stroke and has since been incapacitated to the bed. Her health is excellent. She requires no medication, is aware and alert, and generally in good spirits. She practices standing and taking small steps every day with a walker. Espy is 94 years old, blind, and black.

62   THE BLATANT IMAGE 1983

FÜNF MENSCHEN GEHEN ZUR ARBEIT

● "My friend works for two days at the office and three days at home. Often when he works at home he sits slumped on the couch, and sometimes he only wears his bathrobe. They call this the 'new work.'" Contribution by Sarah, *July 26: New Work*, in Werker Magazine, *365 Days of Invisible Work* (Amsterdam: Werker Magazine; Utrecht: Casco – Office for Art, Design and Theory; Leipzig: Spector Books, 2017).

● Ad van Denderen, 1 a.m. *Peepshow, Reguliersbreestraat*, in Hans van den Bogaard and R. Ferdinandusse, *24 Hours Amsterdam* (Amsterdam: Meulenhoff/Landshoff; London: Thames and Hudson; Köln: DuMont Buchverlag, 1986).

● *Boys: Le Magazine Gay en Bleu Tendre* (Paris: 1978), 13.

● Yuri Mikhailovich Raksha, *My Mother*, 1969, in Elena Viktorovna Nikolaeva, *Art and the Working Class* (Leningrad: Khudozhnik RSFSR Publishers, 1983).

● "'Die deutschen Filipows' – aus der Reportage über die Berliner Bauarbeiterfamilie Fournes, die das Aktiv der Berliner Arbeiterfotografen für die 'AIZ' erarbeitete." Erich Rinka, *Fotografie im Klassenkampf* (Leipzig: VEB Fotokinoverlag, 1981).

ÜBERMÜDET

● The column "Bilderkritik" in *Der Arbeiter-Fotograf: Offizielles Organ der Vereinigung der Arbeiter-Fotografen Deutschlands 3*, no. 8 (Berlin: August 1929).

● "My cell is five feet by eight. In that small space you got to fit a bed, table, toilet, and sink. Sing Sing has the smallest cells of all the prisons, the smallest oldest cells I've ever seen. Sometimes you can't flush your toilet and again at times the toilet will flush without pushing the button. I woke up in the middle of the night and found the toilet flushing." John Conroy, inmate and Sing Sing, quoted in Steven Schoen, ed., *Sing Sing: The View from Within. Photographs by the Prisoners,*

(New York: The Floating Foundation of Photography
and Winter House LTD, 1972).

● "–Attentat– Les enfants de l'immeuble montrent les débris
de l'explosion." Pierre Ciot (A.F.P.), 12.10.1983, Marseille.

● "Image taken and censored by the subjects themselves."
Dar Chabab, *Young Worker's Camera*. From the exhibition
Werker 10–Community Darkroom by Werker Collective at
Fundació Antoni Tàpies, 2017, Barcelona.

● Unknown photographer, *Boy Sleeping*, ca. 1900,
albumen print, Algiers.

● *Spaccapietre che dormono*, ca. 1872, in *Sebastiano Porretta,
Ignazio Cugnoni Fotografo*, (Torino: Giulio Einaudi, 1976).

"DON'T FORGET TO TAKE YOUR PILLS, DARLING"

● James Hatcher, *My Mum Having a Nap, exhibition poster for
Doing Photography: Blackfriars Young Photography Group* at
Half Moon Gallery, 1975, London.

● "Wird sie geliebt, oder buhlt sie um Liebe? Pikante Postkarte
(um 1910)." Ludwig Knoll, *Kulturgeschichte der Erotik. Band
II*. Seite 261. (Stuttgart, Hamburg, München: Deutschen
Bücherbundes GmbH & Co, 1982).

● Postcard gifted to WERKER by Leon Filter. On the back
it reads "Leon Filter reads *Schwuchtel*, Issue 1, 1974, page 3."

● "The boy [...] remained asleep. He lay unashamed, embraced
and penetrated by the sun. The lips were parted, the down on
the upper was touched with gold, the hair broken into countless
glories, the body was a delicate amber. To anyone he would have
seemed beautiful." Quoted in James Gardiner, *A Class Apart:
The Private Pictures of Montague Glover* (London: Serpent's
Tail, 1992).

● *Shrew. Women's Liberation Workshop 3*, no. 9
(December 1971).

● Jo Spence. *Don't forget to take your pills, darling*. ca. 1970, advertisement for *Drugs and Driving*. Jo Spence Memorial Library, courtesy of Birkbeck University, London.

● Susoespai: Creació i Salut Mental, *Herramientas Visionarias*, from the exhibition *Werker 10—Community Darkroom* by Werker Collective at Fundació Antoni Tàpies, 2017, Barcelona.

NIGHTS

● Marjan Klampfer, Ivana Perme, Marjana Pušenjak, *Bizoviške Perice* (Ljubljana: Osnovna Šola Božidarja Jakca, 1996).

● Alison Jell, *Nights: North London 1975*, in *Spare Rib*, no. 44 (March 1976).

● Robert de Hartog, *Kijkboek over gastarbeid* (Utrecht: NCB, 1977).

● "We dress for our own pleasure and get off on each other. It's our own small world; within it we understand and are understood—and we do what we want. When we put on our clothes, we feel free." Gilles Larrain, Ralph Gibson, *Idols* (New York/London: Links Books,   1973).

● Jacob A. Riis, *How the Other Half   Lives* (New York: Dover Publications, 1971).

● *The Blatant Image: A Magazine of Feminist Photography*, no. 3 (1983), 62.

Performing Success While Being Exhausted

29 May 1980, 8:00 a.m.,
de Appel, Brouwersgracht 196, Amsterdam

An appointed doorman wakes the handful of sleepers who occupy the beds aligning the walls of de Appel's performance space. He continues to do this every morning during the two weeks that de Appel operates as a hostel. Outside the entrance, a sign is installed, saying: "GRATIS SLAPEN – FREE DORMITORY in de Appel vanaf/from 22.00–8.00 uur/o'clock 28 mei/May–10 juni/June."

23 November 2016, approx. 9:00 p.m.,
de Appel, Prins Hendrikkade 142, Amsterdam

We are halfway through the second event of *Open Avond(S)* at de Appel's grand white cube space in central Amsterdam, when we present Allan Kaprow's 1974 video *Then*, showing a light bulb melting an ice cube – a playful response to the experience of time. The evening continues, combining live interventions with materials from de Appel's archive.

15 April 2017, approx. 3:30 a.m.,
de Appel, Schipluidenlaan 12, Amsterdam

Another performance commences, waking up the few audience members who have dozed off on inflatable mattresses across the space. With this final event in the *Open Avond(S)* series de Appel opens its new exhibition space, in Amsterdam's Nieuw-West neighbourhood. A move by the city authorities to speed up gentrification of this lower-income area?

7 March 2024, 4:30 p.m.,
de Appel, Tolstraat 160, Amsterdam

As I go through the archive, just moments before the public opening of the newest venue, I discover an epistolary exchange from 1979 between de Appel and Czech artist Jan Mlčoch, discussing his proposal for a free dormitory.

When I first started to research performance art, as a first-year student in art history at the University of Amsterdam, I soon learned about Amsterdam's thriving performance scene of the late 1970s and 80s and the important role de Appel played in it.

I later engaged more closely with the institution and its archive as I worked as a curatorial assistant for *Open Avond(S)*: a series of events inspired by a monthly open stage that took place between 1979 and 1980 at de Appel.[1] The last edition of *Open Avond(S)* took place in 2017 and was part of an overnight programme organized by that year's Curatorial Programme participants, seductively titled *The Night of Exhaustion and Exuberance*. It was the closing event of a four-day programme about underpaid cultural production and the demand for productivity and social self-promotion as 'prerequisites' to get by in 24/7 capitalism.

....

[1] *Open Avond(S)* was initiated by Emma Panza, in reference to the *open avond* events that took place at de Appel in 1979 and 1980. As part of the original series, de Appel offered performance artists an opportunity to show and test their work, on the sole condition they made their proposal at least one day in advance. Following the traces of this tradition, the 2016-2017 *Open Avond(S)* series proposed artists a similarly open space through an open call, and by presenting materials from the archive, Emma Panza and I connected performance history with current practices.

Arie de Fijter and Ksenia Perek for Open Avond(S), curated by Emma Panza & Titus Nouwens, De Appel, 2017. Photo by Carina Erdmann

Upon receiving the invitation to contribute to this publication and write about rest politics in relation to performance, I thought of the overnight event, and how it addressed rest as both something to critically think about and as something to collectively enact. The four-day event engaged with the question of how we perform for one another when in public, a performance perhaps determined by parameters of 'professionalism' and precarity, while the overnight event included the act of sleeping by viewers and performers alike. Moments of sleep were contrasted with performative acts, resulting in a strange merging of performance and reality for an audience who were falling in and out of sleep. At the same time, this event made reference to a project that offered visitors free accommodation and that took place at de Appel in 1980, at a time when housing costs were considerably lower in Amsterdam and the Netherlands had not yet fully transformed from a welfare state to a neoliberal economy.[2] What would such an intervention mean today? What can performance (in its various forms) offer in critically examining the way we – our individual and collective bodies and minds – and the spaces we use for art, function in 24/7 capitalism? How can art, and performance, in particular, propose strategies of withdrawal and critique of high-paced lives characterized by both precarity and constant productivity?

....

[2] Neoliberal undercurrents in postwar Dutch society gradually mutated into a key influence on the policy paradigms of the 1980s and 1990s. This may explain the continuous postwar resistance against the welfare state, the remarkably radical transformation in the 1980s and 1990s of the Netherlands into one of the most liberalized European economies, and the paradoxical manifestation of Dutch neoliberalism in a depoliticized, consensual guise. In the 1970s the Dutch welfare state was in crisis, resulting in a radical reshaping of welfare policies. In the Netherlands, more than elsewhere, neoliberalism was presented technocratically as an inevitable policy, rather than a political choice with far-reaching consequences for the distribution of social welfare. For further reading see: "Market Makers. A political history of neoliberalism in the Netherlands" (1945-2002) at Utrecht University, or Bram Mellink and Merijn Oudenampsen, *Neoliberalisme: Een Nederlandse geschiedenis* (Amsterdam: Boom Uitgevers, 2022).

FREE
SLEEPING

To write about performance means writing about the audience's presence. *The Night of Exhaustion and Exuberance* was a combination of a discussion about performance in the professional sphere, performance as an artistic act (through the artists' contributions), and performance of the audience (by inviting them to take up space in a specific way). The event was a culmination of the aforementioned program of discussions and keynote presentations emphasizing, amongst other things, how cultural producers are often required to shift between underpaid professional labour and social self-promotion at lavish V.I.P. events. The curators referred to what artist Martha Rosler has described as the "demand, in neoliberal economies, for the wholesale invention, performance, and perpetual grooming of a transactional self."[3]

The overnight event proposed what I later came to see as an expanded understanding of performance; how both artworks and viewers have a performative presence, and how we, in essence, always perform when in public; at our jobs, when visiting a gallery, and in any situation when other people are present. US artist Pope.L considered this presence as follows: "The visitor has a role, and that role is to make." He argued that by considering how an audience interacts with a work, one takes into account their agency – what they bring to a work and how they might alter it.[4] With this in mind, does the proposition to use a gallery as a place to sleep, like in the 1980 and 2017 occasions at de Appel, make sleeping a participatory performance?

....

[3] Martha Rosler, "Why Are People Being So Nice?" *e-flux Journal*, no. 77 (November 2016). www.e-flux.com/journal/77/76185/why-are-people-being-so-nice.

[4] Pope.L, "Pope.L: Hospital at the South London Gallery," South London Gallery, 22 December 2023, YouTube video, 03:39, www.youtube.com/watch?v=Q8UepqGF8-M&ab_channel=SouthLondonGallery.

On a research trip in preparation for the seminal international art manifestation *Works and Words* (15-30 September 1979), de Appel founder Wies Smals met Jan Mlčoch and invited him to realize a project, which the artist responded to by turning de Appel into a temporary hostel. The reason may have been Mlčoch's disillusionment with art's purpose, as can be detected in his letter to de Appel: "Such a nice room in the middle of the city should be put to better use than for art," he wrote. And so it happened. Outside the building, a sign with the words "Gratis Slapen. Free Dormitory" was installed, and ten army beds were placed inside the gallery. A 'doorman' would let people in and wake the guests at 8 a.m. every morning, sharing weather updates and any other news that he had learned while listening to the radio during the night. According to the newsletter that was shared by mail by de Appel with their audience upon completion of the project, many people made use of the accommodation, while only one person was aware in advance that it was an artwork.[5]

....

[5] Quote from handwritten visitor's report I found in de Appel archive, possibly written by Piotr Olszanski: "From people who came to visit dormitory (during two weeks) there was only one person who had come with the expectation to see 'art' (he meant performance during night). He was very disappointed seeing 'only' beds in the room. He couldn't understand that it was 'all,' that it fulfilled completely the idea of Jan Mlcoch."

The Free Dormitory project can be seen as a precursor to the 1990s and early 2000s tradition of participatory work that came to be known as relational aesthetics: an artistic tradition highlighting how spaces can potentially be repurposed, even if temporarily and symbolically.[6] The project is an example of how to re-imagine regular uses of exhibition spaces and conventional viewer-artwork relations, through the use of performance. Similarly, in his 1972 *Bed Piece*, US artist Chris Burden, who Mlčoch was in close contact with, proposed to stay in a bed placed in a gallery for the entire 22-day duration of his exhibition.[7] The focus of this work was not the social collective, like in the 1990s participatory works, but the body of the artist himself, like in the body art tradition of the 1970s period. In the passing days, Burden went through a bodily transformation – softening the twitches in his fingers, finding a deep rhythm of breath and moving from heaviness into weightlessness, with an alert mind. "Lying in bed for twenty-two days... there's no element of pretence or make-believe in it," the artist reflects. He was aiming for the communication of an experience where a sense of Self is deeply present. "Burden's control over his mind and body is a rigidly ascetic one," observed art critic Jan Butterfield in 1975. "It is not his body per se which comprises Burden's pieces – but his mind."[8]

....

[6] Nicolas Bourriaud, *Relational Aesthetics* (Dijon: les presses du reel, 2002); Pavlína Morganová, writing about Jan Mlčoch for Artlist in 2003: "in 1980, when he organised a homeless shelter at the Gallery De Appel in Amsterdam, which basically prefigured contemporary participatory art.'" See: Pavlína Morganová, "About the Artist," *Artlist – Center for Contemporary Arts Prague*, 2003, www.artlist.cz/en/jan-mlcoch-3299.

[7] This close contact can be assumed from Mlčoch requesting his artist fee for the project to be paid to Burden, as can be read in one of the letters sent to de Appel.

[8] Christopher Chapman, "THE BOY, THE BED AND THE GUN," *Portrait*, no. 51 (Summer 2016).

THE INDIVIDUAL
AND COLLECTIVE BODY

Much like Burden did, Mlčoch often focused on the human body and the performer's individual agency in relation to a collective audience. Because of the political context in which he produced and presented those works of body art, the question of individual agency is a matter concerning both audience and authorities. In Czechoslovakia under communist rule, strict censorship limited the range of activities that could be carried out in public and performance embodied a possibility of free personal expression, a way of balancing a fragile relationship to the world. In its insistence upon the irreducibility of the human body in an increasingly depersonalized and depersonalizing public sphere, this form of performance art was a politically charged genre.[9]

Performance often entails navigating the space and time that is yours, and the space and time you decide to share with others. This makes me think of how rest and exhaustion are both individual experiences and the result of an economic system that we collectively uphold. A system with little solidarity and with a hyper-focus on the Self that is fully responsible for all outcomes of their livelihood.

....

[9] Lara Weibgen, "Performance as 'Ethical Memento': Art and Self-Sacrifice in Communist Czechoslovakia," *Third Text* 23, no. 1 (2009), 55–64.

Around the time that Mlčoch executed his performances under totalitarian regime, Pope.L took to the street in New York to perform his *Crawl* series, with the aim to address the extreme inequalities and physical suffering that come with progress as measured in capitalist society. In 1970s US, whatever support there had been for homeless people, and for physically and mentally ill New Yorkers, was withdrawn, and many – including the Pope.L's own father, aunt, and brother – ended up living on the streets.[10] For his *Crawl* pieces, he simply crawled on his belly in the street while wearing a suit. Here, performance became a radical act of withdrawal, going against the usual flow of public space and making plainly visible the shortcomings of our economic system.

Such insistence on slowing down presents a strong contrast when done in public space, while in the isolation of a gallery space, for example, it may be a way to push individual boundaries and the viewer's hyper attention. In our current state of capitalism, we seem to erode the 'useless' time of reflection and contemplation: possibly the very thing that art offers? What interests me about Burden's *Bed Piece*, is how it made visible the physical and mental components of rest. At the same time, Burden's piece highlights the interpersonal nature of performance. "In the *Bed Piece* it was like I was this repulsive magnet. People would come up to about 15 feet from the bed and you could really feel it. There was an energy, a real electricity going on," describes Burden.[11]

---

[10] Adrian Searle, "Pope.L review – sublime shipwreck misses its crawling captain," *The Guardian*, 23 november 2023, www.theguardian. com/artanddesign/2023/nov/23/pope-l-review-south-london-gallery.

[11] Quoted in Robert Horvitz, "Chris Burden," *Artforum* XIV, No. 9 (May 1976).

HOW
TO REST

At the time of the free dormitory, de Appel invited Flash Art editor Helena Kortova to share her reflections on Mlčoch's practice. She pointed out his interest in both isolation and interpersonal connection. "The works of Chris Burden were particularly decisive in opening up the entire new world of performance to him. However, his own personal experiments with this expressive form were preceded by a long period of keeping a personal diary, recording experiences, events and dreams which prove remarkably similar to his later work in performance." According to Kortova, the diary notes slowly turned into art pieces, with his first 'piece' executed in solitude, unencumbered by an audience, while it was a "step towards overcoming his total isolation, towards sharing his private existence with the outside world."[12]

Kortova's description notably reflects on an essential component of performance: the relation to the, at times, fragile intimacy of the individual body of the performer and the presence of an audience. Rest is about the physical body, but also about negotiating your own space and time in relation to others, what is yours and what are the   projections and desires of others. Can isolation be a   form of rest? With our modern-day tendency to   fill every minute of the day with activities, scrolling,   absorbing, and producing images, what can we do differently?

....

[12] Letter written by Helena Kortova to de Appel, titled *Between isolation and aggression*, no date.

Whereas Mlčoch proposed an alternative function for the gallery – a place to sleep or rest – and a place to be together, Burden maintained the gallery's usual character as a contemplative space, with himself as the art on view. These propositions exemplify distinct ways performance can question regular uses of our time and attention: two aspects of daily life that are under the influence of a perform-economy pressuring us to deliver, especially in the art world, at all times and at all costs.[13]

An artist whose work encapsulates this condition of our lives today is British artist Abbas Zahedi. In his minimalist installations, he plays with the architectural functions of gallery spaces to create situations that integrate both contemplation and interpersonal connection. Through gestures that centre on the relationship between space, artwork, and body, and between institution and public, Zahedi proposes the gallery as a place where visitors consciously spend time with their emotions, a space for reflection, where they feel supported and connected, by and with each other.

....

[13] During a discussion at de Appel, cultural critic Jan Verwoert argued that everything revolves around delivering, especially in the art world. "We have to deliver at all times, at all costs. Therefore, we perform as hell, causing exhaustion that ends up being the single thing that drives our perform-economy." Corrine van Emmerik, "The exhaustion of being nice," *Metropolis M*, 21 April 2017, metropolism.com/nl/recensie/31352_de_appel_why_so_nice.

In the midst of the Covid lockdown, when galleries were, without hesitation, dismissed as being non-essential and thus closed down, Zahedi proposed to open his site-specific exhibition in central London to frontline workers. As a result, doctors, nurses, and public transport staff – arguably those that are amongst the most essential to society – were able to visit the gallery where they could decompress and have a moment of rest, alone or with one another. A proposition that questions whom and what the exhibition space is really for, who is truly welcome to cross its threshold.[14]

....

[14] In another work, titled *Waiting With {Sonic Support}*, Zahedi similarly explored questions of exclusion and inclusion, by creating an open mic installation at the entrance of the Frieze Art Fair, where participants' contributions could be heard inside the fair. By participating, they received a VIP entry ticket normally reserved for art collectors.

PERFORMANCE,
LIFE

At a time of capitalist co-option of everything that relates to the Self, from self-care to meditation to intimacy, it is important and urgent to consciously create space to just feel, to hold each other, to be with your emotions, as Zahedi proposes. I think performance is the ultimate form to address this urgency of the emotional and the intimate in art. Performance and artistic propositions that employ performative elements (audience participation, for example), have the capacity to make viewers reflect on how we behave and relate to one another in a specific context, and how this, in turn, is reflected in the space outside of it – in social and political realities of the everyday, shaped by the performativity of our words and actions. At the same time, in a reality where individual performance is constantly measured, above all in a working context, performing rest can be a radical act.

By discussing various live works and interventions engaging rest and sleep, I have tried to draw attention to the ways performance can instigate both an intimate experience of the self and one's body, and an experience of being part of a collective, even if temporarily. I believe it is through this combination of the individual and the collective body that performance can be an effective strategy for rethinking systems and spaces in various intersecting ways – physically, mentally, socially, and politically.

Despite the fact that performance, as a form, is in line with (or a product of?) our current stage of capitalism characterized by the commodification of immaterial experiences and activities, its potential for critique may lie in how it can simultaneously divert focus from the individual Self (the Self as entirely responsible for its own livelihood) towards the collective, and bring attention to the individual body and its need for rest.

With this in mind, I think the free dormitory project at de Appel still holds relevance today. Ironically, the piece turned out to be Mlčoch's departure from the art scene, as he was disillusioned with performance becoming part of the art world's modus operandi, being institutionalized in prestigious galleries and international festivals. It was for this reason that, when offered the gallery presentation in Amsterdam, he decided to put the space to practical use. As Czech art historian Pavlína Morganová reflects: "With this symbolic gesture Mlčoch ended his career as an action artist and began to fully focus on life, which sometimes can be more difficult than the most dangerous performance."[15]

---

[15] Pavlína Morganová, *Czech Action Art – Happenings, Actions, Events, Land Art, Body Art and Performance Art Behind the Iron Curtain*, (Prague: Karolinum Press, 2015), 181.

FINNEGAN SHANNON

Do You Want Us Here or Not Drawings

18:35

Walking and standing are hard on my body, so I am very attuned to seating options as I move through the world. I'm always looking for spots to stop and rest. I made these drawings in 2017 after a particularly painful and tiring museum outing. I was frustrated with the scarcity of seating and realized that making artworks that are also functional benches is one way to get more seating into exhibition spaces. The text is a way of channelling some of my frustration and playfully draws attention to the way that the act of sitting itself expresses a need or desire for rest.

My background is in printmaking and drawing and, at the time, my primary ways of working (though drawing continues to be the tool I reach for when I am thinking through an idea). I immediately wanted to make these into actual three-dimensional seating objects, but it would take me over a year to figure out even the basics of how a bench could be built. In the meantime, I circulated these drawings as a zine. Conversations and reactions from friends and colleagues catalysed my interest in seating, and the seed of what is shown here has now grown into a variety of seating experiments around the world.

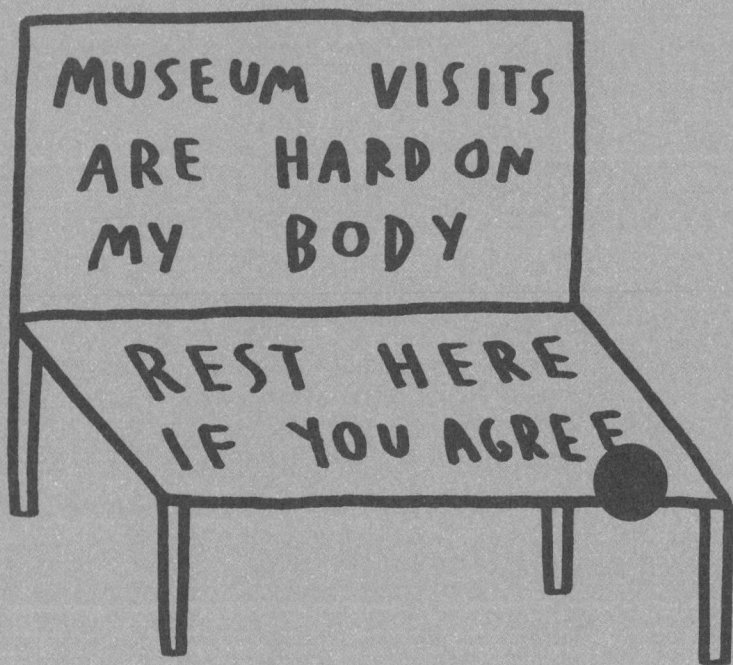

MUSEUM VISITS
ARE HARD ON
MY BODY

REST HERE
IF YOU AGREE

insert title here Or How I Feel Like I Get Nothing Done

The art world we form and frame is something rarely discussed in the written word, but a very popular topic of gossip and complaints amongst cultural workers. We often exchange our dissatisfaction with ways of communication, unfair disappointment with limited personal connections, inability to change the structures in which we function, and lack of funding for 'proper' research. Still, we continue doing the same things in the same ways – over and over and over and over again: curating a solo show based merely on a short conversation with an artist here, writing a text referencing buzz literature we only scanned through there. Sometimes, we even accept unpaid portfolio reviews at privately funded educational facilities, and at other times, we push ourselves over the edge for small-scale grant applications. And I never know why I do these things. Will they actually pay off at some point? Will I be able to live a safe and comfortable life working in this field? Will my body forgive me for working it 24/7?

I have noticed an insane amount of what I can only imagine is 'imposter syndrome' and an underlying need for validation from my peers, colleagues, friends, partners, etc. And it's not because of neediness or because we were 'all told we were special' when we were younger. It's because of a simple mathematical equation even I – *mit kein* tolerance for any mathematics – have to acknowledge.

INPUT > OUTPUT

We work too much and produce too much, yet we're embedded in a system that does not have time to think about the output. We get minimal satisfaction and community-produced validation for our work and efforts. We research, create artworks, set up exhibitions, write texts, give talks, facilitate workshops, and ignore our personal lives to build up our professional ones. The activities, operations, and communities that we once thought made the art world distinct and memorable have given way to a pervasive routinization of its norms and procedures.[1]

So, in the midst of hyper-production and heavy bureaucratization, we complain. It is, as Sara Ahmed puts it, a form of protest or outcry and a way to express grief, pain, dissatisfaction, and bodily ailments. She frames its potential to reveal institutional mechanics and the reproduction of systems within institutions. Complaints can serve as a way to challenge power dynamics, address inequalities, and push for a more just and equal world.[2]

Many have called for change, for slowing down. Lutz Koepnick suggests one can embrace lifestyle choices like supporting local food movements and enjoying leisurely meals, practising meditation for relaxation, promoting walkable urban environments, and seeking alternative travel options; focusing on calmness and repose, and finding ways to fully engage with the present moment. Slowing down isn't about rejecting progress, but about appreciating life's richness and complexity. Koepnick already implies that the ability to embrace slowness is a lifestyle choice of the economically privileged.[3] But will this assist us in changing the way we work, especially if it is only possible for the privileged few? Slowing down only means we're getting to the outcome slower, but we still need to get there, no? And can we make progress without being pressured towards an output?

....

[1] Pamela Lee, *Forgetting the Art World* (Cambridge: MIT Press, 2012).

[2] Sara Ahmed, *Complaint!* (New York: Duke University Press, 2021).

[3] Lutz Koepnick, *On Slowness: Toward an Aesthetic of the Contemporary* (New York: Columbia University Press, 2014).

My question revolves around reimagining this output-oriented way of acknowledgement into a productive and safer environment that favours process over product on an institutional and communal level. This should, in theory, create safer working environments by incorporating space and time for reflection, introspection, and connection. We indulge in setting up exhibitions and projects that are formatted for communities of cultural workers, symposiums, temporary libraries, or resting/co-working spaces, while aiming to communicate knowledge and tools for visitors/viewers/participants.[4] We even see an increase in non-output-oriented residencies, etc.[5] But at the end of the day, we are rushing. Not engaging, connecting. We're pitching. We're not sitting with the material, but scanning it briefly, skimming over it – be it literature, artworks, catalogues, or novels. We don't spend enough time fact-checking, and we rarely get to write texts as we plan to write them. In all the seriousness of what we create, did we forget how to have fun – or, as Martin Herbert recently put it: "Are we having fun yet? If not, there's still work to do."[6]

....

[4] Binna Choi, Annette Krauss, Yolande van der Heide, and Liz Allan, eds., *Unlearning Exercises: Art Organizations as Sites of Unlearning* (Amsterdam: Valiz, 2018); See: Vesna Bukovec, Tia Čiček, and Ana Čigon's artistic research event "Nocturnalities: Bargaining Beyond Rest" during the exhibition *Work in Progress. Reflections on Communities Beyond Capitalism* curated by Andrea Knezović at Škuc Gallery, www.galerijaskuc.si/exhibition/work-in-progress-reflections-on-communities-beyond-capitalism.

[5] Taru Elfving, Irmeli Kokko, and Pascal Gielen, eds., *Contemporary Artist Residencies. Reclaiming Time and Space* (Amsterdam: Valiz, 2019); for example, 1646 – ReCNTR RESIDENCY. Open call, February 2024, 1646.nl/1646-recntr.

[6] Martin Herbert, "Is Contemporary Art a Pleasure-Free Zone?," *ArtReview*, 6 March, 2024, artreview.com/is-contemporary-art-a-pleasure-free-zone-martin-herbert.

Material and immaterial infrastructures must be addressed to ensure safer working environments in the art world. Making funding schemes, connections with individuals and organizations, and knowledge and inspiration sources visible and transparent, are inherent ways of addressing them. This then promotes implementing policies for fair compensation, providing access to resources and support networks, and promoting diversity and inclusion. Clear guidelines for ethical conduct and open communication are also essential.[7] For example: ensuring that everyone involved knows their cooperators understand project timelines, financial capabilities, and distribution; scheduling regular check-ins to allow safe space for reflection and dialogue; while at the same time trying to understand the complexities and vulnerability of individuals' lives. I believe we will find ourselves no longer in managerial roles – aiming to keep projects on track – but in nurturing roles, where we aim for community and individual safety, growth and fulfilment. Integrating these elements into the art world's infrastructure can create a more sustainable and equitable ecosystem for artistic practice and exchange.

....

[7] Karin Zitzewitz, "Infrastructure as Form," *Third Text* 31, no. 2-3 (October 2017): 341–358, doi.org/10.1080/09528822.2017.1380984.

COMMUNITY > INSTITUTION

Does the road forward demand vast institutional reorganization? Bojana Kunst suggests transforming artistic institutions to prioritize solidarity and stability over perpetuating feelings of powerlessness and instability. Cultural workers are encouraged to critically analyse their working conditions, challenge neoliberal ideals of creativity and flexibility, and advocate for fair wages and benefits through collective organizing. This involves engaging with the public sphere to highlight the importance of art in shaping social discourse and resisting prevailing structures of exploitation and precarity. At the same time, we need to emphasize the need for a re-evaluation of artistic work's value that is separate from elite consumption, and the preservation of artistic procedures in the public sphere. Additionally, we must underscore the importance of critical, theoretical reflection to counteract banal conformity and foster intellectual discourse in contemporary culture.[8] Institutions in general, as well as cultural ones, should embrace vulnerability as a means to disrupt the normalization of precarity and challenge dominant social governance. They should restructure as entities akin to plants, deeply rooted in their communities. This rootedness might foster genuine connections and confront the prevailing culture of self-protection. Furthermore, institutions should prioritize community needs over self-interest and aim to foster genuine social engagement.[9]

---

[8] Bojana Kunst. *Artist at Work, Proximity of Art and Capitalism* (Alresford: Zero Books, 2015).

[9] Bojana Kunst. "The Institution between Precarization and Participation," *Performance Research 20*, no. 4 (September 2015): 6-13, doi.org/10.1080/13528165.2015.1071032.

As ever-present and, at times, frowned upon discourses which can provide genuine social engagement, I would argue that queer and feminist methodologies offer valuable frameworks for cultural workers to create safer and more sustainable working methods. These frameworks affect conditions when implemented in actual artwork/exhibition/knowledge production structures: for example, queer methodologies prioritize inclusivity, diversity, and social justice by challenging traditional norms and power structures. If we are constantly aware of the frameworks that limit us, cultural workers can utilize collaborative methods, such as co-creating artworks, exhibitions, events, and knowledge, with individuals and communities to promote diversity and advocate for marginalized voices. Autoethnography allows cultural workers to represent various identities and narratives through authentic personal reflections. It also involves conducting research that focuses on the experiences, using methods like participant observation and interviews with community round tables, challenging traditional power structures and producing knowledge that reflects power dynamics in the contemporary art sphere. Incorporating various voices into exhibition-making and event production encourages reflexivity and positionality, aiding cultural workers in recognizing biases and privileges for more ethical and equitable practices. By not only promoting inclusivity, diversity, and social justice, and challenging unequal societal power relations within exhibitions, events and artworks; but also implementing these methodologies as part of the process of exhibition/event-creating/artwork, we will ensure safer and more sustainable working environments than if we are only viewing the impacts of the final form. This way, we would satisfy the overall need to consider the intersections of gender, race, class, and other social identities in art production, to create inclusive representations and participation, as well as challenge unequal power relations.[10]

....

[10] Catherine J. Nash and Kath Browne, *Queer Methods and Methodologies. Intersecting Queer Theories and Social Science Research* (New York: Routledge, 2016); Zara Saeidzadeh, "Gender Research and Feminist Methodologies," in *Gender-Competent Legal Education. Springer Textbooks in Law*, eds. Dragica Vujadinović, Mareike Fröhlich, and Thomas Giegerich (Cham: Springer International Publishing, 2023), 183–213.

CULTURAL WORKER > CURATOR/ARTIST

The act of examining and redefining cultural work brings forth the examination and redefinition of the cultural worker itself. Be it curators, artists, producers, dramaturgs, or directors, no single person can create an artwork by themselves. At the very least, we reference a book our friends gushed over, and at most, we are embedded in complex structures, or presenting our work to audiences in/outside institutional spaces. The role of the curator is elusive yet highly definitive. They can be a collaborator, promoter, personal therapist, friend, agent, writer, reader; the list goes on and on. The curator's role and tasks really come down to the individual and the communities from which they come, and usually demand more from them than they are capable of giving. Filling so many roles makes them tired but excited, hyperactive yet a perpetuum mobile of consuming and outputting. Don't you dare fall asleep at the wheel; the car itself may just stop existing. Thankfully, the future curator may be envisioned as a facilitator of impactful artistic experiences, advocating for experimentation and inclusivity while addressing systemic issues in the art world.[11] However, the most beneficial role the curator might take on is that of a cultural worker. A worker in and for culture – not one limited by the borders of its nation, but one embedded in fluid and growing communities facing difficulties and celebrating accomplishments along the way.

······················· > ·······················

[11] Manoel Silvestre Friques and Renan Laru-an, "Curators Must Stay Different," interview by Ruth Noack, *open! Platform for Art, Culture & the Public Domain*, 3 December, 2015, onlineopen.org/curators-must-stay-different.

Improving the safety of cultural workers means addressing the instability of freelance and project-based artistic labour. This involves providing stable working conditions, long-term planning, social security, and fair funding, and acknowledging the importance of self-organization and collective action within artistic networks to resist exploitation and maintain autonomy. Today's unsafe conditions for cultural workers stem from post-Fordist labour paradigms prioritizing flexibility and mobility, leading to dependence on temporary projects.[12] This brings us back to the inherent need to change how we do things – how we communicate, write, read, travel, engage, listen, and connect. On the journey from guilds to self-employed individuals, we have lost our humanity, and we have aimed to become the machines/AI that we now fear will replace us. We have strived for so long to become perfect in everything we do; we forget that imperfections are what make us unique.

Failing, breaking, erasing, rethinking, reformatting, and more – all of these should be constant in our practices as cultural workers. To find alternative ways of working and living, we have to unlearn patterns of work and adopt other ways of receiving, sharing, and constructing knowledge. Our inherent striving for 'perfection' must be replaced by the principles of openness, adaptation, and acceptance – in the final phase, even recovery – which we have to understand as central to restructuring a harmful value system in which we are stuck.

Cultural workers unite.

....

[12] Jonas Tinius, "Between Professional Precariousness and Creative Self-Organization. The Free Performing Arts Scene in Germany," in *Mobile Autonomy: Exercises in Artists' Self-organization*, eds. Nico Dockx and Pascal Gielen (Amsterdam: Valiz, 2015), 171-193.

Tracing Lines of Support (An Ongoing Story)

All one can say is, first, that an infrastructure is defined by use and movement; second, that resilience and repair don't necessarily neutralise the problem.
– Lauren Berlant[1]

CERVICAL

Working in art education and artistic practice overall, I have recently started hearing from more and more colleagues and friends that their freelance contracts are being handled by outsourced companies. The names of these automatized 'human resource' platforms often include the word 'flex.' Not long ago, I also started a new, temporary, job in education where I had to deal with that kind of structure. It was the first time I heard of the name of the platform. Not a single document was handed over to me directly, nor did I speak to anyone in person. The interface was there for my flex colleagues and me. While I was filling in my personal details, I imagined tiny anthropomorphic figures jumping around doing artistic gymnastics, figures with malleable spines, who could be bent into a U shape.

....

[1] Lauren Berlant, "The commons: Infrastructures for troubling times*," *Environment and Planning D: Society and Space* 34, no. 3 (2016), 393.

Where in any other art work the existence of a minimum structure would have helped in securing fluid freelance working 'agreements' by documenting and acknowledging invisible labour, this resembled a kind of dystopian version of anonymity. While I received a couple of user manuals to follow in order to receive my salary, everything that was not in there was meant to remain unspoken. Despite being an art institution dedicated to education, the human interaction involved was very poor: where there would have otherwise been an HR employee to talk to, the webpage only made clear that questions are not meant to be asked. The sole responsibility belongs, then, to the hands of the art worker/self-employer/performer. There is nothing flexible about it, except for my spine dreaming of artistic gymnastics.

Flexibility, as the adaptability of workers and learners, is judged on their mobility in the labour market and between businesses, institutions, and/or freelance workplaces. This moving or being moved readily from place to place, across time, of being available 24/7 requires a high level of "workforce versatility."
– Annette Krauss[2]

After endless stomach adventures, food going up and down my oesophagus and acidic liquids haunting the back of my throat, I finally had to discover one more part of the human body. Thanks to my osteopath's brilliance, far from any experience of cold men's orthopaedic hands, I came to meet my vagus nerve. The longest nerve of the human body, the vagus nerve runs across the neck having a big impact on the heart, lungs, and digestive tract.

I want to befriend that nerve.

....

[2] Annette Krauss, "Lifelong Learning and the Professionalised Learner," in *Unlearning Exercises, Art Organisations as Sites of Unlearning* (Amsterdam: Valiz, Casco Art Institute: Working for the Commons, 2018), 81.

THORACIC

A vague but still very clear memory of my teenage years is when I had my first – long-anticipated – moment of physical proximity with a same aged teen. It was one of the most confronting moments of my life so far, even more than a (first!) kiss, to no fault of the person involved. As we got closer during the evening, on the balcony of our classmate's house, he reached out to hold my waist but found a different texture than expected.

A thick layer of plastic was protecting my core. A corset of sorts, holding me tightly and tied behind my back with polyester strips. While I am trying to bring this experience back visually and put it into words, I struggle to find the embodied terms. I want to see that image again, so I google what I think its name could be but find only elegant BDSM-like elastic bands. I search for the ugly massive prosthetic with harsh metal bars with no immediate results. Or did I remember it wrongly, the disproportionate scale created by my young body's memory? I end up on orthopaedic websites where I endlessly scroll through the online fashionable designs instead of digging deeper into my own image of my reflection. I remember the boy's hands getting stopped from touching me further or longer and his frozen awkward face moving back. But that is not where I am heading with this text. The point I am trying to make here while writing in yet another uncomfortable sitting position is how I spent five or six formative years of my young self held by a structure that was supposed to correct my dangerously crooked spine, all the while pushing bit by bit, nanometre by nanometre, day and night, towards a space of breathlessness. Besides the difficulty in breathing, anxiety issues, loss of emotional self, and extreme containment or claustrophobia, I felt held by something bigger than me. When looking back, I find it interesting to think about how the biggest part of this procedure of spine correction was the personal responsibility that came with it. The more I was able to contain and tolerate the physical pain and self-discipline, the bigger and more satisfying the outcome I would enjoy in the future. The more I would sacrifice my body autonomy and social life, the more I would gain in future body autonomy, reproductive capacity, and so on and so forth. It was only very late in my adult professional life that such a rigid structure became a point of reference in understanding embodied experiences of work, leisure, and intimacy.

The vagus nerve(s) serves as the body's superhighway, carrying information between the brain and the internal organs and controlling the body's response in times of rest and relaxation. The large nerve originates in the brain and branches out in multiple directions to the neck and torso, where it's responsible for actions such as carrying sensory information from the skin of the ear, controlling the muscles that you use to swallow and speak and influencing the immune system.[3]

Its parasympathetic character helps us rest, digest, and restore.

I want to befriend that nerve.

LUMBAR

Some years ago, I had the chance to closely follow the work *Molecular Love: (Mestizo) Act 3* by Mercedes Azpilicueta. While coordinating and building up the work in the exhibition that she was part of in Berlin at the Times Art Center, I also prepared the performance on behalf of Mercedes. Several times throughout the rehearsals we played the sonic composition (made by Mercedes in collaboration with Constanza Castagnet) that accompanied the two performers moving through the space amidst the textile installation. Although the performance does not explicitly address questions of labour, it still always insinuates it by thinking with bodily exhaustions within domestic and other types of reproductive work. Mercedes' voice would be heard singing:

----

[3] "Vagus Nerve." *Physiopedia*, www.physio-pedia.com/Vagus_Nerve.

A body is never one
I have a curved back
I am nervous, you are relaxed
A body is never one

You asked me if I write
I say sometimes, sometimes
[...][4]

Echoing these sentences here, they are so close to me. Each single line, if it were a text, would be a new chapter of a book about feminized notions of labour. Within the broad range of art work that I have been doing in the past eight years, I have been called to meet and adjust to multiple working conditions, which necessitate one essential requirement: a sturdy back to lean on. Since day one of practising freelance thinking and making, I constantly move around with a computer hanging from my shoulders. Whether this is to bring it to a workplace or do any freelance work (writing, coordinating, teaching, curating...), the computer – meaning, my entire office – is the continuation of my back and brain. As long as it comes with me, I can be productive and deliver work, or at least in 97 per cent of the cases. This is not new for most of the readers of this text, rather, a very common shared experience of freelance travelling/ work efficiency.

....

[4] Mercedes Azpilicueta, excerpt from the script of *Molecular Love: (Mestizo) Act 3*, 2021.

Mercedes Azpilicueta, *Molecular Love: (Mestizo) Act 3*, installation view at Times Art Center Berlin, 2021. Photo by Yozy Zhang.

I haven't really dived into the statistics of the amount of people that experience serious back problems causing chronic pain and obstacles in adapting to the above lifestyle, it's anyway hard for me to visualize in numbers. However, in the past few years since I officially started working as a freelance worker, I have been observing more and more the multiplicity of sitting locations and positions I have been adopting in order to be able to make a – bare – living. During five to seven days of work per week, I find myself working on my feet, on several beds, on multiple chair designs of which 99,99 per cent are not meant for people to sit on comfortably – like the very one I am sitting on as I am typing this – where I can stay seated for no more than fifteen minutes without being aware of my back's complaints.

Vagus means wandering in Latin and is where the words vagrant, vagabond and vague come from. The name reflects the long pathway and extensive branching of our vagus nerves.
– Theresa Larkin[5]

While thinking of the spine as the core structure of the body, one cannot ignore another long line that runs in parallel to it.

---

[5] Theresa Larkin, "The vagus nerves help us rest, digest and restore. Can you really reset them to feel better?" *ABC News*, 26 August 2023, www.abc.net.au/news/2023-08-26/vagus-nerves-rest-digest-nervous-system-regulation/102771178.

SACRAL

How my spine's support has been tied to my performance
as a flex-ed art worker and therefore success (survival?),
is of central examination here. I grew up convinced by my
orthopaedist that when I would be over thirty I would have
a curved back preventing me from having a normal life (they
were right), I would not be able to give birth without being stuck
in bed for more than nine months with acute back pain (this
I still have to find out), and I would never have a life at all
unless I would go swimming every day for the next – back then
– fifty years (during the summer months I swim in the ocean,
but during the winter I only went swimming once).

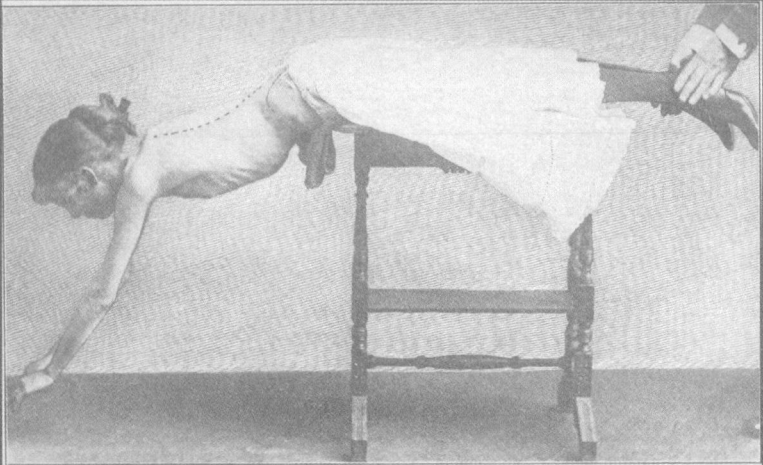

Royal Whitman, *A Treatise on Orthopedic Surgery*
(Philadelphia and New York: Lea & Febiger, 1910),
archive.org/details/treatiseonorthop1910whit.

The vague but material memory of the misogynistic and
highly hostile culture of the paediatric orthopaedist, became
very concrete in a cold basement in the Pagrati neighbourhood
of Athens, in the lab of a man of few words who made two casts
of my thorax once every two years.

The more I try to reconstruct the image of that basement, the more I remember my youth's trembling body lying naked on a 40 cm-wide bed, while being wrapped by the man's big, seasoned hands distributing the wet plaster on my body. While waiting for the plaster to dry, talking or breathing had to be minimized. The discomfort of being touched in that way, of the matter drying up on one's skin while in stillness, causing more stillness, alongside the temperature and lighting of that room, will not be forgotten. Once the plaster was dry, he would then carefully cut the corset by drawing a vertical line with a knife, creating a cast for the new thorax prosthetic. On the same day or the next, I went to the National Gallery with my parents to adore naked Venus' bodies by the hands of Botticelli and friends, while the spring of 2004 was blooming in the city.

COCCYGEAL

Over the past years, I have sat in many cheap chairs owned by my temporary employers, or better, clients. Not cheap in terms of pricing, that I cannot tell. Cheap in terms of welcoming. On the other hand, I have always looked down on the hyper-anatomical office chairs on wheels where you can technically stay seated in front of a screen for twelve hours without noticing. This is too much of a corporate aesthetic for the 'kind of work that I do.' Uncomfortable chairs make me want to get up, or just take a break, and at least I don't need to invest in a chair that will keep me seated and therefore at work. Stools, benches, beds, couches, armchairs, camping chairs, chaise longues, and all kinds of other sitting structures have been hosting my back and my tail, always keeping in mind the temporary solution of the freelance gigs.

In her essay "Exergue," artist Céline Condorelli analyses how support often "wrongly appears as both supplementary and valueless."[6] Condorelli's text takes as a starting point the photos of Adam Broomberg and Oliver Chanarin taken in 2004 in Milo (which happens to be a place that is very dear to me) that document the hundreds of scaffoldings preventing – temporarily – the buildings from falling down two years after the catastrophic earthquake. The scaffoldings, or 'puntellamenti' in Italian, are touching the precarious buildings with the tips of the timber beams. In Condorelli's words: "the scaffolding props up and works to avoid or at least delay the process of failure and collapse. [...] The scaffolding works by trying to compensate for the sheer inability of a building structure to move and adapt to the forces around and within it, an impossibility suddenly made visible but yet always present and threatening beneath the surface of things."[7] I go back to the semi-constructed image of my corset, trying to picture it as hundreds of fingertips pressing my spine and shoulder blades. The cold hands of the man in the laboratory suddenly become soft warm fingers that hold me steady and safe.

The uncomfortable chairs, leading to future X-rays and osteopath visits, and the crooked spine are a constant reminder that support becomes "a moment of pure potential."[8] While turning to my teenage self, I gain and give them comfort that not everything is their own responsibility. And that one should hold each other not only with our labours but during rest as well.

....

[6] Céline Condorelli, "Exergue," in *Support Structures*, eds. Céline Condorelli and Gavin Wade with James Langdon, (Berlin: Sternberg Press, 2009).

[7] Ibid.

[8] Ibid., 397.

Against Mindfulness

States of Anxiety, Minds for Community[1]

At the core of public health lies the formation of the state. Some of its aspects align with Aristotle's views, considering the state as a polis formed for sociability and the common good. Other facets, darker yet more tangible in historical perspective, resonate with Thomas Hobbes' *Leviathan*; a state depicted as a fearsome whale instilling fear and anxiety to prevent chaos and war of everyone against everyone.

....

[1]This chapter summarizes a fragment from my research project *States of Anxiety, Minds for Care* (2019-2020). I aimed to examine mental health as a consequence of the social and political organization of a community. Supported by BAK, basis voor actuele kunst fellowship, I delved into the intricate relationship between mental health and the broader societal and political context. I deeply thank BAK, basis voor actuele kunst, and Maria Hlavajova personally for making this research possible.

In the era of late capitalism, the model for social organization originates in the corporate sector. North American corporate culture significantly influences communication, lifestyle choices, and the 'effective' use of time and space in all spheres of life, all over the world as far as capitalism reaches. Care of the Self has become a commodity intertwined with the notion of human capital. Referring to the spread of so-called entrepreneurship culture, the late Mark Fisher – who himself suffered from depression and imposter syndrome – wrote: "Each individual member of the subordinate class is encouraged into feeling that their poverty, lack of opportunities, or unemployment, is their fault and their fault alone."[2] However, the costs associated with healthcare, particularly mental health, are often left unaddressed. The shift towards private responsibility over collective support is evident in areas like insurance, pensions, and even familial relationships, which are increasingly framed as entrepreneurial ventures, where contracts, budgets, and financial responsibilities are strictly defined.

[2] Mark Fisher, "Good For Nothing," *The Occupied Times*, 19 March 2014, theoccupiedtimes.org/?p=12841.

In his essay "Beyond Satire: The Political Comedy of the Present and the Paradoxes of Authority," drawing inspiration from Dominiek Hoen's work on capitalism and religion, Aaron Schuster emphasizes the precarious nature of labour within the debt economy: One actively strives to include oneself in a system which, by default, one falls outside of.[3] This struggle leads to a sense of gratitude for the simple manifestations of professional recognition, such as getting a job or a project, intertwined with an inherent feeling of guilt. In this paradigm, individuals are compelled to focus on self-improvement and mental health, driven by an infinite debt incurred by the logic of the economic system. For instance, in the art world, the tacit understanding is that recognition from the institution comes with a sense of indebtedness. After submitting a large number of job applications, one finally secures a position as a curator, triumphing over hundreds of international candidates. In such a scenario, not everyone possesses the resilience to negotiate their (often inherently unjust) contract terms, or confront the ethical practices of the institution regarding subcontractors and artists. For artists, receiving an invitation to partake in an institutional project or a fellowship holds immense significance, often rendering them hesitant to address their unfair working conditions. It remains uncommon to receive invitation emails that explicitly outline all aspects of the proposed work, including the fee.

....

[3] Aaron Schuster, "Beyond Satire: The Political Comedy of the Present and the Paradoxes of Authority," in *Sovereignty, Inc. Three Inquiries in Politics and Enjoyment*, eds. William Mazzarella, Eric L. Santner, and Aaron Schuster (Chicago: Chicago University Press, 2020).

The intricate relationship between human capital and time emerges as a crucial factor. Time appears as both a luxury and a scarce resource. It embodies the potential for choice, decision-making, and control, highlighting its significance in navigating the complex landscape of contemporary mental survival. This perception of time becomes entwined with the concepts of mindfulness and the medicalization of emotion. The neoliberal emphasis on individual agency and responsibility positions time as the means to exercise greater control over one's life. Simultaneously, scarcity of time arises as societal pressures and demands create a time deficit for many, intensifying the challenges of achieving mindful reflection and emotional well-being within the constraints of a fast-paced, competitive environment.

Within this logic, individuals are often perceived as either functional or dysfunctional mechanisms, as British psychologist David Smail outlined in his book *Why Therapy Doesn't Work*. The pursuit of mental health is framed as ensuring the efficient functioning of the individual machine, with sports, mindfulness, the 'here and now' approach, and self-help books providing socially condoned forms of therapy for individuals who are always at risk of breaking down.[4]

----

[4] David Smail, *Why Therapy Doesn't Work*, 1st ed. (London: Taylor & Francis Ltd, 2015).

While maintaining a healthy lifestyle is no doubt something positive, the commodification of wellness reflects a competitive corporate impulse. Gyms are not merely places for exercise, but arenas for dietary and sports challenges, turning personal health into an achievement. Gyms and health centres often employ 'challenges' as a promotional tactic. These typically involve participating in specific types of competitions, like running, rowing, or weightlifting. Participants can compete with a friend, bring a colleague, or join open group challenges. For gyms, this marketing strategy serves to foster self-esteem, consistency, and motivation, and as a result maintain retention among club members. However, medical research dating back to the 1970s indicates that integrating competition into daily routines has contributed to the spread of anxiety and depression.[5] Today, mental health issues escalate as social networks amplify anxiety by spreading the achievement and happiness competition globally. It is easy to represent an idealized image of one's life via social media platforms and therefore potentially evoke in others unpleasant feelings of envy, lowering self-esteem, and fostering discomfort and general dissatisfaction with life.[6]

Popular mindfulness advocates like Jon Kabat-Zinn and Eckhart Tolle suggest living in the present and disengaging from the toxicity of the world. While often beneficial on an individual level in times of mental despair, their advice neglects the social dimension of community, mutual engagement, and the long-term perspective for social change.

....

[5] William Davies, *The Happiness Industry: How Government and Business Sold Us Well-being* (London: Verso, 2015).

[6] Philippe Verduyn et al., "Social comparison on social networking sites," *Current Opinion in Psychology 36* (2020): 32-37, doi.org/10.1016/j. copsyc.2020.04.002.

ANXIETY
IN THE WHITE CUBE

Labour in the art sector can be seen as an extremely concentrated example of the above-mentioned problematic dynamics. Historically, artists depended on support from the state, church, or elites. Apart from the church, the rest is still the case. The funding of art is not that visible in times of relative peace, but in times of conflict, war, or political turbulence, patrons start appearing from behind the scenes to demand a specific position, submission, or even silence.

In the last decades of neoliberal framing, art labour has been made into a form of entrepreneurship, thus creating the prospect of a realistic possibility of living from one's art/creative practice. Cultural workers in the Netherlands, led and supported by Platform BK, have been advocating for fair working conditions and remuneration.[7] In the last few years, they have achieved significant results such as formulating and spreading the usage of the Artist Fee Guideline and Calculator.[8] The majority of art institutions in the Netherlands are now following the Fair Practice Code, co-initiated by Platform BK. In Norway, the Norwegian Association of Curators went even further and developed legal descriptions of curatorial practice, guidelines for curatorial wages, and a dream contract for curators, along with other useful resources concerning the legal and economic aspects of curatorial practice.[9]

....

[7] Platform BK is a membership-based association of artists, curators, designers, critics and other cultural producers. It researches the role of art in society and takes action for a better art policy. See: www.platformbk.nl/en.

[8] "Kunstenaarshonorarium," kunstenaarshonorarium.nl/en.

[9] "Wages," The Norwegian Association of Curators, www.norskkuratorforening.no/wages; "Dream Contract for Curators," The Norwegian Association of Curators, www.norskkuratorforening.no/dream-contract-for-curators.

According to a report by the Dutch Centraal Bureau voor de Statistiek published in February 2023, there were around 13,000 visual artists in the Netherlands in the period 2017–2019. Around 35 per cent find themselves in a comfortable financial position, 32 per cent call their financial state reasonable, and 33 per cent call their income moderate or bad.[10] That doesn't sound too bad, but as William Davies argues, in the current system winners suffer too.[11] Any level of success in the cultural sector is often intertwined with high competition and precarity. The relentless pace leaves little room for breaks, parental time, leisure time, non-productive, and sick time. The majority of artists, driven by passion, find themselves working long hours, evenings, nights, and sacrificing personal time for fragile career prospects.

....

[10] "Monitor Kunstenaars en andere werkenden met een creatief beroep," Centraal Bureau voor de Statistiek, www.cbs.nl/nl-nl/dossier/dossier-culturele-en-creatieve-sector/monitor-kunstenaars-en-andere-werkenden-met-een-creatief-beroep.

[11] Davies, *The Happiness Industry*.

In recent years, partially influenced by the global pandemic and partially by general labour fatigue, the arts sector has seen a trend toward creating experiential spaces that incorporate mindfulness practices.[12] Yoga, meditation, Pilates, breathing exercises, and colour therapy have found their way into art spaces and art education environments, challenging the traditional sterility of white cubes and intellectual set-ups of art schools. The 2023 exhibition *84 Steps* at Melly in Rotterdam, featuring amongst other works meditation and relaxation spaces, exemplifies this shift. Another trend is the appropriation of activist and queer self-care exercises. Curatorial projects such as *Sick Time, Sleepy Time, Crip Time: Against Capitalism's Temporal Bullying* (various locations in the USA) by recent Jan van Eyck Academy fellow, curator, researcher, and educator Taraneh Fazeli, are made to feature artist resistance practices against the commodification of wellness. It includes, for instance, references to politics of rest. Another example is *Black Power Naps*; a sculptural installation, vibrational device, and curatorial initiative that takes its inspiration and point of departure from "historical records that show that deliberate fragmentation of restorative sleep patterns were used to subjugate and extract labour from enslaved people and reclaims laziness and idleness as power."[13]

----

[12] Mindfulness practices are usually considered as practices of self-control and self-awareness. They often involve techniques such as meditation, deep breathing exercises, and body scans. The goal of mindfulness is to cultivate greater awareness of one's thoughts, feelings, bodily sensations, and surrounding environment, which can lead to increased emotional regulation, and overall emotional endurance and well-being.

[13] Siestas Negras (@black.power.naps), www.instagram.com/black.power.naps/?hl=en.

Over the last five years, in the context of my work as a docent of curatorial studies at MA Fine Art at the University of Arts in Utrecht, I witness an increasing number of students in need of mental health support. The majority of students work extended hours to pay their life and tuition fees, which leaves them with high-stress levels and minimal time to actually study. With the number of artists already operating in the cultural sector, and anticipated budget cuts by the right wing government, what prospects can art education offer to art students who don't have family wealth or other means to be independent? Art students suffer from anxiety and depression, and teachers suffer from burnouts, thus the educational environment tends to shape itself more and more towards self-healing, breathing, and other physical and mental ways of coping.

The struggle of art spaces to attract higher visitor numbers, much like thriving wellness, gyms, yoga centres, and life and mindfulness gurus and coaches, prompts a reflection on the need for these to be inserted into the white cube. It raises the question of whether cultural workers, burdened with burnouts and various mental health challenges, are exhibiting a call for help instead of proposing an emotional or intellectual experience to their potential audience. The turn to discourses and practices of care and mindfulness are symptomatic, not only of a crisis in societal welfare but of labour conditions in the arts, which they risk further obscuring even as they promise to somehow address them.

It is time that art workers advocate for a deeper individual and institutional transformation of the art field and its relation to power, and take part in shaping the art field from both above and below. Actively participating in labour policymaking and institutional life, practising fair and transparent labour methods, maintaining generous, clear, and fair labour conditions, setting up limits on availability, and taking care of a balance between labour and leisure time; art workers could move beyond complaints and public coping with mental health issues to a mindfulness that is 'socially engaged,' and aimed at building a more equitable and sustainable future.[14]

....

[14] Ronald Purser, *Handbook of Mindfulness: Culture, Context and Social Engagement* (Cham: Springer, 2017).

Finding the Food: Strategies for Curating and Running

The body needs rest and nutrition in order to maintain itself and grow. The mind works in the same way. As a professional curator and amateur athlete, lessons from one discipline impact the other. In a field that usually overlaps little with sports, the connection is a valuable nexus to explore correlations in energy, discipline, and care. Taking a look at hiring calls from the art world reveals that culture has not absorbed much from the recent discourse on care, nor on the curatorial skill of assessing feasibility. Running can help to read between the lines of these calls and address the unhealthy demands that are made at the top levels of institutions.

CULTURE CAN'T
BE MEASURED

In a world driven by statistics, analysis, and quantitative data, the artistic sphere struggles to make a case for proven methodologies. The tendency is for it to be absorbed either into the field of academics via research outputs, or into the market where value can be financially ascribed. Yet, the act of creativity is nowhere to be found in either of these two formulas. In *Two Regimes of Madness*, Gilles Deleuze describes the unpredictability of the creative act predicated on expression and necessity: "Having an idea is a rare event, it is a kind of celebration, not very common. [...] A creator only does what he or she absolutely needs to do."[1] This kind of labour does not exist like fruit on a tree that can be picked, or like the timed labour of the factory – it is a burst that comes and goes without predictability, surrounded by conditions that make it possible or not.

....

[1] Gilles Deleuze, *Two Regimes of Madness, Texts and Interviews 1975-1995*, ed. David Lapoujade, trans. Ames Hodges and Mike Taormina, (Massachusetts: MIT Press, 2006) deleuze.cla.purdue.edu/lecture/lecture-01-21.

Culture is a field of its own that suffers from machine incomprehensibility, and whose workers often find themselves on the precarious outskirts of a production-driven analytical labour network. Within capitalist accumulation, success is measured by quantitative analysis and culture falls outside of this regime. We can look at the rise and fall of NFTs as an example of market speculation and demand having no equivalent cultural value and eventually failing due to the hyperinflated false worth of these objects, compared to the valuable bodies of work of Hilma af Klint or Vincent van Gogh, who never saw success in their lifetimes.[2] The result of incomprehension of how cultural value is made results in cultural institutions (who should represent the top quality of artistic output) often being filled with political imperatives to serve other purposes such as child-care, nightclubs, or community-building spaces for anybody except the local art scene. Political leadership often fails to understand the purpose of maintaining the institution outside of quantitative values such as visitor numbers or revenue.

....

[2] Jane Lindhe, "95% of NFTs are Dead, But Why?" *Forbes*, 24 September 2023, www.forbes.com.au/covers/investing/95-per-cent-of-nfts-worthless-study-finds; While Klint sold her figurative paintings, it is the abstract ones that are most popular today after remaining hidden for decades. See: Anastasiia S. Kiraplov, "What you didn't know about Hilma af Klint", *The Collector*, 22 April 2023, www.thecollector.com/what-to-know-about-hilma-af-klint.

CULTURE IS DEMANDING

Like most disciplines, art requires a certain level of expertise to navigate its history, contemporaneity, discourse, and networks that allow access to the means of production. However, due to the demand for high levels of production with insufficient budgets and time, boundaries between work and life become unclear, and it is difficult to establish well-defined differences between off time and research time, or colleagues and friends. Working in this way requires cultural producers to be tireless – to accept nocturnal cycles of work and to count networking as leisure. Without any possibility of productivity analysis and the tendency to demand self-sacrifice, the industry has struggled to develop any effective labour regulations or contracts for its curators. This even led to a scandal at Tate Modern after it became apparent that institutional curators could earn more if they made coffee instead of exhibitions.[3]

UNFAMILIARITY IS
A NEGATIVE ATTRIBUTE

A large amount of the art world reacts to sports in the same way as most of the population reacts to their first museum visit. Some brush it off with a "not for me," while others openly express disdain. The allergy to physical motion existed in a previous version of myself, so I write this without passing judgement. It was only after self-identifying as an athlete and learning about it from the inside that I began to understand the full depth of this world even from the perspective of a hobbyist rather than a professional. Understanding the basic rules of athletic training is about a lot more than controlling your physical appearance – it is about gaining a deep knowledge of the body, its needs, and the variables that affect everything from your energy levels, to your mental state, to productivity. Training for the marathon is about experimenting with your limits and understanding your own inner mechanics of energy consumption and production.

....

[3] Christy Kuesel, "Tate's 'head of coffee' job posting sparked outrage over curators' low wages," *Artsy*, 30 January 2020, www.artsy.net/article/artsy-editorial-tates-head-coffee-job-posting-sparked-outrage-curators-low-wages.

UNDERSTANDING REST
AND NUTRITION
IS A BUMP IN THE ROAD

A good long run starts the night before. The first considerations are to get enough carbohydrates on your plate and drink enough water to avoid any switch in the body's energy consumption from carbohydrates to protein stored in the muscles. This needs to be done early enough to ensure a full and proper rest. Sleeping is the moment when the body regenerates and repairs itself. Any form of exercise helps muscles to grow through the process of hypertrophy. Training produces small tears in the muscles. During sleep, the torn cells in the muscles multiply, grow into full cells, and fuse with the existing muscle fibres. In running, as in any type of exercise, sleep is crucial: it is the moment of production of increased muscle mass in the body. Furthermore, it is the moment when depleted energy reserves in the muscles are replenished with more fuel. Working out and failing to rest before and after the session could undo all of the work that was done.

RESILIENCE IS A SKILL
THAT REQUIRES YEARS OF TRAINING

In a recent call for applications to fill the vacancy of directorship at the Berlin Biennale, the first sentence strikingly opened like this: "The Berlin Biennale seeks an experienced, resilient, and self-confident leader who represents the institution externally and ensures the further development and future viability of the Biennale with a compelling vision."[4] The language calls for resilience, meaning "the ability of a person to adjust to or recover readily from illness, adversity, major life changes, etc."[5] When it comes to an object, the definition reads that it should have "the power or ability of a material to return to its original form, position, etc., after being bent, compressed, or stretched." Or of institutions: "The ability of a system or organisation to respond to or recover readily from a crisis, disruptive process, etc."[6] This disquieting description of the labour and emotional conditions of this job offer reveals the severity of cracks in considerations of labour and institutional care in the art world. There is an acknowledgement that difficult conditions create impact, but no analysis of what kind of training is needed by cultural workers to increase endurance and resistance. Often, this can stem from industry-wide structural problems which have led to a whopping 76 per cent of millennial museum workers thinking of quitting the industry.[7]

....

[4] "Call For Applications: Director Of The Berlin Biennale For Contemporary Art", *Biennial Foundation*, 15 January 2024. www.biennialfoundation.org/2024/01/director-of-the-berlin-biennale.

[5] Dictionary.com entry for "Resilience," www.dictionary.com/browse/resilience.

[6] Ibid.

[7] Julia Halperin, "Why do US museum workers want to quit?" *The Art Newspaper*, 15 September 2023. www.theartnewspaper.com/2023/09/15/why-do-us-museum-workers-want-to-quit.

ÀNGELS MIRALDA

RESILIENCE REQUIRES
ENDURANCE TRAINING

An untrained, unprepared individual cannot run a marathon, or at least does so at a great risk of permanent injury. Running is a high-impact sport and requires a slow and gradual physical adaptation. During a build-up period which can last years, muscles grow around the joints such as the knees, adding extra padding and reducing damage, while consistent training increases cartilage growth. Internal organs also change considerably, especially the heart whose walls strengthen, increasing the overall efficiency of the muscle, and decreasing the body's resting heart rate. Endurance training is not only about expanding the distance you can run in four-hour stretches, but doing it and not feeling tired afterwards.

DISCIPLINE, CONSISTENCY,
AND SMALL BUT STEADY GROWTH
ARE THE KEY TO SAFE DEVELOPMENT

In the cultural field, this works exactly the same way. Even after these years of training, the body can fail if it is not supplied with the correct amount of rest or nutrition – similar to the equation of experience, time off, and decent pay. Towards the end of the Berlin Biennial's quote above, the viability of the continuation of the Biennial is brought into question revealing the fragility of our institutions. It puts the weight of responsibility of its own survival on a resilient individual without leaving space for an analysis of viability. No institution or project is viable if its staff is working under harsh conditions with no end in sight. Institutions are doomed to remain in long and dragged-out crises if they fail to address the structural imbalances that lead to low pay, and the privileging of social access over proven experience.

RUNNING THINGS IS
A TEAM EFFORT

In the contemporary art field, the importance of social access often trumps experience or resilience – leading to many people being unprepared for the demands of their position. Together, people legitimize the culture of failure. Social hires of people who are well-connected but lack sufficient experience range from low-level employees to directors of institutions.[8] These hires further propel the problem by stretching the limits of institutional resources and the time of other staff members. The body does the same: when there is an imbalance in muscle strength, other muscles compensate, which eventually leads to injury of the stronger muscles. An institution in crisis is a lesioned athlete, whose ambition and desire to do what they did before wears away at existing wounds, never allowing them to heal.

CAN RUNNING A BIENNIAL
BE COMPARED
TO RUNNING A MARATHON?

Like any lengthy process with a finish line or a goal, months of hard work and training are not the beginning of working on the project itself. The work already began long before, during the years of experience with smaller-scale exhibitions that gradually builds up into larger and larger projects. A healthy increase is always incremental, not sudden. The busiest moment, installing together once the artists arrive, is the final two kilometres before the finish line when, despite all of the exhaustion, all of the work behind you, the self-doubt and pain, the finish line is finally in view and gives an extra push of energy that you didn't think you had.

....

[8] Rachel Corbett, "'There's No One on Staff Who Can Lead': Former Detroit Institute of Arts Employees Accuse Its Director of Mismanagement and Ethics Violations," *Artsy*, 17 July 2020, news. artnet.com/art-world/staff-unrest-at-the-detroit-institute-arts-1895307.

NUMBERS SPEAK
FOR THEMSELVES

Data shows that rest is crucial – something that the cultural world's inaction in producing its own evaluative systems makes impracticable. The greatest marathon runner of our times, Eliud Kipchoge, speaks of the importance of 'Vitamin N,' which is not a chemical compound, but the strength to say no and prioritize goals, health, and rest.[9] Anything else can lead to more harm than good. The key is to measure scale and time, effort and process, and analyse methodologies that work and those that don't, in order to organize a season schedule that builds rather than harms. In Kipchoge's home country of Kenya, hundreds of runners wake up early to join group runs, to meet together, exchange tips, and help each other to improve. He credits his community for the support and teamwork which are part of the key components in the mental training for beating world records.

....

[9] Keeley Milne, "Eliud Kipchoge wants you to learn to say no," Canadian Running, 3 November 2022, runningmagazine.ca/the-scene/eliud-kiphchoge-wants-you-to-learn-to-say-no.

SUSTAINABLE CONDITIONS
MUST BE MET

We still lack the conversation and understanding of what a healthy art system is. As long as institutional curators pride themselves in working as gatekeepers, as long as the community aspect is overlooked, and as long as we don't feel brave enough to flag inappropriate behaviours, we will continue to live in toxic competition and overworked unrecognition. The advances that have been made live in a precarious balance of politics in which they could easily be taken away with a shift in electoral results. The art system itself needs to achieve resilience and develop strategies that protect, lift, and build a strong community. This begins with forming our own autonomous systems of evaluating success, verifying written information before hiring, and rethinking the role of the institution from exclusivity to the home of a local community that needs to take a frontal role in improving the conditions of its community; the local cultural and creative scene.

Free Exhibition
Seating Advice

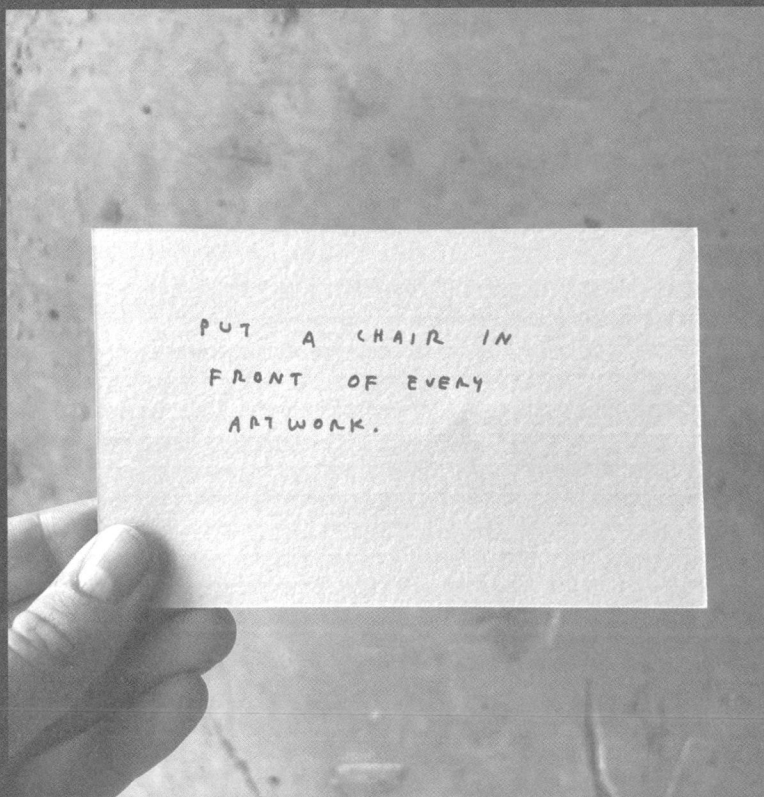

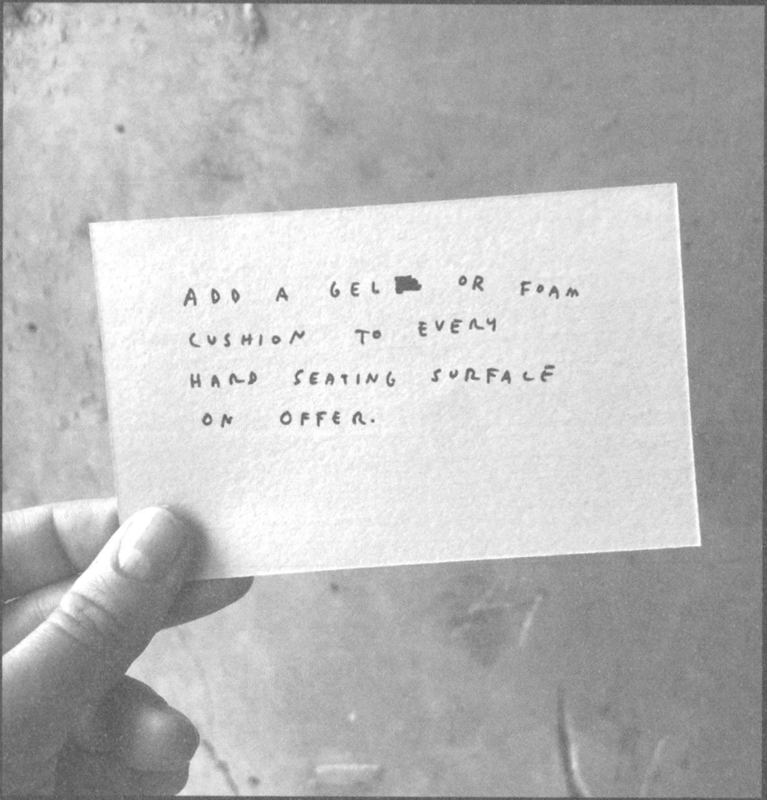

COUNT THE NUMBER OF
BENCHES IN THE GALLERY.
~~NOW~~ DOUBLE IT.
DOUBLE IT AGAIN.

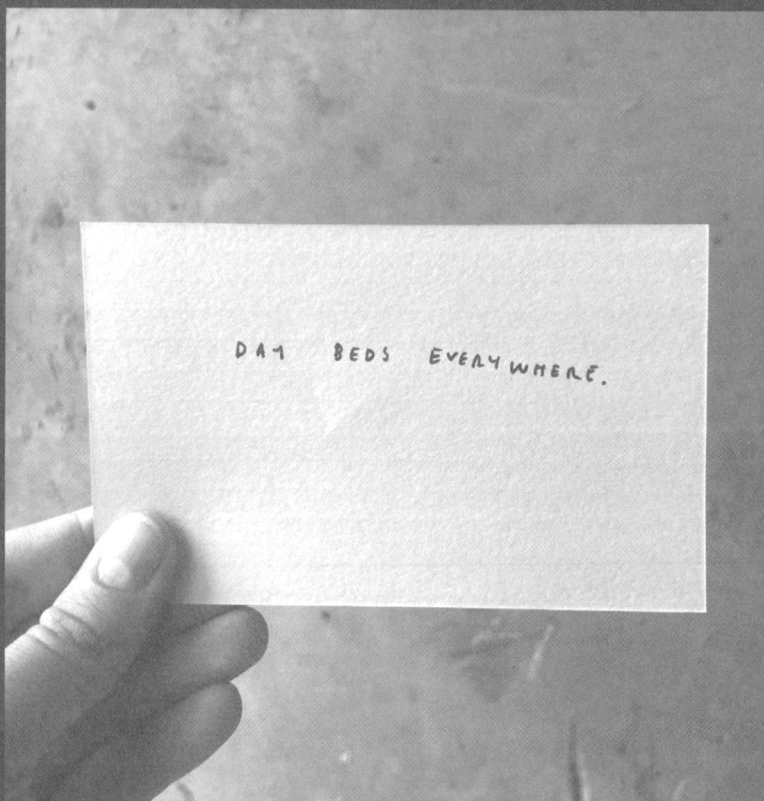

DAY BEDS EVERYWHERE.

This work started as a series of notes to myself. I had been thinking about seating in museums and other semi-public spaces for a few years. I felt (and continue to feel) that a bench is the bare minimum, and that when we start to dream about possibilities, we can think much, much more expansively. I think of this piece as both literal advice and as an incantation.

The Dream Concert

The Dream Concert is an intimate night of music and poetry, curated by multidisciplinary artist Yamuna Forzani, that celebrates and explores themes of queerness and intimacy. The stage for the evening consists of a set design with a large bed covered in frilly satin pillows at its centre. Forzani's custom costumes take on the exuberant identities of the performers, allowing their characters to shine through. This concept was created from a longing for connection, softness, and the safety of being in one's bedroom.

THE DREAM CONCERT

This concept was born from a desire to create an intimate space for my fellow sleepy queers. At the time, I was sober and going to bed early. I realized that there aren't many events that are curated in this way – so I created it.

As someone who worked a lot during the night and collaborated and styled many dancers and DJs, I had a strong desire to do something more gentle and calm. *The Dream Concert* was a way for me to connect with singer-songwriters, poets, and dreamers. I built the set design with a large bed with lots of frilly pillows, draped curtains, and satin bed sheets. Everything was so over the top and camp with different shades of pink and purple. The lineup was a sapphic fantasy, an overdose of lesbian energy (somewhat a rarity but definitely appreciated), with poetry from Zaire and Mojowi, and live music from Sono, Sophia Habib, and ZULU GREEN.

I dressed myself as a 'pillow princess,' matching the set design and introducing the artists. We had a tea corner and no alcohol allowed. The evening finished at 10:30 p.m. and I was in bed by midnight.

I find it very important to connect queer spaces to rest as indeed a lot of queer spaces are centred around nightlife and clubbing. This can be incredibly powerful, cathartic, and transformational, but doesn't always resonate with everyone. I am a big fan of slowing down and sharing intimate moments together. As I get older, my desire shifts more towards resting and recharging. I have a growing appreciation for poetry, workshops, dinners, walks in nature, and smaller gatherings where one can share and connect on a deeper level. I feel that as the world is growing more dire, there is more need for softness.

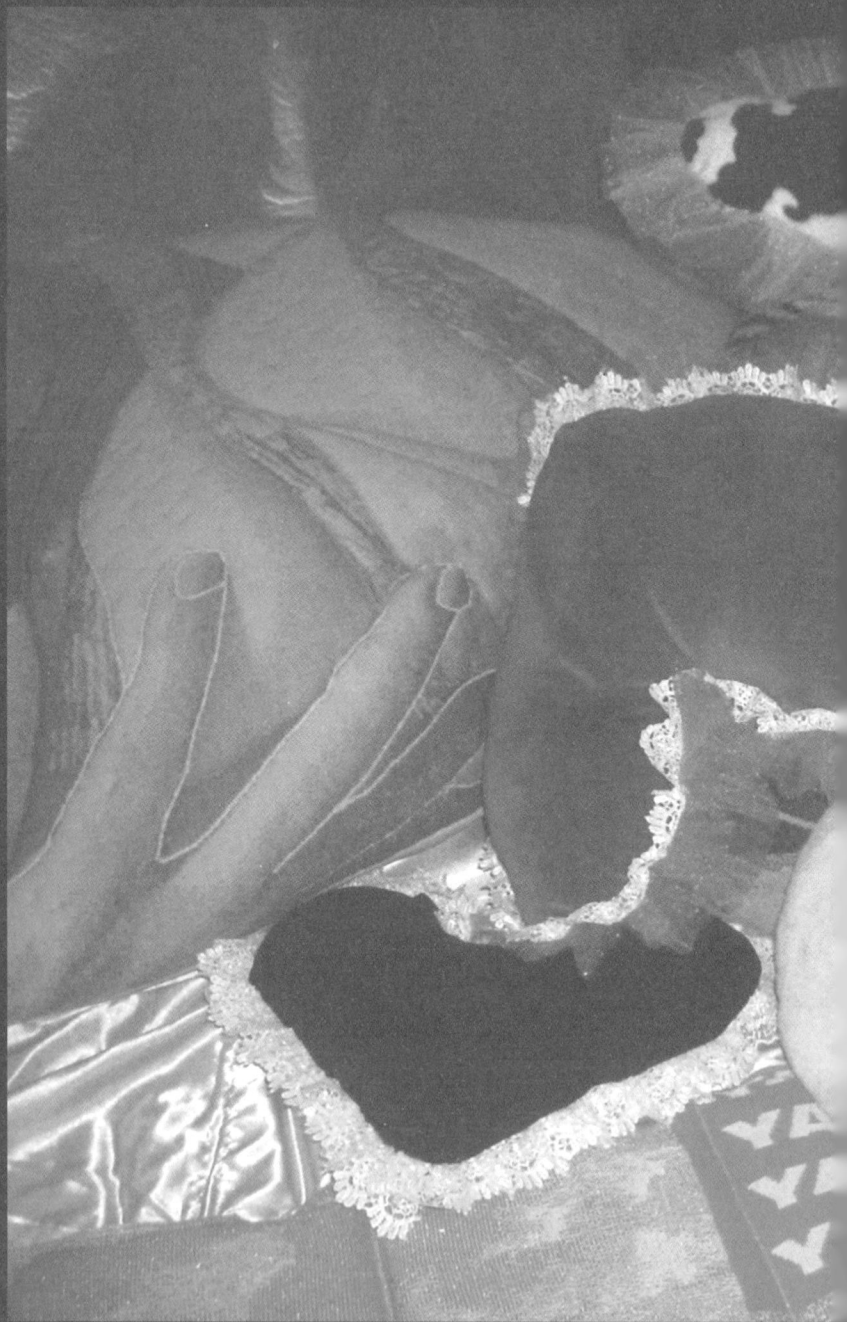

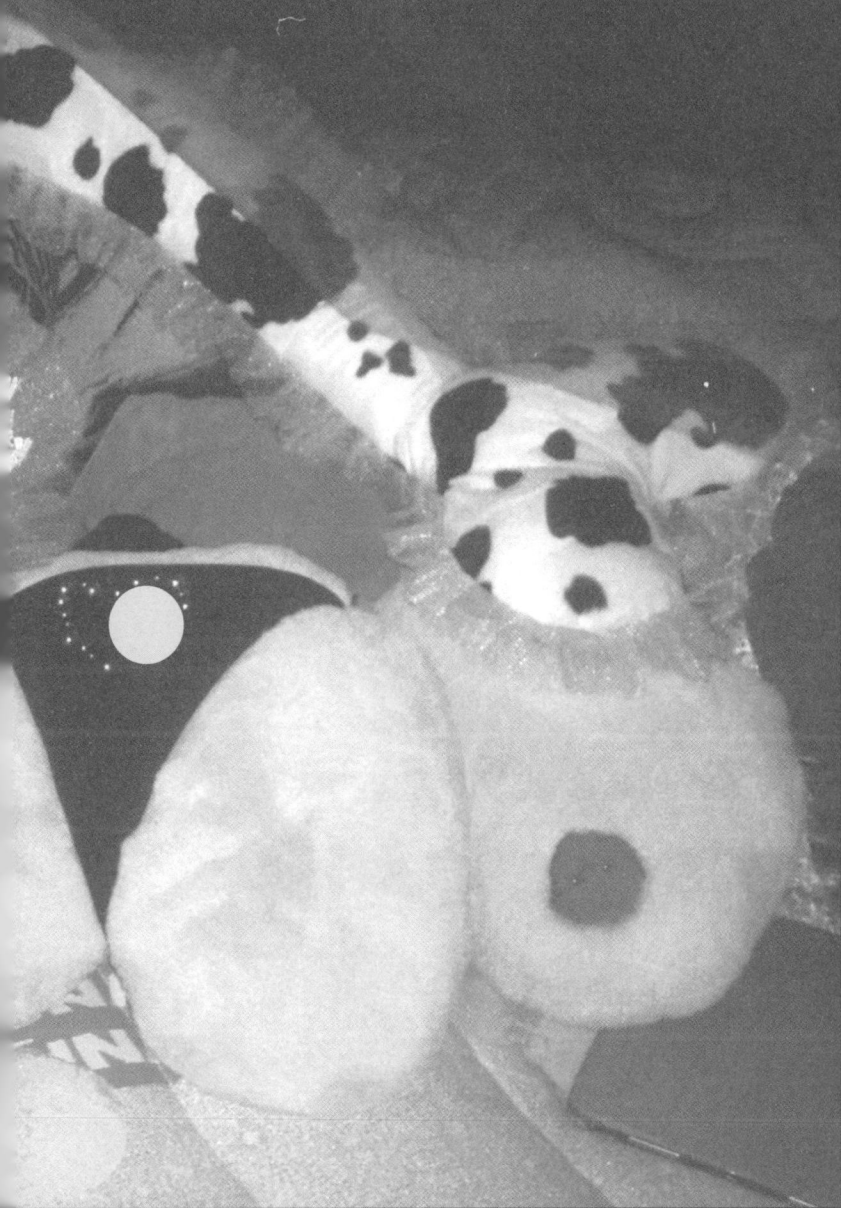

Photographs by YSN STUDIOS (@ysn.studios)

Re: Invitation Institutional contribution for the publication Nocturnalities Bargaining Beyond Rest

Lat
51°   55'

11:23

Long
4° 28' 39.9" E

27.9" N

From: Office | A Tale of A Tub ▓▓▓▓▓▓▓▓
Subject: Re: Invitation: Institutional contribution for the publication Nocturnalities: Bargaining Beyond Rest
Date: 6 May 2024 at 11:23
To: Andrea Andrea ▓▓▓▓▓▓▓▓▓▓▓▓▓▓▓▓
Cc: Agata Bar ▓▓▓▓▓▓▓▓▓▓▓▓▓▓

Dear Andrea and Agata,

I hope you're having a nice start to the week!

Thank you for reaching out about your project. I'm writing you this reply on the first morning back at work after the first exhibition of the new directorship opened this weekend. It has been a whirlwind few months since we began in January, with big structural funding applications, annual reports, learning the organizational ropes, building bonds between staff, our audience, and the neighbourhood in which we reside, and developing and producing the year's programme – all in the space of four months. Given all this, and the topic of your research, it feels most healthy to refrain from contributing anything more than this email –should you want to include it – to your publication. In all honesty, we need a little rest.

Sending warm wishes,
Isabelle

Isabelle Sully
Artistic Director | A Tale of a Tub
Justus van Effenstraat 44
3027 TK Rotterdam
The Netherlands
www.a-tub.org

Sunrise
07:53

DE APPEL

Sunset
19:32

Harvest

Lat
52° 22' 44.4" N

16:36

Long
4° 54' 1.02" E

HOW CAN WE REST WHEN
THERE IS A GENOCIDE TAKING PLACE? →

WHO GETS TO REST?

"REST IS ALSO
MOURNING BR
AND THEN YOU

A MOTHER SLEPT 20 YEARS
WITHOUT A BLANKET WHILE HER
SON COULDN'T HAVE ACCESS TO THE SAME
IN ISRAELI PRISON.

CAN REST BE S
CAN WE REST BY
BY DOING SOMETHIN

YOU HAVE TO ALLOW

ALLOW OTHERS TO SUP

THINK ABOUT

WHAT ABOUT INSTITUTIONAL REST?
IS AUGUST GLOBAL REST? ← EXTREME u
ALSO FORCE

CAN WE THINK OF THE OFFICE AS A FAMILY?
THE SAME STRUCTURES THAT ARE NEEDED TO
SUPPORT EACH OTHER'S REST ALSO ENABLE
ABUSE OF ENERGY/TIME.

REST FROM WORK
REST FROM SOCIALIZATION
REST FROM INFORMATION

NSPONSABILITY
WITNESS.

FOR RESTING/
ING.

MOURNING"
ME EXHAUSTION,
O TO STOP. (OR THE
POLICE STOPS YOU?)
A - RESTED

PERFORMATIVE MOMENTS OF REST.
" YOU CAN'T CHOOSE WHEN TO REST.
IT HAPPENS".

LSE?
A DEMONSTRATION?
THEN NOTHING?

CAN WE FORCE OURSELVES TO REST
WHEN WE GET "VACATION?

TO REST.
REST.

LECTIVELY.

(WE NEED TO STOP THINKING ABOUT REST INDIVIDUALLY)

ONDITIONS CAN

"DURING MOTHERHOOD REST FELT LIKE A
JOB. IF I DIDN'T REST I WOULD DIE.
IT WAS A SURVIVAL MECHANISM"

Harvest (by Maria Nolla)
of a conversation between the members of de Appel's team.

HARVEST

Harvest is the artistic recordings of discussions and meetings. Harvesters listen, reflect, and depict this process from their own perspectives and practices. Harvests can be humorous, poetic, or candid. They can take the shape of a post-it note, a story, drawings, a film, a sound piece, or a meme. It is a way to share collective discussions where the building of knowledge happens through dialogic practices. De Appel has learned harvesting from lumbung and is sharing the practice with participants and visitors of de Appel.

Some Nocturnal Reflections...

Dear Andrea,

I hope your exhibition is taking shape the way you envisioned it and thank you for the invitation to ponder and exchange   some thoughts on your inquiry on 'the politics of rest.'

Our   short dialogue already sparked several conversations in the following days about the notion of rest, what we actually mean when we talk about rest, and why it seems so difficult within the cultural field to implement it, even appearing unsatisfactory once one allows oneself to actually take rest. With this mail I would like to continue our exchange and thank you for the opportunity to reflect together and merge it into the contribution for your publication.

Maybe it is the aftermath of the pandemic, maybe it is my age, or perhaps the growing attention for fair practice in the arts – a feeling of exhaustion is a recurring topic in my weekly conversations with professional peers. It is often a somewhat uncomfortable topic and intertwined with a realization that, despite all efforts to be efficient, inspired, and effective, one has failed by admitting that a break or rest of some sort is necessary. That a personal limit has been reached.

Rest is quickly associated with a break from work, or perhaps a daily routine of productivity. But rest is not the same as leisure, a concept that came into existence symbiotically with the emergence of the modern notion of labour. Rest seems to have a different anatomy than leisure though. There are many factors at play when reflecting on the toll working conditions can take in the cultural field, and plenty of arguments are to be made about how systematic structures create individual casualties, and how organizational bodies reproduce capitalist and extortionist politics just as much as everywhere else in society. Despite all our good intentions to be critical, to know better and to do better...

But there is something I find particularly fascinating, which I would like to share with you: the refusal to take rest. Throughout my conversations and experiences, I wondered why the notion of taking rest is met with such discomfort and even refusal to do so. If one has the choice to do so, especially when one is exhausted, why is it so terribly difficult to surrender to it?

Last week an expression found me: no rest for the wicked. It was uttered with a wink of an eye by a friend who did not have time to continue a lovely meeting because work needed to be done. With our conversation in mind, the figure of speech lingered. Rotted in biblical sources, the saying was adopted in a sermon in 1524 by Johannes Calvijn and references the potential endless purgatory for the sinners and wicked. In true Protestant fashion, the sobering need for constant work and labour to avoid eternal damnation has been deeply embedded in the culture of the country we both have migrated to. It made me wonder; when we talk about rest, do we need to foster a different culture of rest as opposed to a culture of work? Perhaps we could actually divert from its potential relation to labour, efficiency obsession, and even the entanglement it brings with personal identity politics. After all, what we do is who we are.

Perhaps there is another way we need to address rest, not as a way of failing to be productive, but rather as a spiritual practice and accompanying politics. Perhaps, in this way, the connotation of rest as detachment can be reversed as space and time for greater connectivity without moral judgement and ambition – time for oneself, others, and the world. Perhaps we need to brand it as spiritual labour. Perhaps, how we rest is who we become, a way of being.

Some speculative thinking I would be curious to hear if this is in any way of use for your research and publication before I submerge even more. For now, I will keep pondering the different philosophical avenues, and I suppose like with all thoughts that are taking shape: no rest for the wicked.

Warm regards,
Alexandra

PS: For some more collective reflection, I extend this conversation to my colleagues Lua Vollaard and Leana Boven, who were very interested. Hope this is ok for you too, if not – please let me know.

Alexandra Landré
Artistiek directeur
Artistic director

Dear Alexandra,

Apologies for the delayed reply. As you can imagine the frameworks of contemporary artistic labour are quite peculiar these days. Ever since our 'intimate clock' has gotten fused with 'office hours,' and became conditioned by the shifting demand of market trends, project-based lifestyle, and professional nomadism, my life, in fact, our lives, gasps for what modernity craves the most: free time.

However, I presume that the more geographically situated or 'less globalist-oriented' creative practices (whatever that terminology encompasses) are suffering equally from the same late capitalist mentality. Perhaps just embodying different issues within the similar capitalist modus operandi of 'soul' terrorism – or if you will, terror on the very essence of what makes us alive.

I have just returned from a professional trip to Austria and Slovenia, where I participated in the panel talk and the 10th U3 Triennial of Contemporary Art. I have arrived briefly in Amsterdam – the place that has become home now – to recuperate, centre and hold my ground against my own ambitions, before jumping again to Spain, for yet another artistic adventure.

Your letter and contemplations around the politics of rest have truly moved me, especially since I have been equally trying to map, excavate and foresee new articulation and systems around institutional and intimate negotiation of rest, and, consequently, care.

In particular, it struck me how you framed the remark around the refusal to rest. Perhaps withdrawal is something that requires a specific holistic consciousness to begin with, or at least a setting in which demand and expectations are not fiercely knocking at our doorstep. It seems to me more and more, as you formalized it earlier, that the anatomy of rest specifically resides in the unique cultural articulation of the notion of resting. In particular, in its performative assets – especially since we both, as migrants in this country, witness that culture and nurture do dictate the way one assumes rest individually, as well as systemically.

The proposition that rest, as the primary state of every living thing, was and still is gradually co-opted throughout centuries by ever-expanding capitalist strategies by utilizing socio-cultural tropes and dialectics as its primary vessel – is utterly shocking, yet very much true.

That also suggests that the capitalist co-option of rest has already begun before its discursive untangling (which of course is evident from various angles), and has been happening intergenerationally. And that the 24/7 paradigm and the ascendance of cognitive capitalism (what Jonathan Crary and Yann Moulier-Boutang elaborate on) are just recent forms of such culmination. Of course, industrialization followed by techno-political developments and globalization are core engines of such predicaments.

It is indeed true that leisure and rest hold different positions when it comes to their roles; and evidently, it is also related to the frameworks of class, privilege, and meritocratic attitudes. As rest   transcends from the state or a style of being into a   state of intended performance, it shifts its ontological   foundation entirely. Suddenly, we are faced with   circumstances where *rest* becomes a state of merit. Since the notion of labour and performance have been attached to the very essence of the notion of rest, I am afraid, my dear Alexandra, that nobody is safe anymore.

Rest became the ultimate commodity, replacing associations of leisure time as the redundant 'bourgeois fabulation.'

Did we slowly enter the age where we are grieving rest?

Coming back to culturally situated and perhaps more holistic assets of this rhetoric, I would like to mention a very unique Croatian term for a specific state of rest – the word *fjaka* (meaning; a relaxed state of body, mind, spirit, and heart).

The term is similar to the notion of siesta in Spanish, but unlike siesta, *fjaka* can manifest at any point, and it is not related to the time of the day or any type of decision-making. Instead, it is a state of mind and an embodied attitude. *Fjaka* is the persistence of an easy-going perspective where no rush is needed and no rush will be accepted.

On that note, I hope we all persist on *fjaka*, and a future that we do not all have to resist.

Warm regards,
Andrea

The Memory of Rest

The chapel is filled with twelve huge beds with different types of grass. A few days before the opening, I surrender myself to the most attractive green grass and feel the heaviness of my body. Where the fabric of my clothes doesn't cover me, the grass tickles my arms, cheeks, and part of my belly. In this moment I remember Daylin. Daylin is a fifteen-year-old who comes regularly to Hotel Maria Kapel (HMK) with his friends. The friend group makes jokes about each other's body odours and giggles about everything. They mostly come and check out the exhibitions for a quick minute and then disappear to the downstairs cinema where an old drum set is available for them to play.

The cinema, located in the basement directly below my horizontal body in the main exhibition space in the chapel of HMK, is also my hideout place. It's dark, it's isolated from light and sound, and people won't find you easily. I must confess that also there, I sometimes found myself lying horizontally on the soft dark cinema carpet where my heartbeat could slow down.

One day Daylin came to me and asked if he could lie down on the chapel floor and have his friend take a picture from the balcony. He had a series of pictures where he would lie face down in several places, like his classroom, but now also in HMK's chapel. I said this series is definitely art, he answered that he just found it funny. Fair enough. For this issue, I actually wanted to send you this picture of him, but I never received it. Instead, I am sending you the memory in the form of a chain of thoughts that filled up my short moment of rest the horizontal position in the grass granted me.

- Inez Piso-Tuncay, director HMK

Inez Piso-Tuncay lying on the grass of the installation
by HMK's artist-in-residence Amalie "Sveske" Ourø.

Thoughts on Resting

Kunsthuis SYB is beautifully located in a small village in the bilingual province of Friesland. It hosts artists for six-week research residencies and then organizes small-scale exhibitions and workshops aimed at talent development. The artspace was initiated by Sybrand Hellinga in his own house in 2000 and since then a domestic atmosphere has accompanied the methodologies of the team.

Thoughts on resting:

● Travelling back and forth between SYB and home is, for me, a way of digesting what has happened. It's a moment of transition from the working life into the personal life in which I am able to rest. This transition is important to actually feel this 'state of mind' of resting.

● Working from home, there is no transition. It is mixed, and it intertwines with each other – being in the same space as where the office is.

● When I think of rest, I also think about 'the rest;' all the other things or the things that remain. So thinking about rest, it's also all the other things that need to be done. When there is all the rest, there is no rest, restlessness.

● No residencies also mean more space for us to be there, and have moments to rethink.

****

● For most of the resident artists, Kunsthuis Syb is a place to rest and research without the obligation of creating new work. For many, it gives the space to reflect and rethink one's practice in an environment away from the hectic life of the city.

● At the same time, Kunsthuis Syb is a small-scale organization with no full-time staff. Working from home goes hand in hand with being on location at regular intermissions. This often blurs the space of rest and work and finding the right balance is a constant struggle. As it creates a space to think and rest for artists and participants, the small team has to work behind the scenes and prepare the conditions that make resting possible. That is a beautiful thing, but finding the right rhythm is not always easy.

● Going to the bakery; taking a walk to see the first spring flowers; getting some groceries from the supermarket; visiting the cemetery; having a chat at the local bar; cooking pasta al pesto; getting some potatoes from a local farmer; reading that book that has been asking for attention for more than a year; when it's not cloudy, looking at the stars. Forgetting about emails for a bit.

Time Diary

From: Aline Hernández ~~█████████████~~
Subject: Re: Invitation: Institutional contribution for the
publication Nocturnalities: Bargaining Beyond Rest
Date: 15 May 2024 at 18:52
To: Agata Bar ~~█████████████████████~~,
Marianna Takou ~~██████████████~~
Cc: Andrea Andrea ~~██████████████████████~~

Dear Agata and Andrea,

My sincere apologies for not getting back to you earlier.
I never received your first invitation (we were having problems
with our server at the time, and some communication was lost),
and your reminder caught us in the middle of mobilizations for
Palestine in Utrecht.

First of all, thank you for your invitation. I cannot avoid sharing that ironically, the invitation comes at a time when we're feeling overworked and exhausted. In my mind, I dream about writing a reflection around exhaustion from never-ending funding applications and reports. Many years ago, the conversation around exhaustion and reporting informed Arts Collaboratory network's imagination for our funding paradigm shift. Many of the members were also exhausted from writing application after application, followed by never-ending reporting.

Having shared that story, we're sorry to share that, unfortunately, we're running at a low capacity, and it is unrealistic for us as a team to make a meaningful contribution to your publication right now. However, while talking about your invitation my colleague Marianna and I thought that perhaps some excerpts from Casco's Unlearning Exercises could fit well, considering the theme, particularly "Time Diary".

We're keen to hear what you think about this idea. However, we understand if it doesn't work, so please feel free to tell us. Otherwise, it's nice to be in touch and we hope we can collaborate in the future.

Sending all the best,
Aline

Aline Hernández, artistic director
Pronouns: she/her
For information on our activities, projects, and ecosystem visit casco.art and follow us on Instagram
Casco Art Institute: Working for the Commons
Lange Nieuwstraat 7, 3512 PA Utrecht, NL
T: ~~\NNNNNNNNNNN5~~
M: ~~\NNNNNNNNNNN7~~

UNLEARNING
EXERCISES

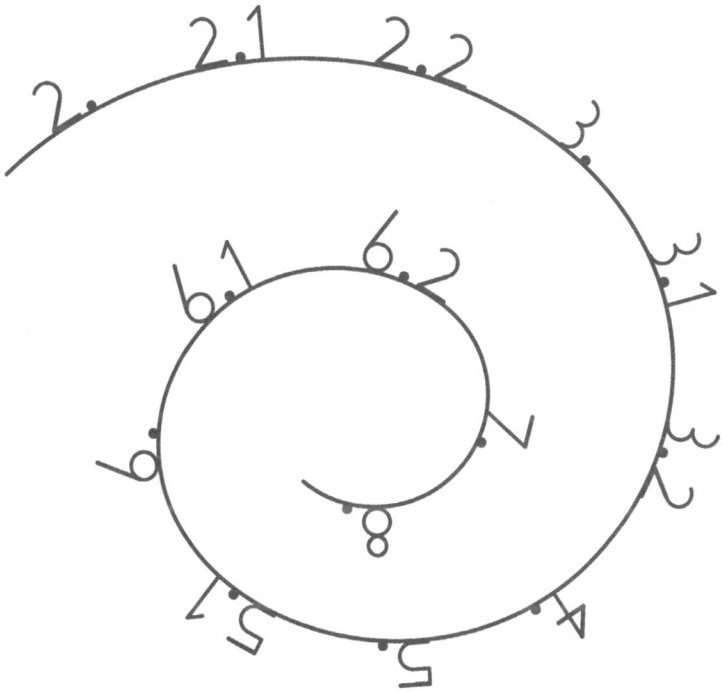

Art Organizations
as Sites for Unlearning

7.
TIME DIARY

UNLEARNING EXERCISE

For a limited period (a few days to a few weeks), every team member makes a record of their day beyond set working hours by noting down what they are doing from time to time. Together we try to distinguish categories; invisible, care, productive, communicative, and "intellectual" for different activities and analyze this by identifying our working habits, breaking down logics of efficiency and productivity, and recognizing other values. We also read aloud together, revaluing our day-to-day activities, especially with respect to what are normally considered unproductive moments, as a means to arrive somewhere else.

WHAT TO UNLEARN

Ways of dealing with time and planning based on logics of efficiency and productivity while undervaluing, or even attempting to kill reproductive time; entanglement between no time, busyness, and business; and struggles with different ways of working and rhythms.

51

Transcript (excerpt)
16 March 2015:
Annette, Binna, Carlijn, Jason,
Sanne, Simone, Suzanne, Ying,
and Yolande.

Binna
So we documented what we do
every day for two weeks. I think
what we enjoyed in common
was appreciating each step of
the working process, realizing
that reproductive dimensions
are constantly generated within
the productivity regime. You get
annoyed when something goes
wrong and you have to fix it—
that's reproduction. If we are
able to appreciate this reproductive labor as part of the process,
part of what do, we may feel
happier, have less frustration.

Ying
Politically, I am not   .
Still, it made sense to ormalize
cleaning. But does it make sense
to formalize these other things?
Or does it take away their value?
Not to forget the control issue.

Annette
It's about abusing this form
of tracking or not, no?

Note
There's some fear attached to sharing
this diary. In fact, it could be considered a
general exercise/method used in big institutions
and companies to control their workers and
make them more efficient. It's important
to articulate again and again the purpose
of writing this diary. There's no fundamental
necessity to share them, though this allows
for the recognition of differences and
collective analysis of the personal as the
political. We are also looking for a more
affective and easy way of doing and
sharing this diary.

52

ACTION	CONTEXT	Self	Friends	Family	Team	Community
Getting ready						
Care						
Cleaning						
Laundry						
Grocery shopping						
Cooking						
Fixing						
Transition btw. places						
Execution						
Deviation						
Daydream						
Shopping						
Eating						
Physical Exercise						
Break						
Networking						
Meeting						
E-mail						
Telephone						
Hosting						
Lobbying						
Writing						
Performance						
Planning						
Infrastructure						
Logistics						
Coordination						
Study						
Research						
Reading						
Report						
Fundraising						
Aplication						
Designing						
Administration						
Archiving						
TOTAL TIME- CONTEXT						
of which combined time: (done at the same time)						53

Rest as Solidarity in Practice

I have been thinking about that: how sometimes we have to stop what we are doing to feel the true impact of something, to let our bodies experience that impact, the fury of an escalating injustice, a structure as well as an event; a history, an unfinished history.

Sometimes to sustain your commitments you stop what you are doing.
- Sara Ahmed[1]

In the context of W139, but also most likely in relation to other cultural institutional voice institutions, this idea of a collective doesn't really exist. In the end, institutions are structures and networks composed of people – people who each have their own lived experiences, their own frameworks and contexts, and their own relationships to the use of their time. With this in mind, we've asked everyone in the organization to contribute some thoughts about their relationship to rest, with each person adding on to the previous one. Some people were not able to contribute because they did not have the time, the energy, they were on holiday, or simply because they did not want to.

* each contribution is separated by a line

....

[1] Sara Ahmed, "Complaint and Survival," feministkilljoys, March 23 2020, feministkilljoys.com/2020/03/23/complaint-and-survival.

In 2022, I accidentally contributed to a book by Alina Lupu about work, with an email that I had written to her where I had to decline her request for me to write a text. In it, I reflected on my freelance work, distributed by one day a week here, two days a week there, and said that "together these jobs take up way more time than that because of course each one-day-a-week job is always more than one day a week. How can we have real sustainability in our working practices if the work is so fragmented and more is always expected of you (and needed from you)? I think the whole cultural sector relies on all this unpaid overwork in order to make things actually happen, since the budgets we are working within are often so unrealistic in relation to the outcomes that are expected."

Looking back on this, it still carries a lot of truth. The cultural field runs on this energy to create, build, develop, manifest – to bring things into being with as few resources as possible, to bring things into being at the expense of ourselves. I think the one thing we've been trying to do at W139 is to scale things back when we see that we don't have the capacity to continue, whether it's due to budget limitations or human limitations. This is a welcome change from the more common tendency of trying to push things through despite a lack of time, money, or resources. It's such a relief when someone says, "Let's pull back" instead of "Let's push through it."

_____

I will pick up the thread from here, and the question of what it means for an institution to rest. From the outside, the way we currently operate at W139, compared to a few years ago, might be perceived as scaling or slowing down. Instead of up to ten exhibitions a year, we currently do four. And still, the organization is not 'at rest.' And with that, neither are the people that work for and with it.

From my perspective, this has to do with balancing our (very) limited financial resources with the number of artists and projects we can accommodate, and the ambitious output we envision for our organization. (This is explained by the fact there are already too few organizations and platforms in the Netherlands to present art. Doing fewer programmes means providing fewer opportunities for artists).

And another part, an – at least for myself – often equally big one, has to do with how one strives to work on programmes with artists, the personal (and institutional) responsibility one has or feels, and the dedication that comes with that.

One of the things I've learnt that I try to take with me from working in the cultural sector over the past three decades in differing settings, informed by various organizational infrastructures and national ecosystems, is that I cannot expect an organization to protect me from working too much. But I do believe that together, we can contribute to creating a supportive environment, questioning what we can and cannot do, and improving circumstances that allow for sufficient rest.

NB: While I write this, quite delayed, contribution on a Saturday morning, I do so at a moment I had reserved for preparing two urgent funding applications which need to be submitted by Monday. The learning continues.

—————————————————————

There's not really a cute word in English for falling into a sudden episode of microsleep – eyes falling shut, a second of unconsciousness, head nod. In Dutch, the word would be 'knikkebollen,' which   is quite literally nodding your ball, your ball being your   head. I never had bad associations with being in a   school class, or at work, sleep deprived because of   stress or a hangover, failing to keep my head on my shoulders; and maybe that is because the word that describes it scores high on the cute scale. So there's me, working at IKEA some years ago, crouched over the white Jubla candles that I just stacked from one pallet to another, thinking I looked absolutely adorable with my sleep deprivation. I drink more coffee now so the 'knikkebollen' has turned into slight eye twitches, and unfortunately, there isn't a Dutch word to cuteify eye twitches. Maybe we should introduce one.

—————————————————————

It's currently 23:20 on a Thursday evening, and I'm sipping tea before going to bed in an attempt to rest, ease my body, and slow down my mind. To wake up the next day and start with a workout at the gym. After that, I will try to do ten things I've tasked myself with, of which I'll probably be able to execute only five. And this is how a usual day unfolds. Not necessarily starting with a workout, but having more things to do than what I can realistically fit into a regular working day. This means that a 10-hour workday is nothing out of the ordinary. 12 or 14 hours of work in a single day is also not unusual.

About five years ago I changed my career from being a performance artist to a visual arts curator and now even an aspiring art dealer. And then to imagine that I sabotaged my performance art career because of the super unhealthy work ethic in the performance art field. Because, to produce and direct theatre or performance art, is even more mental in regards to unhealthy work habits. The average theatre or performance director suffers from insomnia, especially when they enter into editing mode, before the first tryout or premiere. I chose to not go through that kind of suffering and favoured a career in the field of visual arts. At least after an exhibition opens the work is done; but after a performing arts director premieres their piece, they are assumed to go on tour since this is one of the very few ways they can actually make a living. This would be a total suicide scenario for me, and I decided not to go that route.

So here I am, a full-time freelance curator/programmer with two super-part-time contracts, working my ass off because I'm a creative and an artist at heart. If I fail to deliver, there's a whole army of artists/curators ready to take my spot. So I have no choice but to deliver. How do I know? Well, I was selected from a stack of 150 applicants. Every single one of them is waiting to work as hard as I do, if they aren't already.

"I Say This with Love"

—

Stealing Time and Care as a Smoke Screen, All the While I Know That Rest Is Resistance

Lat
51° 55' 27.9" N

15:07

Long
4° 28' 39.9" E

ELOISE SWEETMAN
AND JASON HENDRIK HANSMA
SHIMMER

We've been contemplating the concept of 'stealing time' as the very reason that rest is not possible in arts and culture. This is because it relies on a creative mindset that has traditionally pushed against standardization and institutionalization. When and where is rest possible – given that the boundaries of work are blurred because exhibitions and events are outside of 'normal working hours' (which is the least of our problems, by the way)? By sharing our concerns here, we hope colleagues in the arts can help us navigate the contradictions of rest in the workplace.

Time, the only true material we all share, is often stolen under the pretence of care and leaves many exhausted but unable to pinpoint the exact wording, the exact moment where the stealing began. Say it to one person and it sounds like a complaint, say it to another person and you sound like you have a chip on your shoulder. So you shut up and keep going, drained and confused.

In our view, forms of time theft include sexist and racist slurs, unreasonable demands, lack of empathy, contact at all hours, ghosting, unclear communication, false impressions, broken commitments, emotional manipulation, and empty promises. More subtly, it includes the misrepresentation of practices that claim to be about rest, care, and love but act in the opposite ways. How many times have you found yourself working around broken commitments suddenly wondering how you are going to pay your rent, or why you're now the point of contact because the director has suddenly gone on holiday and is not contactable? You work all night, on holidays, through the weekend, during your parental leave. For what? What's the point of creeds, if there are no deeds?

Many of you likely understand these interactions, where your energy and attention are consumed by someone else's demands, worries, or tasks – all under the guise of their care or love for you or the work. As you get older, maybe you start to wonder if the tables have turned and now you are on the other side stealing somebody else's time, because that is how it's always been. These actions prevent people from living their lives to the fullest. There is no rest when time is stolen from you. You cannot return the time that you stole from someone – and in an ethical sense, stolen time might be worse than a stolen object.

When starting Shimmer, we aimed to build an organization based on care and companionship. Inspired by Deborah Bird Rose's talk "Shimmer, when all you love is being trashed," we sought to create an intimate space fostering reciprocal practice and audience engagement while giving artists room to breathe. However, these principles, while honourable, became a trap. It became an obsessive external focus on what constitutes the right kind of 'care' and for who and when and so on. It left us depleted and led to a loss of critical engagement, causing us to feel distrustful.

We have long wondered how we should safeguard our mental and emotional resources from being burnt out. How can we make sure those who we work with are also protected? Protected from thematics and supported to work in an environment of creativity? As curators, artists, and individuals, managing these encounters in the arts is crucial. Cultural tendencies trap us into time theft, preventing growth, connection and rest. Rest, the very fabric that allows us to connect.

We need to build a community where rest is possible for everyone, not just those who can afford it or are privileged. And we need to remind ourselves that we're allowed to rest and we are not going to disappear if we take a three-day holiday. This does not mean to only allow rest for productivity's sake, in order to have better workers. But to rest without judgement. To set boundaries together, not as individuals. To not move the boundaries when others are not looking or resting. And to recognize that rest is for everyone and the first step in changing the freewheeling blatant theft of another's time is that we say it clearly and in print: rest, when all you love is being trashed, rest.

A Lull Nearby

The title of the work *A Lull Nearby* (2023), alludes both to a lullaby and the word 'lull', or a moment of rest or quiet. Lullabies are excellent examples of communication where subtle details play a significant role. As they are meant to accompany the transition to sleep, words are often of secondary importance, with the melody instead being hummed, for example.

The installation consists of two distinct elements. The first
is a scroll with texts and drawings; visitors are invited to take
pieces of the text home, leaving a gap in the scroll as they do.
This refers to the music storage method of a piano roll, where
the holes in a long piece of paper refer to notes that were played
in the past. The roll is attached to two found armrests that are
examples of 'hostile architecture.' They were placed by Dutch
municipalities on park benches to prevent people from sleeping
there. These armrests decide exactly who gets to sleep when,
where, and how. Arms can rest, but certain bodies, voices,
and thoughts cannot.

Across from the paper scroll are wooden benches that
resemble museum benches. On top of them is a big textile work
that the artist refers to as text(ile) writing, which foregrounds
the textural qualities of language. This textile is made by
a machinic process of writing and consists of a year of notes.
The machinic production of text(ile) writing relates to the
automatic humming of a lullaby. The text and textile work
asks to notice what has moved thoughts, not as the arrest and
capture of those movements but rather to reorient to what can't
be heard right now but might be able to be heard tomorrow.
A lullaby for hoping the world will wake up the next day.
The world as if it were habitable for all.

Photo by Cecilie Fang Jensen.

A *lull*aby for hoping the world will wake up the next day. The world as if it were habitable for a*ll*.

Heavy, metal armrests are enclosing a seat. They decide how to sit upright, not to lean, or lay down. What happens between this imposition of posture? When seen from the side, they look like the letter *l*

Activist group concerned with public space, *Vriendelijke Bankjes Bond*, removes armrests which are put in place to prevent people from sleeping on benches. These armrests decide exactly who gets to sleep when, where and how.

Arms can rest, but certain bodies, voices, and thoughts cannot.

Who can fall asleep between these *l* 's?

Who can *dream?* Who can scream?

There is a collection of images and words that cannot be written or captured. Not because there is no time or no concentration, but because the conditions for articulation are simply rare. They often arise side by side with other works or projects: the amount of works that do not make it to the page, frame, or stage. Nevertheless, they are very important for how the work came about. This is not a matter of nostalgia or a refusal to kill your darlings,

because they simply cannot be called darlings yet.

They are half words, a memor sound, a shape that hasn't closed yet. A painting that is always on stand-by while working on other paintings to catch all the paint that is too much for the one at hand. Or the paper created with all the small pieces of textile that are cut off textile works. Compositions of images and words that need different rhythms or conditions to create. They are audible, but not always intelligible. They work in their own logic of time, happening when least expected.

Heavy, metal bars impose how
to sit, not to lean, or swerve.
What happens between these
restrictions? Words wonder
if they can live between these
violent constraints. Sleep
wonders. *Life still waits.*

A year of notes and thinking in relation. A
scribble in thought, following a line and asking
what it means to share. A year of sketches and
words not on what is learned and shared, but
how it is learned and shared. How knowledge
might come into form. Capturing the year
in notes, noticing what has moved thoughts,
not as the arrest and capture of movements
but to reorient it to what can't be heard right
now, but might be able to be heard tomorrow.
Sharing as a dedication to change a rhythm.

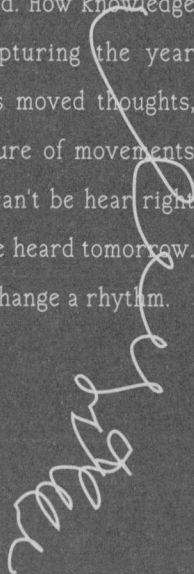

What happens in the ro*ll*ing and
unro*ll*ing of *text*?

Text(ile) writing helps to foreground the textural qualities of language. It also concerns a machinic process of writing. Threads are handled in rhythm and direction and are mirrored to the lines or words written. Small threads are punctured into the fabric during a lengthy process. This machinic production of text(ile) writing relates to the humming of a voice which asks for movement and resonance, rather than semantics. The texture of language as a quality moving into articulation, be it on paper, in air, or otherwise. From reading an enormous textile text that can be felt, heard, smelled, and seen, to crumbling a note in your pocket. Reading and writing not as something that happens individually. More rocks in hands while talking.

Lullabies are traditionally songs for helping an infant to sleep; to accompany them in a shift from waking to sleeping. Repetition through *lulling or rocking* is an important feature. Children learn language through lullabies among other things. Not in a direct way, but by intonation, rhythm and repetition which remind them of linguistic qualities they are already familiar with.

There are many dai*ll*y *lull*abies without a parent holding a child.

Notes notice. Thoughts unro*ll*. Notations follow the trace of sounds. A piano ro*ll*s is a long piece of paper with ho*l*es and gaps referring to notes played. It goes as follows: a pianist plays a piece, and their notes get traced with holes in a paper ro*ll*. For each next performance, the performer is present, but not playing. Rhythm, style, speed of the pianist remains; catching the movements of their past fingers. The music ro*ll*s and unro*ll*s again during the next ghostly performance, and the next one, and next, and next.

A ro*ll*ing of *l*'s a *lull*aby rather

than an imposition of form on words,

postures, and movements.

A *llllll*u*lllll*aby

concerns *resonance,*

haptics, movement, and

sound. It does not solely

concern the song sung

and is not necessarily

for a child.

A *llllllu lllll*aby

proposes language

as movement in a

performance.

*lllllll l*ine following

*llllllll*oop of a

llllll ace

cur*l* of a *l*ine ... *l*

*lllll lull*ing

To join someone in the transition

of falling asleep/falling awake. To

join someone making 100 drawings

of the letter *l* to talk about their

weekend. To find out in the morning:

today is the shape of... whistling,

bubbles, and *lllll* lychees for

breakfast.

The *lullaby* at
someone's birthday
that sends friends into
the night with one last
song.

A dream accompying you through breakfast and lunch, it is shaping the very real qualities that make the day as it is. The experience of relation is irreducible to one single location and time. It's not just that things are connected but that *their coming into relation shifts everything*.

The lullaby of a dancer waking themselves up by humming the song of last night's performance.

The lullaby of a writer that holds their hand on their heart when falling asleep, having no idea where the sleep will take them.

The lullaby of holding a rock in your hand while falling asleep, slowly rocking yourself to sleep.

Photo by Beeldsmits.

On Stillness, Rest, and Darkness (as Blackness)

Rest your body, aabo,
heavy with distention, dreams lost in translation,

dreams of drifting in space, the rings of Saturn
around the neck of Layla, dreams macerated
under grief's gaze. Bless your drowsy blue slumber,
swayed by the patron saint of restlessness
– Warsan Shire[1]

....

[1] Warsan Shire, *Bless the Daughter Raised by a Voice in Her Head: Poems*
(London: Chatto & Windus Penguin Random House Group, 2022), 17.

Sadness and anger manifest as non-rest. What does space to breathe and listen look like in times of mourning and grief? How do we hold each other and ourselves when we are mourning the loss of belief? Why do we search for refuge in the individual instead of in the collective? We come together in the unknown to mourn and to celebrate. We embrace not fully seeing in the dark. We continue to be with it, without (re)presenting it.

FOR THE FUNGAL FLOOR,
WE COME TOGETHER

How can we rest our bodies? By acknowledging unrest and coming together. We organized a performance as part of the recent group show at Buro Stedelijk titled *Manifestation #16: Descent into Fungal.*[2] Every Thursday evening, we came together in Buro Stedelijk's Central Space where different artists performed for the mycelium floor and for the public. Hereby we collectively took care of the mycelium floor that was part of a large installation by Dutch design brand YUME YUME. On Thursday evening, 7 December 2023, musician Ranie Ribeiro played the harp for the fungal floor and the public, and shared a meditative, wholesome, and restful performance.

----

[2] I have chosen to speak from a 'we' that grounds me in the experience of what I am, which I share with many others and also don't, for 'we' are each feeling-beings in our own ways, informed by being and holding different identities. The artwork in question makes me feel I could belong to a 'collective we,' one that few feel often at any given moment – but in writing about this artwork, I feel for a moment that 'we' belong together. Because so many readers of this piece have wanted me to define this 'we,' I will do so, bringing back Glissant's notion that we not succumb to the compulsion to understanding, a pathology, which Édouard Glissant, and Fabienne Kanor after him, actively address in naming their studies 'poetics' rather than, say, 'philosophies,' as in Glissant's *Poétique de la Relation* (1990) and Kanor's *La poétique de la cale: Variations sur le bateau négrier* (2022). The 'we' I craft here builds and refers to a malleable 'we' that cannot be defined. It might call some of us in and others out. A 'we' that grounds me, and others. It is a 'we' that allows you to decide how you receive it: "#16 DESCENT INTO FUNGAL," Buro Stedelijk, burostedelijk.nl/manifestations/16-descent-into-fungal.

INFORMED BY ETYMOLOGIES,
WE COME TOGETHER

Following the Cambridge dictionary, 'rest' means "to (cause someone or something to) stop doing a particular activity or stop being active for a period of time in order to relax and get back [...] strength."[3] Thus, it is a temporary state between more active ways of being. However, in her blog post "The Stillest," cultural programmer and writer Simone Zeefuik – referring to Thomas J. Price's sculpture *Moments Contained* – writes: "It's a beauty we often miss or rush past because we have been made to believe that stillness is a waste of time rather than a part of it.[4] This stillness, the motionlessness, is where rest manifests. To recharge but, for all we know, also to stay in that particular state. To embrace the motionless rest.

RELINQUISHING UNDERSTANDING,
WE MIGHT (ALL) COME TOGETHER (BETTER)

Sometimes rest means giving up trying to understand, becoming comfortable with not knowing and finding respite in that. Could rest mean not showing up? And what might rest manifest as for women, trans, queer, and queered bodies working in the cultural field?

Might it sometimes mean opting out, and opting out of what? And at other moments, opting in to other ways of organizing or attending moments of joy, of fun? How do we find collectivity and even togetherness in a field that relentlessly puts forward individuality and 'personal wins?' How can we find true collaborative (curatorial) practices in the work we do?

....

[3] "Rest," Cambridge Dictionary, dictionary.cambridge.org/dictionary/english/rest.

[4] Simone Zeefuik, "The Stillest," *laZeefuik*, 11 May 2023, lazeefuik.com/?s=rest.

ON STILLNESS, REST, AND DARKNESS (AS BLACKNESS)

THANKS TO COLLECTIVE SILENT GRIEF,
(VARYING CONSTELLATIONS OF SOME OF US)
COME TOGETHER (AS WE INVITE OTHERS TO ACCOMPANY
US IN THE STILLNESS THAT IS ALSO SOLIDARITY)

What does rest look like when work is exhausting, and when the working conditions are not made for you to exist but rather to sharpen your anxiety, your fatigue, almost inviting you into the indented failure-narrative of a 'burnout?' Thoughts I am not too eager to share because of the vulnerability, the almost intentional aggression to make me feel shame, which are barren of lexica to acknowledge the magnitude of resilience that is part of the Black and female experience. As Zora Neale Hurston states so profoundly in her novel *Their Eyes Were Watching God*: "If you are silent about your pain, they'll kill you and say you enjoyed it."[5] There is a lot of rest in accepting the mourning and grief that surrounds the work we do. This doesn't mean we discount the love and joy we encounter; it merely means we refuse to be silent about the pain.

....

[5] Zora Neale Hurston, *Their Eyes Were Watching God* (London: Virago Press, 2018).

MAY DEATH AS LIFE GRACE US,
(THOSE OF US OPEN TO IT), SO WE (MIGHT) COME TOGETHER

In her famous book *All About Love*, bell hooks starts the chapter "Loss: Loving into Life and Death" with the sentence: "Love makes us feel more alive," and follows with a sentence that undergirds this: "Living in a state of lovelessness we feel we might as well be dead; everything within us is silent and still."[6] Here, I focus on the stillness, the motionlessness of lovelessness and the strong difference between the stillness of death and that of rest. Death doesn't have to be loveless or even motionless. Death holds the potentiality of new life, new forms of being, new ways of holding each other; and through this, love doesn't die. We can find rest in mourning; find togetherness in mourning and propose motion as a part of rest. I return here to the memory of the fungal floor that we collectively took care of at Buro Stedelijk for eight weeks; but more so, as Anna Lowenhaupt Tsing states in *The Mushroom at the End of the World: On the Possibility of Life in Capitalist Ruins*, that "global landscapes today are strewn with this kind of ruin. Still, these places can be lively despite announcements of their death; abandoned asset fields sometimes yield new multispecies and multicultural life. In a global state of precarity, we don't have choices other than looking for life in this ruin."[7] Let us find a nocturnal kind of rest that happens when we are together in motion. Perhaps in mourning in the dark, while feeling the vibrations through our fibres and understanding that rest, sometimes, doesn't have to do anything with sleeping or stillness but rather with moving, touch, and collectivity. Such as Ranie Ribeiro's performance on the harp inside Buro Stedelijk's Central Space, or Popcaan's concert in the Melkweg on 4 December 2023, but also S*an D. Henry-Smith's performance *tremor (thunder)*, or Thomas J. Price's sculpture *Moments Contained*.

....

[6] bell hooks, *All About Love: New Visions* (New York: William Morrow, 2000).

[7] Anna Lowenhaupt Tsing, *The Mushroom at the End of the World: On the Possibility of Life in Capitalist Ruins*, (Princeton: Economics Books, Princeton University Press, 2015), 6.

ACKNOWLEDGING SHAME, ALL OF US,
SO THAT WE MAY COME TOGETHER

Artist Simnikiwe Buhlungu said in collective conversation that: "The only way to move forward is to embrace the experiences that come to you, even the ones that are not pleasant." We're encouraged to acknowledge the painfulness of experience and hereby own it, share it, and diminish the shame around it. Love is an action, according to hooks, not simply a feeling.[8] Love is a political action, and abuse and neglect are the opposite of love. As we participate in both mourning and joy, in rest and in action, as active witnesses in this confrontation, what we engage with is the complex and contradictory form of intimate work that can be shared publicly. Just as Tina Campt helps us to 'listen to images,' and to fully embrace 'the Black gaze,' by referring to Deana Lawson's work, Campt helps us to sit with the possible discomfort and complexity we might encounter. Lawson's images stage encounters that require work.[9] Rest in this instance is work just as work in this instance is rest.

DARKNESS NOT AS TEMPORALITY
THAT SHOULD BE FIXED BY LIGHT,
DARKNESS' DISCOMFORT AS FULL POTENTIAL

Darkness has the capacity to elude capture, generate alternative relations to space, and resist, interrupt, and disturb. This rethinking through a lens of potentiality and vitality provides possibilities to recover darkness, indeed, to recover Blackness, into the restorative of darkness' stillness – Blackness is inseparable from darkness – from being overdetermined by its negative signifier. We sit with the discomfort of not knowing, of being in the dark, and of holding this not knowing with its full potentiality instead of searching for the light. Being with the discomfort, we are thereby not alone. Together we rest.

....

[8] hooks, *All About Love*, 4-5.

[9] Tina Campt, *Listening to Images* (Durham: Duke University Press, 2017); Tina Campt, *A Black Gaze: Artists Changing How We See* (Massachusetts: MIT Press, 2021).

Other Indias
Bloom at Night

AN INTERVIEW BY
MEGHANA KARNIK

For Nocturnalities, *I interviewed*   *Amsterdam-based
collective other indias. As a group of*   *interdisciplinary
artists, academics, and cultural workers from the Indian
subcontinent, other indias' goals are to resist ethno-nationalism
and centre voices that embrace the nuances of caste, the
Northeast, Kashmir, and interconnected liberation movements
that are systematically pushed to the margins. Their organizing
unfolds in a context of stressed and destabilized communal
relations. As a counter-hegemonic project, they must face and
process casteism, patriarchal violence, oppression of religious
minorities, and historical trauma of partition as these issues
arise in real-time, within the group, to make way for a coalition.*

Our paths crossed during Hope is a discipline, *an exhibition and research network that brings together cultural workers who practice hope as communal labour.*[1]*Inspired by Hala Aylan's recent essay on ´diasporic witnessing,´ an account of a Palestinian-American poet bearing witness to atrocity from a distance, I felt called to speak with other indias in relation to this idea.*[2]*How are they resolving labour strategies in their movement for a politics of rest, specific to the Indian subcontinent? How do they navigate perpetual, intra-communal unrest? This interview was conducted in March 2024 with two of the collective's initiators, who opted to remain anonymous. It has been edited for brevity.*

---

[1]The exhibition *Hope is a discipline* took place between 6 October and 23 November 2023 at de Appel in Amsterdam, Netherlands. Also see: www.deappel.nl/en/archive/events/1202-curatorial-programme-2023-hope-is-a-discipline.

[2]Hala Aylan, "I am not there and I am not here," *The Guardian*, 28 January 2024,

MEGHANA KARNIK: I remember it was a protest that brought other indias together. Was it in 2022?

other indias: We met in front of the Indian Embassy in The Hague, at a protest opposing the demolition of activist Afreen Fatima's house.● It was our first time interacting with the group who was present there. We're very shy people and it is actually kind of unlikely that we would end up initiating a collective. We cooked pulao and took it to the protests so people could eat. We were all sitting a little far away from the embassy, on the staircase that led to a park of sorts, eating and talking. It was because of that moment, we assume, that other indias began, because after the protest and speeches, everyone felt this energy and urgency. There was a conversation about how we could continue. It seemed like a lot of people had gathered from the universities in The Hague, and we felt we missed this space in Amsterdam. There was a gap.

Bringing the pulao to the protest was key. What was quite clear from the interaction was that while it was important for us to keep responding to the atrocities of the Indian state, how are we able to care for each other? How are we able to sustain a movement? Because you can't sustain a movement without caring for each other. The food and community aspects showed us this.

....

●Zafar Aafaq, "India activist Afreen Fatima says her house bulldozed 'illegally.'" *Al Jazeera*, 13 June 2022, www.aljazeera.com/news/2022/6/13/act-of-vendetta-afreen-fatima-on-her-house-bulldozed-in-india.

A month and a half later, we took all of these questions to a picnic that we organized in Flevopark for Independence Day on 15 August. An open invitation was shared amongst our networks and with people we had kept in touch with after the protest. We hadn't named ourselves yet. We didn't know if this was going somewhere, we just wanted to continue the conversation because, until that moment, there was no space in Amsterdam to share. During the picnic, we asked ourselves if we could become a collective. Who is 'we,' when we say we, in terms of Indians? So it was a bit uncomfortable. It was not like we were there for a happy occasion, nor that we came together with shared values. The intention was also to make our urgencies explicit.

MEGHANA KARNIK: I'm curious, why do you think people joined the Independence Day picnic? How did it go?

other indias: To give you an idea; it was a small group, less than twenty. We spent many hours getting to know each other through a round of introductions; why are you here, how long have you been in the Netherlands? It became clear that most who came didn't have this kind of space to gather with other Indians before. There were layers of positionality – across caste, class, religion, geopolitics. People were talking about privilege, but also about getting consumed by privilege and not knowing how to move ahead. One of the reasons we gathered is because we didn't just want to be reactionaries, but to have more sustained movements. We talked about rest, actually, because that was something one of us had been working on already. That's when a lot of different perspectives started coming up. Rest is a privilege to some people, especially for marginalized groups in India.[4]

---

[4] A helpful resource for developing literacy on caste equity is "What is Caste?," *Equality Labs*, www.equalitylabs.org/what-is-caste.

There was a dichotomy: one group said the personal is personal, and we must focus on the political because the urgency is immediate. Another group said, urgency will remain immediate, so we have to find ways to keep going, to consider aspects of rest and joy, because this has a revolutionary potential. How do we make space for joy within our movements? If we can afford to rest, shouldn't we opt for that as a way to sustain ourselves?

MEGHANA KARNIK: So, the first meeting immediately opened some long-standing debates of revolutionary struggle.

other indias: Exactly. Everyone wanted to continue meeting, and we recognized everyone had different ideas, starting points, and needs for why they wanted to access a space like [other indias]. So we posed the question of, let's say we become a collective or a more regular group that met and did things together? An active Netherlands-based collective that was referenced quite a bit was Sehaq Queer Refugees Group (focused on experiences of refugees from the MENA regions), due to the kind of community activities they were hosting. We took them as an example. We wanted to work on film screenings and learn to communicate our values. And then, people started offering up spaces that they were involved in – that's how we did our first screening, *Dr. Babasaheb Ambedkar* (2000). We just used the resources we had, by word of mouth, expanding by talking to people.

MEGHANA KARNIK: Some South Asian spaces seek to decentre India. Tell me about the name, about India's significance in this work, in the context of South Asian organizing.

other indias: The name 'other indias' came from a professor here in Amsterdam, who would talk about the concept behind *Mother India* (1957). Have you seen it? It's a Bollywood film. We don't necessarily recommend it. Taking a leaf from the title, she proposed, "What if the group was called 'Other India?'" India seemed very limiting. We wondered, could we make room for the plurality of this group? It goes back to the first meeting, the context of diasporic being.

Plurality also feeds the understanding that India is not homogeneous. The Indian state has been desperately pushing for the idea of 'one India,' right? So, to not fall into that same trap of saying 'we're all one,' but actually acknowledging our differences – especially with caste, Kashmir, or the Northeast – we ended up with the name 'other indias.' By the end of 2022, we started drafting a document that we call constituting other indias. It's an open-access, continuously changing document, with many of our ideas. There's a line: "We are working to find ways to care for each other better; despite our differences, because of our differences." That part was important to us. There is an uncomfortableness to deal with, to make room for meeting new people with disparate experiences.

Since we attended the *March Meeting 2024: Tawashujat* at Sharjah Art Foundation, we have been reflecting on the name. We have continuously made space for movements and thinking from the Indian subcontinent, but we have not been able to give much space to South Asia as a region, as a whole. However, we are not shy to call ourselves a South Asian space. There's an artist, Himali Singh Soin, who writes about this in the manifesto, *Subcontinentment* (2020), "we are a part of, and apart from." It's a wonderful document and I recommend it because it articulates where we're coming from better than we could here. We also want to hold the Indian state accountable, so we have to use its name. Like last year, when we hosted the *Solidarity Vigil* at Framer Framed, which was in response to ongoing violence in Manipur and other regions. We collectively wrote a statement for the press release. A short excerpt from our statement goes: "We are here, we too belong, we too are India, we are other indias and we call other indias everywhere to join us."

MEGHANA KARNIK: I remember that line well.

other indias: We also recognize that there is a movement decentring India's focus, and that there are people who are joining our group because of the name itself, because of these questions. We're very open to changing the name, actually. This is something we started reflecting on during the *March Meeting*. Someone made the comparison with Palestine to Kashmir.

Are we imagining India as it once was? What about the future of India, as an ethno-nationalist state, is that something that aligns with us? We are sitting with these questions, and if we end up realizing this is not a good way to represent ourselves, we will change the name.

MEGHANA KARNIK: other indias will be two years old in June 2024. What have been some of the reasons people gather with you, when you look back on it?

other indias: It's a really good question. We started to ask ourselves this question of our greater intentions together, and have been thinking about defining an intention for each gathering. In the beginning, there was a shared need for a community space, where people could hang out, have chai and talk, but that isn't the purpose of our events. One thing, in terms of a generic intention or purpose, is our responsibility as a diasporic Indian community. If we are quiet, we're complicit. We aren't knowledge or culture makers. We are vehicles for existing movements, voices, and ideas that were already resisting the hegemony of the state.

An example of a reason for a gathering was a wish to explore joy as resistance. We had this idea of a 'joy party,' but we didn't want it to be a party. We wanted to be able to root everything in the politics of our community, in the geography of our community. We formed it to become the *Queer Muslim Joy Party* at Bar Bario (2023), where we invited artists to host a poetry workshop, a kleicha (Iraqi   Eid cookies)- making session as a collective ritual of   remembrance, and screened a recently-released   tender film by an Indian filmmaker that centres the   daily life of an extended working-class family in a Muslim quarter in the heart of Ahmedabad. The funds raised with this programme were directed to Sonzal Welfare Trust, an NGO that supports and advocates for trans people in Kashmir. Perhaps it is redundant to say, but we were exploring our privilege of being able to gather to celebrate (as a queer, interfaith group).

MEGHANA KARNIK: How do you navigate different positionalities and fault lines?

other indias: Well, this will be our most candid answer. Because for a good year, there were only two of us able to continuously talk and marinate these questions and perspectives, to bring them back to a core intention. Two people who get along with each other, who have similar belief systems. We did not want to impose a structure that replicated the same issues plaguing capitalist spaces, or leftist spaces we had each participated in before. Later, in the constituting other indias document, we made a table, asked people to put down roles and resources they could offer, in terms of skill, knowledge, and capacities. And, it remains empty, which is funny and also telling. It remained unstructured. We didn't want to impose a structure, so instead, we would organize things, and if people wanted to organize something under this umbrella, they could let us know. We started to have two groups: an other indias group and an organizing group. These groups are fluid, you can jump in and out. The group discusses what we are thinking about, and we open it up for some days or weeks, to see who has the capacity or shares the urgency. There is no forced expectation in the group. It's not like you're in, only if you're able to contribute.

When we first gathered, we said we wanted to have a sustained movement. Someone had to keep doing things. Because we know this movement-building is not something that just happens [on its own]. You know, once you decide it happens, it happens. That's what happened with the *Queer Muslim Joy Party* – we had a really good turnout. That's when a more collective ideation started, of "Oh, what are the possibilities?" Between that event and *Hope is a discipline* (October–November 2023) at de Appel, our organizing group expanded from three, to five, to now about thirteen. It was impressive.

MEGHANA KARNIK: Ola Hassanain speaks about the 'preparatory work´ needed for solidarity. How does the group make decisions together? What do you want people to understand about other indias, in its relationship to nocturnality and rest?

other indias: At the moment, what has become common practice is that if any ideas are circulated by members of other indias in the larger group, someone walks up to us and says: "Hey, I want to do this with other indias," then puts it up to the organizing subgroup. This group now deals with the questions of, "Do we have time, space, energy for this? Why are we participating? What's the intention? What are we organizing?" It's not a perfect process in any way. Compared to last year, we have more questions and more feelings, actually, than answers. With thirteen people in the organizing group, our differences are more on the surface. This year, we had a general meeting to introduce new people to other indias; where we talked about all the things we've done in the past, what resources we have currently, and what urgencies are arising that we find ourselves responsible to organize or respond to. We noticed that there is as much interest in being involved in organizing, as there are people who just want to access the community.

At the beginning, there was more frustration with that, when there were only two organizers. Thinking of the initial table of roles and resources in the *constituting other indias* document; we're starting to recognize that everyone who comes plays different roles. Some bring people, some organize, and some just show up. It's a lot of work, actually, to show up consistently. There are important roles being played, even though we don't know some people in the group personally. There is no one way to be an activist, no one right method. There's also frustration that spaces like this already existed [in Amsterdam], a few years ago, maybe a decade ago. We heard there were two groups that had different values, so they didn't want to interact with each other. And that story made us so sad because that's literally what the criticism of the left is about: we can't even get along with each other. We cannot keep having the same expectation of how people show up in their activism. Our role as facilitators is just to bring these people together, absorb the feedback, keep conversations that are happening going, and put it into organizing.

This is a volunteer-run initiative, without funding, without a legal status. We don't have an online presence and come together by word of mouth. We aren't homogeneous; we are researchers, academics, artists, and cultural workers. We keep each other informed. This ambiguity is practical, it allows us some stealth, but is also generative for us. Coming back to nocturnality, we have to maintain anonymity like this for safety reasons, but anonymity and ambiguity has also opened possibilities of collaborators, such as the invitation to Sharjah. Though we are different from the artists and cultural practitioners usually invited to the *March Meeting*, we'll take our agenda there. It's also in the way we facilitate our events, the introduction we give. We choose to not talk as much about who we are, as what we do. For example, with *Pickling for Posterity* at de Appel [which addressed social reproduction, caste, food, and land justice], we chose to create a path towards the direct testimonies of women, through screenings of Dolly Kikon's *Seasons of Life* (2020), Jumana Manna's *Foragers* (2022), and Bhargav Prasad & Ain Contractor's *Fight With Care* (2023).

MEGHANA KARNIK: How do you reflect on Mariame Kaba's idea of hope as a discipline and communal labour?

other indias: Before reflecting and situating it in the past, it's something that we have to sit with today. As of two days ago, the Citizenship (Amendment) Act (CAA) became an act.[5] It's real, it's there [in India] now. We are far away geographically but our minds are there, our hearts are there. There are conversations about organizing in the future. But we're all sitting in this reality that this big thing just happened. They just pulled it out of thin air. What kind of energies are we then channelling to meet, now? It's something we're asking ourselves every day, even today.

It goes back to food and nourishment, right? The idea that the urgency of the now will remain. How are we able to sustain ourselves in showing up? How are we able to build resilience as a community, in showing up? And that was why the first one and a half years until now we have been centring this question of "How are we able to care for each other better?"

....

[5] BBC News, "CAA: India's new citizenship law explained," 12 March 2024, www.bbc.com/news/world-asia-india-50670393.

There is a practice of friendship within the movement we're trying to build, because it is people that make movements. How do we keep relying on each of those friendships, as a way to find and regain our strength, again and again? Without friendship, hope is even more distant. So, hope is a discipline. It truly is. It's a practice.

At our general meeting, we asked members what other indias meant to them and turned it into a small zine. One line that directly answers the prompt says, "I joined and continue to engage with other indias as it gives me a sense of belonging, hope, and safety as I learn to expand my imagination and ways one can resist and move through the world with love." So I guess in a way, other indias was the space for people to hope, it was a manifestation of that desire.

MEGHANA KARNIK: There is a line by Eula Biss about how we are each other's environment[16] The idea is basically one of interdependence, that we can't just practice 'self-care' and hope to be immune to looming catastrophes. I wonder about your response to that. What does it mean to be organizing against the Indian state, in this environment, in the Netherlands?

other indias: Our practice is directly connected to our being here in the Netherlands. It's impossible to imagine outside of that fact. It has also brought a lot to the surface when we talk about solidarity amongst friends outside of the group, or at work. It has exposed a lot of layers to the Indian subcontinent and diaspora. This year and in the future, our focus is to build a movement together with the Indo-Caribbean diaspora, because so far we haven't made an attempt to directly engage with them in Amsterdam. Now, our organizing will constitute exactly this, of learning each other's environments, learning each other's politics and social context, to build this movement together. Because it's not like the Hindutva/Brahminical/patriarchal/capitalistic ethos is still limited to the geography of India. It's here, in Dutch politics.

....

[16] "However we choose to think of the social body, we are each other's environment. Immunity is a shared space – a garden we tend together." Eula Biss, *On Immunity: An Inoculation* (Minneapolis: Graywolf Press, 2014). Recommended by Marina Christodoulidou.

So how can we engage with the social circumstances here?

They say necessity is the mother of invention. Perhaps this politically engaged group begins with strategies of care and sustenance precisely because of the absence of support structures in the Netherlands context. The geographic shift of diaspora from one set of conditions to another, produces a new politics of rest, with new positionalities taking up care work for a collective that is in formation. Their organizing must attend to structural casteism, patriarchal violence, oppression of religious minorities, and the historical trauma of colonial partition as it arises in real time, within the group dynamic. Notably, other indias' members don't consider themselves to be culture-makers as much as conduits.

Listening to other indias speak about bringing pulao to a protest, I think of how much the collective identifies with social reproduction – of cooking, to feed people partaking in direct action, or using a picnic to shift individual silos into a communal space. These are some of other indias' first acts. The idea strikes me that the group is not a solar entity, which is to say, projecting itself outward and claiming territory/authorship; but a nocturnal one, oriented to facilitate receptivity, deep listening, and making space to process. Someone wakes up before dawn breaks and prepares a home for its inner workings.

As the group's core organizing circle expands from two to thirteen, it contends with new questions and shifts a focus from the Indian subcontinent to Indo-Caribbean communities who have long lived in the Netherlands. It continues its work in the context of counterinsurgency, of manufactured polarization of South Asian diasporic communities. How will other indias continue digesting and alchemizing the structural violence of the times? How does the necessity of the space they create, and its need to transform, speak for exhausted and failed states?

Fuelling Constant Resistance

A CONVERSATION WITH
RASHA DAKKAK BY AGATA BAR

In the context of *Nocturnalities*, many conversations revolved around the privilege associated with rest. The right and means to care for oneself and take a pause are privileges often intertwined with race, gender, and class, not just economics. Audre Lorde captured this in 1988 when she wrote, "Caring for myself is not self-indulgence, it is self-preservation, and that is an act of political warfare.[1]

How does this concept translate into rest strategies during times of actual warfare? Particularly when experiencing conflict from a distance, from the safety of the Netherlands, while constantly being confronted with   it? What is the role of art and design education   and practitioners in times of crisis?
To explore this, I spoke with Rasha   Dakkak, a Palestinian graphic designer, researcher, educator, and Head of the Graphic Design Department at the Gerrit Rietveld Academy in Amsterdam. She shared her insights on rest and self-care strategies, especially in the months following 7 October 2023.

----

[1] Audre Lorde, *A Burst of Light and Other Essays* (Mineola, NY: Ixia Press, 2017), 95.

AGATA BAR: Andrea Knezović and I initially contacted you because we were inspired by the title of an event organized in solidarity with Palestinian people that took place at Vleeshal.[2] *We Who Believe in Freedom Cannot Rest* is a sentence from a resistance song written by Sweet Honey in the Rock as a tribute to civil rights activist Ella Baker. You and I are both working at the Gerrit Rietveld Academy. It's early July, and we both are closing an academic year in the pursuit of rest. Each year, we get a number of weeks to heal our exhaustion and to reset before the academic year starts again in September. But can you actually rest? There is an expectation to continue the fight and activist work, even beyond our exhaustion.

RASHA DAKKAK: Yes, it does feel that way. The Palestinian struggle is relentless and ever-evolving, and the unending strife for justice surely keeps us restless. Pursuing justice demands continuous action, but we must recognize that rest is a vital form of resistance. Taking a break, whatever that break means to oneself, is not a sign of abandoning the fight; it is essential for maintaining strength and ensuring the longevity of our efforts. Believing that one can sustain the same energy and intensity indefinitely is a recipe for burnout. Rest could allow us to return with renewed vigour, enhanced effectiveness, and new strategies.

....

[2] *We Who Believe in Freedom Cannot Rest*, event at Vleeshal Center for Contemporary Art on 7 December 2023, vleeshal.nl/archive/we-who-believe-in-freedom-cannot-rest-event.

Reflecting on the recent academic environment, we've witnessed student uprisings globally, as well as at our institution where we experienced a six-week encampment. I think this intense period has given us a lot to think about regarding new forms of advocacy. After such a prolonged occupation, I find it necessary to consider alternative approaches that build on what we've learned. I would say that the next phase should steer away from the same formats we've relied on in the past. While occupations and encampments have their place and can be powerful, they're also physically exhausting and unsustainable in the long run. These methods can wear down those who participate and deplete resources that might be better used elsewhere.

AGATA BAR: With student encampments, I was thinking how they operate nocturnally. How the police violence we witnessed in the last months happened at night.[3] How allowing the encampment to stay overnight was the ultimate goal of the student body, and how the goal of institutions like the police, the boards of our universities, and the municipality is to deprive students of rest.

RASHA DAKKAK: I read the encampment's decision to stay overnight as a representation of their commitment to not rest till they achieved what they set out to do, and this drive for justice is what kept them going, even when they were exhausted. And yes, those who oppose such goals might seek to thwart the efforts of others during the night, as lack of rest can lead to discouragement.

....

[3] On 6 May 2024, students from the University of Amsterdam (UvA), Amsterdam University College (AUC), and the Vrije Universiteit (VU) set up an encampment at Roeterseiland in solidarity with the people of Palestine. This action was inspired by similar encampments that had emerged on university campuses across the United States and around the world in the preceding month. Students faced shocking violence from police, with hundreds arrested in Amsterdam and Utrecht. Bulldozers destroyed barricades protecting liberated campuses in Amsterdam, while riot police used batons, pepper spray, and dogs against the crowds. The protests and different types of encampments continued for weeks in different locations and were regularly met with more police violence.

Back in 2021, I began wrestling with some questions about activism and protest.[4] The world is overflowing with injustice, and suffering is happening everywhere all the time. It made me wonder: what role should I play in this vast landscape of oppression? Should I be out on the streets protesting every day? How do I weigh the significance of all these atrocities, and how can I distribute my care fairly? These questions were really weighing on me. As I thought more about it, I realized that I needed to find a way to integrate these fights for justice into my everyday life, into my daily practices, and within my skill set.

AGATA BAR: In the nine months since the war in Gaza started, have you participated in any actions or forms of support that you think have contributed to more sustainable activism?

RASHA DAKKAK: In recent months, I've taken on different roles within the academic realm and through my artistic practice, involving research, writing, and public talks. One example is a workshop I designed called *Beyond Despair: To Stand for Something*.[5] As the global humanitarian crisis continues, I've observed a widespread feeling of helplessness and uncertainty among those around me who are struggling with how they can make a meaningful contribution. The ongoing Israeli war on Gaza and the rest of Palestine, which has persisted for over one hundred days, has intensified these feelings of despair and stressed the need for concrete action. Many people find the idea of taking action intimidating, often questioning their depth of knowledge and the authenticity and impact of their potential contributions. This workshop was created in response to these urgent concerns, aiming to help guide the overall sentiments of helplessness that many of us are experiencing.

....

[4] In late April and May of 2021, a rapidly unfolding chain of events included protests against Israeli plans to ethnically cleanse the Palestinian neighbourhood of Sheikh Jarrah in Jerusalem, days of violent Israeli raids and hundreds of injuries at the Al-Aqsa Mosque, and a bombing campaign on the Gaza Strip.

[5] The workshop took place at the Royal Academy of Art (KABK) in January and at Gerrit Rietveld Academy in April 2024, both at the bachelor's level in the Graphic Design department.

During the workshop, participants were encouraged to engage with texts narrating the lived experiences of Palestinians, both within Palestine and in the diaspora. These narratives, rich with personal accounts of life intertwined with music, imagination, dreams, education, and institutional interactions, served as a foundation for participants to connect with their own realities. By drawing parallels between their experiences and those depicted in the texts, participants could cultivate a deeper empathy and understanding, fostering a more sustainable and personal form of activism.

The second edition of the workshop featured designers Engy Aly and Ghalia Elsrakbi, who provided a historical context of visual resistance through prints and publications from the Middle East between the 1970s and the 1990s. This historical perspective not only enriched the participants' understanding, but also illustrated the enduring legacy of visual resistance and its evolution over time.

I suspect that such an approach, which focuses on building personal connections, historical awareness, and utilizing already acquired skills and assets, could present a sustainable model of activism. It shifts the focus from short-term reactions to long-term engagement and resilience, enabling participants to contribute meaningfully and authentically to a cause they care about. This method not only sustains the momentum of activism but also ensures that it is rooted in genuine understanding and personal relevance, thus making the support of activism more enduring and impactful.

....

The texts are a collection of excerpts taken from Rasha Dakkak, et al., eds., *Durable Discussions. Essays from the Disarming Design Department* (Onomatopee, 2022), including "How to Regain Freedom" by Jara van Teeffelen, "Celebration as Resistance" by Karmel Sabri, "Sifting Through Design Memory" by Rasha Dakkak, and "The Arming Act: Reflections on Cultures of Popular Education" by Saja Amro.

AGATA BAR: It makes me think about these sessions organized by Learning Palestine,[7] an initiative of artists, academics, intellectuals, and community members that uses education as a way of talking about what happened or what's happening in Palestine. While attending one of their performative lectures with quite a diverse group – there was a Lebanese person, some Dutch and German people, and I am Polish – we all realized that none of us ever learned at school about what happened in 1948, what happened throughout the 75 years since the establishment of Israel and what happened to Palestinians. Even if you ask clear questions, the answers aren't straightforward because, in the end, only a small group of people are actually educated on the topic.

RASHA DAKKAK: To effectively counter opposition, being well-informed is essential. This not only involves a broad understanding, but also a nuanced grasp of the subject. Understanding the struggle and recognizing how we can contribute from our unique positions and professions is crucial.

As an image maker, I had a pivotal realization when I first encountered early Zionist posters. These posters, which depicted Palestine as an uninhabited paradise, showcased the land's potential while intentionally ignoring the existing Palestinian population. By portraying Palestine as an empty land of opportunity and promise, these posters appealed to various aspirations, from agricultural pursuits to urban living or historical connections.

For me, this highlighted the immense power and influence of visual and print media in shaping perceptions and narratives. The posters' ability to cater to different motivations for migration underscored the critical role of image-making in advancing ideological agendas. It led me to think of an endless list of notions on how visual communication can be employed to oppress people. Exclusion and the omission of certain groups from visual narratives can render them invisible and deny their existence and contributions.

....

[7] Learning Palestine, learningpalestine.hotglue.me.

Stereotyping can eternalize discrimination, and using demeaning representations can dehumanize a group. Repeatedly showing traumatic images of a group can desensitize the public to their suffering. Controlling the visual narrative can maintain a specific historical interpretation. Recognizing such notions can help challenge and dismantle visual oppression.

This insight is relevant across various fields, whether in visual communication, art, medicine, or law. Unfortunately, traditional education often overlooks these perspectives, favouring a more consumerist approach. Understanding multifaceted histories as well as contemporary realities empowers us to contribute meaningfully.

AGATA BAR: You mentioned the visual resistance before. While researching the subject of rest, I found Tricia Hersey's book particularly inspiring.[8] Her perspective on rest as a form of resistance against white supremacy and the capitalist system deeply resonated with me. Rest and self-care as a soft force in opposition to fighting physically; it is something that you do individually, but also spread within your community. This approach to self-care involves recognizing the source of the pressure to act or perform, rather than just engaging in mindfulness as promoted by neoliberal ideals.[9] I'm really inspired by this part where she creates awareness about the historical implications of rest deprivation and preaches that people of colour should claim their rest as a form of reparations for their ancestors' forced labour. It is almost an intergenerational debt within the Afro-American population when it comes to rest. And I'm also wondering if that can translate to what you are talking about, as an opposition to the actual fight on a front line?

....

[8] Tricia Hersey, *Rest Is Resistance* (London: Aster 2022), 34-38, 144-145.

[9] The neoliberal Self embraces mindfulness as a form of capitalist spirituality, ideal for its preservation, while promoting the notion that each person should manage their own 'self-care' to stay employable and productive. See: Ronald E. Purser, *McMindfulness: How Mindfulness Became the New Capitalist Spirituality* (London: Repeater Books, 2019).

RASHA DAKKAK: The past few months have been unbearable, with each day bringing a new battle. Such battles have been a constant confrontation with my Palestinian identity, which now blazes like an open wound laid bare for all to see. This wound is sometimes met with empathy, other times with discrimination, and other times with indifference. Before this period, there was a time when this wound remained concealed, hidden from the relentless public gaze. That concealment occasionally provided a form of solace from the endless scrutiny.

I've been contemplating the metaphor of camouflage and how my family has navigated this struggle over the last few decades. They weren't front-line fighters; instead, they blended in, revealing their true intentions selectively to protect themselves from the immediate pressures of oppressive systems. This approach mirrors Hersey's advocacy for rest and self-care, offering a way to resist without constant visible struggle. Camouflage can enable tactical retreats and healing, empowering communities to fight on their own terms.

I've also been reflecting on the potential differences among fighters. As a Palestinian refugee who has never set foot in Palestine, my experience is shaped by a prolonged absence from the homeland. Our existence outside Palestine has trained us, through lived experience, to navigate a different web of identities and struggles compared to those living within its borders. Each context tells a different story, demands a unique form of resilience, and shapes a distinct way of being. This multifaceted existence is something I continually think about concerning the ongoing struggle today.

AGATA BAR: Would you say that this is your strategy to protect yourself and protect your energy?

RASHA DAKKAK: Absolutely. This path we walk is not a sprint but a marathon. We must always find ways to ensure that we remain resilient and persistent for the long haul. The future of our cause depends on our ability to persevere, which means taking care of ourselves and each other every step of the way.

The space for a break.

And a moment
that is only yours.

Steering Crip Time

BY MELT (REN LOREN BRITTON, IZ PAEHR)
AND HACKERS & DESIGNERS (PERNILLA MANJULA PHILIP,
ANJA GROTEN, HEERKO VAN DER KOOIJ)

In June of 2024, Hackers & Designers (H&D) and MELT (Ren Loren Britton and Iz Paehr) hosted a *Criptastic Hack Meeting*; a hands-on workshop that brought together MELT's imaginative and speculative design approach to dreaming up anti-ableist technologies with H&D's hands-on hacking approach to imagining regenerative and equitable techno-futures.[1]

....

[1] "Criptastic Hack Meeting: Riding / Snorkeling / Surfing and Burrowing into Time Undercurrents," Hackers & Designers, hackersanddesigners. nl/criptastic-hack-meeting-riding-snorkeling-surfing-and-burrowing-into-time-undercurrents.html.

Inspired by a lineage of crip technoscience – practices that critique, hack, and remake our material and discursive world to promote anti-ableist technologies and knowledge production – the approach to the session was both practical and imaginative.[2] We aimed at resisting tech-solutionism and fostering diverse conceptions of time, proposing 'crip time' as a leading principle. The term crip is a political reclamation of the derogatory label cripple. The phrase 'crip time,' coined by feminist, queer, and disability scholar Alison Kafer, refers to the need for a new understanding of time that recognizes different lived experiences.[3] It emerged from the experiences of disabled people and addresses how disabled, chronically ill, and neurodivergent people perceive time. According to Kafer, crip time bends the clock to accommodate disabled bodies and minds, rather than disabled bodies and minds bending to meet the clock.

Together, MELT and H&D developed this workshop over the course of several work sessions, getting to know each other in the making process through engaging in each other's research and practices, by spending time together in Berlin, Amsterdam, and online, and by sharing and preparing readings for each other.

With this contribution, we would like to share the workshop script that we developed throughout this exchange. We hope that by (re)publishing it, it will provide collective energies, imaginaries, and practices around crip time, and perhaps new workshop iterations can evolve from it in the future.

....

[2] ANTI-ABLEIST TECH, meltionary.com/antiableisttech.

[3] Alison Kafer, *Feminist, Queer, Crip* (Bloomington, Indiana: Indiana University Press, 2013).

WORKSHOP SCRIPT:
STEERING CRIP TIME

We invite you to ride the unruly/unexpected/fantastic undercurrents of crip time with us and create other collective imaginaries for interfacing with crip time that counter the universalist assumption that all bodies and minds experience time and space similarly.[4] Compulsory technocapitalist paradigms of time efficiency, consistent, seamless labour performance and presumed able-bodiedness, pattern time structures that are inaccessible for many people.[5] Ren Britton writes: "My bodymind is expected to move quickly, to keep up with turbo-capitalist computational clock time that counts to the millisecond."[6]

....

[4] Christine Miserandino, "The Spoon Theory," ButYouDontLookSick.com, butyoudontlooksick.com/articles/writtenby-christine/the-spoon-theory.

[5] See the exhibition *Sick Time, Sleepy Time, Crip Time: Against Capitalism's Temporal Bullying* at Bemis Center, curated by Taraneh Fazeli in 2018, www.bemiscenter.org/exhibitions/sick-time-sleepy-time-crip-time-against-capitalisms-temporal-bullying; Terri Williams, "Trans Temporalities," Edinburgh University Press, 27 April 2017, euppublishingblog.com/2017/04/27/trans-temporalities; Sarah Sharma, *In the Meantime: Temporality and Cultural Politics* (Durham: Duke University Press, 2014), doi.org/10.2307/j.ctv11cw801.

[6] Ren Loren Britton, "On Rehearsing Access. Making space for non-normative time with Access Riders," Futeress, 16 April 2024, futuress.org/stories/rehearsing-access.

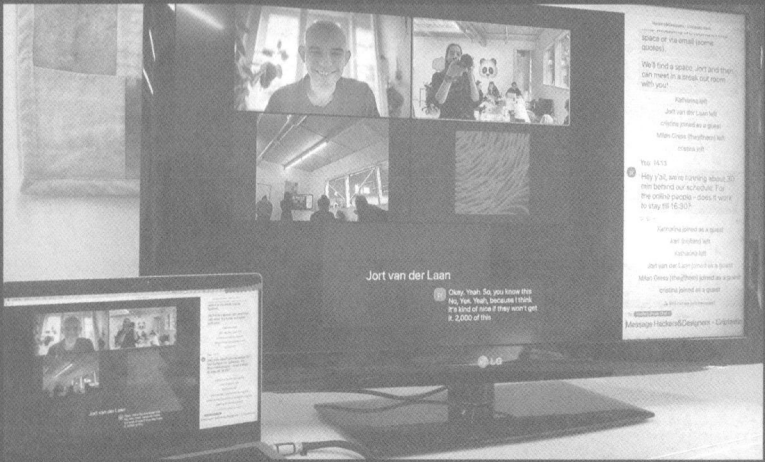

Pernilla Manjula Philip who is in the physical workshop space
is making a picture of the online participants.

We propose hacking as a way to counter the notion of
universal time and tune into crip time.[7] Crip time shows that
there are other ways of being in time: slow, in attunement
with pain or symptoms, with JOMO (joy of missing out),
in resistance towards capitalism's temporal demands.[8]

....

[7] Ellen Samuels, "Six Ways of Looking at Crip Time," *Disability Studies
Quarterly 37*, no. 3 (August, 2017), doi.org/10.18061/dsq.v37i3.5824.

[8] never odd or even, overexposed.sonicacts.com/neveroddoreven/map.

Workshop participants presenting their clocks/steering wheels in an enclosed workshop space. There is a screen on the right, where online participants are following. Others are standing around in the physical space following the presentation.

We invite you to imagine and prototype clocks that work against Gregorian clock time – clocks that are sensitive to interfacing with crip time. We are also working with the concept of the 'steering wheel.' For the workshop, these steering wheels come in the form of prompts and materials to prototype with. Their purpose is to help us approach the body as something that is constantly changing, that may go through and stay in states of illness, exhaustion, and disability. Steering wheels are something you need in order to interact with/make sense of otherwise timelines. The prototyping methodology is about bringing conceptual or theoretical ideas to life and exploring their potential for navigating and attuning to different individual and collective temporalities.

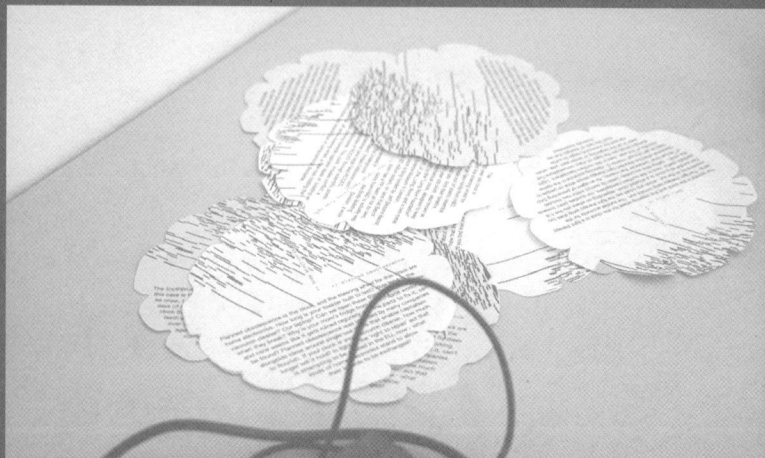

A pile of worksheets. The worksheet contains descriptions of the
steering wheel components and are cut out in the shape
of an imperfect circle.

We invite everyone to engage in a small ritual with us for
giving up temporal dependencies. As a start, we ask you to
decide upon one timely device that you would usually depend
on and that is attached to Gregorian time. This could be your
smartphone, smartwatch, regular watch, your morning alarm,
a calendar reminder, your social media push notification. You
can choose something that you are okay with giving up for the
duration of the workshop, however large or small.

THE STEPS ARE:

1) Place your Gregorian clock/object/entity in front of you.

2) Promise your object that you will pick it up again
in the future.

3) Put it into your backpack or somewhere else where you won't
be in touch with it for the next few hours. This could also just
mean: closing your email programme, or stopping your alarms.

Thank you – we are now ready to dive into the ocean of
crip time.

[Here we take some time to contextualize the notion of crip
time and what it means to us. If crip time is a new concept
for you, we invite the reader and fellow workshoppers to visit
the proposed references in the bibliography to familiarize
yourselves with crip time. Iz shares that "Crip time exists
because many people have expectations about time: How long
should something take? What is a normal amount of time?
Many disabled people say: Crip time is normal for us. In this
workshop we say: For crip time we need new clocks."]

STEERING WHEEL
AND CLOCK COMPONENTS

On a ship on the ocean, steering wheels are used to find a new direction. The steering wheel is how the clock is in operation for the context of this workshop. Some clocks are steering wheels at the same time, others are distinct. Think of your clock and its steering wheel as the what and the how. The clock is the 'what' and the steering wheel is the 'how.' These steering wheels modulate normative time by being slow, by engaging shifting materials, by inventing other temporal patterns, or by incorporating noise/rhythm. They are invitations/portals/wormholes/custom controllers to interface with the crip time ocean. We invite you to build these otherwise clocks from materials we have brought. While we do this, let us be mindful of some parts of the oceans where sharks swim – these places we ask you not to visit. For example, please don't use your steering device/clock to interface with a disability experience that you do not personally have to prevent nondisabled assumptions. We ask you to start from your own experience and how you would interface with the crip time ocean. We have prepared different materials for you that represent 'clocks' (what) and 'steering wheels' (how). Those are the components that you can use to start working on your clock, in smaller groups or individually if you prefer.

>> HOURGLASS +
BUCKET OF SAND

The hourglass is the clock, and the steering wheel for this clock is a bucket of sand. A bucket of sand is broken down from the hardest mountains, crumbling into boulders, slabs, hefty rocks, smaller rocks, pebbles, granules and eventually – sand. The transformations of sand from mountains, hammer away at the disintegration of matter from the literally massive into the particulate. Hourglasses and the sand they hold pose a specific kind of material time, it's both the amount of time of the sand moving from one bulbous shape to another, and the holding of what could be seen as mountains, worn down by time, in a small glass bulb.

>> DOWNLOADS –
LOADING TIME

Downloads is the clock, and the steering wheel for this clock is the load time. How long does each download take? Do you need multiple plugins to make that download work? How about updates to the software? How many programmes have you had to download to make that one other programme work and how long did it take? And how about your trash bin? What about all those installers you had to install... Do you still need them now that the programme is downloaded? How long did it take? And could you find that link again if you needed to?

>> TIME CRYSTAL –
CRYSTAL OSCILLATOR

The crystal oscillator is the clock and the steering wheel is crystals. Crystal oscillators are part of many digital circuits because of their ability to generate a stable pulse and therefore create a clock signal. With a reputation for being high-precision, this slab-cut power stone is connected to its environment and able to adapt thereafter. Temperature, power supply, and other components (neighbours) affect the quart's rhythm. What changes your rhythm, and how does that affect your dance, your talk, your songs? What/who resonates with your pulse and what sets its frequency?

>> TOOTHBRUSH +
TOOTHBRUSH

The toothbrush is a steering wheel of time that comes regularly. The clock in this case is the same as the instrument. Depending on your habits it might be once, twice, thrice a day – or every other day. Sometimes, after a few days of not engaging the toothbrush, your teeth may feel grimy; as a clock, the toothbrush freshens you up, gets into the nooks between teeth and needs to be replaced regularly. Toothbrushes, over time, lose their usefulness for teeth and may become agents of cleaning – the edges of tiles and corners may be easily cleaned by using a toothbrush and in this way, its function changes over time.

>> SUNDIAL –
LIGHT LAMP

The sundial is the clock and the steering wheel for this clock is a light therapy lamp. The light therapy lamp mimics the sun. The sundial accounts for the movements of the sun, which you could say the light therapy lamp does too. The sundial as a clock is a situated clock, depending on where you live it is partially useful. Here in the northern hemisphere, our sundials point towards the north – telling time accurately (when it's sunny) within two minutes of 'actual time' (whatever that means). As an agent for preventing SAD (seasonal affective disorder), light therapy lamps shine on people to help them get enough vitamin D, replacing sunshine in the darker months of the year, here in the northern hemisphere.

>> PUSH NOTIFICATIONS –
SCREENSHOTS/SCREEN TIME

Push notifications is the clock, and the steering wheel for this clock are screenshots/screen time. Just think of all of the notifications of space/place/time/reminders that pop up on your phone. And the reminders of your material connection to screens through the screenshots we take of where we need to be, and how, when and why. And the screen time notifications that tell us how many hours we have laboured in front of this screen, daily, weekly, and monthly.

>> EGG TIMER –
EGG TIMER

The egg timer is the clock, and the steering wheel for this clock is also an egg timer. Timing around three minutes in Gregorian time, this span of time indexes just about how long it takes for an egg's innards to transform from liquid to soft-medium or hard-boiled, depending on how high the altitude is at which you cook. This timer clicks down, and rings like a school bell, loud – and finished – at the end.

>> PLANNED OBSOLESCENCE –
HOME ELECTRONICS

Planned obsolescence is the clock, and the steering wheel for this clock is home electronics. How long is your toaster built to last? How long is the vacuum cleaner? Our laptops? Can we open these things up and fix them when they break? Why is your mom's fridge from the 1970s still working, and mine seems like it gets ruined regularly and the parts to fix it can't be found? Planned obsolescence was invented by many companies alongside ideas around single-use items that enable capitalism to nourish. If your clock is your vacuum cleaner, how much longer will it hold? In light of the 'right to repair' act that has been proposed to the European Parliament and Council, now – what kinds of home electronics stand to allow their innards to be exchanged?

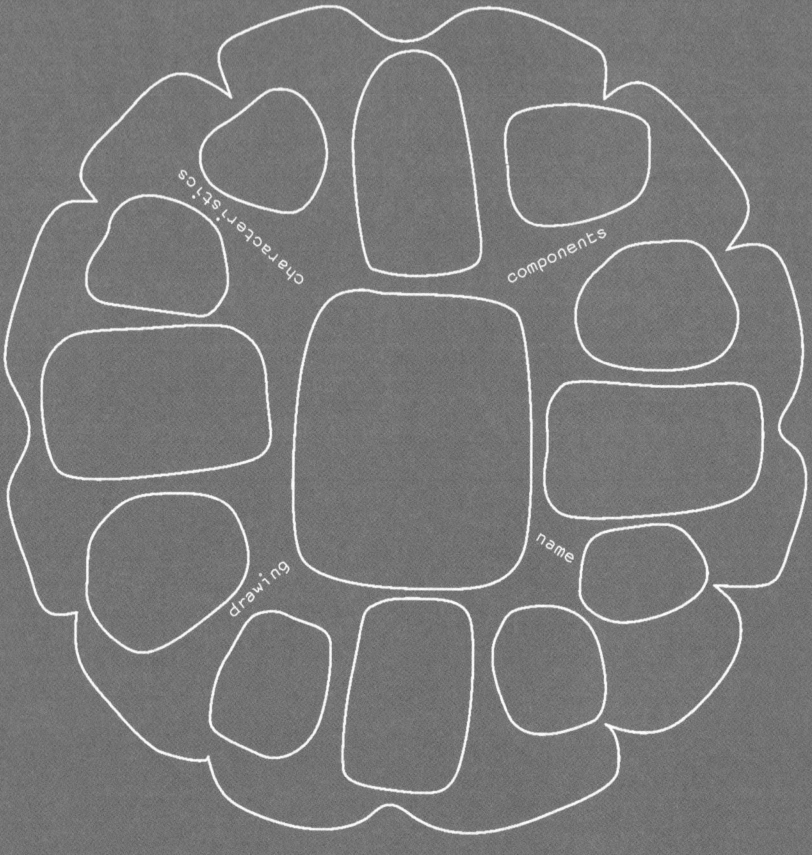

A worksheet with input fields for the name, characteristics, and components of the clock, and one to add a drawing of it. The shape of the worksheet is round with imperfect edges.

Rest, Refusal, and Resistance: On the Politics of Rest and the Invisible Labour of Art Workers

Lat
46° 3' 0.09" N

9:39

Long
14° 30' 29.4" E

When Andrea Knezović and Tia Čiček first invited me to be part of the conversation during the all-night-long event *Nocturnalities: Bargaining Beyond Rest*, in Gallery SKUC in Ljubljana, I thought to myself, "There's so much work to do, there's no time to rest!" But that thought was immediately followed by another: "But without rest, we cannot do any work," a principle I was taught from a very young age by my parents who made sure I knew and employed the distinction.

For example, first I had to do my (school) work and other duties before I could play – which was the best form of rest during my childhood in socialist Yugoslavia in the late 1970s and 1980s. My first-generation college-educated parents, from a proletarian peasant background, enjoyed the socialist welfare-state standards; which meant not only that they had stable full-time jobs, but that they had regular paid vacation and plenty of time to rest and play after work; and we, the kids, played outside without any special supervision. We only had to be back home by 7:10 p.m. when the cartoons were on TV. Afterwards, we went to bed so the parents could watch the 7:30 p.m. evening news. Without exceptions or excuses, my (school) work was done before playing, my school bag was ready, and all notebooks packed for the next day at school. All I had to do after returning home from playing was to brush my teeth, put on my pyjamas, watch the cartoon, and go to sleep.

Little did I know that the distinction between work and play would eventually play an important role in my life as an adult. But first, it had to be undone by mystifications and other convenient ideologies that, to this day, make conversations about the politics of rest absolutely necessary. While we struggle to reclaim our rest and time, however, it is equally important to understand a less visible side of the politics of rest and our struggle for free time, which comes on the heels of refusal to work and class struggle over what is socially necessary labour time. Under capitalism, the flip side of this social necessity – or shall we rather say the capitalist imposition to work – is the time to rest/not work that has been won over by organized workers. The refusal of work underwent problematic distortions during the past few decades, as ideas about a post-work society and the apocalyptic pronouncement of the end of capitalism abound on vertiginous announcements about the technologically automated future.

These prognoses are a symptom of the ways in which a refusal of work became divorced from the reality of class analysis and the labour movement. The illusions about the automated future also signal why it remains important to understand to what extent the refusal of work relates to the workers' struggle to nullify the relationship between wage and productivity in the 1970s, and the capital's pushback to reassert control over labour processes. Moreover, the refusal to work is central to the recognition of variegated forms of wage and wageless labour that are inscribed with diverse forms of exploitation.[1] It is easier to blame or celebrate the robots for taking over our jobs than to come to terms with the cyclical nature of capitalist crises and the fact that workers and their labour time are central to the accumulation of capital. Equally important is to anchor the politics of rest in a recognition of the invisibility of labour in the sphere of cultural production and to recognize it as a terrain of exploitation, but also of class struggle.

Since you might already be attuned to the normalized fact that art workers mostly work for free and that they do so quite willingly, you might wonder what kind of class struggle this is or even that art production is not a terrain of class struggle at all. Why do we think that if we have the privilege to work for free, do what we love, and choose to live precariously, that exploitation is not taking place? Are the exigencies of capitalism not pertinent in the sphere of cultural production and does the value-generating characteristic of human labour not take place in the arts? Is this kind of thinking a sign of privilege or is it simply the mirage created by the debilitating ideology of free labour?

---

[1] Alessandra Mezzadri, "Value Theories in Motion: Circular Labour Migration, Unfinished Land Dispossession and Reproductive Struggles Across the Urban-Rural Divide," *Environment and Planning F*, no. 0 (2024), doi. org/10.1177/26349825231224027; Jairus Banaji, *Theory as History: Essays on the Modes of Production and Exploitation* (Leiden: Brill, 2010).

As I entered the field of art and cultural production in the early 2000s there was no talk about exploitation of labour nor class struggle. Instead, a notoriously disappearing line between work and play/rest, or we might even say 'non-work,' enchanted me like a siren. It sang to me of the magic of freedom and flexibility. I was convinced that I had all the power to determine when I would work and when I would have free time, that I could have a Sunday on a Wednesday, and so on. This ostensible freedom was way better than my parents' white-collar labouring lives with its regimented work week and hours – from Monday to Friday, from 7 a.m. to 3 p.m. – despite the free time including the weekends they enjoyed. But my Sundays didn't take place on a Wednesday, if they took place at all, and the fact that I enjoyed my work was conveniently exploited to pay me poorly for the work that I did. The amount of free labour (and amount of my earnings) was inversely proportional to the meagre amounts of free time. A familiar story, isn't it?

My anecdote exposes the effect of an ideology that emerged during the 1990s and continues to the present day. It is produced and reproduced by influential leftist academics and epitomized by notions such as 'post-work' or 'end of work' or in a more sinister version a 'jobless future.'[2] In his astute critique, George Caffentzis already showed twenty-five years ago the ways in which this scholarship was "antediluvian and forgetful of work's capitalistic meaning."[3] That is, all work in capitalism is value-producing (paid or unpaid) and subject to exploitation. Time for rest or, if you will, suspension of work becomes the key strategy to resist this impersonal yet very real predicament in which we live under capitalism.

---

[2] See for example Jeremy Rifkin, *The End of Work: The Decline of the Global Labor Force and the Dawn of the Post-Market Era* (New York: Putnam Publishing Group, 1995); Antonio Negri, *Marx Beyond Marx* (New York: Autonomedia, 1991); Kathi Weeks, *The Problem with Work: Feminism, Marxism, Antiwork Politics, and Postwork Imaginaries* (Durham: Duke University Press, 2011)

[3] George Caffentzis, "The End of Work or the Renaissance of Slavery? A Critique of Rifkin and Negri," *Common Sense* 24 (1999): 23.

Quite in line with the fetishist character of the capitalist mode of production, those who talk about a jobless future focus on the job rather than on the labour process. "Although its salience is unmistakable, the job marks off, often quite conventionally and even with dissemblance, a part of the work process."[4] Moreover, Caffentzis warns us that those who claim that we are approaching the end of work, completely overlook the "manifold of work" that came on the heels of "a conceptual revolution [...] concerning the meaning of work," most significantly the Marxist feminist uncovering of housework, or the "great Other of capitalism."[5] The invisibility of reproductive labour that was excluded from the realm of commodity production and omitted as value–generating labour, for example, became central for a revised understanding about the ways in which our work becomes a very special commodity called labour–power under capitalism. The revision by feminists of the early social reproduction analyses is crucial, however.[6] Even if certain activities become declared as non–work and redefined as a natural calling, and although they are unpaid – they generate value and are central for capitalist accumulation.

....

[4] Ibid., 22.

[5] Ibid.

[6] Mariarosa Dalla Costa and Selma James, *The Power of Women and the Subversion of the Community* (Bristol: Falling Wall Press, 1972); Silvia Federici, *Wages Against Housework* (Bristol: Falling Wall Press, 1976); Leopoldina Fortunati, *The Arcane of Reproduction: Housework, Prostitution, Labor and Capital* (New York: Autonomedia, 1995); Silvia Federici, *Caliban and the Witch: Women, the Body and Primitive Accumulation* (New York: Autonomedia, 2004).

Labour-power, that is our capacity to work, is a central value-generating substance that we workers would like to sell, but capitalists want to appropriate at zero cost if possible, and for the longest time possible. Moreover, in this set-up, it is even better if we don't conceive of our work as labour solely to earn our living and ensure the basic necessities of life. The less we think about what we do as a form of work that allows us to survive under capitalism, the more likely it is that we ascribe to problematic ideological notions that dissolve the notion of work and replace it with other ideas, for example, in the context of art, creativity, love, passion, need for self-expression, or self-realization. Invisibility of labour and exploitation go hand in hand, especially, as feminism taught us, when you become your work. Nonetheless, the presence of a wage is not central for capital valorization. "[C]apitalism is not defined by the presence or absence of wage-labour. The wage is only one form in which the pricing of capitalist labour can occur," cautions feminist political economist Alessandra Mezzadri.[7] This is why forms of exploitation are variegated and can also be wageless. An excellent example of this condition is precisely the case of labour within the sphere of cultural production – that I term art work – and the reason why we need to consider its predicament of invisibility when discussing the politics of rest.

....

[7] Mezzadri, "Value Theories in Motion," 5.

Rest, or, a suspension of work, is one of the most basic ways in which people under capitalism resist exploitation and, consequently, resist the role their work has in the valorization and accumulation of capital. To rest and to strike are two sides of the same coin. The history of International Labour Day celebrated across the globe on May 1st is a testimony to this connection and a reminder of why rest, pause, and repose are central tools with which we divorce from productivity and the capitalist valorization process. As one of the few secular holidays, May 1st came to be celebrated precisely because workers wanted to celebrate not only the power of organized labour and the power of the working-class people, but also to dismantle the guilt connected to protestant work ethics and to give rest a positive, political meaning.[8]

In the context of art, however, art workers appear to not need rest because they willingly accept the 24/7 paradigm and passionately subject themselves to its uninterrupted process. Their labour process is the epitome of what Jonathan Crary, the inspiration for Knezović's project *Nocturnalities*, describes as '24/7' capitalism to emphasize the extent to which our lives have been dehumanized and adapted to "the uninterrupted operation of markets, information networks, and other systems."[9] In Crary's own words, "24/7 is a time of indifference, against which the fragility of human life is increasingly inadequate and within which sleep has no necessity or inevitability. In relation to labour, it renders plausible, even normal, the idea of working without pause, without limits."[10]

---

[8] Rosa Luxemburg, "What Are the Origins of May Day?," Marxist.org, April 2002 [1894], www.marxists.org/archive/luxemburg/1894/02/may-day.htm.

[9] Jonathan Crary, 24/7: *Late Capitalism and the Ends of Sleep* (London: Verso, 2013), chap. 1.

[10] Ibid.

   In the past decades, numerous studies have shown that
art workers don't distinguish between work and life; they
normalize free labour and self-exploitation while remaining
economically and socially insecure.[11] Art workers tend to not
see the invisibility of their work as a form of exploitation. In the
field of cultural production or the so-called 'creative sector,' art
workers create and do not work, or if they do work, they tend to
consider it a labour of love or 'sacrificial labour' where the joy
and love supplement insufficient or even absent remuneration.[12]
From ideas about free autonomous creativity, we have come to
the point where work is no longer a way to provide subsistence,
but an avenue for self-realization or self-expression. Do what
you love, love what you do – no rest necessary here and we don't
care about the paycheck either. The economic discount that
results from the sacrifice or love is proportionate to the blurring
of work and play, love and labour that often results in lack of
sleep, exhaustion, and no time to rest. This kind of thinking
is a powerful weapon in the class struggle waged against art
workers, especially those who can't afford to work for free.

---

[11] Jaka Primorac, Valerija Barada, and Edgar Buršić, "Creative Workers
in Permanent Crisis: Labor in the Croatia's Contemporary Arts and
Culture," *Industrialization of Creativity and Its Limits*, eds. Ilya Kiriya,
Panos Kompatsiaris, and Yiannis Mylonas (Cham: Springer, 2020);
Vahida Ramujkić and Milan Đorđević, eds., *Rad u umetnosti. Zbornik
udruženja likovnih umetnika Srbije* (Belgrade: Udruženje likovnih
umetnika Srbije, 2021); "A study on the financial state of visual artists
today," The Creative Independent, 2018, thecreativeindependent.com/
artist-survey.

[12] Andrew Ross, "The Mental Labor Problem," *Social Text* 18, no. 2
(2000): 1-31.

Art work, the process and not the result (artwork), or the invisible labour of artists and art workers, is one strand in the manifold of work not fully recognized as a form of labour, and tends to be excluded from consideration about labour exploitation.[13] Furthermore, the invisibility of art work is of the same 'nature' as housework, or the essentialized work by a 'housewife.' Just like housework, which was historically and socially constructed as a natural attribute of female subjects or as a 'labour of love,' the labour of an artist was historically defined as embodied creativity, an inborn faculty of a genius who can create just like a god *ex nihilo*. In both cases, particular skills get essentialized, declared, or culturally constructed as naturally stemming from the subject's essence or nature. Neither is defined as work; they are invisible in relation to production. Similar dynamics connected to the rise of capitalist production that established the housewife were also at work for the ideological separation of artists from artisans, and for redefining art work as creation.[14] Just as housewives were relegated to the sphere of home or reproduction, artists and their practice were elevated to an 'autonomous' social sphere, ruled by freedom of expression and free of financial concerns. Despite the glittering heights of such a promotion, the unwaged exploitation befalls artists as much as housewives.

----

[13] Katja Praznik, "Autonomy or Disavowal of Socioeconomic Context," *Historical Materialism* 26, no. 1 (2018): 103-135; Katja Praznik, *Art Work: Invisible Labour and the Legacy of Yugoslav Socialism* (Toronto: University of Toronto Press, 2021)

[14] Larry Shiner, *The Invention of Art: A Cultural History* (Chicago: The University of Chicago Press, 2001); Federici, *Patriarchy of the Wage*, 96-107.

While we owe it to Marxist feminists who demystified the essentializing principle that turns housework into non-work and becomes the fulcrum of exploitation and oppression of women under capitalism, the discourse of aesthetics and art theory uncritically perpetuates ideas about art work as non-work or creativity – it erases the labour process and mystifies it. Art workers are prime candidates to study the politics of rest as they appear to rest on their laurels while in fact their labour rests on voluntary self-exploitation. Why is that the case, you may wonder? Essentialization in the case of art work is perceived as positive (unlike domestic labour), and it makes art look natural (so, not work); it therefore legitimizes the invisibility of art work in a way that is worse than with domestic labour. When the positive valence of art work is associated with an essentialism that maintains the difference and exceptional nature of each 'creative' art worker, it makes it harder to rebel and want to reform this circumstance. It makes it easier to accept self-exploitation because it is not experienced as such. Thus, looking at art work as a form of invisible labour helps us to start to understand wageless and exploited art work as a political question and a site of struggle for labour standards, including the possibility of rest, paid vacation, and leave for art workers.

Rest is resistance, but how do we employ it if we don't situate art work into the economic relations of production under capitalism? Rest is resistance only when we recognize that work in the arts is also subsumed in capitalist relations, and that it is part of the value generation rather than removed or disavowed from the economic process. Until we do, we are offering free labour with no emancipation or rest in sight. Recognizing and defining our position as workers within the economic relations of capitalism gives us the power to bargain for rest and to recuperate the value of art work. That is why there can be no politics of rest without reckoning with the invisibility of art work.

Nocturnalities

Bargaining

Beyond

Rest

Nocturnalities

Bargaining

Beyond

Rest

Nocturnalities

Bargaining

Beyond

Rest

Lat
52° 21' 41.4" N

20:02

Long
4° 53' 26.8" E

253

AGATA BAR is a managing editor and publications producer based in Amsterdam, working primarily in the field of photography, art, and culture. She has been part of the organization and production teams of Photomonth in Krakow and Unseen Amsterdam and managed the production and distribution of *Foam Magazine.* In the past years, she worked with Noor Images as an editorial director and coordinated publications for Manifesta Biennale. In 2022, in response to the Russian invasion of Ukraine, she co-founded the publishing initiative Growing Pains. Next to her freelance practice, she also coordinates the Design Department at Sandberg Instituut in Amsterdam.

agatabar.com

DE APPEL (Amsterdam) is a daring institution founded in 1975. It soon became internationally known as an alternative institutional model, born out of artists' need to present performance and video art. Today, de Appel continues to act as a host for artistic and curatorial experimentation. Through a programme of Embedded Art in schools and society, a thirty-year-old Curatorial Programme, and an active archive, de Appel brings people together to practise a mutual exchange of knowledge through exhibitions and live activations.

deappel.nl/en

AURÉLIEN LEPETIT is a visual artist who works with textile-based craft techniques on two- and three-dimensional physical and digital surfaces. He uses craft as a tool to heal and transform by exploring the slowness of handmade techniques, keeping the techniques alive as a connection to his family lineage.

The artworks Lepetit creates are emotional, poetical, and visual and exist at the intersection between physical, spiritual, and digital realms. He intertwines mathematical diagrams, computer language and technologies with protein fibres. He uses chromatic language inspired by flora and a slower production rhythm in sync with natural cycles. Lepetit is inspired by painting and the way traditional painters create and compose their own colours. His art delves into the human pursuit of limitless life and energy, the embodiment of emotional restrictions, and the use of the grid as a systemic typology of control.

Aurélien Lepetit's work has been shown in exhibitions at NN Galeria, La Plata, Argentina; de Appel Art Center, Amsterdam, the Netherlands; Het Nieuwe Instituut, Rotterdam, The Netherlands; Centro Cultural Franco-Moçambicano, Maputo, Mozambique; and Kunsthall Zürich, Zürich, Switzerland. His art is collected by various private collectors in France, the Netherlands, the Caucasus region, and the Middle East. Lepetit is the recipient of Villa Formose – Nouvelles écritures 2024, a residency programme in collaboration between Bureau Français de Taipei and the National Taiwan Museum of Fine Arts.

aurelienlepetit.com

NICOLA BARATTO and YIANNIS MOURAVAS are an artist duo that specializes in 'archaeodreaming'; a research-based practice that blends archaeology with the dream world. Their work explores the intersection of history, mythology, and subconscious experiences, creating non-linear, poetic narratives. These stories are expressed through mixed-media installations, including films, artist books, and sculptures. They are alumni of the Dirty Art Department and former research fellows at the Sandberg Instituut Amsterdam.

barattomouravas.com

CASCO ART INSTITUTE Working for the Commons (Utrecht) is an experimental platform where art invites a social vision. Art and the commons are two key tools that serve as models for non-capitalistic ways of living together. Casco Art Institute works for this vision of art and the commons by creating a space or 'casco,' (meaning 'basic structure' in Dutch) for change, co-exploration, and study with collective art projects and organizational experiments.

casco.art

....

TIA ČIČEK holds a Master's degree in Art History and has curated exhibitions that examine and experiment with alternative processes and collaborations that interrogate the circumstances, tasks, and relationships in contemporary arts. Due to their interest in curatorial methodologies and knowledge exchange, they attended the Thinking With Works of Art course under the mentorship of Ruth Noack and Grace Samboh at the International Summer Academy of Fine Arts Salzburg. In 2020, they completed the World of Art School for Curatorial Practice and Critical Writing (SCCA-Ljubljana). Since May 2021, they have been part of the international fluid curatorial collective bad curating inc. Together with philosopher, theorist, and curator Maximilian Lehner, they run the reading and reflection workshops *Work, Curator, Work!*, where a space is created for the equal sharing of knowledge and experiences in the field of contemporary art and personal hardships. Since January 2020, they have been the artistic director of Škuc Gallery, and since July 2022, with Lara Plavčak and Urška Aplinc, they co-run the World of Art School. In May and June 2024, they will take part in MQ AIR in Vienna, with the support of ERSTE Foundation.

RASHA DAKKAK is a Palestinian researcher and maker whose work explores the intersection of imagery, language, and education, locating the power dynamics that shape canons and influence knowledge accessibility. With a background in visual communication, her practice spans publishing, curation, and writing, seeking to redefine design discourse and highlight underrepresented histories. Currently leading the Graphic Design department at Gerrit Rietveld Academy in Amsterdam, Rasha is committed to using design to challenge dominant narratives and reshape our understanding of the world. She holds graduate degrees in fine art and design from Sandberg Instituut, Basel Academy of Art and Design FHNW, the University of Illinois Chicago, and the American University of Sharjah.

YAMUNA FORZANI is a multidisciplinary artist and queer activist whose practice revolves around a desire to build her queer utopia that centres and celebrates her community, making them a part of, and inspiration to, her creative outputs. Yamuna's work takes form through textile, and she explores the medium in collaboration with other design, artistic, and social initiatives. This often involves organizing events and dance performances, which are embedded in fashion and costume, public art and versatile installations. The events she hosts merge practices of other creative fields such as theatre, music, performance art, and social design. These events serve as platforms where Forzani seamlessly amalgamates her creative endeavours, allowing her to be a queer activist, which becomes central to her creative practice. As a part of the Kiki House of Angels in the Netherlands and an international member of New York's House of Comme Des Garçons, she internationally represents the Netherlands in the ballroom scene.

yamunaforzani.org

HACKERS & DESIGNERS (H&D) is a non-profit workshop initiative that organizes activities at the intersection of technology, design, and art. By creating shared moments of hands-on learning, H&D stimulates collaboration across disciplines and technological literacy across different levels of expertise. H&D is a decentralized organization that distributes power over finances and decision-making. Current members of H&D are Loes Bogers, Selby Gildemacher, Anja Groten, Heerko van der Kooij, Juliette Lizotte, Karl Moubarak, Pernilla Manjula Philip, slvi.e and vo ezn.

hackersanddesigners.nl

MELT (Ren Loren Britton & Isabel Paehr) study and experiment with shape-shifting processes as they meet technologies, sensory media, and pedagogies in a warming world. Meltionary (derived from 'dictionary'), is a growing collection of art-design-research engagements that cook up questions around material transformations alongside impulses from trans* feminism and Disability Justice. Melting as a kaleidoscope-like phenomenon touches upon multiple topics at once: climate change, the potential for political reformulations, change over time, and material transformation.

meltionary.com

ANOUK HOOGENDOORN is an artistic researcher who is currently undertaking a PhD with the Centre for Culture and Creativity at Teesside University, UK in collaboration with the Department of Performing Arts and Film at Zürich University of the Arts, Switzerland. They were formerly part of *PEERS* '22/'23 (pre-PhD) at Zürich University of the Arts, studied Artistic Research (Research MA) at the University of Amsterdam and Image and Language (BFA) at the Gerrit Rietveld Academie. Anouk's practice always has an important collaborative and experimental orientation to it. Their (spoken) texts, textile works, sketches, movements, and sounds are moments of process rather than presentations that are fixed once and for all. Their main current interests include radical pedagogies as well as the notions of intimacy and proximity grounded in queer and disability studies.

anoukhoogendoorn.com

BIOGRAPHIES

HOTEL MARIA KAPEL (Hoorn) is an artist-in-residence, exhibition space, and cinema for contemporary visual art in the city centre of Hoorn; a historic town 40 kilometres north of Amsterdam, the Netherlands. Hotel Maria Kapel is a non-profit organization that aims to assist young as well as more established artists from all over the world in the production of new work and promote exchanges between national and international artists, cultural institutions, and the public.

hotelmariakapel.nl

....

MEGHANA KARNIK explores the paradoxes between art and social change, spirituality and economy, lived experience and institutional process. Her research plays out across modalities as a curator, arts administrator, artist, and writer. She is currently based in New York, stewarding a new iteration of *Hope is a discipline* (2024) as Lower Manhattan Cultural Council's inaugural Curatorial Fellow. Her first book, *Process-As-Practice* – written with Shawné Michelain Holloway, Elena Levi, and Maggie Wong – is being published by For The Birds Trapped in Airports in late 2024. Formerly, she was Manager, Grants & Artist Initiatives at Art Matters Foundation (New York), where she helped implement *Artist2Artist*, a grant programme that gives philanthropic power to artists; Associate Curator for FRONT International: Cleveland Triennial for Contemporary Art (*Oh Gods of Dust and Rainbows*, 2022); and Associate Director of EFA Project Space (New York), a cross-disciplinary venue hosting guest-curated exhibitions and *SHIFT:* A Residency for Arts Workers. She participated in the 2023 de Appel Curatorial Programme, holds a MA in Arts Administration from Teachers College, Columbia University, and a dual BA in Political Science and Art History from Case Western Reserve University.

storefrontpsychic.com

ANDREA KNEZOVIĆ is a conceptual visual artist and researcher with a research master in Artistic Research from the University of Amsterdam and a bachelor's degree from the Academy of Visual Arts, Ljubljana. Knezović's research centres around the politics of care, its institutional implications and psycho-cultural aspects. Between 2022-2024, Knezović was chair of the board of the Salwa Foundation and co-founder of the art and research platform MARC Amsterdam (2021-2024). She contributed to various discursive journals including *MIT Thresholds Journal, Lish Journal*, and *simulacrum*. She exhibited in places such as the Museum of Contemporary Art Metelkova, Ljubljana; the 10the edition of U3 Triennial at Museum of Modern Art Ljubljana; BAK, basis voor actuele kunst, Utrecht; Cukrarna, Ljubljana; MIT Keller Gallery, Cambridge, MA; Nieuw Dakota, Amsterdam; 12 Star Gallery, London; The Israeli Center for Digital Arts, Holon; Kiribati National Museum, Tarawa; Marx Halle, Vienna; and others. In 2023/2024 she was selected for the BAK Fellowship for Situated Practice in Utrecht. Her works are part of numerous museum and corporate collections, including the Museum of Modern Art Ljubljana, NLB Bank, and the SCCA-DIVA Archive. In 2013 and 2015, she was nominated for the Essl Art Award. She lives and works in Amsterdam.

andreaknezovic.com

KATIA KRUPENNIKOVA is a curator, educator, yoga practitioner, and mother based in Amsterdam. As an independent curator, her current interests include rearranging difficult political narratives and exploring radical education and experimental mental healthcare. She is a tenured lecturer in Curatorial Studies at the MA Fine Art programme at HKU, University of the Arts Utrecht, in the Netherlands.

Krupennikova has collaborated with various institutions, including the V-A-C Foundation/GES-2 (Moscow, Russia), Ujazdowski Castle Center for Contemporary Art (Warsaw, Poland), A Tale of a Tub (Rotterdam, the Netherlands), Oude Kerk (Amsterdam, the Netherlands), Württembergischer Kunstverein (Stuttgart, Germany), Nest (The Hague, the Netherlands), and the Latvian Center for Contemporary Art (Riga, Latvia), among others. In 2019, she was a member of the core group of curators for the Bergen Assembly, *Actually, The Dead Are Not Dead,* in Bergen, Norway.

Krupennikova is a founding member of the Oo(y)ster Mums collective and serves on the editorial board of *Errant Journal.* She has participated in local and international juries, including Apexart (2024–2025) and Rietveld Review (2022). She has been honoured with fellowships at de Appel Curatorial Programme (2011-2012) and BAK, basis voor actuele kunst (2019-2020). As an author, Krupennikova occasionally collaborates with Metropolis M magazine.

....

KUNSTHUIS SYB (Beetsterzwaag) is an artist residency that encourages research, experiment, and cooperation. Artists are invited on the basis of a project proposal to work and stay in the house for six weeks.

kunsthuissyb.nl

SILVIO LORUSSO is a writer, artist, and designer based in Lisbon, Portugal. He published *Entreprecariat* (Onomatopee) in 2019 and *What Design Can't Do* (Set Margins') in 2023. Lorusso is an assistant professor and co-director of the Center for Other Worlds at the Lusófona University in Lisbon and a tutor at the Information Design department of Design Academy Eindhoven. He holds a PhD in Design Sciences from the Iuav University of Venice. Lorusso's work touches upon visual communication, memes, post-digital publishing, entrepreneurship and precarity, digital platforms, design culture and politics, creative coding, art and design education, and video games. His practice combines a variety of media such as video, websites, artist's books, installations, and lectures. This activity is further stimulated by writing essays, curating exhibitions, and organizing public programmes. Lorusso has been a member of Varia, the Center for Everyday Technology, as well as part of the editorial board of Italian graphic design magazine *Progetto Grafico.* Among other venues, his work has been presented at Het Nieuwe Instituut (Rotterdam), MaXXI (Rome), Transmediale (Berlin), The Photographers' Gallery (London), and Kunsthalle Wien (Vienna). His writing has appeared in several magazines and publications, including *Volume, Real Life Magazine, Metropolis M,* and *Esquire Italia.*

silviolorusso.com

···

ÁNGELS MIRALDA is a writer and curator living in Amsterdam and Barcelona. Her work focuses on artistic production as a metaphor for global processes of circulation and trade. She has organized exhibitions at Something Else III (Cairo Biennale), Radius CCA (Delft), P////AKT (Amsterdam), Garage (Nicosia), Tallinn Art Hall (Estonia), Latvian Center for Contemporary Art (Riga), MGLC (Ljubljana), GMK (Zagreb), Museu de Angra do Heroísmo (Azores), and the Museum of Contemporary Art (Santiago, Chile). She is editor-in-chief of *Collecteurs Magazine* (New York), and was a writer at *Artforum* from 2019 to 2023.

angelsmiralda.com

BIOGRAPHIES

TITUS NOUWENS works as a curator, writer, and producer at the intersection of visual art and performance. He holds degrees in Art History and Curating from the University of Amsterdam and the Royal College of Art in London. He is the founder of Amsterdam-based platform Prelude (prelude.nu).

··

RITA OUÉDRAOGO is an Amsterdam-based curator, researcher, and writer. She develops ongoing experimental and collaborative projects and public programmes on collaboration, archives, colonialism, African diaspora, institutional power, counter-culture, popular culture, and social issues. She holds an MSc in Cultural Anthropology and Development Sociology from the University of Amsterdam. Ouédraogo worked on various projects aimed at making museum collections more widely accessible as well as on projects outside of institutional structures. She researches questions related to cooperation and solidarity that explore modes of collaborative practices across power differentials, especially within a decolonial framework. She is the co-founding curator of Buro Stedelijk, Stedelijk Museum's project space.

instagram.com/ritaouedraogo
burostedelijk.nl/collaborators/rita-ouedraogo

KATJA PRAZNIK is the author of *Art Work: Invisible Labour and the Legacy of Yugoslav Socialism* (University of Toronto Press, 2021) and *The Paradox of Unpaid Artistic Labor: Autonomy of Art, the Avant-Garde and Cultural Policy in the Transition to Post-Socialism* (Založba Sophia, 2016). She is an Associate Professor at the University of Buffalo's Arts Management Program and Department of Global Gender and Sexuality Studies. Her research and political work are dedicated to the demystification of creativity and the emancipation of art as a form of labour, including the labour-organizing of art workers. She is a co-founder of the freelance art worker's union Zasuk and the initiator of A Cultural Work Inspection. Her essays and articles have been published in edited volumes and peer-reviewed journals, including *Historical Materialism* and *Social Text,* and in numerous international publications dedicated to issues of fair payment and labour standards in the field of art and cultural production.

instagram.com/praznikarci
utorontopress.com/9781487508418/art-work

....

MARIO SANTAMARÍA is an artist based in Barcelona whose work has been shown in La Panera (Lleida), àngels barcelona, Aksioma (Ljubljana), Württ. Kunstverein Stuttgart, and arebyte Gallery (London), among others. He has participated in group exhibitions, such as *Songs of the Sky. Photography & the Cloud* at C/O Berlin (2022), *Writing the History of the Future* at ZKM Karlsruhe (2021), *Infosphere* at CENART Mexico (2017), and *Species of Spaces* at MACBA Barcelona (2015). Santamaría is a university lecturer at BAU and Elisava, Barcelona, and has also been a visiting professor at universities such as Trinity College Dublin, Universität Bremen, ISIA Urbino, and UC Berkeley. Santamaría was awarded the Premi Miquel Casablancas (2020), was a finalist of the Fotomuseum Winterthur Post-Photography Award (2016), and has been artist-in-residence at Sarai Nueva, Delhi (2012), Hangar, Barcelona (2014–2015), and HISK, Ghent (2016).

mariosantamaria.net

BIOGRAPHIES

FINNEGAN SHANNON is an artist who experiments with forms of access. They intervene in ableist structures with humour, earnestness, and rage. Some of their recent work includes *Alt Text as Poetry,* a collaboration with Bojana Coklyat that explores the expressive potential of image description; *Do You Want Us Here or Not,* a series of benches and cushions designed for exhibition spaces; and *Don't mind if I do,* a conveyor-belt-centred exhibition that prioritizes rest and play. They have done projects with MUDAM Luxembourg, the Queens Museum, moCa Cleveland, the High Line, MMK Frankfurt, MCA Denver, and Nook Gallery. Their work has been supported by a Wynn Newhouse Award, an Eyebeam fellowship, a Disability Futures Fellowship, and grants from Art Matters Foundation, Canada Council for the Arts, and the Disability Visibility Project. Their work has been written about in *Art in America, BOMB Magazine, the Believer,* and *Out Magazine.* They live and work in Brooklyn, NY.

shannonfinnegan.com

....

SHIMMER (Rotterdam) located in the Port of Rotterdam, noted for its beautiful sunsets caused by industrial pollution, is a curatorial studio set within the contradiction of oil-riggers and wind-turbine-installing ships. The contradiction of a changing industrial environment informs their adaptive and transformative outlook. Established in 2018, Shimmer was founded by Eloise Sweetman and Jason Hendrik Hansma.

shimmershimmer.org

....

STROOM (Den Haag) has been the expertise centre for art, society, and the public domain since 1990. Together with contemporary artists, they explore the culture of coexistence, examine forward-looking societal perspectives, and stimulate the imagination of the public.

stroom.nl

A TALE OF A TUB (Rotterdam) is a non-profit institution for contemporary art and culture located in the former washhouse and bathhouse of the Justus van Effencomplex in Spangen, Rotterdam. The complex was designed in 1922 by Dutch architect Michiel Brinkman as a social housing project for the city's dock workers and is named after the eighteenth-century journalist, italic writer and translator Justus van Effen (who, importantly, translated the political satire *A Tale of A Tub* to Dutch for the first time).

a-tub.org/en

ANGELIKI TZORTZAKAKI is a writer, curator, and tutor based in Amsterdam. Her practice materializes in multiple, often performative ways, and overall looks at narratives that wish to break the nature-culture binary.

Recently, Angeliki (co-)curated the programme *Touching Faultines* (All of Greece One Culture, 2024), the 2024 Sonic Acts Biennial *The Spell of the Sensuous,* and the solo show by Yorgia Karidi at THF RAW. Previously, she contributed to *A Rave Down Below* at 2023 ELEVSIS, and was part of the curatorial team of *School of Waters,* the 19th Mediterranea Biennial in 2021. In 2021-2022, Angeliki received the SNF Curatorial Fellowship ARTWORKS while she previously was a research fellow at the nomadic programme *A Natural Oasis?* (2018-2020). Since 2019, Angeliki has collaborated with Mercedes Azpilicueta to develop and coordinate her projects. Between 2019 and 2023 Angeliki was part of the artist-run residency *bi-* and the performance group Scores for Gardens. Other – collaborative – writing and performance work has been presented at HIAP (Helsinki), Künstlerhaus Büchsenhausen (Innsbruck), Theatrum Mundi/Onassis Foundation (London, Athens), Italian Institute of Culture (Tokyo), JaJaJaNeeNeeNee (Amsterdam), PARADISE AIR (Matsudo); and been published by Arts of the Working Class, Flash Art, Roots-Routes, Fries Museum, de Appel, Archive Books, Building Fictions, and Lugemik.

ELOÏSE VO is a French artist and designer based in Geneva who graduated from the School of Art and Design of Strasbourg and a post-master programme at the DIU EUR ArTeC (Université Paris 8/Nanterre). Since 2022, she has been a PhD candidate at the Hes-So HEAD – Geneva and EPFL. Though trained as a graphic designer, her work has branched into performance, media installations, publishing, and writing, alongside design commissions. By looping back to John C. Lilly's experiments, her PhD research explores the 'Echo(re) locations of the Dolphin House' to recall alternate histories of synthetic intelligences. Knitting together labour theory, the history of design, science and technology with xenofeminist perspectives, she tends to (re)define the planetarity conditions of the wetware and its unnatural solidarities by exploring the technologization of animality and femininity. Her work has been exhibited at Le Signe, National Center for Graphic Design in Chaumont and in the group show *La Relève IV* at the Parallèle Festival in Marseille. She is a resident at Le Wonder, an independent artist-run space based in Bobigny.

instagram.com/eloise_vo

WERKER was founded in Amsterdam in 2009 by Marc Roig Blesa and Rogier Delfos. Inspired by Die Vereinigung der Arbeiterfotografen (the Association of Worker Photographers), a group of politicized photo clubs that emerged in Germany in the 1920s, the artist collective follows in the footsteps of the first socialist photography experiments in the USSR, extending to Europe, the United States, and Japan. Their methods revolve around self-representation, self-publishing, image analysis, collective authorship, and counter-archiving. WERKER has realized projects for, among others, Gropius Bau in Berlin (2023); Manifesta 14 in Kosovo (2022); Sonsbeek 20>24 in Arnhem (2020), the 5th Ural Industrial Biennale of Contemporary Art, Yekaterinburg (2019), and so far published ten issues of *Werker Magazine.*

werkercollective.net

W139 (Amsterdam) is a leading production and presentation space for contemporary art in the centre of Amsterdam that has been paving the way for experimentation and new modes of autonomy, self-organization, and collectivity within the arts for 44 years.

w139.nl

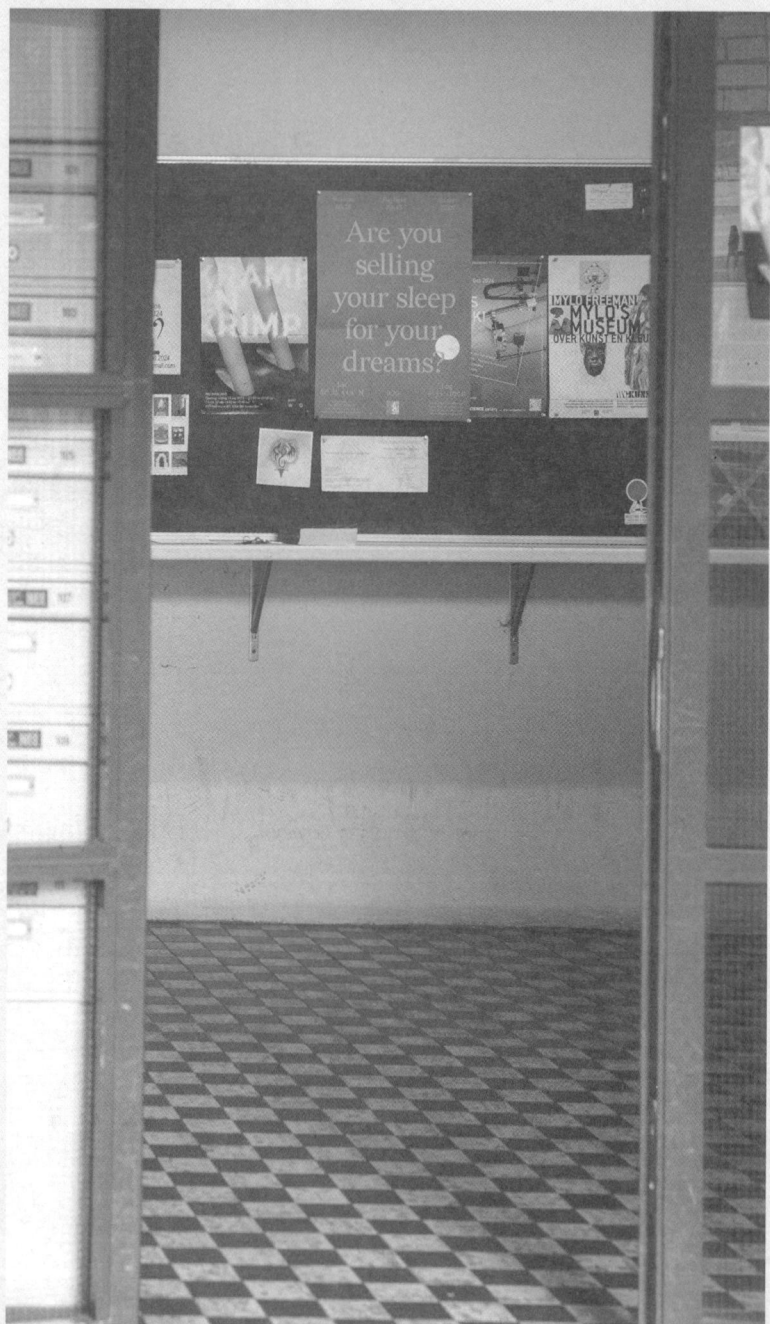

Nocturnalities
Bargaining
Beyond Rest

Lat
52° 21' 41.4" N

20:02

Long
4° 53' 26.8" E

Nocturnalities
Nocturnalities
Nocturnalities
Nocturnalities
Nocturnalities
Bargaining Beyond Rest
Onomatopee #260

EDITED BY
Andrea Knezović
Agata Bar

WITH WRITTEN
CONTRIBUTIONS BY
Tia Čiček
Rasha Dakkak & Agata Bar
Silvio Lorusso
Meghana Karnik
Andrea Knezović
Katia Krupennikova
Ángels Miralda
Laura Mrkša &
Sepp Eckenhaussen
Titus Nouwens
Rita Ouedraogo
Katja Praznik
Angeliki Tzortzakaki
Eloïse Vo

WITH VISUAL
CONTRIBUTIONS BY
Yamuna Forzani
Hackers & Designers × MELT
Anouk Hoogendoorn
Aurélien Lepetit
Baratto & Mouravas
Finnegan Shannon
Mario Santamaria
Werker

WITH INSTITUTIONAL
CONTRIBUTIONS BY
A Tale of a Tub
Casco
de Appel
Stroom Den Haag
Hotel Maria Kapel
Kunsthuis Syb
Shimmer
W139

PUBLISHED BY
Onomatopee Projects,
Eindhoven,
The Netherlands
Jesse Muller &
Natasha Rijkhoff

COLOPHON

GRAPHIC DESIGN
Miquel Hervás Gómez

PHOTOGRAPHY
Roman Ermolaev

COPY EDITING
Irene de Craen

PROOFREADING
Agata Bar
Jesse Muller
Annemarie Wadlow

TYPEFACE
Redaction, inspired by
Titus Kaphar &
Reginald Dwayne Betts.
Designed by Jeremy Mickel.

PAPERS
Munken Lynx 90grs
Metsaboard Prime
FBB Bright. 255g

PRINT & BOUND BY
Printon OÜ

EDITION
1,800

YEAR
2025

ISBN: 978-94-93382-09-1

WEB DEVELOPMENT &
REST ARCHIVE
François Girard-Meunier
Justus Gelberg &
Lukas Engelhardt
Sascha Krischock

THIS PROJECT IS
GENEROUSLY SUPPORTED BY

AFK amsterdams fonds voor de kunst

creative industries fund NL

M mondriaan fund

www.Nocturnalities.com
www.Nocturnalities.com
www.Nocturnalities.com
www.Nocturnalities.com
www.Nocturnalities.com
www.Nocturnalities.com
www.Nocturnalities.com
Bargaining Beyond Rest
info@nocturnalities.com

9 789493 382091